Varieties of Nothingness

Edited by Dean Rickles & Leslie Stein

CHIRON PUBLICATIONS • ASHEVILLE, NORTH CAROLINA

www.ChironPublications.com

Cover design by Celeste Stein
Interior design by Danijela Mijailovic
Printed primarily in the United States of America.

ISBN 978-1-68503-245-6 paperback
ISBN 978-1-68503-495-5 hardcover
ISBN 978-1-68503-244-9 electronic

Library of Congress Cataloging-in-Publication Data Pending

Table of Contents

Artistic and Cultural Forms

Theological Expression

List of Contributors

Vismay Agrawal has primary interests in exploring the mind, meta-awareness, phenomenology, and epistemology. He graduated with a B.Tech. Hons. & M.Tech. in Biomedical Engineering Design from the Indian Institute of Technology (IIT) Madras. Currently, he is embarking on his PhD studies at Monash Centre for Consciousness and Contemplative Studies (M3CS) under the supervision of Dr. Jakob Hohwy, Dr. Adeel Razi, and Dr. Ruben Laukkonen. Additionally, he is a Research Analyst at the Integrated Research Literacy Group (IRLG), where he is working on several projects related to psychedelic therapy for mental health. Previously, he has published research papers in medical imaging, deep learning, and signal processing domains.

Harald Atmanspacher is an emeritus member at the Chair of Philosophy at ETH Zurich, honorary professor at the University of Essex, and honorary member of the International Association of Analytical Psychology, and faculty or board member of several other institutions. He serves as the President of the *Society for Mind-Matter Research* and is editor of its journal *Mind and Matter*. Main topics of his work are non-reductive relations between different scientific domains (contextual emergence), non-commutative approaches in cognitive science (quantum cognition), and novel accounts of mind-matter correlations (dual-aspect monism). His most recent monograph is *Dual-Aspect Monism and the Deep Structure of Meaning,* with Dean Rickles.

David Chai is Associate Professor of philosophy at the Chinese University of Hong Kong. He is the Series Editor of *Daoism and the Human Experience* and his books include: *Daoist Resonances in Heidegger: Exploring a Forgotten Debt* (2022); *Reading Ji Kang's Essays: Xuanxue in Early Medieval China* (2021); *Daoist Encounters with Phenomenology: Thinking Interculturally about Human Existence* (2020); *Dao Companion* to *Xuanxue (Neo-Daoism)* (2020); and *Zhuangzi and the Becoming of Nothingness* (2019). Prof. Chai has also published numerous articles on ancient and medieval Chinese philosophy, and comparative philosophy.

Ian Durham is Professor and Chair of Physics at Saint Anselm College. His recent work has focused on attempting to understand what role, if any, quantum mechanics may play in consciousness as well as the causal efficacy of consciousness on quantum systems. He has helped contribute to a quantum mechanical extension of a key component of integrated information theory and, most recently, he and collaborators have extended the work of Chalmers and McQueen on consciousness-induced collapse of the wavefunction. He is currently exploring the implications these results may have for causal physical theories more broadly.

Gerard Guiton ('Guyton'), a Quaker, lives on Bundjalung country in the Northern Rivers region of N.S.W.. He is a former schoolteacher, and aid & development worker. He is also a spiritual director/companion, and long-time peace activist and environmentalist. He holds degrees from Manchester (U.K.), Sheffield (U.K.) and Monash universities. The author of *The Growth and Development of Quaker Testimony* (Lewiston, NY: Edwin Mellen, 2005)—a version of his doctorate—*The Early Quakers and the 'Kingdom of God'* (San Francisco, CA: Inner Light Books, 2012), *Stillness* (Melbourne: Morning Star, 2016 [1994]) and *What Love Can Do* (Melbourne: Morning Star, 2016), his upcoming book is *The Spiritual Nature of Consciousness: Peace, Justice & Compassion for the Earth & Humanity*.

James W. Heisig is professor emeritus of the Nanzan University in Nagoya, Japan, where he has worked since 1977 at the Nanzan Institute for Religion and Culture. He has written extensively on philosophy and religion, with a special focus on Japanese philosophy and its interface with western thought. His recent books include *Of Gods and Minds* (2020) and *In Praise of Civility* (2022). In 2023 he was awarded Japan's Order of the Sacred Treasure.

Daniela K. Helbig is a faculty member at the School of History and Philosophy of Sydney at the University of Sydney, Australia. She works on a range of questions that connect the history of technology and intellectual history, e.g. 'La Trace de Rome? Aerial Photography and Archaeology in Mandate Syria and Lebanon' (*History of Photography*, 2016), 'Life without toothache: Hans Blumenberg's Zettelkasten and history of science as theoretical attitude' (*Journal of the History of Ideas*, 2019), or 'Gebäude auf Abbruch? The digital archive of Kant's opus postumum' (*Aisthesis*, 2020).

Ruben Laukkonen is a principal investigator and lecturer at Southern Cross University and holds honourary fellowships at the Vrije Universiteit Amsterdam and The University of Queensland. Ruben's research uncovers empirically grounded and experientially authentic models of meditation, insight, and non-duality. Using a combination of methods including behaviour, neuroimaging, machine learning, and phenomenology, he is investigating some of the rarest states of consciousness available to human beings. Ruben's research is deeply theoretically driven and traverses multiple levels of explanation, from neurons to psychology. He has published articles in leading journals, has won numerous awards for his research and teaching, consults for the Organisation of Economic Cooperation and Development, and has written on topics that range from artificial intelligence to psychedelics.

Ken Parry is Honorary Senior Research Fellow, Department of History and Archaeology, Macquarie University, Sydney. He researches and publishes in the fields of Late Antiquity, Byzantine Studies, and Eastern Christianity. He is the author of *Depicting the Word: Byzantine Iconophile Thought of the Eighth and Ninth Centuries* (1996), and editor of *The Blackwell Dictionary of Eastern Christianity* (1999), *The Blackwell Companion to Eastern Christianity* (2007), and *The Wiley Blackwell Companion to Patristics* (2015). He has contributed to *The Cambridge Intellectual History of Byzantium* (2017), *Brill's Companion to Byzantine Iconoclasm* (2021), and *Brill's Companion to Byzantine Philosophy* (forthcoming). He is currently editing and contributing to *Brill's Companion to John of Damascus.*

Graham Priest is currently Distinguished Professor of Philosophy at the Graduate Center, City University of New York, Boyce Gibson Professor Emeritus at the University of Melbourne, and International Research Fellow at the Ruhr University of Bochum. He is known for his work on non-classical logic, metaphysics, the history of philosophy, and Buddhist philosophy. He has published nine monographs and over 300 articles. For further details, see www.grahampriest.net.

Paul Redding is Emeritus Professor of Philosophy at the University of Sydney. A major strand of his work over three decades has been devoted to questions concerning the metaphysical commitments of the German idealists and, in particular, of G. W. F. Hegel. His recent work has focussed on Hegel's logic, and in 2023, his *Conceptual Harmonies: The Origins and Relevance of Hegel's Logic* was published by The University of Chicago Press.

Dean Rickles is Professor of History and Philosophy of Modern Physics in the School of History and Philosophy of Science at The University of Sydney, where he is also a co-director of the Centre for Time. His recent books include *Life is Short: An Appropriately Brief Guide to Making it More Meaningful* (Princeton University Press, 2022) and *Dual-Aspect Monism and the Deep Structure of Meaning* (Routledge, 2022 - co-authored with Harald Atmanspacher).

Leslie Stein trained as a Jungian Analyst at the C.G. Jung Institute in New York and is in private practice as a psychoanalyst in Sydney, Australia. His books include: *Becoming Whole: Jung's Equation for Realizing God* (New York, Helios); *Working with Mystical Experiences in Psychoanalysis: Opening to the Numinous* (Routledge); *The Self in Jungian Psychology: Theory and Practice* (Chiron) – winner of the IAJS Award for the best book on Jungian theory, 2022; *The Journey of Adam Kadmon: A Novel* (Arcade, New York); *The Psychoanalysis of Dr Seele* (Arcade, New York); Editor, *Eastern Practices and Individuation: Essays by Jungian Analysts* (Chiron); and Editor with Lionel Corbett of *Psychedelics and Individuation: Essays by Jungian Analysts* (Chiron). He is on the Board of Directors of the Philemon Foundation, responsible for publication of the previously unpublished works of Jung. He is also an Adjunct Professor at the Department of Urbanism in the Sydney School of Architecture, Design and Planning at the University of Sydney with a long career of advising governments in many countries and the UN on mental health outcomes in urban areas, as to which he has written 4 books, and has been the principal advisor on urban planning reform to the NSW government.

Inja Stracenski is lecturer and coordinator of the School of Jewish Theology at the University of Potsdam, Germany. She works on various topics related to Jewish thought and philosophy, e.g. 'Spinoza's Compendium of the Grammar of the Hebrew Language' (*Parrhesia: Journal of Critical Philosophy*, 2020), and a book manuscript based on her 2020 PhD dissertation, *Spinoza's first philosophy and the knowledge of God*.

Nathan Wolski is the Liberman Family Lecturer in Jewish Studies with the Australian Centre for Jewish Civilisation, Monash University, Australia. He is the author of *A Journey into the Zohar: An Introduction to the Book of Radiance* (SUNY, 2010), the translator of *The Zohar: Pritzker Edition*, Volume 10 (Stanford, 2016), and with Joel Hecker, *The Zohar: Pritzker Edition*, Volume 12 (Stanford, 2017), and most recently, *Kabbalistic Yiddish: Aaron Zeitlin's Mystical-Messianic Poetics* (Cherub, 2020).

Editors' Introduction

Dean Rickles and Leslie Stein

Leibniz famously asked, "Why is there something rather than nothing?" A young Wittgenstein believed that contemplating this problem (*why* the world is, rather than *how* it is) constituted the basis of a mystical experience (*Tractatus*, 6.44). This binary distinction (being and nothingness), this impossible conundrum, yields the inevitable conclusion, expressed in a succinct form in Parmenides's maxim that *Nothingness Cannot Be,* yet there are a great many other options hidden from Western eyes.

Nothingness is there somewhere. It is the question that exists in all disciplines, all thought, all wonder. It exists in fullness and emptiness, presence and absence, being and nonbeing. Into this apparent void, the contributing authors came together in retreat to breathe into nothingness from their own disciplines; to make it rise to the surface, examine it, say what it could be before it falls back into oblivion. It was held aloft objectively for observation, turned over for inspection, and permeated each of us as we sat in the great vastness of the Blue Mountains outside of Sydney, Australia, in January 2023. The approaches come from cultural influences, spiritual inquiry, psychological understanding, neuroscience, physics, religious and esoteric practices, consciousness, Heidegger and Hegel, logic, apophatic reasoning, bringing concentrated insights into something so obvious, yet so obscure.

Starting off the collection of essays, Dean Rickles argues for a position he calls "quantum existentialism" in which the fundamental basis of reality is nothingness, understood in a sense similar to Schelling's Godhead in which ultimate reality is contained in the fullness of potentiality. However, observer-participators are essential in this scheme to manifest actuality (and objectivity) from pure potentiality. The human role is to rise to this special capacity. The basis for this transduction of potential to actual is illustrated in ongoing attempts to make sense of quantum mechanics, making quantum mechanics a theory of this nothingness.

Ian Durham also draws inspiration from physics, elaborating points of contact with existentialism. He focuses on the duality of existence and nothingness, in which each derives its meaning by oppositional relation. This flows into all things, which exist through their relations to other things, implying that the whole edifice of worldly reality is built on nothing (no ultimate things). This is consistent with an Eastern perspective, and Durham considers the links between physics and these other ontological versions of reality in which the notion of *things* is empty (corresponding to *śūnyatā,* a concept that recurs throughout this collection). In an attempt to ground his thesis, Durham follows the quasi-Buddhistic path of reducing reality to phenomenal experience (with cause-effect built in).

Harald Atmanspacher also focuses attention on phenomenological aspects, though in this case the idea of the experience of nothingness itself (rather than on *things* that somehow vanish through deeper analysis, as in Durham's account), which he subjects to a highly systematic treatment employing ideas from dynamical systems theory. Here, mental processes are represented by motion in a kind of potential-energy landscape of mental states that might be experienced by a self (including the energetically costly state in which a loss of selfhood is experienced). This is naturally related to the idea of mystical mental states involving the oceanic dissolution of self. The experience can be modeled as an unframed, noncategorical state, which Atmanspacher compares with Jean Gebser's idea of "acategoriality." Here too we find a curious incursion of existentialism with a novel understanding of death anxiety presented through this framework, where death (deep nothingness) is understood as that peculiar gap sitting between the mind's "thoughts [that] jump out of it like numbers out of a black hole" (as he approvingly quotes from the novelist Robert Musil). Yet this gap is also where ego-freedom lies and, as Atmanspacher argues (developing Gebser's ideas), a better future for our civilization.

Leslie Stein also places the experiential aspect of nothingness center stage, though examined from the perspective of the psychoanalytic encounter. What emerges is much along the lines of Musil's black hole, a timeless instant of emptiness (a "winking out" in Stein's words) in which there is both terror and freedom coexisting and coming out of nowhere.

This is the root of many classical mystical experiences. Stein gets to the bottom of what it is that can be said to *have* such experiences, given their black hole character. Part of this process involves a *post hoc* interpretation, imbuing the experience with *meaning*. Stein connects this phenomenon to the Sufistic idea of the divine witnessing itself through the polished mirror of an ego as well as that of *kenosis*, in which emptiness must be achieved to receive revelations. In order for such metaobservation and interpretation to take place, Stein argues, there must be a higher-order form of mind behind our ordinary states. This metalevel is taken to be what Sri Aurobindo and others label "That" and is seen to be part of a primordial plan of the cosmos to evolve, using us as vehicles for its highest self-expression: the great *ipsissimus* project of the most high!

Vismay Agrawala and Ruben Laukkonen shine an experimental light on the black hole experience of "winking out of existence," which they relate to *nirodha*, namely a *cessation* of or *cut* in consciousness. Here, as Stein discusses, these dives into nothingness seem to bring with them a clarity and peace. Indeed, they relate this rebooting of consciousness to Theravada Buddhism in which it constitutes a key step to go beyond suffering. Their empirical approach mixes the scientific with the spiritual and proceeds by measurement of cessation states, especially those able to sustain longer cessation periods (or *nirodha samāpatti*). The empirical component amounts to finding the neural correlates of no-thingness (emptiness) and nothingness (cessation) states. The experiential aspects of mystical states are bound up with the inhibition of the default mode network in the brain, responsible for the sense of self and its grounding and motion in space, time, and modality. Likewise, the salience network, more associated with the feeling of embodiment are well expressed in a computational model (based on predictive processing methods) that Agrawala and Laukkonen employ, in which the suffering of the mind essentially comes from its search for equilibrium. Playing around with these, as in psychedelics and meditative practices, can lead to direct experience of no-thingness beyond a merely abstract idea which might be so powerful as to trigger psychosis. The nothingness experience, they suggest, might require a thoroughgoing dissolution of the brain's software, with a new program installed. Charting the existence of such breaks, using electroencephalograms (EEGs) (in a master in *nirodha samāpatti*) and the like, is only a first step in this interesting new area of study, which can be further fine-tuned to detect the various stages of turning off the mind's various levels of structure.

Graham Priest presents an account of nothingness that thoroughly substantivalizes it, so that *everything* comes from *nothing*, the very antithesis of *ex nihilo nihil fit*. His discussion turns on a logical ambiguity between nothing as a quantifier (an amount) and nothing as a noun (a thing). Much of the confusion over the concept of nothingness, argues Priest, comes from this ambiguity. Yet, Priest argues we should simply accept the paradox and, indeed, accept the contradictions that we seem to be drawn into when saying things, such as nothing is something (indeed: everything = all being). The problem can be traced back to a Western insistence on the absence of paradox (especially to Aristotle who enthroned it as a principle of good reasoning to avoid contradiction). If we can accept this contradiction, then we can avail ourselves of nothingness as a ground of being, and Priest outlines an account whereby nothingness provides the necessary contrast-class for something to make sense metaphysically. We might express this simply as without nothing, no something.

Paul Redding takes up a famous philosophical account, that of Hegel, that comes to a similar conclusion to Priest, but for different reasons. While Priest argues that nothingness is a *ground* of being (with a necessary distinction between the two), Hegel argued that nothingness just *is* being: There is no distinction at all. This seems even more paradoxical than Priest's paradox and appears to be saying something like 1=0! The contradiction is resolved by Hegel in saying that neither being nor nothingness is fundamental: Incessant *becoming* is the truth about reality. Being becomes nothing, and nothing becomes being in an Heraclitan strife of opposites. Like Priest, Redding traces the problems back to the Greeks, with their distaste for zero ("nullophobia"). The Indian/Asian use of zero created greater conceptual possibilities that were simply unavailable to those systems rooted in the Greek framework. However, Redding notes that Hegel's work ultimately spoils this account, especially evident in Hegel's discussion of the reality of infinitesimals, in which Hegel appears to synthesize the two systems of thought. The notion of an infinitesimal (not quite nothing, but not quite something), from the early days of calculus, was steeped in controversy and mystery. Hegel's treatment of these curious quantities was a blend of East and West.

Inja Strecenski and Daniela Helbig bridge the philosophical and literary aspects of nothingness by pulling together a pair of thinkers, Martin Heidegger (a philosopher) and Georges Perec (a novelist), contrasted in obvious ways (one an anti-Judaist, the other a Jewish Shoah-survivor), but aligning on their treatment of the perplexities of nothingness, in particular the quotidian experience of being as somehow entangled with nothingness. Heidegger is quite possibly the philosopher most associated with nothingness, though often for the frustrating impenetrability of his writings on the matter. Heidegger gives free rein to the paradox of the status of nothingness. Perec, it is shown, does something similar, showing how what we think of as merely nothing in our everyday lives is full of contingent somethings that usually sit below the threshold of awareness. Indeed, the very attempt to speak of nothing automatically frames it as a something. Indeed, there is an inescapable kind of creation from nothing in this process, which Perec is seen to capture with humor and without the heavy load associated with philosophy. Just as filling a blank page with words offers a creation out of a lesser, kind of nothing, so the filling in of an experience of the world that might appear to offer *nothing* is a creative act.

Turning to the visual arts and the empty space of the canvas rather than the page, David Chai discusses a little-known "brush with nothingness" of ink-wash master Jing Hao (c. 850-911) in whose works there is an attempt to capture something like nothingness (construed as ineffability) through specific strokes embodying the breath of nature (the vital breath) in the potentiality of the brush/canvas. It is an impossible task to capture the full dynamic nature of a scene since one is faced with a formless form. Rather than aiming for realism, there is something like a minimal capture of the numinous experience of such a scene, with a resonance established between the painter and the painted (and, later in viewing, the viewer and the painting). Here the links to Taoism and the idea of a cosmic unity are readily apparent, with the act of painting in this case amounting to a mystical experience.

James Heisig keeps us in the realm of Eastern thought, focusing on the very significant role of the concept of nothingness in Japanese philosophy. The Japanese view is, like some already mentioned, bound up with the idea of *becoming* or flux rather than *being* as the mark of the real, once again generating an apparent paradox: To be is to become. But against what does this flux operate? Here, says Heisig, is where nothingness comes into play offering a ground somewhat akin to that described by Priest, though in this case it does not get its own existence via a contrast with being, since there is no being. Rather, it is the ultimate basis of reality, and as such has rather more in common in this sense with Schelling's ideas, as discussed by Rickles. Indeed, Heisig notes that the Kyoto school, based around Nishida Kitarō (1870–1945), were influenced by the German idealists including, unsurprisingly given Hegel's own considerable work on the history of Asian philosophy. What is clear from this discussion is that recent Japanese philosophy is especially concerned with the concept of nothingness to such a degree that it is really the core theme rather than a mere appendix, as Heisig puts it.

Gerard Guiton also discusses the idea of formlessness as being the essence of reality and at the heart of the contemplative life and the way into several meditative practices and a deeper understanding of several key concepts in Sufism. What emerges is a view in which nothing is not something to be worshipped (a point also made by Priest), but something that stands against the gift of its opposite we are presented with. Hence, Guiton defends *somethingism*.

Ken Parry examines the themes of negative theology (apophaticism, or characterizing something by listing what it is not) and being godlike, focusing on Meister Eckhart and Nicholas of Cusa. The basic idea is that since we cannot know God directly, we must resort to apophaticism as the only way to say *anything* at all. In contrast to Guiton, rather than approaching something to gain an appreciation for the divine, on these apophatic accounts one must detach in order to allow space for the divine to enter; what remains after all has been removed is God. In so doing one becomes Godlike. Going further, Nicholas of Cusa argues that the something (finite creation) itself emerged via a contraction of God, creating in itself a space for us to enter.

The final chapter by Nathan Wolski considers the Zoharic treatment of nothingness, or *Ayin*, which involves a highly detailed analysis of its nature and its preeminent role in the kabbalistic theology, sitting, as Wolski puts it, at the apex of the Godhead. One path is a variant of the apophatic approach of Eckhart, in which one gets to *God is the Not* by extending negative theology to its limit, though one does not achieve understanding in this way, but only a statement of existence. Wolski describes the stages of the generation of being from nothingness through a Yiddish creation myth (*Der Kadmen*) by author Der Nister (a pseudonym meaning *the hidden one*), in which God's own becoming from nothingness is expressed as a kind of tale of divine individuation matching the kabbalistic story of emanation. As with Nicholas of Cusa, we find the idea of a contraction of infinity to create a space for finite, temporal beings, but now the infinite (the *Primordium*) desires to know itself in the finite which is clearly problematical. The myth allows us to sympathize with a God faced with inevitable "solipsistic madness" as Wolski puts it. But there is also what Der Nister calls "the Silence," which functions as the nothingness required for being to become, for the divine contraction to occur, which is written as a sacrificial act for *something* to be. However, the Silence appears as a more necessary being than creation, since even if all is destroyed the Silence (nothingness) must remain. It is, as many of the chapters have also argued, ontologically fundamental, at odds with the classical, Western view we mentioned at the outset, that nothingness cannot be.

The conference from which these essays are drawn was part of the larger project *Wandering Mazes Lost: Investigating Arguments over the Problem of Existence*, funded by The John Templeton Foundation. It was an attempt, successful as these essays show, to bring together the physical reality of matter with the realm of spirit, to explore the hidden and the unsayable.

Existential Grounding

1

Your Cosmos Needs You!
From Nothingness to Quantum Existentialism

Dean Rickles

"Objects are only lifted out of nothingness by a human point of view."

Johann Wolfgang von Goethe

Jakob Böhme, the shoemaking theosophist of Gorlitz, conceptualized humans as a kind of cosmic ordering force, saving creation from collapsing into the chaos of a divine abyss. Without our reflecting capacities, there is no way for the world to manifest itself. After all, what would it be manifested *to?* As Böhme understood it, God "hath manifested himself by the externall World in a similitude, that the spirit might see itself in the Being essentially, and not so onely, but that the Creature likewise might contemplate and behold the being of God in the Figure, and know it" (Böhme, *Epistles* 5:14 - in Ellistone, ed., 1886). This idea is a common feature of several well-known philosophical and mystical thinkers,[1] and it also finds its way into more contemporary thought (not least C.G. Jung's work) through Lucien Lévy-Bruhl's (1926) notion of *participation mystique*. However, what is less well known, and this will form the main focus of this paper, is that modern physics is well on its way to incorporating something like this basic feature of reality into its fundamental core. If successful, and we believe it has every right to be so,

---

[1] It is a core tenet of Sufi thinking, for example, as described in the metaphor of the perfect individual as a mirror (see Sells, 1988 and Laude, 2018). But the same idea, of a desire to be known, a yearning for self-revelation, can also be found in, e.g., Plato's *Timaeus*, in Schelling's *The Ages of the World*, and elsewhere. It is this very desire that triggers creation as "a will that wills something" (Schelling, 1813, 143).

it will turn the current paradigm of scientific epistemology on its head. Fundamental to such a viewpoint is the breaking down of the division between subject and object (or observer and world), and in this sense we are drawn also toward elements of existentialist thought. The notion of a participator in reality's construction takes this existentialism further (I call the position "quantum existentialism"), rendering the observer no passive spectator, not simply an actor in the grand drama of creation, but an author too (perhaps as part of a writing team; perhaps with a hierarchy and a principal author).

We all know of the famous line of William Blake, who took so much inspiration from Böhme: "If the doors of perception were cleansed everything would appear as it is: infinite" (*Marriage.* pl.14, E39). It is perception that selects, through attention, what becomes manifest from the chaos, narrowing infinity down to a finite picture of reality. As Lord Kitchener puts it, with some paraphrase, "Your cosmos needs you!" Your cosmos needs you, that is, to carve out order from chaos; to lower the entropy of a world that constantly strives for equilibrium (i.e., maximum entropy and therefore maximal noncreativity and stagnation); to transduce infinite potentiality into some particular feature or event. The chaos here is the nothingness, understood in a radical sense, as a state in which there is not yet any manifestation of anything at all, including both events and their negation. Without this depth of nothingness, in which all possibilities are stored, there could not be any creation of a world. Time in this case becomes part of the conversion of potentiality to actuality. Here, again, we find that quantum mechanics provides a similar viewpoint, in which (for some interpretations at least), the nature of this conversion is formalized in terms of collapse of a superposition of possibilities into some specific outcome, generating a process as it develops.

This paper will explain this curious confluence of old and new ideas, showing how nothingness is the key concept that links them, with quantum mechanics being shown far more than just a theory of physics; rather, it is a deep principle of the cosmos and creation.

Another message of the paper is that such ideas of cocreation are not to be consigned to far-out philosophical (or, worse, new age) speculation. I want to indicate that, properly understood, quantum mechanics is a theory that works through this deep notion of nothingness. Nothingness is really the central and most important feature of the theory. None of the results (especially the so-called "no-go theorems," but also the indeterminacy and the idea of phenomenon creation) really make much sense without it. Moreover, we then see very clearly why quantum mechanics is so hard to understand: Its nonunderstandability is on all fours with the nonunderstandability (ineffability) of nothingness. No wonder we struggle to make sense of it! One can't help getting into a tangle because we are trying to describe what cannot be described, trying to view the ineffable as belonging to the categories of Being and Non-Being.

1. Nothingness and Novelty

Jorges Luis Borges begins his short story *The Immortal* by quoting from Francis Bacon's *Essays*, LVIII: "Salomon saith, 'There is no new thing upon the earth.' So that as Plato had an imagination, that all knowledge was but remembrance; so Salomon giveth his sentence, that all novelty is but oblivion." (Borges, 2004, p. 118). Yet, we might put some pressure on Salomon's remark here. We might wonder what counts as a "thing" ('somethingness') and what counts as "new." We might question, too, exactly what "remembrance" (*anamnesis*) consists of. Certainly, a very nontrivial ontology is being presupposed here, which includes both a theory of time and modality. The implication is that everything possible is actual (the principle of plenitude), and there is infinite time (with no initial creation). Given these conditions, there will indeed be a repeated cycling through all possibilities. Any being sampling such possibilities would indeed do so over and over again, and would only be able to experience "the new" by drinking the draft of forgetfulness and inducing oblivion. However, if this is the first run of events, with an initial creative act, such that we are building as we go, then the conclusion does not follow. Each actualization of a possibility is bringing it into being. In this case, we still need a robust notion of nothingness for there to be newness: It must not "preexist" in whatever it is born from. The new is seen as coming out of nothing. If this were not the case, it would not be new, but would be at best "latent."[2]

---

[2] We return to this issue later, since there is some broad sense in which even an extreme notion of nothingness will have all possibilities *in potentia*. But they will not have being in this case, nor will they have nonbeing. They will be *beyond* being and nonbeing.

We find a version of this problem in what is often considered to be the first philosophical writing on the problem of being and nothingness, in the fragments of Parmenides (see Gallop, 1991). Our usual binary way of thinking in which being and nonbeing are the only possible states, as well as the idea that nothing comes from nothing (*ex nihilo nihil fit*) can indeed be found well-expressed in Parmenides. The context is instructive, for Parmenides was battling against the views of other Greeks. In particular, Anaximander's idea of the boundless *apeiron*, which was postulated to be eternal and changeless, yet it was said to *generate* the opposites, and so the manifest world of duality, which it did so in cycles, as in an eternal recurrence theory. Parmenides's view is similar, viewing the opposites, plurality, and change as a kind of illusion, but sees the generation and dissolution of the manifest world itself as illusory: appearance rather than reality. The opposites cannot exist latently in the changeless, boundless entity lest this simply becomes just another pluralist theory—this is a problem Parmenides identified in other Milesian so-called "Monistic" cosmologies: They are not true monisms since they require this same latent existence of whatever is generated from the monistic basis. Instead, the One-substance cannot change according to Parmenides: What is just is and can't *have been* or can't *come to be*. Again, if such opposite characteristics (e.g., wet and then dry) existed prior to being *separated out*, then the Boundless was not a true unity after all, but if they *did not exist* prior to being separated out, then how could they possibly come into existence without violating the principle of *ex nihilo nihil fit?*[3] Parmenides could not understand how generation/corruption could be meshed with unity.[4] The underlying logic has passed into modern philosophy. But, we will see, other systems of logic allow this. Before we turn to these alternative ideas, let us briefly indicate how the modern debates have been influenced.

J.S. Mill argued, in his *A System of Logic*, that most of philosophy was based on a simple linguistic/logical mix-up of the verb *To Be* in its functions as a copula on the one hand and as implying existence on the other. The separation of subject and attribute/predicate was first formulated in what is called the "Port Royal logic" (devised by Antoine Arnaud in his

---

[3] Anaxagoras would state that *nous*/mind gives the chaos a push into form. This is an early avatar of participatory realism, in which the mind stands outside of the world of things.

[4] Aquinas and Avicenna had a near-identical battle about God's ability to create somethings, with Aquinas playing Parmenides (see Acar, 2002).

The Art of Thinking). One affirms or denies a predicate of a subject through the verbs *Is* or *Is Not*, so that "X exists" means "X is a thing" (propositions here are triples: <subject, join, predicate>). If "to be" and "to exist" have the same meaning, then we may say that from "X does not exist" it follows "There exists an X that does not exist" which gives something that both exists AND does not exist. Here lies the basic Parmenidean contradiction in which we are forced to impute being to a condition of nonbeing:

> Whatever is, is (being—DR) and whatever is not, is not (non-being—DR). As a result, whatever constitutes the nature of reality must always "have been" since nothing can come into being from nothing. Furthermore, reality must always "be" since being (what is) cannot become nonbeing (what is not). … [I]t can neither be thought nor uttered that anything is not. (Fragment 17)

Obviously, this is seen to be problematic when we are asking such questions as "Could there *Be* Nothing?" since we seem to be pushed into talking about positive attributes of Nothing. This takes its most famous shape in the context of Leibniz's problem of "Why is there Something rather than Nothing?" in his essay on "The Ultimate Origin of Things." The very way of posing it in this form shows that Leibniz is stuck in the binary of being and nonbeing and the specter of Parmenides's contradiction looms large—i.e., we are being asked to consider why it is not the case that nothing *exists*.[5]

2. The Being and Nothingness Binary

Charles H. Kahn (Kahn, 2003, p. 109) traces the start of all this debate (Being versus Nothingness / Appearance versus Reality, and so on) to Parmenides:

---

[5] For Leibniz, any explanation of the world must stand outside of it. The ultimate ground, that is, must lie in something external to what is being explained, and this ground itself must be metaphysically necessary rather than contingent. Furthermore, since the reason for an existing thing must come from something that also actually exists, it follows that there must exist some one metaphysically necessary entity (i.e., God) responsible for the world's existence and about which we can probe no deeper in explanatory terms.

> The notion of Being, as formulated by Parmenides, seems to come from nowhere, like a philosophical meteor with no historical antecedents but profound historical consequences. It would be difficult to overstate the influence of this new conception.

But this seems to be simply based on an unnecessary restriction to the Greeks. Indeed, it seems more likely that Parmenides himself was writing as part of a much older context mixing mystical ritual (initiation) and intellect. When we probe more deeply into the source of Parmenides's views, we find a deeper notion of nothingness that better serves issues of creation and better fits the nature of our world. Certainly, Parmenides's fragment is not in the style of modern philosophy but is written rather as a poem, *The Way of Truth* (as opposed to the way of mere opinion, that is), describing an underworld journey (*katabasis*) to visit "The Goddess" in her abode, passing through "the halls of the night" (fr. 1.9). When writing of the goddess he explicitly casts himself as an initiate (one who died while still alive) into still-then ancient mysteries, entering the place intended for souls after death while not suffering that fate (fr. 1.26- 27).

The alternative context for Parmenides's poem looks alien relative to the modern binary "being/nonbeing" distinction. However, Kahn is surely correct about the influence that the binary view has had. If we consider a pair of modern creation stories from physics, we see both the role it plays and how quickly it leads to problems. First, in general relativity, Einstein's theory of space, time, and gravitation, succinctly summarized as "Mass tells space how to curve and space tells matter how to move," is behind the Hubble expansion model of our universe, with its reverse extrapolation to the Big Bang origin. Running the tape of our universe backward seems to lead to a point before which space and time cease to make sense. It looks as if we can extrapolate, theoretically, all the way back to a zero-dimensional point: nothing. However, there is a very basic problem here, which leads to a breakdown of the theory which, as Peter Bergmann (Einstein's research assistant) once remarked, shows that general relativity contains the "seeds of its own destruction" (namely in the form of singularities). As a mass shrinks, e.g., in stellar collapse, the energy density increases. Yet without any reason (e.g., a force) to stop the collapse, there will be no limit, either to the smallness of the collapsing star or the energy density (which will itself result in infinite spacetime curvature, and so a singularity that we associate with a black hole which is understood to be a fully collapsed star in which the matter has been transmuted to pure mass-energy). This has led some physicists, notably John Wheeler, to suggest that there must be a deeper layer than the physics of space, time, matter, energy, and the laws linking them hiding inside the black hole horizon (or the corresponding early and small state of the universe). This layer would be "prephysics," or "prespace," and it tries to get beyond physics in a sense, looking for the raw materials from which the physical world is constructed, which tend to locate the answer in really basic logical entities rather than anything spatiotemporal:

> Glass comes out of the rolling mill looking like a beautifully transparent and homogeneous elastic substance. Yet we know that elasticity is not the correct description of reality at the microscopic level. Riemannian geometry likewise provides a beautiful vision of reality; but ... is inadequate to serve as primordial building material.
> Wheeler, 1977, p.544

In other words, while we ordinarily think of reality as being essentially spatiotemporal, this is inadequate, and we must push beyond such descriptions, which indeed take us further away from things and closer to something like nothing.

Let us now consider another popular origin story, based this time on quantum field theory. The basic idea of the theory is that there is a quantum vacuum whose fluctuations in energy correspond to the generation and corruption of the particles that make up our world. Because of the nature of quantum field theory *qua* quantum theory (and so being subject to the uncertainty principle, which inversely relates some so-called "conjugate" quantities, such as position and momentum or energy and time), there is always a little energy at each point of the vacuum, and so always a little motion.[6] For large times there can be small fluctuations in energy (which can correspond to the production of a particle of some mass). For very short times there is the possibility of enormous fluctuations, including, the creation model[7] goes, the entire universe emerging from one of these. This cosmogony is curious from the point of view of being and nothingness, since the vacuum, functioning as physics's nothingness, is quite clearly very far from a bland, featureless void. It is teeming with life. What we (as good philosophers) might want to ask is: Why is there this quantum vacuum, together with the various laws governing its behaviors, and so on, rather than nothing (in the sense of *no thing whatsoever*)? I point out these examples to indicate that we do not seem to have made progress in the understanding of being, nothingness, and creation: quite the opposite, in fact.

3. Older Conceptions of Nothingness

Curiously, we find that the older conceptions are, in some ways, more sophisticated. For example, the Pyramid and Coffin texts go back almost to 2000 B.C.E. and reveal a depth of understanding of the issues surrounding matters of nothingness and its role in creation. Recall, also, that the Parmenides fragments were written from the point of view of an initiate and so constituted an expression of perennial wisdom of the ancients (possibly predating the Egyptians too). We find a distinctly Parmenidean prototheory in these early "texts," with one coffin text creation story claiming:

---

[6] The details are not important for this paper, but the idea is that the more we try to localize position, the less grasp we have of momentum. A similar complementarity holds for energy and time, so that the more we localize to a small time, the larger the possible fluctuation in energy.

[7] The model is outlined and defended as a complete solution to Leibniz's problem of why there is something rather than nothing in Krauss (2012). Krauss was explicitly aiming to produce an atheistic solution, in contrast to Leibniz's own interventionist model. Again, it fails miserably since it simply assumes a wealth of machinery from our world which is the very stuff we are trying to explain, thus violating Leibniz's idea (and a basic requirement of noncircular reasoning) that we should not help ourselves to what we are trying to explain in an explanation. We might place into this same category any theory that suggests fully Godlike powers of humans (or future versions thereof): From whence the material that is being worked with? From whence the laws, the possibilities?

Nothingness cannot Be.
Nor, however can nothingness be Many.
Many must be something.

While epigrammatic in their simplicity, these ideas are clearly tuning into the same concepts as Parmenides and more modern thinkers. The Egyptians also had a notion of ONE, in which there was no change or division, timeless and which was "before" duality, in which opposites unified:

> O noble ones who are before the Lord of the universe ("the All"), behold, I have come before you. Respect me in accordance with what you know. I am he whom the Unique Lord made before two things ("duality") had yet come into being in this land by his sending forth his unique eye when he was alone, by the going forth from his mouth … when he put Hu ("Logos") upon his mouth. … I brought forth my spell myself. Magic [ḥk3w] is my name. Papyrus BM 10188, Coll. 28/22 (my emphasis)

This deeper level, in which opposites are unified (i.e., before duality), obviously corresponds to something like Nothingness in the sense of No-Thingness, since things are always characterized by some specific attributes that serve to distinguish them from other things, which are grounded in duality.[8] Without such distinctions, there can be no division. But, of course, there appears to be division in our manifest experience. The story was that at the beginning of time, the god *Atum* emerged from

---

[8] This unity of opposites was often represented by a hermaphroditic being, Phanes (or Protogonus), who created the other nonhermaphroditic deities. The Orphic Egg in the Ancient Greek Orphic tradition is viewed as the cosmic egg from which Protogonus emerges—the egg is often depicted with the serpent, Ananke, coiled around it, symbolizing the necessity of a material order governing what is created from the cosmic egg, through Ananke's marriage with *Chronos* (time). In the Upanishads there also exists a supreme being, Parameshwara, but Brahman is the analogous being to Phanes (qua neuter entity). Again, this is such a being that cannot be defined conceptually because that would limit it (it is "*neti neti*": "not this, not that"). The creation then involves the splitting of Brahman through something like the Principle of Plenitude: "from a possibility of plurality, it came." In the Rg veda, rather than an egg, there is the universal womb called "*Hiranyagarbha*": the source of manifest and, ultimately, illusory reality.

the waters of chaos, known as *Nu*, to stand on the initial dry land, *Benben*, to commence the act of creation. *Heka* (related to *spell* or *hex*, indicating that the magical, creative act resides in the word) was the power used—*ka* is the vital spirit which the gods possess. The idea that the creative act involves some kind of breath or sound emission (the word/s of god) was replicated in various other creation stories, where *Hu* becomes *Om,* for example—and, of course, the logos is part of the biblical creation story. *Heka,* too, finds parallel in the *Nous* concept of Anaxagoras, though the passing on of the concept is far stronger in *Heka's* role as the patron god of medicine (a role represented by two snakes).

We find an even more concrete example that suggests a realm beyond the being and nonbeing binary in the *Rg Veda* (1500 B.C.E.). "The Hymn of Creation" is very explicit on this:

> There was neither non-existence nor existence then;
> Neither the realm of space, nor the sky which is beyond;
> What stirred? Where? In whose protection?
> There was neither death nor immortality then;
> No distinguishing sign of night nor of day;
> That One breathed, windless, by its own impulse;
> Other than that there was nothing beyond.
> *Rigveda, Nasadiya Sukta* 10.129 (Abridged, Tr: Krame)

"Neither nonexistence nor existence" is simply not part of the conceptual structure of Western, classical logic: Leibniz's "Why is there something rather than nothing" (Parmenides's being or nonbeing logic) simply cannot conceptually cope with this expanded set of options. We have Not(P) together with Not(NotP), which plainly violates Aristotle's Law of Exclusive Middle.

More recently, we find Plotinus's notion that emanation proceeds from The One, but through a relationship of logical dependence, rather than a temporal process—The One does not *need* to emanate into plurality, and so the splitting through emanation is not one of necessity, as it is with the splitting of Brahman. But, similarly to the neutral foundations we have seen, The One generates *Beings* rather than being, so it *grounds* being (as well as grounding the conditions for nonbeing). It seems we are led to transcendence in terms of emanations of plurality. The *power* coming from The One is not the *same* as The One. Once again, we appear to face the problem that Parmenides found in Anaximander: If there is truly One, then how can a plurality emerge if it is not already precontained, latently as a plurality in that One? We will see that the solution is that the unconditioned realm, while having the *potentiality* for all possibilities (including negative ones), by that very fact (i.e., having the potential for being and nonbeing) cannot be properly said to *have* or *be* either, even in a latent state: They have no existence as actual events or things.

> The One is not being but the generator of being. This, we may say, is the first act of generation: the One, perfect because it seeks nothing, has nothing, and needs nothing, overflows, as it were, and a superabundance makes something other than itself. Plotinus, *Enneads*, V. II, 1, 7-9

Why the emanating in the first place then, we might ask? To not be alone: It's a gift, but one like buying a present for the receiver that benefits the giver. The important point is, however, that the gift that is *gifted* is not a world: It is *a space of real potentialities* that can be worked with by the intelligences and souls that are emanated. However, as is a common theme in discussing such an unconditioned, ineffable realm, Plotinus follows the practice of remaining silent about the deeper first principle from which emanation comes. Again, however, it is important to note that whatever it is, it is not simply nothing, and not simply being, but rather some intermediate or alternative condition.[9] Moreover, this alternative is not to be understood as an absence, but rather a fullness. Indeed, even the naming of it as One is not correct, since being beyond quality it is also being unity and plurality (*cf.* Massie, 2010, p. 155, and also Banner, 2018).

---

[9] Here we might point to what Pascal Massie (2024, p. 143) has labeled "the ontology of non-actuality" which is precisely that which is not actual but not reducible to nonbeing. What I have been calling "potentiality" fits this mode. Massie also uses the term "virtuality," though this term, to my mind, has too much of the very properties Massie is trying to deny, namely essential qualities or facts that can be pinned down—indeed, see Lehman-Wilzig (2022) for an argument suggesting that reality and virtuality are "two sides of the same coin." Of course, we also speak of "virtual reality," which would then be an oxymoron. Massie ultimately subsumes both virtuality and potentiality into what he calls "*Spielraum*" or "play."

4. Nothing Is Real?

> The pre-Socratic Greek philosopher Parmenides taught that
> the only things that are real are things which never change…
> and the pre-Socratic Greek philosopher Heraclitus taught
> that everything changes. If you superimpose their two
> ways, you get this result: Nothing is real.
> Philip Kindred Dick[10]

There is ambiguity in this amusing quote. It could mean that nothing is
real (i.e., nothing has a kind of reality of its own) or that there simply is
no reality at all. Modern thinkers tend to go Parmenidean, as mentioned
already: Nothing can't be part of being, since that is a contradiction. But,
as already intimated, there are realms of thought—Western and otherwise
— that put nothingness as the most real: the ground of being and nonbeing
beyond the Parmenidean binary. When you are dealing with something
that grounds even opposites such as being and nothingness, you're
obviously in for a hard time as a thinker. As Heidegger puts it nicely:
"contradiction is the destruction of all thinkability"—if you're dealing
with something beyond both being and nonbeing, then that is a kind of
hyperdestruction for which there are no words.[11] And, indeed, the fact
that one must seek alternative means of expression is well known in those
lines of thinking that splintered off, running in parallel to most Western
philosophy. In esoteric theology, for example, we find the following (here
from an Irish barrister who had a transformative experience, causing him
to believe he was a messenger of God):

> [T]he state of Being of the Infinite and Absolute
> Reality—the Eternal Parent—during this state of the
> Infinite Unmanifest cannot be expressed in words, for it is
> beyond words. It can be thought of only symbolically—
> by means of Its only possible symbol, i.e., that of Infinite

---

[10] Philip K. Dick, January 1978 talk titled "How to Build a Universe that doesn't fall apart
two days later." Reproduced in: Dick, 1995.
[11] Hegel has an alternative means to bridge the Parmenidean-Heraclitean chasm: His
notion of absolute (pure) Being is, as he put it, for all practical purposes, the same as
Nothing, since no attribution of properties can be given. To this he suggests a synthesis:
The absolute (nothingness) is *becoming*.

> Space. Even symbolized, it can be thought of only in
> terms of negation; for being in the state of Absolute
> Being ... cannot be thought of as possessing any of the
> qualities, attributes, or properties of Thingness.
> Kenealy, 1867, p. 109

Thus, we find a necessary turning to a symbolic representation of
something behind the symbol that cannot be directly indicated. This was a
common theme of Rosicrucian thought, as, for example, in the following:

> Strictly speaking, the Infinite Unmanifest is a "Nothing"
> rather than a "Thing"; and yet not such a "Nothing"
> as implies "not-ness" or "naught," but rather such a
> "Nothing" as implies "The Possibility of Everything, yet
> without the limitations of Thingness."
> Magus Incognito, 1918, p. 25

Again, we find the Heideggerian tangle that occurs in trying to describe
something that sits outside of being and nonbeing. The crucial remark
here, for our purposes, is that of a ground that provides for the possibility
of everything (including absence). These examples are still within
what might be from a Western perspective (despite their obvious wider
provenance). In ancient Chinese thought, we find discussions remarkably
close to these recent accounts, including Heidegger, though with a great
deal more wit. From the fourth century B.C.E. we find the following:

> Now, I have something to say. I don't know if with this
> I am positing a category or not positing a category. But,
> since "positing a category" and "not positing a category"
> themselves involve creating a category, then there is
> nothing with which to distinguish them. Nonetheless,
> allow me to try to say it: "There was a beginning. There
> was not yet beginning to have something beginning.
> There was not yet beginning to have a not yet beginning
> to have something beginning. There was something.
> There was Nothing. There was not yet beginning to
> have Nothing. There was not yet beginning to have a

not yet beginning to have Nothing." Suddenly we have
Something and Nothing, but I don't yet know, with this
Something and Nothing, which is Something and which
is Nothing. Now, as for me, I have already referred to
something, but I don't know yet if I have said something
or if I have said nothing.
Zhuangzi, *Qi Wu Lun,* 2001, p. 55

What is interesting about this line of thinking, which, of course, centers
on the notion of *Tao,* is that it does not involve a creator as such but is a
cosmic ordering power or force. The *Tao* underpins being and nonbeing,
so nonbeing is also something created here. The overarching idea is to
understand oneness, restoring harmony to the world. The system of
thought is as much a guide to good living as it is a cosmology; the two
facets (micro- or human and macro- or cosmic) are not independent of one
another. The above passage from Zhuangzi forms part of a kind of *reductio
ad absurdum* argument against origin stories (which would themselves
involve an attempt to make rational sense of an unconditioned reality). If
something had a beginning, then *before* such a beginning was something
that was not yet beginning, and off to a regress we go—even trying to
rationally distinguish "something" and "nothing" is seen to be problematic,
because it must be founded on something. This way of thinking is thus
opposed to the entire project of cosmogony (of why something rather than
nothing) since such projects exceed what can be said.

    Yet, there is pressure in modern philosophy to always explain and
represent. This is one major source of the so-called Analytic/Continental
split, which Heidegger was placed in the middle of, thanks to his much-
lambasted remarks on the reality of nothing—namely: "Even nothingness
itself is not present without being—The Nothing itself *Noths!*" ("*das
Nichts nichtet*"). His claim basically agrees with Parmenides in one sense
(that nothing cannot be) but disagrees in another (nothing is substantive).
Of course, this looks like a contradiction and was largely laughed at in
analytic philosophy circles, but unfairly I think.[12] If you probe this deeply,

---

[12] Rudolf Carnap was the driving force of the critique in his 1932 manifesto that forged
Logical Positivism in which philosophy must involve claims that are either directly
observable or provable through logic (remodeling itself after the natural sciences): "The
Elimination of Metaphysics Through Logical Analysis of Language." See Chapter 3 of
(Chase, 2013) for a discussion of this historical episode.

it's hard to express and eventually becomes impossible to express—that is part of the point and the trouble: hence, Wittgenstein's earliest mystical phase, where he tells us to just stop talking at a certain point. Misinterpreted perhaps, by Cambridge cronies as: Don't bother even considering anything that cannot be formulated precisely in first-order logic. We are only just emerging from this barren wasteland which only split apart the virtues of clear-thinking from the deep questions that need to be asked and that form the lifeblood of philosophy.

5. From Schelling's Godhead to Quantum Superpositions

While it might look superficially as though modern philosophy and science are completely at odds with these alternative ways of thinking about reality, they are closely aligned at a deeper level. The link can be found even in Heidegger. In particular, Heidegger's study of Friedrich Schelling, which informed much of his thinking about the expanded concept of nothingness. What we find is that the notion being outlined has the exact properties of the quantum state in quantum mechanics. This might sound far-fetched, yet we will see that the notorious interpretive problems of quantum mechanics (e.g., the measurement problem) are on all fours with the problems being tackled by the likes of Heidegger and Schelling.

The same problem of ineffability plagues both. But it is not simply ineffability: There is a close match between the closest formulations we can manage of both the quantum state and the state of nothingness. Consider the following characterization from Schelling:

> The Godhead, in itself, neither is nor is not; or in another
> expression … the Godhead is as well as is not … it neither
> has being nor does it have not being … it has being as
> that which neither has being nor does not have being.
> Schelling, 1815/2000, pp. 26-27)

If we replace "Godhead" with "Quantum State" here, we would have a perfect description of a superposition state in quantum mechanics. Moreover, we can find, if we go down this line of thinking, an explanation for the indeterminacy of quantum mechanics: It is of a kind with human freedom and creativity (which was Schelling's target). Both can exist only because of this deeper ground. It is essential for creativity and creation. Human freedom does not come from quantum indeterminism, as is often erroneously supposed; rather both come from the state of real possibility.[13]

Clearly in these cases there is something beyond classical logic. There are connections in fact to the "*Catuṣkoṭi*" of Indian logic, involving a *tetralemma* with four alternatives rather than the usual classical pair. Like Indian music, this logic affords us some more space to move, with four points (*koṭi*) rather than just the affirmation and negation of the Parmenidean binary. While Aristotle held a principle of the excluded middle, according to which any statement must be either true or false with no third possibility and the two alternatives exclusive, here the *Catuṣkoṭi* gives us an additional "both" and "neither."[14] These four are still mutually exclusive in most applications, yet what Schelling calls "the Godhead," appears to have them *all,* together, simultaneously. What is quite remarkable is that this set (which perfectly matches Schelling's description) is like a density matrix in quantum mechanics describing the state of some quantum system while in an unobserved superposition. In this situation there is entanglement between the alternatives (the best-known example being Schrodinger's cat in the box linked to a quantum process, which has the classical alternatives Alive and Dead). This means that there is *interference* between the two classical alternatives that we would expect to observe on looking into the box so that it can't be said to *be* one or the other until we look, and neither can it said to not be. We can visualize the connection as follows (where A is being and ~A is nonbeing):

---

[13] I might note here that there is an interesting possibility regarding Quantum AI, in which machine learning is linked to quantum computers. In this case, because the AIs would be drawing from this deeper ground, as encoded in quantum states, they might well have access to states of true freedom and creativity like humans.

[14] Hamlet's soliloquy wouldn't sound nearly so good according to this logic, rendered as "to be or not to be, or [to be *and* not to be], or [neither to be nor not to be]? That is the question." Clearly, the principle of noncontradiction also seems to be a casualty of this revised logic.

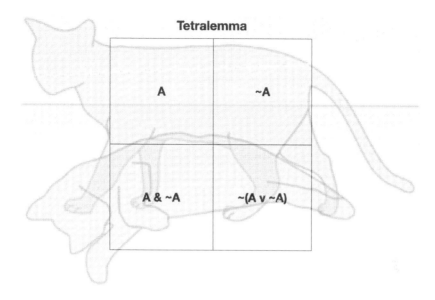

What is interesting about this, and many other approaches that involve "the unconditioned," is that they take the formed reality, the apparently solid world of classical options, as illusory (*Maya*) and the formless, ineffable realm as the *most real*, since it is the ground of the informed world. Quantum reality would provide a version of this idea, with the additional element of a process that shifts the unconditioned reality into a conditioned world (even if this world is nonfundamental). We turn to this additional process next, since this is where the participatory element enters.

6. *Quantum Mechanics and Reality Revelation versus Creation*

A common intuition is that when we observe some object, make a measurement, we are revealing how the world is. Though there might be some slight disturbance, depending on what it takes to make the measurement, the world was in some condition of its own before we made the measurement. As the physicist J.S. Bell put it: "When it is said that something is 'measured' it is difficult not to think of the result as referring to some pre-existing property of the object in question" (Bell, 1990, p. 209).

It was Bell who came up with the theorem that appears to show that this is not how things are in reality: The world does not have preexisting properties and things of its own. This was the real root of Einstein's famous distaste with quantum mechanics. It was not probability (despite his saying "God does not play dice with the Universe"). It was more case of God not needing man to create the world.[15] Einstein wanted a fully objective description ("physical reality"): If we remove man, all runs smoothly. Einstein assumes that there *is* a state of the universe as it is: an "objective universe out there" that measurements and observations reveal to us. Subjectivity can appear in the world, but it is illusory. Niels Bohr, by contrast, argued that the problematic nature of quantum phenomena resulted precisely from the attempt to picture the world as it really is *apart from observation*: a view from nowhere. Even what we would think of as the *results* of experiments, which then seem to be physically objective, are also merely "abstractions" constructed to describe phenomena in terms of observer and observed when that distinction doesn't exist at a fundamental level, since they form a relative pair, rather than a relationship between absolute realities. For Bohr, quantum theory grasped a fundamental truth about epistemology, namely that it is always relational in this way.

However, Bohr tended to follow the path of silence about the nature of reality outside of this relational link between observer and observed. Quantum theory was as much a description of the limitations of knowledge as it was about the world itself. He notes "that all departures from common language and ordinary logic are entirely avoided by reserving the word 'phenomenon' solely for reference to unambiguously communicable information" (Bohr, 1963, pp. 5-6). That is: We must situate ourselves within the Parmenidean binary if we wish to speak to one another and make sense. This was taken to mean that Bohr was only concerned with the results of measurement and so was an instrumentalist. Nothing could be further from the truth. It was one of Bohr's protégés, John Wheeler, who developed Bohr's ideas further into a theory of the participatory nature of reality, beyond the pure phenomenon. To make sense of this idea, let us briefly mention a simple example of quantum mechanics in which we can see at work the idea that the quantum world does not have its being or nonbeing fixed

---

[15] John Wheeler claimed that "Nothing made [Einstein] more unhappy than the thought that the observer-participator has anything to do with the establishment of what one is accustomed to call reality." (1986, p. 373).

independently of some additional participatory process involved that specifies how it is to manifest itself.

This situation has much in common with existentialism. Consider the following description of this position, which is most useful for our purposes:

> The existentialist position challenges the traditional Cartesian view of a world full of objects and of subjects who perceive those objects. ... The existentialist position cuts below this subject-object cleavage and regards the person not as a subject who can, under the proper circumstances, perceive external reality but as a consciousness who participates in the construction of reality.
> Yalom, 1980, p. 1

This bears much in common with Bohr's insistence that the world cannot be divided from the observer of that world. However, whereas standard existentialism focuses on human identity and values, which do not preexist the acts of creation and construction leading to them, in the case of quantum mechanics neither does the world preexist acts of creation.

A new approach, taking the baton from Wheeler, who took it from Bohr[16], is QBism (developed primarily by Chris Fuchs). This approach states that the theory of quantum mechanics is a kind of tool for an agent navigating the world. The quantum states themselves are subjective. The world "out there" is unknown, but quantum mechanics can tell you things about what you will experience given certain interventions and experiments. So, quantum states are states of information, knowledge, belief, pragmatic gambling commitments, not states of nature. The quantum system represents something real and independent of us; the quantum state represents a collection of subjective degrees of belief about something to do with that system (even if only in connection with our experimental kicks to and from it). The structure called quantum mechanics is about the interplay of these two things—the subjective and the objective. What is "outside" of this is ineffable, something QBists avoid by simply denying that their theory is about anything other than

---

[16] Wheeler (1986, p. 373) claims that Bohr, 30 minutes before his death, admitted that "was an objective description" of reality, rather than simply a scheme for communicating measurement results.

experience, so that the external world, strictly speaking, is not modeled. Harvey Brown has argued that this renders the view untenable and, in fact, empirically incoherent. As he puts it: "QBism ... does not deny the existence of an observer-independent reality ... But I find the ineffable nature of the external world in QBism troubling" (Brown, 2019, p. 80). Indeed, it is troubling, in the same way that philosophers are troubled by the notion of nothingness along the lines of Schelling.[17]

Brown misunderstands that what is empirical comes out of this ineffable chaos[18], and it must: Quantum mechanics *requires* a being before being, because it contains what would otherwise be contradictions such as the Cat-Alive + Cat-Dead, which cannot be or not be in an ordinary sense. Hence, the deeper nothingness is a ground of the empirical world and empirical science.

> [O]ur actions matter indelibly for the rest of the universe," for quantum mechanics "signals the world's plasticity ... [w]ith every quantum measurement set by an experimenter's free will, the world is shaped just a little as it participates in a kind of moment of birth.
> Fuchs, 2011, p. 172

Realism usually means there is a "world out there" (independent of the subject). Let us give a simple example that makes some of these ideas clearer, by looking at the double-slit experiment:

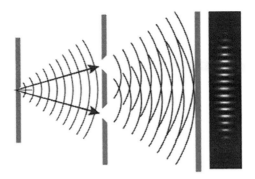

---

[17] Little wonder that John Wheeler claims that he was "driven crazy" by the unobserved world (mentioned in an interview in *Alcade* magazine, November/December 1985, p. 12).
[18] As Jung puts it: "The multiplicity of the empirical world rests on an underlying unity [*Unus Mundus*], and that not two or more fundamentally different worlds exist side by side... Rather, everything divided and different belongs to one and the same world." (Jung, 1955-56, para. 767).

We have a source that can emit light, at a rate of one photon at a time (alternatively, one can use electrons, which also have wavelike properties in quantum mechanics). Beyond this is a diffraction screen with two slits, intended to generate interference effects, much as if water were passing through. Beyond that is a detection screen which will indicate what happened in the experiment by revealing a definite *phenomenon* that can be communicated, according to Bohr's idea. Now, depending on where you put measuring equipment, you will manifest a different feature of reality (i.e., a different phenomenon will appear).

This is what we might label an "informational approach": The asking of one question stands in a *complementary* relation to the asking of another. If we are measuring at the slits, then we make a "where is the particle?" measurement and generate a response from the world according to that frame. Measuring at the screen, we measure wave aspects (momentum), and generate a response according that frame instead. We cannot do both simultaneously.[19]

The world hasn't yet decided what it is in such scenarios: It is full of possibility, and creation (understood now as the manifestation of a phenomenon) occurs only when we enjoin ourselves to it in some way. Note that this is not idealism: It does not reject "a world," we don't get to decide *which*, properties are manifested, but only what kind of properties. We still have the quantum indeterminacy. Neither, of course, did we make the stuff of reality itself. But it is not quite e*xistence* preceding essence, as in orthodox existentialism; it is subtly different from such views. If anything, it is nothingness that precedes existence and essence, and nonexistence. This is akin to William James's "possibilism": There is real possibility in the world, and what that means, ultimately, is that there is a state (call it what you will) in which no thing is manifest. What is this other than freedom.

Referring back to *participation mystique*, we find Jung expressing almost the same idea as participatory realists:

---

[19] On a more technical note, one can build up quantum mechanics from such ideas. The reception of an answer to a question put to the world demands *distinguishability*. The mathematical analysis of distinguishability demands probability amplitudes. Complementarity demands that these probability amplitudes be complex. Which leads a long way toward quantum mechanics itself. See Wootters (1983).

> If God's consciousness is clearer than man's, then the
> Creation has no meaning and man no *raison d'etre*. In
> that case God does not in fact play dice, as Einstein says,
> but has invented a machine, which is far worse.
> C.G. Jung, letter to James Kirsch, 28th May 1953[20] Jung,
> 1975, pp. 117-8.

What we can draw from this is that if the creation does have meaning, then we are playing our part in it: This *is* our meaning (or at least a very significant component). And yet, Einstein is suggesting precisely a preference for a machine, with no space for play: everything already laid out once and for all, a logically closed system, no part of which could be altered without collapsing the whole edifice. This is quite clearly antiexistentialist. There are true essences on Einstein's account (hidden variables).

We find John Wheeler writing along these same lines, in adopting a role for participation mystique in physics:

> Nature at the quantum level is not a machine that goes
> its inexorable way. It is wrong to think of the universe
> as "sitting out there." Instead, what we get depends on
> what question we put, what experiment we arrange,
> what registering device we choose. We are inescapably
> involved in bringing about that which appears to be
> happening.[21]
> Wheeler, 1983, p. 184

However, again, this is clearly not standard existentialism. Jean-Paul Sartre would say "The world is a mirror of my freedom," but this isn't

---

[20] Similarly: "Without the reflecting consciousness of man the world is a gigantic meaningless machine, for in our experience man is the only creature who is capable of ascertaining meaning at all" (Jung 1975, letter to Neumann, 10th March, 1959, p. 494). William James earlier made strikingly similar remarks: "The scientific world-picture vouchsafes a very complete understanding of all that happens—it makes it just a little too understandable. It allows you to imagine the total display as that of a mechanical clockwork, which for all that science knows could go on just the same as it does, without there being consciousness, will, endeavour, pain and delight, and responsibility connected with it—though they actually are" (James, 1983, p. 96).

[21] Further clear remarks along these lines include: "Participatory Observership as the Source of All Useful Meaning" (Wheeler, 1977, p. 21) and "meaning itself powers creation" (Wheeler, 1986, p. 366).

quite correct. We and the world share the same kind of freedom, and both cocreate one another. A world that is purely quantum mechanical would have no definite properties. It would be *dead*, as Blanchard and Jadczyk put it (1996, p. 613). But without the quantum mechanical world, we would be in the same condition. It is the relation, the participation that breathes life into the dead world.[22] Wheeler seems to agree, writing that:

> The vital act is the act of participation. 'Participator' is the incontrovertible new concept given by quantum mechanics. It strikes down the term *observer* of classical theory, the man who stands behind the thick glass wall and watches what goes on without taking part. [T]he observer-participator converts conceivability into actuality. Wheeler, 1980b, p. 5

Because of the split, it appears as though the subject-agent is involved. And they are: no agent-no phenomena, as Wheeler might say. There is a necessary precondition for quantum existentialism: One must have *REAL possibility* to have real creation, for there to be something *New* under the sun. Conversion of pure potentiality (in the sense of the deeper nothingness) into actuality is what creation is all about.[23] There must be true chance. Something must be able to take place without a cause. Wheeler gives an amusing drawing[24] explaining the situation we find ourselves in as seekers of knowledge interacting with the world:

---

[22] In Rickles (2022) I explain how an understanding of our own death is required to breathe this life into the cosmos, since without the limitation on choice there is no necessity to bring some specific path or property into actuality, and one could sample the whole space, which leads to a dead world again. A deeper analysis of Wheeler's position can be found in Atmanspacher & Rickles (2022).

[23] This is comparable to the Greek notion of *entelecheia*, which Leibniz's philosophy made such deep use of. They are that which realizes or makes actual what is otherwise merely potential. This is similar to Aristotle's distinction between matter and form, according to which each thing is decomposed into the elements of which it is composed (which primal stuff not yet an actual thing) and the form which makes it the thing it is. For living beings, the matter must be informed by a vital function or soul, which is the entelechy of the living being.

[24] Bohr's Great Smokey Dragon according to Wheeler: tangible at the teeth and tail, but unknown in between. (Wheeler 1980a, p. 358).

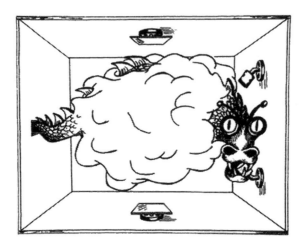

As he explains:

> We have to recognize a new animal in the zoology
> of nature: beyond particle, beyond field of force,
> beyond spacetime geometry, the elementary quantum
> phenomenon. This great smokey dragon, Bohr's
> phenomenon, has its tail sharply localized at the point
> of entry to the apparatus. Its teeth are sharply localized
> where it bites the grain of photographic emulsion. In
> between it is utterly cloud-like, localized neither in space
> nor in time. The search for the message of the quantum
> is a continuing pilgrimage, marked so far by three
> great way-stations: indeterminism, complementarity,
> phenomenon.
> Wheeler, 1983, p. 142

It is my belief that the nothingness, understood along the lines of
Schelling's beyond being and nonbeing, can serve to ground all three
waystations and can include the freedom of the observer-participator.
It provides the "something deeper than geometry, that underlies both
geometry and particles [which] must provide the Universe with a way to
come into being" (Wheeler and Patton, 1975, p. 538). We can, in fact, view
this waystation triple as a kind of flowchart: Start from indeterminacy,
then add will-choice/participator (which involves posing questions to the
world), and then get a definite, manifest world out (= Phenomenon or

Tangible Reality). Wheeler spoke of "definiteness out of indeterminism," and this provides a way of thinking about what that might mean. There is a sense in which the nothingness contains all worlds, if only in *potentia*. It takes a relation-with-an-agent to select/realize: We (or beings with self-awareness and freedom) are the crucial component in rendering potential actual. Wheeler quoted approvingly from James's The *Dilemma of Determinism*:

> Actualities seem to float in a wider sea of possibilities from out of which they were chosen; and somewhere, indeterminism says, such possibilities exist, and form part of the truth.
> Wheeler, 1974, p. 683

We require a nothingness from which to select what is not yet anything or nothing, and we must be part of that same realm if such acts are to be free.

Again, we find a curious parallel between Jung and Wheeler here:

> Man, I, in an invisible act of creation put the stamp of perfection on the world by giving it objective existence. This act we usually ascribe to the Creator alone, without considering that in so doing we view life as a machine calculated down to the last detail, which, along with the human psyche, runs on senselessly, obeying foreknown and predetermined rules. In such a cheerless clockwork fantasy there is no drama of man, world, and God; there is no "new day" leading to "new shores," but only the dreariness of calculated processes.
>
>   My old Pueblo friend came to mind. He thought that the *raison d'etre* of his pueblo had been to help their father, the sun, to cross the sky each day. I had envied him for the fullness of meaning in that belief, and had been looking about without hope for a myth of my own. Now I knew what it was, and knew even more: that man is indispensable for the completion of creation; that, in fact, he himself is the second creator of the world, who alone has given to the world its objective existence— without which, unheard, unseen, silently eating, giving

birth, dying, heads nodding through the millions of years, it would have gone on in the profoundest night of non-being down to its unknown end. Human consciousness created objective existence and meaning, and man found his indispensable place in the great process of being.
Jung, 1989, pp. 255- 256

William James summarized the situation as: "The universe = God and Company, Ltd" (2012, p.154). Wheeler, ever the Jamesian, writes that we are a "participator in genesis" (Patton and Wheeler, 1975, p. 538). I began with a mention of Jakob Bohme. Cosmogenesis is, for Böhme, the divine's own quest to become whole, with us humans participating in this attempt, helping God through our focus. Böhme's cosmology places a heavy responsibility upon humanity, as the completion of the sevenfold cycle depends upon our active cooperation. In this new participatory approach, quantum existentialism, is meaning and opportunity: We can see a rosier future if we can see ourselves as participators involved in what happens next and if we understand that the future is not yet written. This viewpoint is making its way into normal channels:

> Theodore Roosevelt's decision to build the Panama Canal shows that free will moves mountains, which implies, by general relativity, that even the curvature of space is not determined. The stage is still being built while the show goes on.
> Conway & Kochen, 2006, p. 1472[25]

The problem is making the world *en masse* aware of this responsibility they have, so as to stop the damage to the environment, for example. I find quantum existentialism offers up, not only a viewpoint closely aligned with a rich history of ideas from across time and space, but also one closely aligned with societal engagement and the future of humanity.

---

[25] The quote comes from a discussion of the authors' "free will theorem," which states that if the experimenter can freely choose the directions in which to orient his apparatus in a certain measurement, then the particle's response (to be pedantic—the universe's response near the particle) is not determined by the entire previous history of the universe (Conway & Kochen, 2009, p. 226).

Note that this is not the common "humans are Gods" idea here. There is more humility since the entire approach is based on a basic recognition that we are limited in what we can know about reality. The source is forever hidden from view. Let us then leave the final word to Edwin Arnold (Arnold, 1891, p. 211), who perfectly summarizes the situation we find ourselves in:

> Measure not with words the Immeasurable;
> Nor sink the string of thought into the Fathomless.
> Who asks does err; who answers, errs;
> say naught!
> Shall any gazer see with mortal eyes?
> Or any searcher know with mortal mind?
> Veil after veil will lift—but there must be Veil upon Veil behind!

References

Acar, R. (2002) *Creation: A Comparative Study Between Avicenna's and Aquinas' Positions*. Ph.D. Dissertation, Harvard University.

Atmanspacher, H. & Rickles, D. (2022) *Dual-Aspect Monism and the Deep Structure of Meaning*. London: Routledge.

Arnold, E. (1891) *The Light of Asia, or the Great Renunciation (Mahâbhinishkramana): Being the Life and Teaching of Gautama, Prince of India and Founder of Buddhism (as Told in Verse by an Indian Buddhist)*. Boston: Roberts Brothers.

Banner, N. (2018) *Philosophic Silence and the 'One' in Plotinus*. Cambridge: Cambridge University Press.

Barad, K. (2007) *Meeting the Universe Halfway: Quantum Physics and the Entanglement of Matter and Meaning*. Durham, NC: Duke University Press.

Bell, J. S. (1990) Against 'Measurement.' In J. S. Bell & Aspect (eds.), *Speakable and Unspeakable in Quantum Mechanics: Collected Papers on Quantum Philosophy* (pp. 213-231). Cambridge: Cambridge University Press, 2004.

Blanchard, P. & Jadczyk, A. (1996) Time of Events in Quantum Theory. *Helvetica Physica Acta*, 69, 613-635.

Borges, J. L. (2004) *Aleph and Other Stories*. London: Penguin.

Brown, H. (2019) The Reality of the Wavefunction: Old Arguments and New. In A. Cordero (ed.), *Philosophers Look at Quantum Mechanics* (63-86). Berlin: Springer.

Chase, J. (2013) *Analytic Versus Continental: Arguments on the Method and Value of Philosophy*. London: Acumen Publishing.

Conway, J. & Kochen, S. (2009) The Strong Free Will Theorem. *Notices of the American Mathematical Society*, 56, pp. 226-232.

—————. (2006) The Free Will Theorem. *Foundations of Physics,* (10)36, 1441-1437.

Dick, P. R (1995). *The Shifting Realities of Philip K. Dick: Selected Literary and Philosophical Writings*. New York: Vintage.

Ellistone, J. (1886) *The Epistles of Jacob Boehme*. London: John Thompson.

Fuchs, C. (2017) Participatory Realism. In Durham, I.T. & Rickles, D. (eds.), *Information and Interaction* (113-134). Berlin: Springer.

Gallop, D. (1991) *Parmenides of Elea: A Text and Translation with an Introduction*. Toronto: University of Toronto Press.

James, W. (1983) *The Principles of Psychology, Volumes I and II*. Cambridge, MA: Harvard University Press.

————. (2012) *The Will to Believe and Human Immortality*. Mineola, NY: Dover Publications.

Jung, C. G. (1955-56). *Mysterium Coniunctionis*. The Collected Works of C.G. Jung, Vol. 14, R.F. Hull, trans. Princeton: Princeton University Press.

————. (1975) *Letters, Volume II* (G. Adler & J. Jaffe, eds.). Princeton, NJ: Princeton University Press.

————. (1989). *Memories, Dreams, Reflections*. G. Adler & A. Jaffe, eds. R. & C. Winston, trans. New York: Vintage Books.

Kahn, C. H. (2003) *The Verb 'Be' in Ancient Greek. Indianapolis:* Hackett Pub. Co.

Kenealy, E. V. (1867) *The Book of God. An Introduction to The Apocalypse of Adam-Oannes*. London: Reeves & Turner.

Krauss, L. (2012) *A Universe from Nothing*. New York: Free Press.

Laude, P. (2018) *Shimmering Mirrors: Reality and Appearance in Contemplative Metaphysics East and West*. New York: State University of New York Press.

Lévy-Bruhl, L ([1912] 1926) *How Natives Think* (Translated by Lilian A. Clare). London: Knopf Collection.

Magus Incognito (1918) *The Secret Doctrine of the Rosicrucians*. Chicago: Advanced Thought Publishing Co.

Massie, P. (2010) *Contingency, Time, and Possibility: An Essay on Aristotle and Duns Scotus*. Lanham, MD: Lexington Books.

————. (2024) Reality, Virtuality, and Play. *Phenomenological Studies*, 8, 143-166.

Patton, C. M. & Wheeler, J. A. (1975) Is Physics Legislated by Cosmogony? In Isham, C.

Penrose, R. and Sciama, D. (eds.), *Quantum Gravity: An Oxford Symposium* (538-605). Oxford: Clarendon Press.

Rickles, D. (2022) *Life Is Short: An Appropriately Brief Guide to Making it More Meaningful*. Princeton, NJ: Princeton University Press.

Schelling, F.W. J. (1815/2019), *Ages of the World*. J.M. Wirth, trans. Albany, NY: SUNY Press.

Schilpp, P. A. (1951) *The Philosophy of Alfred North Whitehead*. New York: Tudor Publishing Company.

Schlosshauer, M., ed. (2011) *Elegance and Enigma: The Quantum Interviews*. Berlin: Springer.

Sells, M. (1988) Ibn 'Arabi's Polished Mirror: Perspective Shift and Meaning Event. *Studia Islamica*, 67, 121-149.

Wheeler, J.A. (1974) Perspectives: The Universe as Home for Man: Puzzles attached to consciousness, the quantum principle, and how the universe came into being suggest that the greatest discoveries are yet to come. *American Scientist*, 62(6), 683-691.

—————. (1977) Genesis and Observership. In Butts, R.E., Hintikka, J. (eds.), *Foundational Problems in the Special Sciences* (3-33). Dordrecht, Netherlands: Springer.

—————. (1980) Pregeometry: Motivations and Prospects. In Marlow, A.R. (ed.), *Quantum Theory and Gravitation* (1–11). Amsterdam: Academic Press.

—————. (1980b) Beyond the Black Hole. In Woolf., H. (ed.) *Some Strangeness in Proportion* (341-375). Reading, MA: Addison-Wesley.

—————. (1981) The Lesson of the Black Hole. *Proceedings of the American Philosophical Society*, 125(1), 25–37.

—————. (1983) Law without law. In J.A. Wheeler and W.H. Zurek (eds.), *Quantum Theory and Measurement (*183–213). Princeton, NJ: Princeton University Press.

—————. (1986) Hermann Weyl and the Unity of Knowledge. *American Scientist*, 74(4), 366–375.

Wootters, W. (1983) A Measure of the Distinguishability of Quantum States. In Meystre, P. and Scully, M. O. (eds.), *Quantum Optics, Experimental Gravity, and Measurement Theory* (145-154). Boston: Springer.

Yalom, I. (1980) *Existential Psychotherapy*. New York: Basic Books.

Zhuangzi, *QiWu Lun* (A. C. Graham, trans., 2001), *Chang Tzu: The Inner Chapters*. Indianapolis: Hackett Publishing Co.

2

On Mind and Void: Understanding the Duality of Existence and Nothingness

Ian T. Durham

1. The Duality of Existence and Nothingness

What is nothingness? By definition, one would think it isn't anything. Isn't that the point? But then that begs the question, what is "anything"? For that matter, what is "*is*"? As Whitehead once said, "Philosophy is an attempt to express the infinity of the universe in terms of the limitations of language" (1948, p. 21). Language, of course, is naturally recursive; every word in a dictionary is defined in terms of other words that are also defined in that same dictionary. As Russell points out,

> Since all terms that are defined are defined by means of other terms, it is clear that human knowledge must always be content to accept some terms as intelligible without definition, in order to have a starting-point for its definitions.
> 1919, pp. 3-4

Is nothingness such a term?

Editors of dictionaries make valiant attempts to avoid overt acknowledgement of this but cannot escape the vagaries and nuance of human experience and our attempts to describe it. The *Oxford English Dictionary*, considered by many to be the definitive catalog of the English language, says this about nothingness:

nothingness, *n*. (1) a. The realm of non-existence; that which is non-existent. b. The state or condition of being non-existent... c. Absence or cessation of consciousness or life. d. *Philosophy*... In existential thought: non-existence or the non-existent as an ontological category considered in relation to human existence. (2) a. The futility or vanity of a thing or activity; the worthlessness or vapidity of. b. That which has no value or worth; the condition of being worthless or vapid. (3) Insignificance or unimportance. (4) As a count noun: a non-existent thing, a void; a state of non-existence or worthlessness; a worthless, insignificant, or unimportant thing, action, etc. (5) *Buddhism*. Also in form no-thing-ness. = *sunyata n*. [3]

In the first and fourth definitions, nothingness is defined in contrast to existence. The fifth definition is more subtle; it references the concept of *śūnyatā*, which has a variety of meanings in Indian philosophical traditions (not just Buddhism). In the sense implied here, while *śūnyatā* can be interpreted as a kind of "voidness" representing ultimate reality, it is perhaps better interpreted as the undifferentiated unity from which all apparent distinctions arise. Understood in those terms, it is more a complement to existence than a negation of it. Neither does it necessarily deny "thingness," which is a property that calls to mind categorical distinctions in the manner of Heidegger. That is, "no-thingness" is about denying the property of "thingness" rather than denying that — "thing" — which possesses that property. Rather, it is "no-thing-ness" that denies "thing." Existence, in the form of an undifferentiated unity, is taken for granted.

Perhaps more accurately, existence is *experienced*. We experience our own existence and we do so as an undifferentiated whole. That is, our experience is "this" and *only* "this"; it is never "that." Put another way, we do not experience a chair, say, separately from the floor or the air in a room. While we can certainly *describe* separate interactions with these things, the fact is that our experience of them is simultaneous and undifferentiated as far as our conscious selves are concerned. The concept of individual "thing," as regards our experience, is an emergent, categorical labeling of various parts of that experience.

That is not to say that there is no difference in a physical sense. You can no more breathe in a chair than you can sit in air. The categorical labeling is necessary for us to make sense of and navigate through our experience. Rather, the question here is one of existence in a metaphysical sense as a means of understanding nothingness. But what, then, is existence?

The question itself lies at the very heart of philosophy as a discipline. Eddington (physicist and astronomer by trade) had this to say:

> Existence seems to be a rather important property, because I gather that one of the main sources of division between different schools of philosophy is the question whether certain things exist or not. But I cannot even begin to understand these issues, because I can find no explanation of the term 'exist.'
> Eddington, 1939, p. 154

He attributes some of this confusion to the myriad ways in which we use the term. But he also makes it clear that ambiguity in the definition is not the only problem here. He gives the example of an overdraft on a bank account. From the standpoint of the bank and the customer whose account has been overdrawn, the overdraft certainly possesses a particular kind of existence. But it's not quite the same thing as the existence of the bank itself since the overdraft is fundamentally a negation.

Likewise, there is the problem of tense. Do the past and future exist? Sartre's character Antoine Roquentin in *La Nausée* thinks not:

> The true nature of the present revealed itself: it was what exists, and all that was not present did not exist. The past did not exist. Not at all. Not in things, not even in my thoughts. It is true that I had realized a long time ago that mine had escaped me. But until then I had believed that it had simply gone out of my range. For me the past was only a pensioning off: it was another way of existing, a state of vacation and inaction; each event, when it had played its part, put itself politely into a box and became an honorary event: we have so much difficulty imagining nothingness. Now I knew: things are entirely what they

appear to be—and behind them . . . there is nothing.
2007, pp. 95-96

Roquentin has come to the conclusion that our belief in the ontological existence of the past is rooted in our inability to imagine nothingness. He maintains that this belief in the past is an illusion; there really is nothing beyond our immediate experience of the present.

And therein lies Eddington's point. Existence is a classification assigned to things in different contexts by different sorts of people. By and large, we rarely run into problems; philosophers who might professionally deny that an overdraft "exists" in a philosophical sense are likely to grudgingly admit to a certain kind of existence if it is their bank account that has been overdrawn. Likewise, Roquentin might be forced to accept a certain type of past as having existed when confronted with its consequences. But that belies a deeper issue regarding the notion of existence.

There is a certain sense in which "exists" is synonymous with "is." To exist means *to be*. Sartre's magnum opus, *Being and Nothingness*, could just as easily, though perhaps not as poetically, been titled *Existence and Nothingness*. Eddington explains:

> For me (and, it appears, also for my dictionary) 'exists' is a rather emphatic form of 'is.' "A thought exists in somebody's mind," i.e. a thought is in somebody's mind—I can understand that. "A state of war exists in Ruritania," i.e. a state of war is in Ruritania—not very good English, but intelligible. But when a philosopher says "Familiar tables and chairs exist," i.e. familiar tables and chairs are..., I wait for him to conclude. Yes? What were you going to say they are? But he never finishes the sentence. Philosophy seems to me full of half-finished sentences; and I do not know what to make of it.
> 1939, p. 156

Eddington sees existence as an equivalence, which is to say it defines a *distinction*. A chair is a chair, not a hedgehog; if chairs were hedgehogs, then the difference between them would be purely semantic. That is, the existence of something implies that *it is not something else*. This suggests a certain relativism to existence in the following sense: Something exists only in so much as it can be distinguished from something else; that which cannot be distinguished does not exist.

But what about the very concept of existence itself? Nothingness seems to be dual to the *concept* of existence rather than to the existence of a specific thing. Nothingness either implies a void, in the more traditional sense, or an indistinguishability in the śūnyatā sense, which, in both cases, contrast with what we might term "somethingness." It seems the concept of existence is relative to the concept of nothingness. Indeed, it would be difficult (if not impossible) to define one without reference to the other.

The depth and importance of this idea cannot be understated. To reiterate, the existence of some thing only makes sense in relation to some *other thing*. Likewise, existence itself only makes sense in relation to nothingness and vice versa; they represent a fundamental duality.

2. The Metamathematics of Structure

The fundamental duality of existence and nothingness represents a form of *structuralism,* which, broadly construed, claims that objects are only interpretable in relation to a larger system. While often applied to human culture, there is a mathematical form that claims that what matters to a mathematical theory is not the nature of its objects, be they numbers, sets, functions, etc., but rather their relation to one another and to the broader context set by the theory.

Taking the śūnyatā notion of "no-thing-ness" as implying the emergence of "thing" from the categorical labeling of the various parts of our unified experience, we can attribute to these categorical labels, a set of symbols, e.g., A, ρ, $\bar{\chi}$, etc. This is not mathematics; it is merely taxonomy. But taxonomy by itself is meaningless. The point of taxonomy is to compare things. We label this "A" and that "B" in order to distinguish them. But distinguishability is really a comparison of properties and qualities. Categorical labeling, then, is ultimately a relational notion.

It is quite possible, of course, for two things, A and B, to differ in more than one way. Thus, it may be necessary to label the various relations, to which we can associate another set of symbols distinct from the first. Likewise, it may be our experience that A can *become* B (and potentially vice versa). This is an action that is predicated on a certain type of relation between *A* and *B*. There may be many such actions in our experience, and thus again we may find it helpful to label these separately from the relations and the things. Patterns may emerge, and we may find it further helpful to compare relations to relations and actions to actions, which would require even more symbols. But to be clear, we are still squarely in the realm of taxonomy. We are simply *labeling* the different parts of our experience. Nevertheless, there is a sense in which our labeling becomes more and more abstract. There is undoubtedly a level of abstraction at which the veritable sea of symbols we may have collected begins to resemble something wholly unto itself, entirely separate from the things it represents. That is, at some point the sea of symbols takes on a certain structure.

For example, suppose that we decide that a certain collection of things from our experience is similar enough to warrant being grouped together in a set that we will label X. We may likewise decide that there is a second collection of things from our experience that also warrants being grouped together in a set that we will label Y. It's entirely possible that there could be overlap between the two sets, e.g., X might stand for all citizens of Poland, and Y might stand for all citizens of Canada. There are undoubtedly people who hold citizenship in both countries, but there is nothing that *requires* there to be overlap.

In any case, depending on the nature of X and Y, there may be many relations between the elements of each. One could argue that systematically articulating the nature of these relations is the domain of mathematics. For example, in mathematics we say that a "function" *from* the set X to the set Y assigns to each element of X, exactly one element of Y. This is, of course, only one possible relation between the two sets. It might be that each element of X could have multiple elements of Y assigned to it, but then it would not be called a "function" in mathematics.

In that sense, we can think of a mathematical function, *f(x)*, as a kind of input-output device that takes one element x from the set $X=\{x_0, x_1, x_2,...\}$, which we denote $x \, i \in X$, and converts it to one (and only one) element y from the set $Y=\{y_0, y_1, y,...\}$, which we denote $y_i \in Y$. Hence, we have the familiar notation $y=f(x)$. Crucially, what sets this apart from simply labeling our experience, is that *something has happened*. We began with $x_i \in X$, turned a proverbial crank, and got $y_i \in Y$ in return. Something from our experience transformed into something else. It is an action.

Our experience is filled with such transformative actions: Seeds turn into flowers, chemical compounds turn into medicines, our younger selves turn into our older selves. But it is also possible for the actions themselves to transform. Evolution, for example, could be interpreted as a transformation of transformations, e.g., the life cycle of a therapod, which itself is a transformation, transforms, over time, into the life cycle of a bird. Mathematically, this is called a "higher-order function" $F(f)$ that takes an element, $f_i(x)$, from a set of functions $F=\{f_0(x), f_1(x), f_2(x), ...\}$ and converts it to an element, $g_i(x)$, in the set of functions $G=\{g_0(x), g_1(x), g_2(x), ...\}$.

At some point in the above it is clear that we have crossed the Rubicon into the realm of mathematics. We have acquired, if not a sea, certainly a small pond of symbols. The properties and general behavior of these symbols define a certain structure that is distinct from that of which it is composed. Individually, the symbols are merely labels, but taken as a whole, they define something richer and more complex, albeit more abstract. This is the essence of mathematical structuralism.

There is a special type of higher-order function that, when it takes itself as an input, outputs itself again. We refer to such a function as *idempotent*. Figure 1 gives a visual comparison of an idempotent function to a standard function in the context of simple input-output devices. The figure gives one a sense of there being an infinite regress in idempotent functions.

standard function   idempotent function

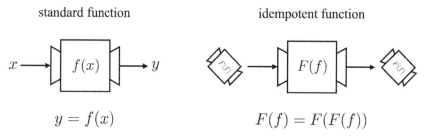

$$y = f(x) \qquad\qquad F(f) = F(F(f))$$

FIG. 1. A standard function *f(x)* takes some element *x* and transforms it into some element *y*. An idempotent function *F(f)* takes itself as input and produces itself as output.

In any case, consider the simple function:
$$f : x^2 = x.$$

This function, which is idempotent, has only two solutions: $x=1$ and $x=0$. Here we have the very essence of existence and nothingness in a single expression. Either x exists ($x=1$) and is thus *something,* or it doesn't ($x=0$). Neither solution is given preference over the other. Existence and nonexistence are intrinsically linked. In fact, existence is the *only* structure possessed by a single element. At the most fundamental level, things either exist or they do not; either they may be differentiated and labeled, or they may not. But, fundamentally, the two concepts are *dual.* There is not just one solution to the equation; there are two.

A further implication of this is that existence is unitary.[1] We could go further still and claim that existence is a singular whole in the *śūnyatā* sense of "no-thing-ness." While we can dicker about the existence of individual things, our experience tells us that at least *something* exists.

But let us dicker anyway. Our experience is clearly of a differentiated whole, and it thus bears asking about the nature of the relations between the differentiated parts. In the simplest sense, a relation between two thing —call them x_1 and x_2—only exists if the things themselves exist. There is a mathematically convenient way to represent this. Formally, it is called a *binary operator,* but the essence is quite simple. Since any can only take on a value of 1 or 0, a relation r_{12} between two things (x_1 and x_2) is easily described by a product,

$$r_{12}{:}x_1{\cdot}x_2.$$

The existence or nonexistence of the relation is determined by the values of x_1 and x_2. That is, if x_1 and x_2 both exist, their values are 1, and thus the value of r_{12} is $1\times1=1$, i.e., it exists. But if either or both of these things do not exist, then at least one of the values in the product is zero, and thus the value we assign to r_{12} must be zero, i.e., it does not exist. More formally, a mathematician would say that if $x_1, x_2 \in \{0,1\}$ then r_{12} if and only if $x_1=x_2=1$. Otherwise, $r_{12}=0$. Conversely, if r_{12} and x_1 is something, then x_2 must be something else.

The existence of a relation implies three things: (1) nonexistence in the manner described herein; (2) the existence of something; and (3)

---

[1] In this context the term is taken as being synonymous with 'singular.' It is not meant in the mathematical sense of unitary operators.

the existence of something else.[2] But the latter immediately suggests *that there is more than one thing*. That is, the existence of a relation suggests a concept (two things) that is distinct from mere existence itself (one thing). In the terms described by Peano, the relation's existence thus implies the existence of three primitive concepts: zero, number, and successor (cf. Russell, 1919). This is not a trivial point; the degree of abstraction here is surprisingly high.

In any case, much as we did with the multiplication of things, we can continue with the multiplication of relations. That is, the act of distinguishing two relations is itself a relation that only exists if the relations it is comparing also exist. The existence of such would then require the existence of a third thing. In other words, at this most primitive of levels, the existence of more than one relation requires the existence of more than two things. We quickly arrive at a universe that seemingly consists of things and relations, but, upon further inspection, is really a differentiated whole that is interdependent. Each thing or relation only exists in contrast or comparison to something else. This is "no-thing-ness" in the *śūnyatā* sense; all things exist together, interdependently. Conversely, "nothingness" is the nonexistence of *everything* (see Figure 2).

These are deeply philosophical claims. In fact, it is not even clear that they are fully consistent. For example, suppose we have the set of everything—all things and all relations— that exist: $1=\{x_1=1, x_2=1, x_3=1,\ldots, r_{12}=1, r_{23}=1,\ldots\}$. Does 1 exist? If it does, by definition, it should contain itself, i.e., 1 should be an element of 1. But since 1 does not, itself, possess a value, it is neither a "thing" nor a relation and therefore is not a member of itself. Even more tricky is the set of all things and relations that *don't* exist: $0=\{x_1=0, x_2=0, x_3=0,\ldots, r_{12}=0, r_{23}=0,\ldots\}$. Does 0 exist? If so, shouldn't it be a member of 1? But it, too, is neither a relation nor a thing and so it shouldn't exist. But then if it *doesn't* exist, it should be a member of *itself*, which it clearly is not.

There are accepted responses to these contradictions in the philosophical literature, but we could equally easily dispense with them by simply declaring mathematics to be purely descriptive. All descriptions are, in some sense, inadequate. They rarely capture the true essence of that which they describe. Our world of experience includes qualia which

---

[2] I am ignoring self-relations here, that is relations between something and itself.

may not even be mathematically representable in a complete and coherent way. This is the very essence of the hard problem of consciousness. Nevertheless, important philosophical questions must be addressed. In particular, if things do not have an independent existence, how do they arise, and what does this say about the nature of causality?

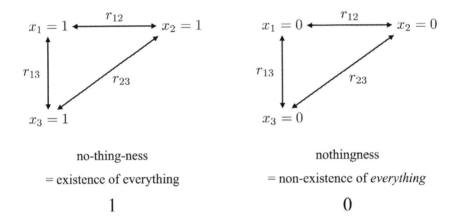

no-thing-ness

= existence of everything

1

nothingness

= non-existence of *everything*

0

FIG. 2. A universe of things in which everything exists is "no-thing-ness" in the *śūnyatā* sense whereas a universe in which nothing exists is 'nothingness.'

3. An Indo-Tibetan Buddhist Perspective

Certain Indian Buddhist texts, particularly those that serve as a foundation for Tibetan Buddhism, provide a potential—and uniquely non-Western—perspective on these issues. Of particular note is the Buddhist concept of *dependent origination,* or *pratītyasamutpāda*, and its deep relation to causality. As Jinpa notes:

> The law of causality and the system of dependent origination represent, out of the four principles of reasoning, the *principle of dependence* and the *principle of function*. These two matters are accorded crucial importance in the Buddhist tradition. It is on the basis of causality and dependent origination that the origin of everything is explained, from the larger evolution of the cosmos and its inhabitants to specific discrete events

such as the fall of rain in a particular place at a particular time.
2018, p. 60

In essence, all things originate from causes and are thus dependent in their origination on those causes. This is surprisingly close to the Eleatic notion of continuous, unending causation. As Parmenides famously stated, "nothing comes from nothing" (*ex nihilo nihil fit*). While later Western philosophers tended to use this idea to support a notion of "first cause" or to make the "cosmological argument" for a prime mover (cf. Reichenbach, 2004), it seems much closer to dependent origination in the Buddhist sense. However, the Eleatics expressly denied the existence of a void. The very concept was deemed illogical (cf. Sedley, 1982). In contrast, the Madhyamaka school of Buddhism, founded by the influential Buddhist philosopher Nāgārjuna, has as its central tenet the

> … concept of emptiness, a radical relativistic standpoint that maintains that nothing exists outside the world of dependent origination; nothing, in other words, exists independently or possesses an intrinsic nature.
> Jinpa, 2018, p. 41

Herein lies the ultimate notion of *śūnyatā*: "Nothingness" is "no-thing-ness" and vice versa. In plain language, the very concept of emptiness *is fully commensurate with the idea of dependent existence*. No *thing* exists independently of other *things*.

The concept of dependent origination is exceptionally deep and multifaceted (cf. Jinpa, 2023, pp. 195-212, 339-358). For the purpose of building a cohesive narrative around the duality of existence and nothingness that is commensurate with the notions of idempotency and structuralism, understanding our use of it here may benefit from a simple example. Imagine a universe that only contained a single thing. It would be meaningless to even talk about properties of this thing since that would imply we could describe different aspects of it, each of which could be interpreted as a "thing" in its own right. Even more simply stated, the existence of a property implies the existence of a comparison, e.g., "red" only has meaning in relation to other colors. In other words, the existence of something (x_1) implies the existence of something else x_2 from which it is distinct and to which it may be compared and contrasted via a relation r_{12}).

　　We will take dependent origination, then, to be the idea that independent existence is meaningless and thus all things arise dependently on and thus *in relation to* one another. But the Buddhist tradition also assumes that (i) in order for something to exist it must possess causal power and (ii) the universe must be causally closed (Jinpa, 2018, p. 60). Thus, the existence of everything that possesses causal power must coarise with the relations *that represent that causal power*. One could imagine the unity of existence, i.e., the set of everything, —"no-thing-ness"—as a complex web of connections that is entirely self-contained and thus "closed."

　　In metaphysics, the notion of causal closure is often assumed to roughly mean that physical effects cannot have nonphysical causes (Montero 2003). Popper and Eccles took this to imply a certain strong form of materialism (Popper 1984). Indeed, one of the many criticisms of causal closure is that it somehow places unnecessary limits on discussions of subject and object. If, for instance, consciousness were not physical, then causal closure would suggest that it could have no physical power. An even stronger interpretation would be that a causally closed universe must necessarily be a deterministic one. But neither of these views is necessarily true. It certainly appears true that a causally closed universe might require a hard adherence to monism, but monism is not pure physicalism or materialism, e.g., dual-aspect monist theories could be viewed as a way around any such assertion (cf. Atmanspacher & Rickles, 2022).

　　In any case, there appears to be no reticence about causal closure being inherently tied to the physical or material in the ancient Buddhist writings. Even in the *Cittamātra,* or "Mind-Only," school of Buddhism, which could be interpreted as the very antithesis of physicalism and materialism, causal closure is still assumed. That is, the Buddhist writers seem to see any such boundary between physical and nonphysical as meaningless. The only meaningful thing one can say about something is that it either exists or it doesn't. But what about the existence of itself? Does it not also require the existence of something to which it may be compared and contrasted? We, of course, already have such an entity in the form of 0. Existence and nothingness are thus dual—one is meaningless without the other—and, as suggested by Figure 2, *together represent a fundamental idempotency.*

4. Conscious Experience as a Minimal Ontology for Existence

It's not enough to understand existence and nothingness as a fundamental idempotency. In that sense structuralism perhaps misses an important point: In order to relate two things, we must understand how they differ, which ultimately entails understanding *what they are*. Since we're trying to understand existence and nothingness, we're dealing with the most fundamental of structures. Understanding what they are, then, necessitates establishing a minimal ontology that captures that deep fundamentality. One approach to this is to ask ourselves if there is anything whose existence is absolutely certain *to us*. After all, we're the ones performing the analysis here.

The answer, of course, is that there *is* one thing of which we are each, individually, absolutely certain and that is that we, ourselves, exist. To be clear, this is not meant in the broader sense that we can be certain that all human —us, ourselves—exist. Rather, each of us is certain that we individually exist. We may believe that everyone (and everything) around us is an illusion and we may (if we experience one or another psychological or neurological condition) even believe that we are not alive, but we most certainly believe that we exist in the following sense: *We are having an experience—we have awareness*. In that sense Descartes was absolutely right and, as Sorensen has noted, "[e]ven a solipsist agrees there is at least one thing!" (Sorensen, 2022). Conscious experience can therefore serve as a minimal ontology for existence. To be clear, it is a *minimal* ontology and does not preclude additional, possibly emergent ontologies.

But what is conscious experience? Can we describe it in a systematic manner that is consistent with dependent origination and the causal structures described by Buddhist philosophers? One potential answer to this question lies in integrated information theory (IIT), which is currently the most mathematically well-developed theory of conscious experience. The most recent version of IIT begins with a set of five axioms associated with what is called *phenomenal* existence (Albantakis et. al., 2022). Phenomenal existence is *experienced*. That is, first and foremost, existence manifests itself to us through phenomena that we experience. What one might refer to as the "zeroth" axiom of IIT states quite simply that "[e]xperience *exists*: there is *something*" (Albantakis et. al., 2022, p. 3). The other five axioms then proceed from this self-evident observation.

Of particular interest to the present discussion are the axioms of *integration* and *exclusion*. Integration captures the idea that experience is *unitary* in the sense that it is *whole* and *irreducible*. That is, our experience of it is simultaneous and connected. We do not experience different aspects of a given moment separately. Our senses process our surroundings in a unified manner that places everything in a singular context. In this sense, every seemingly individual thing in a given, singular unified experience had to dependently arise precisely because it is part of this irreducible whole. A given experience doesn't form piecemeal. If you are in a room and you look around in order to observe what is in that room, you are actually having a *series* of experiences rather than a singular experience. If you become aware of a chair after having become aware of a table, then you have experienced the chair and table separately.

Exclusion is then the idea that our experience is definite in that it is *this* whole and not some other. Put another way, we cannot simultaneously have two irreducible experiences. It would be akin to experiencing two different moments in space and time at once. That being said, this does not preclude the differentiation of different aspects of a singular experience. While we may simultaneously become aware of both a table and a chair in a given room (if, for example, they both happen to appear in our field of vision at the same time), we are nevertheless able to tell that one is a table and one is a chair. The difference is established by a relation which manifests *with* the table and chair. That is, the relations are an integral part of the unified whole. In that sense, IIT encapsulates phenomenal experience or its absence in something like Figure 2.

The transition to *physical* existence in IIT is accomplished by adding cause-effect power to each of the axioms of phenomenal existence. For something to physically exist in IIT, then, it must both *have* causal power and *accept* causal power, i.e., *be* affected by something else. One might assume that the relations just defined must be the "carriers of cause and effect," but that is only partially true. Some relations may merely be comparisons that allow for the individual things to be differentiated from one another. That is, a relation between a table and a chair is a comparison of the properties that distinguish them. There is not necessarily any causal power inherent in that relation. The causal power is introduced in the time evolution of the system from one instant to the next, i.e., *in the relation between different experiences*. A distinct part of a unified, singular experience (e.g., a dark cloud in the sky) may cause a distinct part of a *different* unified, singular experience (e.g., rain a moment later). Each experience follows the exclusion axiom in that each is the only experience we are having at a given moment, yet the cloud and the rain are only portions of those respective experiences. In that sense, Figure 2 is a somewhat "flattened" or "timeless" representation of reality as regard the relations.

The claim that physical existence arises from phenomenal experience and cause-effect power is surprisingly similar to Buddhist teachings. In addition to the fundamentality of cause and effect in Buddhist thought, as Jinpa notes, "... in general existence and nonexistence are defined on the basis of whether something is established by valid cognition" (2018, p. 84).

More specifically, in the Nālandā[3] tradition

> ...inference reliant on reasoning based on objective fact
> was accorded greater importance than inference based
> on valid scripture or testimony, yet when compared with
> inference based on objective fact, the valid cognition of
> direct perceptual experience was granted higher priority.
> ibid., p. 57

But an emphasis on phenomenal or perceptual experience would seem to deny any notion of objective truth. Is this necessarily true, though? Is there no such thing as objective reality?

5. Selective Subjectivism

At a certain level, objective reality is potentially unknowable. That is, someone could always argue that everything that we think of as objective reality is nothing more than our own mental construct. There's really nothing that we, as individuals, can do to prove to ourselves or anyone else for that matter, that, at any given moment, we're *not* actually dreaming or that everything we're experiencing is *not* simply a mental construct. But

---

[3] Nālandā was a Buddhist monastic university that operated from 427 to 1197 C.E. and is considered the world's first residential university.

that's hardly helpful if we're actually trying to understand the regularity that seems to mark this experience. On a more practical level, it doesn't help us to navigate our perceived world. We can, for example, argue philosophically about the existence or nonexistence of an overdraft on a bank account, but that won't likely stop the bank (real or imagined) from attempting to recover its money. Or, perhaps more bluntly, would you bet honest money that taxes are merely an illusion?

Perhaps the objection here is to the term "objective." If all that exists dependently arose together, then perhaps the term "intersubjective" is a better choice. Either way, it is hard to claim, with a straight face, that one is doing "science" if one believes that everything is purely subjective. Why bother doing research in the first place? It would at least be dishonest to argue the point since, by arguing it (the subjectivity of reality), one would presumably believe the statement itself to be objectively true, which is a contradiction.

But the tension may not be entirely necessary. In fact, it is possible to get something that resembles an objective reality out of a set of subjective observer states. For example, in recent work, Müller used algorithmic information theory to show that, under certain conditions and assumptions, "… it appears to observers as if there was an external world that evolves according to simple, computable, probabilistic laws" (2020, p. 301).

But this comports well with the view that science, as an anonymous reviewer in *Philosophical Magazine* once said, is the "rational correlation of experience" (as quoted in Eddington, 1939). Though the term "rational" here is open to interpretation, it calls to mind the Buddhist notion of "valid cognition."

In either case, it places the emphasis on our *knowledge* of reality rather than reality itself. Eddington referred to this scientific philosophy as "subjective selectivism." He says:

> '[o]bjective' is essentially a negative characteristic (non-subjective) of knowledge, although we regard it as a positive characteristic of the thing to which the knowledge refers; and it is always more difficult to demonstrate a negative than a positive conclusion. I accept an objective element in physical knowledge on, I think, reasonably

strong grounds, but not with the same assurance as the
subjective element which is easily demonstrable.

Selective subjectivism, which is the modern
scientific philosophy, has little affinity with Berkeleian
subjectivism, which, if I understand rightly, denies
all objectivity to the external world. In our view the
physical universe is neither wholly subjective nor wholly
objective—nor a simple mixture of subjective and
objective entities or attributes.
ibid., p. 27

In fact, it is this philosophical stance that he uses to justify the mathematical
structuralism of idempotency as a basis for understanding the duality of
existence and nothingness. While acknowledging the problems inherent
in the word "objective," it nevertheless denies the extreme Berkeleian
view. Likewise, while Buddhist philosophy accords perceptual experience
priority, it nevertheless also requires a certain objective truth that is
manifest in fundamental logic.

6. A Convergence of Ideas

So where does that leave us in regard to this fundamental duality? There
certainly seems to be an interesting convergence of ideas here, with
ancient Buddhist writings, mid-20th century philosophy of science,
and contemporary neuroscience all suggesting something similar: Our
knowledge of reality is based on intersubjective phenomenal experience
that is carefully correlated and obeys fundamental logical principles, most
notably cause and effect. Crucially in the Buddhist tradition this is taken
to *require* a notion of dependent origination. The existence of something
causally depends on the existence of something else. When seen in the
context of *śūnyatā,* which denies the notion of individual "thingness" at
the most fundamental level, it becomes clear that the distinctions and
relations inherent in this dependent existence, must arise together. That
is, their individual existence is really an illusion.

But we can extend this idea further to the notion of existence
itself. In order for existence to possess some meaning as a concept, we
must also have a concept of *non*existence or nothingness. The two are

inextricably linked. In the dictionary, the latter is even defined in terms of the former. In Eddington's mathematical structuralism, they represent a fundamental idempotency. In Buddhist philosophy, nothingness is an undifferentiated unity or wholeness rather than a true void in the more Western sense. But in either case, existence and nothingness are fundamentally dual concepts. One is meaningless without the other. If existence is then grounded in phenomenal experience, we are brought back to the words of Sartre's Roquentin: "Now I knew: things are entirely what they appear to be—and behind them ... there is nothing."

References

Albantakis, L., Barbosa, L., Findlay, G., Grasso, M., Haun, A. M., Marshall, W., Mayner, W. G., Zaeemzadeh, A., Boly, M., Juel, B. E., et al. (2022) Integrated information theory (IIT) 4.0: Formulating the properties of phenomenal existence in physical terms. arXiv: https://arxiv.org/abs/2212.14787.

Atmanspacher, H., & Rickles, D. (2022) *Dual-Aspect Monism and the Deep Structure of Meaning*. London and New York: Routledge.

Eddington, A. S. (1939) *The Philosophy of Physical Science*. Cambridge: Cambridge University Press.

Jinpa, T. (2018) *Science and Philosophy in the Indian Buddhist Classics, Volume I: The Physical World*. New Delhi: Simon & Schuster.

Jinpa, T. (2023) *Science and Philosophy in the Indian Buddhist Classics, Volume IV: Philosophical Topics*. New York: Wisdom Publications.

Montero, B. (2003) Varieties of Causal Closure. In S. Walter and H.-D. Heckmann (eds) *Physicalism and Mental Causation: The Metaphysics of Mind and Action* (173-189). Exeter, England: Imprint Academic.

Müller, M. (2020) Law without Law: From Observer States to Physics via Algorithmic Information Theory. *Quantum*, 4, 301.

Oxford English Dictionary (2023) 3rd Ed. Oxford: Oxford University Press.

Popper, K., & Eccles, J. C. (1984) *The Self and Its Brain: An Argument for Interactionism*. London and New York: Routledge.

Reichenbach, B. (2022) Cosmological Argument. In Zalta, E. N. & Nodelman, U. (eds.) *Stanford Encyclopedia of Philosophy*.

Russell, B. (1919) *Introduction to Mathematical Philosophy*. London: George Allen & Unwin, Ltd.

Sedley, D. (1982) Two Conceptions of Vacuum. *Phronesis*, 27, 175-193.

Sartre, J.P. (2007) *Nausea*. New York: New Directions Publishing.

Sorensen, R. (2023) Nothingness. In Zalta, E. N. & Nodelman, U. (eds.) *Stanford Encyclopedia of Philosophy*.

Whitehead, A. N. (1948) *Science and Philosophy*. New York: Philosophical Library.

Experiential
Possibilities

3

Varieties of Experiencing Nothingness

Harald Atmanspacher

"Everything is interesting; but perhaps nothing is more interesting than nothing."

Graham Priest[1]

1. Introduction

The title of this essay relates to the title of the conference at which it was presented: nothingness. The theme of nothingness offers an immense range of approaches, interpretations, cultural backgrounds, intellectual positions, and traditions, reflected by numerous scholars East and West, across the ages. It speaks to this extraordinary width that even the comprehensive entry on nothingness in the renowned *Stanford Encyclopedia of Philosophy* (Sorensen, 2022) falls short of many of its aspects—especially those from non-Western contexts.

Some of those often disregarded aspects are the topics of the collection to which this essay contributes. My own focus in this collection is directed at the phenomenological dimension of the subjective experience of nothingness, somewhat related to what William James attempted in his classic *Varieties of Religious Experience* (James, 1902). In addition to this dimension, however, I will try to provide a system-theoretical account of mental states and mental representations that may be viewed as a mildly formal background to the phenomenology.

This system-theoretical account also has its roots in William James, this time in his *Principles of Psychology* (James, 1890). In chapter

---

[1] In Gabriel & Priest 2022, p.38.

IX of Volume 1, where he addresses the stream of thought, we find the
following passages (pp. 243f, italics in the original):

> When the rate [of change of a subjective state] is slow we
> are aware of the object of our thought in a comparatively
> restful and stable way. When rapid, we are aware of a
> passage, a relation, a transition from it, or between it and
> something else ...
> *Let us call the resting places the "substantive parts,"*
> *and the places of flight the "transitive parts" of the*
> *stream of thought.* It then appears that the main end of
> our thinking is at all times the attainment of some other
> substantive part than the one from which we have just
> been dislodged. And we may say that the main use of
> the transitive parts is to lead us from one substantive
> conclusion to another.
> Now it is very difficult, introspectively, to see the
> transitive parts for what they really are. If they are but
> flights to a conclusion, stopping them to look at them
> before the conclusion is reached is really annihilating
> them. Whilst if we wait till the conclusion be reached,
> it so exceeds them in vigor and stability that it quite
> eclipses and swallows them up in its glare. Let anyone
> try to cut a thought across in the middle and get a look at
> its section, and he will see how difficult the introspective
> observation of the transitive tracts is. ...
> The results of this introspective difficulty are baleful. If
> to hold fast and observe the transitive parts of thought's
> stream be so hard, then the great blunder to which all
> schools are liable must be the failure to register them,
> and the undue emphasizing of the more substantive parts
> of the stream.

The following Section 2 gives a terse introduction into one property
of dynamical systems that is of fundamental significance for their
understanding in general: *stability*. The study of stability in dynamical
systems dates back to the work of Lyapunov, Poincaré and others at the
turn of the 20th century. It is the conceptual core of much recent work

that originated from a set of seminal ideas first put forward by Haken (1977) under the umbrella notion of *synergetics*. States of a dynamical system (such as a mental system) can be stable, and they can be unstable, depending on the potential hypersurface that constrains and governs their dynamics in a suitably chosen state space.

Different kinds of stability or instability characterize different kinds of mental states and representations. They entail, importantly, the systematic distinction of different kinds of dynamics: States typically evolve on timescales that are short as compared to those of representation changes. As a consequence, one can discuss the time evolution of states "adiabatically," i.e., for a quasifixed collection of representations modeled by a potential hypersurface. This leads to a threefold classification of states (first proposed by Atmanspacher, 1992, inspired by Gebser, 1986): categorial states (activating mental representations); noncategorial states (in the absence of representations); and acategorial states (between nonactivated representations).

Categorial states activate mental representations in a way that is experienced by both intentional and phenomenal content. While the intentional content of a representation is about what it represents, its phenomenal content is about what it is like to experience that representation. Both noncategorial and acategorial states do not activate representations, but they can nevertheless be experienced. As will be discussed in detail, they do not provide intentional content, but they may provide phenomenal content. In the noncategorial case, where representations are absent altogether, this phenomenal content is experienced as nothingness type I (Section 4.1). In the acategorial case, where representations exist but are not activated, the phenomenal content is experienced as nothingness type II (Section 4.2).

2. Stability of Mental States

The introductory quote by William James shows that the idea to study the dynamics of mental states by stability criteria is everything else than new. "Substantive states" à la James are stable "resting places" of a mental state, while "transitive parts" of the stream of thought are unstable. James correctly recognizes the problem that the unstable nature of transitive (transient) epochs in the dynamics of mental states makes their observation and registration utterly difficult. As a result, psychology and cognitive science have focused on studying stable substantive states, to the expense of unduly but understandably disregarding unstable states.

Recent decades saw a steady trend to bring unstable parts of mental dynamics back into the focus of consideration. This could be achieved by progress in our understanding of dynamical systems in general, and the resulting option to describe the behavior of mental (as well as neural) systems as nonlinear dynamical systems. Freeman (1979) was the first to introduce corresponding approaches, for other accounts see Beer (2000), Fell (2004), van Gelder (1998), Kaneko and Tsuda (2001), or Atmanspacher and Fach (2005). The following subsections present some basic material to understand how this approach works, and which benefits it brings about for a more comprehensive understanding of the stream of thought.

2.1 Dynamical Systems: Some Formal Elements

The state of a dynamical system, evolving continuously as a function of time t, is characterized by a number n of properties (technically speaking, observables) that are represented as the coordinates of an n-dimensional state space. The trajectory of the state) in its state space represents the evolution of the system. The stability of dynamical systems under small perturbations or fluctuations can be evaluated by a stability analysis.[2] Such a stability analysis yields so-called Ljapunov exponents λ_i $(i=1, ..., n)$, quantifying how and to which extent initial perturbations or fluctuations are changing as time proceeds.

Positive Ljapunov exponents indicate an exponential growth of fluctuations, whereas negative ones indicate that fluctuations are damped exponentially. The sum of all Ljapunov exponents is negative for dissipative systems and vanishes for conservative systems. In the dissipative case, there exists a subspace of the state space, onto which the trajectory of the system is restricted (after an initial "transient" phase). This subspace is called the *attractor* of the system. Another (larger) subspace, which covers all those (initial) states asymptotically

---

[2] See, e.g., Guckenheimer and Holmes (1983) or Leven et al. (1994) or other relevant literature for details of this procedure; see also Atmanspacher and Fach (2005) for an introduction into their usage in cognitive science and psychology.

evolving into the attractor, is called the *basin of attraction*. For a given attractor, the Ljapunov exponents are invariant with respect to continuous transformations of the coordinates of the state space.

In the simplest case, an attractor is a "fixed point" in state space, and all λ_i are negative. If there is no other attractor in the state space, the entire (admissible) state space is the corresponding basin of attraction. More interesting (and more complicated) are situations in which the sum of all λ_i is negative, yet individual λ_i are positive. In this case one speaks of "strange attractors" or "chaotic attractors." Even if the behavior of such systems is governed by strictly deterministic equations, it appears "chaotic"—which is the origin of the notion of *deterministic chaos*.

The stability of attractors can be studied *qualitatively* using a method also introduced by Ljapunov (see Alligood et al. 1996, Chap. 7.6). In order to do so, a function $V(x) \geq 0$ is considered in a neighborhood G of a reference state x_r.[3] The significance of V is that of a potential, which does *not* need to be a (physical) energy, whose extremal properties in G determine the stability of state x. The first derivative $\nabla V = dV(x)/dx$ of $V(x)$ with respect to x describes the change of $V(x)$ in G, and the second derivative $\nabla^2 V(x) = dV^2(x)/dx^2$ indicates a local maximum ($\nabla^2 V(x) < 0$) or minimum ($\nabla^2 V(x) > 0$). The following definitions of stable and unstable states can be formulated.

1. A state x is *stable* if $\nabla^2 V \geq 0$ in G. In this case, V is called a Ljapunov function.

    (a) A state x is *marginally stable* if $\nabla^2 V = 0$ in G.

    (b) A state x is asymptotically stable if $\nabla^2 V > 0$ in G.

2. A state x is *unstable* if $\nabla^2 V < 0$ in G.

For the simple example of a fixed-point attractor in one dimension, Figure 1b illustrates case 1b for a quadratic potential $V(x) = \alpha x^2$, $\alpha > 0$, which is concave in the neighborhood of the minimum of $V(x)$ ($\nabla^2 V > 0$). This minimum is an asymptotically stable fixed point with one negative Ljapunov exponent. In case 1a, the gradient of the potential vanishes, $\nabla V = 0$, and the second derivative too, $\nabla^2 V = 0$, so that each point for this potential is marginally stable (Figure 1a), corresponding to a vanishing Ljapunov exponent.

---

[3] For the sake of simplicity, we consider $V(x)$ as a function of only one variable x. This can be generalized to any number n of variables.

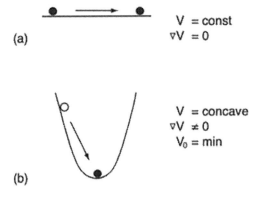

Figure 1: Kinds of stability of a state: (a) marginal stability for a constant potential V with $\nabla V = 0$; (b) asymptotic stability at a critical point V_0 of a concave potential with $\nabla^2 V > 0$ (and $\nabla V = 0$ at V_0).

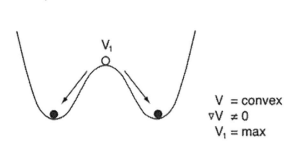

Figure 2: States in the neighborhood of a critical point V_1 of a locally convex potential are unstable and relax into adjacent potential minima.

A combination of case (2) with case (1b) is illustrated in Figure 2. In the neighborhood of x_r, at the local maximum, V is convex ($\nabla^2 V < 0$), whereas V is concave ($\nabla^2 V > 0$) around the potential minima. A state at or around the local maximum is therefore unstable. If the system is in such a state, it will spontaneously relax into one of the two asymptotically stable minima. During this relaxation, the potential difference ΔV will be converted into the motion of the state. The regions left and right of the local maximum are basins of attraction for two coexisting attractors. (For potentials with more than one independent variable, V_1 is often a saddle point rather than a local maximum.)

For physical systems in thermal equilibrium the potential V has the concrete meaning of free energy, its derivative with respect to temperature is entropy, and the second derivative is specific heat. However, under conditions far from thermal equilibrium, which are compulsory for pattern formation in general and the behavior of living systems in particular, the observables and laws of equilibrium thermodynamics are typically not well-defined or simply do not apply. As a consequence, attempts to describe far-from-equilibrium systems by free energy and related equilibrium observables are conceptual category mistakes and nonstarters for serious research.

For this reason, Haken (1977, Chap. 6.7) suggested to use a generalized terminology where potentials replace free energy, control parameters replace temperature, action (output) replaces entropy, and efficiency (output as a function of input) replaces specific heat. The state distribution for a given potential is related to the potential by a maximum information principle. The state dynamics follows the gradient of the potential—or of the entire potential hypersurface if there are multiple coexisting attractors.

Note that the distribution of an ensemble of states at some fixed time equals the distribution of one state over time if and only if the considered system is ergodic. Living systems far from thermal equilibrium typically violate ergodicity (Molenaar, 2008), so that ensemble average and time average (taken over sufficiently long time, i.e., asymptotically) differ. Additional problems arise since the time evolution of most complex nonequilibrium systems in nature is only piecewise stationary or not stationary at all (see Priestley, 1988).

2.2 Mental States and Mental Representations

The central idea of a dynamical-systems account for mental systems (cf. Nicolis, 1991) is that internal mental representations, basic elements of a mental system, play the role of attractors (in the sense of Section 2.1) for external (sensory) or internal stimuli. The relation between the description of mental systems and the formal theory of dynamical systems can be characterized by three points:

1. The mental system, which is physically realized by a neural network, is treated as a dynamical system S.

2. Mental representations within the mental system are treated as coexisting attractors of S with particular stability properties of corresponding potentials V.
3. Internal or external stimuli for the state x of the mental system are treated as initial conditions x_0 whose temporal evolution $x(t)$ leads to an attractor.

In this scenario, mental processes are represented by the mapping of a stimulus onto a mental representation, illustrated by the motion of a state in a potential hypersurface (more colloquially, a potential landscape). The form of the potential characterizes the stability properties governing the dynamics of states of the considered system. Mental states and their associated observables can be conceived as correlated with states of the neural system constituted by neuronal assemblies and their dynamics—notwithstanding the fact that these correlations are often poorly understood.

Our subsequent discussion focuses on mental states of a mental system (which may, in principle, be conscious or unconscious). Their state space remains unspecified insofar as there is, to the best of our knowledge, no (canonical) formalization of mental observables. Furthermore, there is no analytic form of the dynamics of states $x(t)$ and of representations $V(t)$, because no corresponding equations of motion are known.[4]

2.2.1 Mental Representations and Stable Categorial States

For conceptual clarity it is not only helpful but compulsory to distinguish mental representations from mental states. While mental representations are modeled by potentials V constructed over a state space, mental states x moving across a set of representations (a potential hypersurface) can acquire different kinds and degrees of stability. The dynamics of states and of representations typically operate at different time scales: State changes (e.g., thinking) are expected to be fast as compared to changes of representations (e.g., learning).

---

[4] In physics the potential V can usually be identified as some form of (potential, kinetic, free, etc.) energy, formally expressed by a Hamilton function, but the interpretation of the potential V in mental systems remains open. There is no uncontroversially established definition of something like mental "energy."

A state x can be located anywhere on a potential hypersurface, which defines whether a state is stable or unstable at its location. This means that mental representations (potentials, attractors) provide boundary conditions for the motion of a mental state $x(t)$ as a function of time. If a mental state is located in the minimum of a potential (i.e., on an attractor), the corresponding mental representation is said to be "activated," meaning that both its intentional and phenomenal content are experienced.

If a mental state is located in a particular mental representation, it is (asymptotically) stable with respect to perturbations (compare Figure 1b). The measure of stability can be quantified, e.g., by Ljapunov exponents. Representations with shallow potential minima stabilize mental states less than those with deep potential minima. Accordingly, less or more effort is necessary for a mental state to "leave" a particular representation. If this happens, the corresponding mental representation may be considered as "deactivated," but it stays intact for future "reactivation."

Effectively deactivating a mental representation means that the state $x(t)$ has to be changed to such an extent that it leaves not only the attractor but also its basin of attraction. In a situation of multiple coexisting attractors, the state will then move toward another attractor to eventually arrive there. A corresponding dynamics of $x(t)$ obviously exceeds the conceptual repertoire of a situation with only one single representation (as in Fig. 1b).

However, not only states can temporally change, $x = x(t)$, but also potential surfaces $V = V(t)$ can evolve. Not only can the dynamics of a state activate or deactivate an already existing mental representation, but new representations can be generated, or existing ones can be altered. New representations are created when the mental system generates new potentials; old representations are changed when the corresponding potentials are deformed.

It should be pointed out again that the illustration in Figure 1b refers to an especially simple special case, a cartoon picture as it were. Mental representations are not limited to fixed point attractors or limit cycles (periodic processes), but in general correspond to chaotic attractors (Skarda and Freeman 1987). Any asymptotically stable state, which activates such a mental representation with intentional and phenomenal content, is called a categorial state after Gebser (1986, p. 285; see also Atmanspacher, 1992):

> Every categorial system is an idealized ordering schema
> by which actual phenomena are fixed and absolutized;
> as such it is a three-dimensional framework with a static
> and spatial character. Such categorial systems are able to
> deal with the world only within a three-dimensional and
> conceptual world-view.

In the representational account of mental systems due to Metzinger (2003), stable categorial states and mental representations (potentials, attractors) that they may activate are the key players. The model of reality that a subject develops consists of two major components: a *self-model* and a *world-model*. They are differentiated so that they can map all internal and external experiences individuals learn to model in order to successfully cope with their environment, i.e., to survive and reproduce.

By being "fixed and absolutized" à la Gebser, the established repertoire of stable categories that a mental system has at its disposal executes a "censorlike" or "filtering" function (Emrich et al, 2006)[5]. This function attributes experiences to acquired representations, but it fails to explain how new representations may be formed and existing ones may be changed, and how states move across representations. If a mental system would be composed of nothing else than categorial states in static representations, this would exclude a manifold of experiences that we will address in the next subsections.

2.2.2. Marginal Stability of Noncategorial States

Marginal stability of a state x as illustrated in Figure 1a characterizes the limiting case in which V is constant anywhere in the neighborhood of x. This case can be interpreted as an "unbounded" state which cannot activate any representation, simply because there is none. Consequently, no intentional content will be experienced. Nevertheless, such states can

---

[5] Note that this kind of filtering is at variance with the notion of the "filter" metaphor often ascribed to the 19th-century psychologist Myers. In her knowledgable study of Myers's work on the mind-body problem, Kelly (2007) finds that, rather than being due to Myers himself, the metaphor was launched and popularized by Bergson, Broad, Huxley, and others to address the interface between the ordinary conscious experience of an individual and what Myers called the "subliminal self," the *tertium quid* beyond mind and body. For a detailed account of such a dual-aspect monist picture, see Atmanspacher and Rickles (2022).

be experienced phenomenally, and it feels somehow if they are. In this respect one can speak of a noncategorial (or precategorial) state in the absence of representations. Smallest perturbations, which are neither damped nor amplified, will cause x to change.

Metzinger (2003) discusses such states at considerable detail in Chapters 4 and 7 of *Being No One*, mostly in relation to his main target: the representation of the self, the phenomenal self-model. It is Metzinger's thesis that the self-model can be modified or lost in altered or pathological mental states. As an example, he refers to the phenomenon of "oceanic" self-dissolution, which he relates to "mystical" states. The associated loss of the self-model does not only presume a change of perspective but rather abolishes any experience of intentional content.

However, phenomenal experience can occur despite a lost self-model. Here, a limiting case of experience is activated, a minimal or basic kind of phenomenal content capable of being subject to experience. In Section 4.1, this is discussed as nothingness of type I. Because no representations are involved in this limiting case, the experience is entirely unstructured, a uniform atemporal nowness without the perspective of a first person[6]. Since this scenario abstains from any categories, it refers to noncategorial states.

Noncategorial states in the absence of particular representations are examples for a certain subclass of experiences with *nonconceptual content*, a topic that has gained momentum ever since it was introduced into the philosophy of mind by Evans (1982). A comprehensive review of this development is due to Bérmudez and Cahen (2015). For more detailed discussion of nonconceptual content as nonpropositional attitude in connection with noncategorial states, see Feil and Atmanspacher (2010).

2.2.3 Mental Instabilities and Acategorial States

Insofar as categorial mental states are asymptotically stable, a transition from one representation to another is possible via an unstable intermediate

---

[6] The experience is subjective in the weak sense that it is based on an internal model of reality (Metzinger 2003, p. 559). What is experienced is a "ground of reality" —the unstructured fundament of the manifold of structured aspects of reality that emerge due to the formation of representations.

state, as illustrated by Fig. 2. To effect the transition, $x(t)$ has to overcome the potential barrier ΔV. The higher the barrier and the steeper the gradient of the potential, the smaller is the probability of a spontaneous transition and the longer the dwell time of $x(t)$ in the potential. In James's terminology, the process leading from one to another "substantive" state corresponds to a temporal sequence of "transitive" states. The unstable point at V_1 in the bistable example in Fig. 2 is a "transitive" state distinguished by a local maximum of V.

This is a clear call to the study of unstable, transitive states, but it is also clear why this is hard to do. It's a matter of time scales. While stable states are (usually) adopted long enough to become a subject of conscious experience, this is (usually) not the case for unstable states. Gebser addressed transitive states at a local maximum of with his concept of "acategoriality" and emphasized their temporal, dynamical aspect (Gebser, 1986, p. 308):

> Something with a temporal character cannot be spatially
> fixed. It cannot be fixed or prescribed in any form, and if
> we attempt to do so we change it by measurement into a
> spatial quantity and rob it of its true character. This is a
> clear indication that the qualities of time which are today
> pressing toward awareness cannot be expressed in mere
> categorial systems.

Gebser's unfixable "temporal character" can—in a more prosaic way—be related to the evasive, transient behavior of dynamical systems around instabilities. Even if there were known equations of motion to govern the system's dynamics in its potential hypersurface, its trajectory in the vicinity of instabilities would not be predictable by them.

Acategorial states offer a second option to look at so-called "mystical" experiences, in addition to what Metzinger focuses on. As the ground of experience can be activated by noncategorial states in the absence of representations, acategorial states can activate experiences without intentional content in the presence of (neighboring) representations. The corresponding phenomenal content is discussed as nothingness type II in Section 4.2. It differs from the ground experience in noncategorial states insofar as it is not experienced as an unstructured background, but partial representations remain intact and coexist as possibilities within the experience. In this case, the self would not be experienced as dissolved but as a sustained yet nonactivated possible representation.

In acategorial states an experience of both representational ground and particular representations is possible simultaneously. It is possible if a mental state is not located within a representation or category but, for instance, between them. In such "in-between states" different representations can be experienced as a bunch of possibilities without being individually actualized. Dynamically speaking, the continuous representational ground of a mental system can flash up between individual actualized representations and become consciously and phenomenally accessible.

3. Three Main Implications

There are three main implications of the dynamical-systems approach to mental dynamics. They follow from the option to separate mental states from mental representations, so that one may talk about mental states that activate the experience encoded in a representation and mental states that don't activate such an experience. However, only mental states activating a representation are asymptotically stable ones, while marginally stable and unstable states do not activate representations.

If the distinction of states and representations remains unconsidered, this entails a confusion of states and representations to the effect that they become seen as exchangeable. A great many discussions in cognitive science and the philosophy of mind do not respect this distinction. This leads to the undue emphasis of stable mental states that James properly criticizes. A dynamical-systems approach allows us to also consider mental states which do not activate representations in their own right.

The first implication resulting from this is that we can address the dynamics of mental states and the dynamics of mental representations separately in one and the same formal framework: $V = V(t)$ for representations and $x = x(t)$ for states. This is highly plausible, as a state can change between representations taken as unchanging, or representations themselves may change, e.g., due to learning. If the concepts of states and representations are used exchangeably, the corresponding lack of differentiation easily stimulates a lack of understanding or, more technically speaking, leads to category mistakes.

The dynamics of mental states, $x = x(t)$, typically is much faster than the dynamics of mental representations, $V = V(t)$. A representation can change if it is more or less often visited by a state, and this change appears as an increase or decrease, respectively, of the stability of the representation, i.e., as the depth of the potential V. However, new representations can form as a result of changes of their surrounding representations, i.e., as a consequence of an overall changing potential landscape.

Mental states, on the other hand, usually change as a result of changing stimuli within a given potential landscape. Therefore, if stimuli change rapidly, mental states change rapidly, but the potential landscape doesn't. This entails a significant time scale separation for states and representations, which makes it generally easy to treat them separately (e.g., similar to a kind of adiabatic approximation). Exceptions might arise when new representations are formed, and states in their vicinity immediately follow corresponding modifications of the potential landscape.

The second implication is a distinction between different kinds of experiences that are connected with mental states in representations and outside representations. Stable, categorial mental states activating a mental representation imply the experience of the content of that representation together with its quality. In other words, the experience is that of both an intentional and a phenomenal content. By contrast, noncategorial and acategorial mental states that are only marginally stable or unstable do not activate representations, so that no intentional content will be experienced. Nevertheless, phenomenal content may well be at stake.

That mental states outside mental representations cannot express intentional content is a consequence of the fact that intentional content is bound to representations. However, this does not follow for phenomenal content. The next section proposes two special types of experiences of phenomenal content without intentional content. Illustrated by a number of examples, I suggest that noncategorial states in a potential with vanishing gradient, i.e., without existing representations, can nevertheless be subject to experience. And I suggest that acategorial states at a local maximum of a potential with neighboring local minima (i.e., neighboring representations) can also be subject to experience, although of a different kind.

The third implication of the dynamical-systems framework is that it allows us to distinguish between different kinds of experiences of phenomenal content. Categorial states have intentional content plus the phenomenal content associated with the intentional content of an activated representation. For instance, the intentional content of a broken leg is accompanied by the phenomenal pain content of it.

By contrast, both noncategorial and acategorial states have only phenomenal content, and the lack of intentional content is interpreted, for the purpose of this essay, to be responsible for an experience of nothingness. Due to the absence of representations and the resulting marginal stability, the phenomenal content of noncategorial states is one of nothingness type I. Due to the lack of stability and due to the neighborhood of existing representations, the phenomenal content of acategorial states differs essentially from that of noncategorial states. It is denoted as nothingness type II.[7]

mental state	categorial	non-categorial	acategorial
stability	asymptotically stable	marginally stable	unstable
potential	concave $(\nabla^2 V > 0)$	flat $(\nabla V = 0)$	convex $(\nabla^2 V < 0)$
representation	activated	inexistent	not activated
content	intentional & phenomenal	phenomenal	phenomenal
experience	something	nothing type I	nothing type II

Table 1: Synoptic overview of different kinds of mental states with respect to their stability, their role for mental representations, the contents of representations, and the corresponding kinds of experience. (Note that this tablular summary bears the same risks and adverse effects as any other rigid classification system).

---

[7] In the Appendix to this paper, a striking similarity of these two types of nothingness is outlined with the thoughts of the German philosopher Karl Jaspers about faith and revelation (Jaspers 1967).

4. Nothingness

4. 1 Nothingness Type I

The experience of nothingness type I in the present essay relates to the kind of experience a subject has in a noncategorial mental state under marginal stability. More formally expressed, this is the situation in which the gradient $\nabla V \approx 0$: The potential landscape characterizing mental representations is (approximately) flat. In other words, there are no representations that the state can activate, and its change under perturbations does not (considerably) change the kind of experience.

4.1.1 Dissolution of Representations

Infants of early age (or even under neo- or prenatal conditions) are not born with a fully established categorial system of concepts. After early ideas about how concept formation works by Piaget and others, numerous recent studies have revealed more and more details about category formation in perception and cognition (for review, see Alessandroni and Rodriguez 2020). Roughly speaking, the dynamical-systems point of view would predict an overall picture of category formation as the development of a varied landscape of potential hypersurfaces V (multiple coexisting attractors) out of an approximately flat initial situation.

It has been speculated (Thompson, 2015; Windt et al., 2016) that states of dreamless sleep, although without intentional content, are not phenomenally blank. This could be an indication that such states populate a subspace of their state space which has no potential differences, i.e., no attracting subsets. This would satisfy the criterion for noncategorial states, and experiencing deep sleep would be an instantiation of nothingness type I.

For awake adults, usually operating with an established system of representations at their disposal, an experience of noncategorial states is everything else than occurring spontaneously. System theoretically, this would require a process during which the potential V becomes flat, $V(t) \rightarrow const.$ Such a process corresponds to a dissolution of representations. Depending on the stability of existing representations, it can be fairly intricate and elaborate to be realized successfully.

A recently presented way to understand the experience of dissolved representations is due to Metzinger (2020) with his notion of "minimal phenomenal experience" (originally proposed by Windt, 2015). Interestingly, he relates such experience to an "unpartitioned epistemic state space"— a clear reference to a lack of separate representations in the dynamical-systems framework. Mystical states as comprehensively discussed in the classic monograph by Stace (1960) serve as case studies in Metzinger's account. Other significant works on the same theme are Forman (1998), Marshall (2005) or Shear (2007).

Metzinger's minimal phenomenal experience suggests that such experience may be understood as a noncategorial undifferentiated phenomenal "ground state" underlying other, more explicit and refined experiences in categorial states. This has been related to another much-discussed notion in similar contexts, namely that of nondual awareness. As Josipovic and Miskovic (2020) argue, minimal phenomenal experiences may be induced by techniques that manipulate the subject's arousal level by enhancing tonic or phasic alertness, while nondual awareness should predominantly be considered as the target of contemplative and meditative practices independent of arousal level. In particular, they distinguish nondual awareness from "constructed or altered states of consciousness"—e.g., constructed by mind-altering substances, sensory deprivation etc.[8]

In the history of Western philosophy, a number of authors addressed several kinds of mystical states. Among them, it is particularly worthwhile to focus on Spinoza (1677), whose third kind of knowledge through intuition (*scientia intuitiva*) aligns our limited cognitive activities to an "adequate knowledge of the essence of things" and their position within the whole "in one glance." As is well known, such ultimately adequate knowledge for Spinoza is knowledge of the (impersonal) divine, understood as the coincidence of *natura naturans* and *natura naturata* from a pantheist perspective. Within the present account, this knowledge is expressed through the experience of an undifferentiated phenomenal ground of all less fundamental experience.

The French philosopher Deleuze, with his deep knowledge of Spinoza's philosophy, called such experiences immanent. His reference

---

[8] A recent monograph by Letheby (2021) offers in-depth guidance to the use of psychedelics as agents of insight and spirituality in empirical and philosophical respects.

to immanence as the "vertigo of philosophy" (Kerslake, 2009)[9] expresses its status beyond standard (categorial) cognitive experience and beyond any abstract metaphysics of transcendence, thus emphasizing its concrete experiential nature. In the final opus *Mysterium Coniunctionis* by the Swiss psychologist Jung (1977), this same idea can be found in the third type of *coniunctio,* where mental consciousness merges with the collective unconscious and, through synchronicity, with the external physical world (for more detailed discussion, see Atmanspacher and Rickles, 2022).

4.1.2 Plenitude of Nothingness

The work mentioned in the preceding subsection reflects some selected insights and directions of research that are clearly situated within philosophical traditions developed in the Western hemisphere. However, Eastern spiritual systems have a much longer history, including very detailed descriptions of states of nothingness type I and instructions of how they might possibly (but not necessarily) be achieved. These systems often are less metaphysically grounded (in the sense of Western metaphysics and ontology) than experientially oriented. A particular example will be outlined in the following.

In his essay on "oriental nothingness," Hisamatsu (1959) presents his view of the Japanese (Zen) Buddhist notion of nothingness[10]. In contrast to the ontological mainstream of Western philosophy, its central question is not about being, but rather about nothing. The Japanese notion of *mu* for nothingness is connected to both the Indian Buddhist notion of *sunyata*, emptiness, and the Chinese Daoist notion of *wu*, nothingness. It is to be understood as an absolute nothingness which does not refer to non-being as the opposite of being but transcends both being and non-being as a non-dual term without an opposing other. It can be (and has

---

[9] The forceful figure of the vertigo appears explicitly in the freedom essay by Schelling (1809). It is picked up by Kierkegaard (1844) in his essay on anxiety which is briefly discussed in Section 4.2.4.

[10] Shin'ichi Hisamatsu (1889–1980) was a professor of philosophy at Kyoto University loosely related to the Kyoto school, teaching a Japanese form of Mahayana Buddhism. Hisamatsu's influential essay on "oriental nothingness" of 1939 was first published in Japanese in 1946, then in English in 1959, and in German as "Die Fülle des Nichts," *The Plenitude of Nothingness*, in 1975. The English translation (by Richard de Martino) is accessible online at http://www.fas.x0.com/writings/hisamatsu/toyotekimunoseikaku. html. For more details see van der Braak (2019).

been) characterized by six key features, each subset of which, however, would be insufficient in isolation.

1.   Nothingness as "not a single thing," or "no thing": Nothingness is non-discriminating and does not refer to the non-being of individual subjects or objects.

2.   Nothingness as "empty-space": Nothingness is omnipresent, impartial, formless (independent of space), permanent (independent of time), and pure (without afflictions).

3.   Nothingness as "mind-in-itself": Nothingness is living and possesses awareness; but it is different from mind in the ordinary sense, which would contradict (2).

4.   Nothingness as "self": Nothingness according to (3) could be misunderstood as something outside of mind-in-itself, but it is an ongoing ground of conscious activity.

5.   Nothingness as "freedom": Nothingness is, by (2), not afflicted by desires but it is ultimately capable of controlling such desires freely.

6.   Nothingness as "creative": Nothingness according to (4) is its own creative source, so that such nothingness is also, paradoxically, an unlimited and infinite plenitude.

Criteria (1) and (2) can straightforwardly be related to the structureless situation of non-categorial states in a potential with vanishing gradient, where no representations exist. Nevertheless, the non-categorial state has its own phenomenal content, as in (4). This content has been proposed as minimal phenomenal experience, or "pure experience," by Metzinger (2020), who relates the corresponding experience to various kinds of mystical states. However, Josipovic and Miskovic (2020) assert that Metzinger-type minimal phenomenal experience is different from nondual awareness, which they see more tightly aligned with Eastern contemplative and meditative practices than with Western concepts of (empirically) manipulated states of consciousness.

A classic Daoist anecdote illustrates in particular criterion (3), the absence of an ego-like mind. It is about a conversation between a monk and Kuan, his student, and goes like this:

The monk: Where is the Dao?
Kuan: Directly before us.
The monk: Why don't I see it?

> Kuan: You cannot see because of your egoism/
> The monk: If I cannot see it because of my egotism, is
> Your Reverence able to see it?
> Kuan: As long as there is an "I" and a "You," this makes
> the situation difficult and no Dao can be seen.
> The monk: Can it be seen, when there is neither "I" nor
> "You"?
> Kuan: When there is neither "I" nor "You," who should
> be able to see it here?

Nothingness according to (5) and (6), freedom and creativity, are themes that play extraordinarily important roles in Spinoza's and Schelling's philosophies (Spinoza 1677, Schelling 1809).[11] For closer looks into these, which are beyond the scope of this essay, I have to refer the reader to abundant pertinent literature.

4.2 Nothingness Type II

The experience of nothingness type II in the present essay relates to the kind of experience a subject has in an acategorial mental state. This state is unstable: The potential landscape at such a state shows a local maximum. In formal terms, this means that $\nabla V \approx 0$, and $\nabla^2 V < 0$ in the vicinity of that state. A small perturbation is sufficient to let the unstable state decay into one of the neighboring categories where it turns into an asymptotically stable state with $\nabla V \approx 0$ and $\nabla^2 V > 0$.

In such a picture, nothingness of type II is not a dissolution of representations, where $V = V(t)$ becomes flat as in nothingness of type I. Rather, it has to be described as a deactivation of representations, which is achieved by the state dynamics $x = x(t)$. A state in a potential minimum, activating a representation, moves out of the minimum toward a neighboring local maximum, so that the previously activated (and experienced) representation is deactivated (and the corresponding experience is lost).

---

[11] It also resonates strongly with Jung's notion of the "pleroma" as "nothingness or plenitude" simultaneously in his *Septem Sermones ad Mortuos* of 1916 (Jung 1963, App. 7), a sequence of inner dialogs about life and death, unity and multiplicity, good and evil.

4.2.1 Bistability

Bi- or multistable perception (see Kruse and Stadler 1995) is a long-known phenomenon that characterizes the unstable perception of stimuli with ambiguous content. One of the best-known and most studied examples is the Necker cube, discovered by the Swiss geographer Louis Albert Necker (1832) and depicted in Fig. 3. The Necker cube leaves it to the perceiver whether it is seen in one of two possible perspectives, from above or from below, and its perception switches spontaneously between these perspectives on a typical timescale of a few seconds.[12]

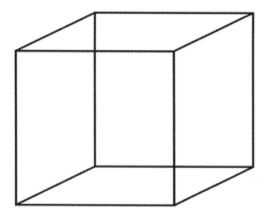

Figure 3: Ambiguous Necker cube

Looking at the perception of the Necker cube in more detail, it can be seen as the switch of a mental state from one representation (cube from above) to another (cube from below). In other words, we have a transition from a substantive (stable) state in one potential minimum to another substantive (stable) state in another potential minimum. After leaving the first minimum and before arriving at the second minimum, the state has to move through a transitory (unstable) state at the local maximum located

---

[12] A comprehensive review of the neuropsychology of Necker cube perception is due to Kornmeier and Bach (2012). Interestingly, ambiguous stimuli play a significant role in Wittgenstein's philosophy of language, where the interpretation of a linguistic term, its meaning, often varies upon a context-induced aspect change (Fortuna 2012).

between the minima. As James properly speculated, the intermediate transitory state is too unstable to be consciously perceived and registered; its lifetime has been estimated on the order of a few 10 msec.

The situation we are confronted with by this elementary example leads to an oscillation between the two perspectives of the cube, hence the notion of bistable perception. Typically, the unstable state decays too fast to become consciously aware to subjects. Is it possible to decelerate the decay to such an extent that its lifetime becomes long enough for conscious perception? For instance, one may imagine some kind of "mental acrobatics" that balances the attracting forces of the neighboring representations.[13] It is likely that certain meditative practices, designed to empty the mind toward the experience of nothingness, are based on the realization of such a kind of procedure.

A comprehensive mathematical model for bistable perception, set up in analogy to the "quantum Zeno effect," is the Necker-Zeno model (Atmanspacher and Filk 2013). It relates the contributing dynamics at three different time scales and matches numerous experimental results, some of them highly nontrivial. The model also predicts windows of temporal nonlocality, with no temporal order (and no causal sequences of events)—a kind of atemporal presence that has been speculatively addressed by Bergson, James, Whitehead, Husserl, and others. The gist of this outstanding feature is that time (as much as space in quantum nonlocality) loses its character as a fundamental category in our understanding of nature.

Subjects sometimes report that they perceive a planar structure of lines as an intermediate image between the three-dimensional perspectives of the Necker cube. This must not be misunderstood, however, as the genuine experience of the unstable acategorial state but rather points to the result of a cognitive activity that almost instantaneously attempts to form a new category as soon as nothingness (type II) is in the offing. In this way, the local maximum between existing representations is deformed into a local minimum representing the planar structure, which is then experienced as a substantive, stable state. As is well known in meditative

---

[13] This reminds us to the strategy of "controlling chaos" (Ott et al. 1990), where an unstable (chaotic) state can be stabilized by external pushes adapted to act against the inherent instability. A different idea is a stabilization of locally unstable states due their properly fine-tuned internal environment, without external tracking, see, e.g., Atmanspacher and Scheingraber (2005).

practices, all kinds of other "ancillary" in-between representations may emerge as evasive maneuvers to avoid the *horror-vacui* experience of true nothingness type II.

In his novel *The Confusions of Young Torless*, Robert Musil gives us his impression of a state of nothingness type II proper. His allusion to the state of death illustrates why the experience of nothingness may indeed be associated with deep anxieties—at least at first glance, as we will see further below in Section 4.2.3. Here is the text passage by Musil (2014):

> We live from one thought to another. For our thoughts and affects do not flow quietly as a stream, but they "occur to us," they fall into us like stones. If you observe yourself accurately, you feel that the soul does not change its colors gradually, but thoughts jump out of it like numbers out of a black hole. Now you have a thought or an affect, and suddenly another one stands there as if it jumped out of nothing. If you are attentive you can even sense the instant between two thoughts, in which everything is black. This instant, once recognized, is nothing else than death for us.

4.2.2 Paradox

Other than the ambiguous Necker cube, a paradoxical cube (Fig. 4) is not ambiguous but "impossible." It does not lead to oscillations between two possible representations but rather offers a stimulus that has no stable (or metastable) representation at all. Therefore, its perception is not bistable but does not allow any consistent global perception. Focusing on part of it locally, for instance on the upper right corner and its vicinity, may allow us to infer how it should look like globally. But as soon as the focus is moved toward the center of the figure, this global structure becomes rejected immediately.

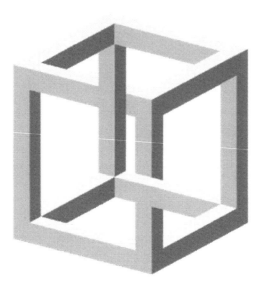

Figure 4: Paradoxical cube

In terms of a potential representation, this can be seen as a process of an ongoing interplay between stabilizing and destabilizing tendencies (as in Fig. 2). Perceiving any local part of the stimulus creates an attracting force toward the corresponding attractor, which is immediately turned into a repellor due to an attracting force toward the other attractor. As a result, the perceptual dynamics never reaches one of the attracting minima but is alternately pushed out of them toward the unstable state in between.

Another, more involved pictorial representation of the figure of paradox is the lithograph *Belvedere* (of 1958) by the Dutch artist M.C. Escher (see Fig. 5). It includes the paradoxical cube that can be seen in the hands of a man sitting at the entrance to the building, with a diagram of the Necker cube at his feet. The two-dimensional image of the three-story building itself is constructed in such a way that the two upper floors look locally consistent but globally aren't so that the woman and the man at the balustrades cannot help but see different parts of the environment. The paradoxical construction makes it possible that a ladder leads from inside the middle floor to outside of the top floor. The ridge in the background belongs to the Morrone Mountains in the Abruzzo region (Italy).

Figure 5: Belvedere by M.C.Escher

Roger Penrose proposed a way to analyze paradoxical (or impossible) figures using the mathematical concept of cohomology (Penrose and Penrose 1958, Penrose 1992).[14] The key idea here is to consider a cohomology group $H(Q,G)$ (first cohomology H^1, to be precise), where Q is the planar support of the figure and G is the so-called ambiguity group. Let Q be pasted together by those n separate parts Q_1, ..., Q_n of the figure that make it globally appear paradoxical. As the eye of the perceiver pursues the lines of the figure at the transition between adjacent Q_is, sudden changes occur in the interpretation of the distance $d \in R^+$ of the object from the perceiver, so the ambiguity group $G = R^+$.

---

[14] This idea has also been applied to other paradoxical scenarios, e.g. the so-called "Condorcet paradox" where individually consistent comparative rankings lead to global inconsistencies; see Abramsky et al., 2015.

Now define points $\{A_{ij}, A_{ji}\}$ in regions where adjacent Q_i index i overlap and determine the distance d for these points. Due to the change of d in those regions d is ambiguous, but the ratio d_{ij} of pairwise distances for each couple $\{A_{ij}, A_{ji}\}$ is the same for each region (for the paradoxical tribar as an illustrative example see Penrose 1992). As a consequence, they can all be rescaled to unity by the same factor. In this case, the set $\{d_{ij}\}$ is called a coboundary. If the coboundaries yield the unit element of $H(Q, R^+)$, this implies that the considered figure is paradoxical.

The punchline of this brief excursion is that the unit element in a cohomology group provides a crisp definition of whether an object is globally inconsistent, hence paradoxical (though, to be sure, H does not tell us much about the phenomenal experience of the object). If the object were ambiguous rather than paradoxical, there would be two mutually exclusive consistent representations rather than global inconsistency. In the ambiguous case, each of the two representations can host a stable state—or a meta-stable one, for that matter—that can be maintained for a certain time, leading to spontaneous oscillations between the representations.

Another example for a paradoxical stimulus is the liar paradox, briefly the "liar," the simplest version of which is the sentence "this sentence is not true." The liar is not a perceptual stimulus but a cognitive one. If the sentence holds true, then it is not true, i.e. false, by what it expresses; but if it is false, then it is obviously true. Cognitively processing the liar happens in time. It amounts to an oscillation of the two truth values of Boolean logic which is forced by the analysis of its content, so it is not spontaneous as in the Necker cube. Yet, neither of the temporally oscillating cognitive states true/false does ever become stable under the (usual) assumption that a sentence cannot be true and false simultaneously (law of noncontradiction).

The Munich-based philosopher Ulrich Blau (2008) offered a comprehensive (almost 1,000-pages) discussion of the liar and its ramifications in different logical frameworks, unfortunately in German, but see also Beall et al. (2016) for review. A most radical way out of the liar paradox has been advocated by Priest (2006), who suggests to give up on the law of noncontradiction, so that a sentence can be true and false simultaneously; such a sentence is called a *dialetheia*.[15] Note that this differs from giving up the law of the excluded middle, allowing for truth values such as "undetermined" in addition to true and false, as in quantum logic or other non-Boolean logical systems with more than two truth values.

Abandoning the law of noncontradiction has been denoted as dialetheism, and it lies at the heart of paraconsistent logic. In the dynamical-systems framework it would correspond to a deformation of the local maximum between two minima for true and false in such a way that the maximum turns into a third intermediate minimum, providing stability for the cognitive state in the mind of the dialetheist. In this way, the unstable state for classical-logic approaches would attain (weak?) stability within paraconsistent logic. In the experience of the dialetheist, nothingness of type II would become something.

4.2.3 First Person Singular

One of the most basic mental representations is the category of the first-person singular, the ego. The stability of the corresponding categorial state is crucial for the experience of identity over time. Alterations of the experience of being an ego with identity are to be expected if the stability of the mental state activating the first-person representation changes. This is possible if the representation itself changes, or if the mental state leaves that representation, $x = x(t)$ so that it gets deactivated.

An extreme case of a change of representation has been discussed in Section 4.1.1: the complete (or approximate, or partial) dissolution of the ego representation (see Millière 2020 for more detailed discussion). If this becomes a permanent condition, it is usually seen as a psychopathological impairment implying a regressive loss of one's sense of being an ego. However, Section 4.1 also indicates alternative interpretations, such as

---

[15] In Indian philosophy, it is not unusual that the law of noncontradiction is abandoned. One of the foremost thinkers in this tradition is Nagarjuna (around 150-250 C.E.), who developed and employed the system of *catuskoti* with four options for a proposition p: (i) p is true, (ii) p is false, (iii) p is both true and false, (iv) p is neither true nor false—where (iii) characterizes a dialetheia. Nagarjuna's tetralemma, as it is also called, has been influential for much of Mahayana Buddhism. See Bagger (2007) for related uses of paradox in Western mysticism.

minimal phenomenal experience or nondual awareness in the sense of nothingness type I.

Another kind of changing ego representation amounts to its disintegration. This means that one egoic base representation is split up into different ones, representing partial egos, often with different properties. Such scenarios have been traditionally called multiple personality disorder, currently redefined as dissociative identity disorder. There are impressive accounts of it, both in psychological case studies (Thigpen and Cleckley, 1957) and in narrative literature (Stevenson, 1886). Not to forget the masterful analysis combining the history of medicine with political and moral struggles by Hacking (1995).

In view of nothingness type II, however, changes of the mental state within the landscape of representations are more significant. The paradigmatic case of such situations is a mental state that departs from the ego representation. Since this representation must be assumed to have an extraordinarily deep minimum, endowing the state in it with extraordinary stability, a high amount of ΔV must be expended to leave that minimum. Alluding to the title "Being No One" by Metzinger (2003), Scott Jordan (2018)[16] composed a song expressing the arduous way out of the ego with the ironically appropriate line "it's hard work being no one".

A mental state leaving an ego representation induces the experience of leaving the ego behind; the experience of being an ego with a certain identity is deactivated. This can be a dramatic and sometimes traumatic experience which, for instance, may accompany "rites of passage" between stages of life (childhood to adult) or social roles (single to married) much discussed in anthropology and ethnology. As the mental state of the concerned individual does not activate the old ego anymore although this ego is still present as a representation, such a state is acategorial.

An interesting contrast between loss of ego and freedom from ego has been emphasized by Gebser, who suggests that this difference indicates a difference between entire structures of conscious experience. For Gebser, operating on the basis of categorial states is the main

---

[16] Likewise in spirit, Arendt (1978, p. 7) quotes Cicero (1928, p. 17) quoting Cato, when she wrote about the *vita contemplativa*: "Never is a man more active than when he does nothing." She also discusses nothingness as seen by Plato, echoed by more recent philosophers such as Spinoza, Kant, Schelling, Heidegger, and Sartre, at length in Chapter 15.

instrument of what he calls mental consciousness, which in his diagnosis dominates the level of consciousness in much of current civilization worldwide, up to its recognizable deficiencies. He anticipates an integral kind of consciousness as the next step in the evolution of consciousness structures, a consciousness which is less rigid and more flexible so that humans may develop novel aptitudes and skills to cope efficiently with themselves and their environment.

Referring to the discussion of ego representations, Gebser (1986, p. 532) explicates:

> Only the overcoming of the "I," the concomitant overcoming of egolessness and egotism, places us in the sphere of ego-freedom. ... Ego-freedom means freedom from the "I"; it is not a loss or a denial of the "I," not an ego-cide but an overcoming of ego. Ego-consciousness was the characteristic of the mental consciousness structure; freedom from the "I" is the characteristic of the integral consciousness structure.

If one wants to reflect this quote back to the two kinds of nothingness distinguished in this essay, ego-freedom in acategorial states would be in line with the phenomenal experience of nothingness of type II. In contrast, the notion of ego-loss would be associated to noncategorial states and the experience of nothingness of type I.

A particularly fascinating and deep account of the experience of freedom generally, not focused on ego-freedom, through a state of nothingness of type II is due to Kierkegaard, translated from his *Concept of Anxiety*. Kierkegaard (1844, S. 2.2) associates a tight relationship between freedom and anxiety with the acategorial transition between categorial states:

> One can compare anxiety with some kind of vertigo. He who must look down into a deep abyss will feel vertiginous. But what is the reason for this? It is both his eye and the abyss – because what would be had he not looked down? In this sense, anxiety is that vertigo of freedom which occurs if the spirit is about to set the synthesis.

Freedom now looks down into its own possibility and, then, seizes finiteness in order to stick to it. In this vertigo, freedom collapses. This is as far as psychology can reach out, and it does not want to reach out farther. In this instant everything is changed, and when freedom rises again, it recognizes that it is guilty. Between these two moments lies the leap which science neither has explained nor will be able to explain.

In the terminology of dynamical systems, Kierkegaard claims that an acategorial state of freedom cannot be attained without overcoming the anxiety that goes along with the deactivation of its categorial predecessor and its corresponding destabilization. Destabilization is psychologically coupled to uncertainty and insecurity, which in our cultural setup are both connoted with utterly negative valence, so anxiety is their proper relative. Once the acategorial state is reached, anxiety turns into freedom, and this act of liberation allows to "look down" into all adjacent categorial possibilities, into one of which it will decay "to stick to it."

However, it would be wrong to believe that the acategorial state itself is "just a possibility." No, it is as real as it could be, even though unstable. Moving from it into a stable category, it loses the freedom out of which it is capable of "seizing finiteness." Kierkegaard's guilt is the unavoidable loss of freedom that results from leaving the infinite possibilities of an acategorial state: Choice is inseparably connected to sacrifice.[17] Yet another cycle of leaving a category through instability, insecurity, and anxiety may lead to another regained state of freedom.

Both James and Kierkegaard were understandably skeptical about a "scientific" explanation of the transitory leap between substantive representations. Taking unstable behavior seriously beyond a fixed landscape of rigid representations moves our insights about this leap a step forward. And perhaps we can, as a consequence, develop a stance toward instability which is less pejorative and puts more emphasis on its creative potential.

---

[17] By now it should be clear that the existential notion of freedom discussed here has nothing to do with the astonishingly superficial studies of volitional acts of human agents in current neuroscience and neurophilosophy.

5. *Conclusions*

This essay is not primarily a metaphysical treatise about nothingness. Rather it explores its experiential dimension, starting from the background of a representational philosophy-of-mind approach that distinguishes between intentional and phenomenal content of mental representations. However, starting there does not mean staying there. The representational framework can be expanded beyond representational, propositional knowledge by applying some formal ideas taken from the theory of dynamical systems.

The expanded framework makes possible a distinction between categorial, noncategorial, and acategorial states with different stability properties, which can be used to discriminate between two basically different kinds of the experience of nothingness. Such experience arises if a mental state is not accompanied by the intentional content of a representation. This can be the case in two ways, either because representations simply are absent or because the state does not activate representations that are present.

The theme of nothingness borders on the discussion of ineffability. The notion of ineffability plays a significant role in religious studies but also has a place in the philosophy of language. And, not to forget, it also figures in aesthetics and the arts. A recent collection of essays edited by Weed (2023) provides an informative overview of contemporary approaches. Wittgenstein's famous dictum in his *Tractatus* can be understood as instigating a link between them: "Whereof one cannot speak, thereof one must be silent."

But there are several ways to understand this phrase; see for instance Shen (2011). Is it an attempt to delineate (or save) philosophy from mysticism? Or to ban the latter from reasonable discourse altogether? Or is it a hint that there is something beyond language (and the "linguistic turn") that deserves attention even if it cannot be expressed in words? Or was the author, at the age of about 30 years at the time, just ignorant enough to see that much insight and wisdom can be found in a realm of experience that transgresses the limitations of the so-called propositional attitude?

In the spirit of the present essay, the experience of nothingness is nonpropositional or apropositional. Non- or a-categorial states can be accompanied by the experience of phenomenal content: It feels somehow to be in such states. The lack of intentional content implies that the experience of nothingness is not about some represented referent. This lack, so the proposal, is interpreted as an experience of nothingness which allows the subject to become aware of an experiential ground that is usually occluded by intentional content.

As described in this essay, there is a variety of ways to experience nothingness, which illustrate the limitations of conceptual discourse by emphasizing an experiential ground underneath it. I think it is quite appropriate to understand this ineffable ground in the spirit of numerous spiritual traditions: as a non- or a-conceptual plenitude of presence that ultimately rises out of nothingness.

Appendix:
Jaspers on Transcending the Subject-Object Split

In 1962, the German philosopher Karl Jaspers published his *Der philosophische Glaube angesichts der Offenbarung*, translated into English as *Philosophical Faith and Revelation* by E.B. Ashton (Jaspers 1967). The title makes it evident that faith is a philosophical term for Jaspers, not a theological one. Bernd Oelmann directed my attention to the book, and I soon realized that Jaspers discusses the way the subject-object split can be transcended in surprising similarity with the notions of nothingness type I and II in Sec. 4. Here is the relevant text passage, pp. 135f in the German original (translation HA, italics original):

> If we become aware of appearances as they are facilitated by the subject-object split, we recognize this split, which alone shows us what is, as a prison. Although the clarity that is possible for us arises only through the split, we also want to break out of the prison. We want to transcend the subject-object split and reach its ground, the origin of all things and ourselves. This exit from prison is possible in two ways.
>
> *First, by mystical experience*. The mystical unio of subject and object lets the ego disappear together with all objects. Together with the split, all language and communication is abandoned, and everything that could

be in communication as well. Seen from the view point of our world of appearances with the split, there is nothing, only miraculous experiences, to be described psychologically, without any collective meaning. One gets immersed in a private state described as infinite bliss, as the perfect lucidity of clear light, which is not attached with any sense of community.

Second, transcending the split can occur by becoming aware of the encompassing as such. If this transcending is performed in the condition of human thinking itself rather than in abstract clues, then this philosophical base operation implies a transformation of human self-awareness. While in fact we remain within the subject-object split, we become aware of it in such a way that we reach the horizon at which we realize our state within the encompassing as the reality whose realization transforms us. Knowing about the prison while in prison does not liberate us from reality in time, but it liberates us through thinking by recognizing a power that determines us without recognizing our origin and goal. In this way, the split illuminates appearances, the encompassing becomes present within them. The prison is not forced open, as in an unio mystica that lets us fall into incomprehensibility. However, if the prison is recognized as if seen from the outside, it becomes itself ablazed with light. The unfolding of appearances in time in the light of the encompassing makes the prison less prison.

The somewhat enigmatic notion of the encompassing that is central to Jaspers's metaphysics refers to a dimension of existence beyond the world of space and time. Jaspers uses the difference between immanence and transcendence to denote the difference between the world of appearances and its encompassing reality. The notion of the encompassing suggests to replace a kind of "hierachical" groundedness of existence with an embeddedness within a wider, transcendent reality.

Jaspers highlights the second way of transcending the subject-object split (our nothingness type II) as superior, not least insofar as he sees its capacity for transformative effects on the human condition.

By contrast, he thinks that the first way, the blissful experience (our nothingness type I), leaves us with an ineffability that defies thinking and communicating, base operations of the human condition. Be this as it may, the spirit of Jaspers' deliberations can be mapped almost one-to-one to the distinction of the two types of nothingness in the present paper.

References

Abramsky, S., Barbosa R.S., Kishida K., Lal R., and Mansfield S. (2015) Contextuality, cohomology and paradox. *Leibniz International Proceedings in Informatics, 41,* 211-228.

Alessandroni, N. and Rodriguez, C. (2020) The development of categorisation and conceptual thinking in early childhood: Methods and limitations. *Psicologia: Reflexão e Crítica, 33,* 17.

Alligood, K.T., Sauer, T.D., & Yorke, J.A. (1996) *Chaos. An Introduction to Dynamical Systems.* Berlin: Springer.

Arendt, H. (1978) *The Life of the Mind.* New York: Harcourt.

Atmanspacher, H. (1992) Categoreal and acategoreal representation of knowledge. *Cognitive Systems, 3,* 259-288.

Atmanspacher, H., and Fach, W. (2005) Acategoriality as mental instability. *Journal of Mind and Behavior, 26,* 181-206.

Atmanspacher, H., and Fach, W. (2013) A structural-phenomenological typology of mind-matter correlations. *Journal of Analytical Psychology, 58,* 219-244.

Atmanspacher, H. and Filk, T. (2013) The Necker-Zeno model for bistable perception. *Topics on Cognitive Science, 5,* 800-817.

Atmanspacher, H. and Rickles, D. (2022) *Dual-Aspect Monism and the Deep Structure of Meaning.* London: Routledge.

Atmanspacher, H. and Scheingraber, H. (2005) Inherent global stabilization of unstable local behavior in coupled map lattices. *International Journal of Bifurcations and Chaos, 15,* 1665–1676.

Bagger, M. (2007) *The Uses of Paradox: Religion, Self-transformation and the Absurd.* Ithaca, NY: Cornell University Press.

Beall, J., Glanzberg M., & Ripley, D. (2016) Liar paradox. In Zalta, E.N. (ed.) *Stanford Encyclopedia of Philosophy.* Accessible at https://plato.stanford.edu/entries/liar-paradox/.

Beer, R.D. (2000) Dynamical approaches to cognitive science. *Trends in Cognitive Sciences, 4,* 91-99.

Bermúdez, J., and Cahen, A. (2020) Nonconceptual mental content. In Zalta, E.N. (ed.) *Stanford Encyclopedia of Philosophy*. Accessible at https://plato.stanford.edu/entries/content-non-conceptual/.

Blau, U. (2008) *Die Logik der Unbestimmtheiten und Paradoxien*. Heidelberg: Synchron.

Cicero, M.T. (1928) *On the Republic, Book I.* Translated by C.W. Keyes, accessible at https://www.attalus.org/cicero/republic1a.html.

Emrich, H.M., Leweke, F.M., and Schneider, U. (2006) Systems-theory of Psychosis—Relevance of "internal censorship." *Pharmacopsychiatry*, *39*, 52-53.

Evans, G. (1982) *The Varieties of Reference*. Oxford: Oxford University Press.

Feil, D., and Atmanspacher, H. (2010) Acategorial states in a representational theory of mental processes. *Journal of Consciousness Studies*, *17*(5/6), 72–104.

Fell, J. (2004) Identifying neural correlates of consciousness: The state space approach. *Consciousness and Cognition*, *13*, 709-729.

Forman, R.K.C. (1998) What does mysticism have to teach us about consciousness? *Journal of Consciousness Studies*, *5*(2), 185-201.

Fortuna, S. (2012) *Wittgensteins Philosophie des Kippbildes*. Berlin: Turia + Kant.

Freeman, W.J. (1979) Nonlinear dynamics of paleocortex manifested in the olfactory EEG. *Biological Cybernetics*, 35, 21-34.

Gebser, J. (1986) *The Ever-Present Origin*. Columbus: Ohio University Press.

Guckenheimer, J., and Holmes, P. (1983) *Nonlinear Oscillations, Dynamical Systems, and Bifurcations of Vector Fields*. Berlin: Springer.

Hacking, I. (1995) *Rewriting the Soul*. Princeton, NJ: Princeton University Press.

Haken, H. (1977) *Synergetics. An Introduction*. Berlin: Springer.

Hisamatsu, S. (1959) The characteristics of Oriental Nothingness. *Philosophical Studies of Japan*, *2*, 65–97.

James, W. (1890) *Principles of Psychology Vol. 1*. New York: Henry Holt.

James, W. (1902) *The Varieties of Religious Experience*. Cambridge, MA: Harvard University.

Jordan, J.S. (2018) It's hard work being no one. *Frontiers of Psychology*, 9, 2632.

Josipovic, Z. and Miskovic V. (2020) *Nondual Awareness and Minimal Phenomenal Experience. Frontiers of Psychology*, 11, 2087.

Jung, C.G. (1963) *Memories, Dreams, Reflections*, New York: Random House.

Jung, C.G. (1977) *Mysterium Coniunctionis. Collected Works of C.G. Jung Vol. 14*, Princeton, NJ: Princeton University Press.

Kaneko, K., and Tsuda, I. (2001) *Complex Systems: Chaos and Beyond*. Berlin: Springer.

Kelly, E.W. (2007) F.W.H. Myers and the empirical study of the mind-body problem. In Kelly, E.F. et al. (eds.), *Irreducible Mind* (47-115). Lanham, MD: Rowman & Littlefield.

Kerslake, C. (2009) *Immanence and the Vertigo of Philosophy*. Edinburgh: Edinburgh University Press.

Kruse, P., and Stadler, M., eds. (1995) *Ambiguity in Mind and Nature*. Berlin: Springer.

Kierkegaard, S. (1844) *The Concept of Anxiety*. Princeton: Princeton University Press.

Kornmeier, J. and Bach, M. (2012) Ambiguous figures – What happens in the brain when perception changes but not the stimulus. *Frontiers in Human Neuroscience*, 6.

Leven, R.W., Koch, B.-P., and Pompe, B. (1994) *Chaos in dissipativen Systemen*. Berlin: Akademie.

Letheby, C. (2021) *Philosophy of Psychedelics*. Oxford: Oxford University Press.

Marshall, P. (2005) *Mystical Encounters with the Natural World*. Oxford: Oxford University Press.

Metzinger, T. (2003) *Being No One. The Self-Model Theory of Subjectivity*. Cambridge, MA: MIT Press.

Metzinger, T. (2020) Minimal phenomenal experience: Meditation, tonic alertness, and the phenomenology of "pure" consciousness. *Philosophy and the Mind Sciences*, *1*(1), 7.

Millière, R. (2020) The varieties of selflessness. *Philosophy and the Mind Sciences, 1*(1), 8.

Musil, R. (2014) *The Confusions of Young Törless*. Oxford: Oxford University Press.

Necker, L.A. (1832) Observations on some remarkable optical phaenomena seen in Switzerland; and on an optical phaenomenon which occurs on viewing a figure of a crystal or geometrical solid.

London and Edinburgh Philosophical Magazine and Journal of Science, *1*(5), 329–337.

Nicolis, J. (1991) *Chaotic Information Processing*. Singapore: World Scientific.

Ott, E., Grebogi, C., and Yorke, J.A. (1990) Controlling chaos. *Physical Review Letters*, *64*, 1196-1199.

Penrose, L.S. and Penrose, R. (1958) Impossible objects: A special type of visual illusion. *British Journal of Psychology*, *49*, 31-33.

Penrose, R. (1992) 'On the cohomology of impossible figures. *Leonardo*, *25*(3/4), 245–247.

Priest, G. (2006) *In Contradiction*. Oxford: Oxford University Press.

Priest, G. (2022) Everything and nothing. In Gabriel, M. and Graham, P. (Eds) *Everything and Nothing*. Cambridge: Polity. 19-38.

Priestley, M.B. (1988) *Non-linear and Non-stationary Time Series Analysis*. New York: Academic Press.

Schelling, F.W.J. (1809) *Philosophical Investigations into the Essence of Human Freedom*. New York: SUNY Press.

Shear, J. (2007) Eastern methods for investigating mind and consciousness. In Schneider, S. and Velmans, M. (eds) *Blackwell Companion to Consciousness*. Malden, MA: Wiley, 697–710.

Shen, A. (2011) *The Limits of Language, A Comparative Study of Kant, Wittgenstein, and Lao Tzu*. Lewiston, NY: Edwin Mellen Press.

Sorensen, R. (2022) Nothingness. In Zalta, E.N. (ed.) *Stanford Encyclopedia of Philosophy*. Accessible at https://plato.stanford.edu/entries/nothingness/.

Spinoza, B. (1677/1996) *Ethics*. New York: Penguin Classics.

Stace, W.T. (1960) *Mysticism and Philosophy*. London: Macmillan.

Stevenson, R.L. (1886) *Strange Case of Dr. Jekyll and Mr. Hyde*. London: Longman, Green and Co.

Thigpen, C.H. and Cleckley, H.M. (1957) *The Three Faces of Eve*. New York: McGraw Hill.

Thompson, E. (2015) *Waking, Dreaming, Being*. New York: Columbia University Press.

van der Braak, A. (2019) Hisamatsu Shin'ichi: Oriental nothingness. In Kopf, G. (ed.) *The Dao Companion to Japanese Buddhist Philosophy*. Berlin: Springer, 635–647.

van Gelder, T. (1998) The dynamical hypothesis in cognitive science. *Behavioral and Brain Sciences, 21*, 615–661.

Weed, L.E., ed. (2023) *Mysticism, Ineffability and Silence in Philosophy of Religion*. Berlin: Springer.

Windt, J.M. (2015) Just in time—Dreamless sleep experience as pure subjective temporality. In Metzinger, T.K. and Windt, J.M. (eds.) *Open MIND*. Frankfurt: MIND Group.

Windt, J.M., Nielsen T., and Thompson E. (2016) Does consciousness disappear in dreamless sleep? *Topics in Cognitive Science, 20*, 871–882.

4

Who or What Experiences Nothingness? Reflections from Psychoanalysis

Leslie Stein

The day I was to sit down to write this paper, already lost in the mystery this question presents, a patient reported this experience:

> I was sitting on the sofa, preparing some notes for a lecture. I closed my eyes as I felt disoriented, confused, and had a sense that something alien was entering my mind. I almost panicked but then, for an instant, I stopped thinking—I started going blank, then felt the weight of my life, my troubles and physical pain, as well as the panic, vanish. I then opened my eyes and understood that everything in that room, the desk, my furniture, and everything outside the window, were all fused together— all interconnected, just one thing really, with only an artificial line causing the illusion that turned that one thing into many. I can't say how long it lasted, maybe a second or a few seconds.

This is a mystical experience: the realization of the reality of interconnectedness and oneness, emerging from a timeless instant of emptiness. The question I seek to address was presented to me in this experience: Was it he who experienced that moment of emptiness, the cessation of thought, the vanishing, or was it that something alien?

Psychoanalysis is an appropriate lens to examine this question as it is focused on subjective experiences that therefore include mystical experiences. These experiences are presented, upon the telling, as a single narrative, much as one would set out a dream, but there are different constituent stages. When I interviewed 29 mystics, those who have made mystical insights their primary focus and served as the subjects of my book, *Working with Mystical Experiences in Psychoanalysis* (Stein, 2019), I was intrigued by the distinct stages of subjective states that occurred as the experience unfolded. I had chosen committed mystics for that study because they all had had multiple mystical states, so they were able to explain the progressive stages more easily than one, such as the patient, who has a single overwhelming occurrence.

I could differentiate and describe six stages within every mystical experience with as much precision as such events allow and language permits (ibid., pp. 62-3). They are, in summary, the initial onset of the experience, what occurs immediately after the onset, the state occurring just prior to the peak being reached, the peak itself, the ending of the experience, and, finally, the evaluation of the occurrence after the fact.

The first stage, the initial onset of the experience, even for advanced meditators or committed spiritual practitioners, came upon them suddenly by surprise, unbidden, and completely overwhelmed whatever was transpiring in the conscious mind, so the event could not be stopped or rejected. As Rudolph Otto so long ago explained (Otto, 1923), this overwhelming event can create awe, fascination, but also fear, confusion, and disorientation, as occurred for the patient. This first stage takes place with full awareness that there is a significant event that is occurring, but with little framing of what it is.

The second stage, immediately after the onset as the experience continues to overwhelm the conscious mind, and most likely for the ego to maintain a sense of itself, a preliminary view, a premature hypothesis arises as to what is transpiring. This view can be positive, such as "I am having a mystical experience," as it was for the 29 mystics as these experiences are consistent with their life's purpose, or frightening, such as "I am suffering a stroke," where there is no prior framework. It is observable in clinical practice that a positive hypothesis at this stage is more consistent with greater long-term integration of the experience than a negative view that results in it being discounted after the event.

Most importantly for this paper, a third stage occurs where the mind is further overwhelmed as the autonomous process continues, overwhelming all vestiges of thought, so there is a moment of no duality, no sense of oneself, or anything that is associated with mentation. It is here, in this timeless instant, that the previous conscious position is lost, leading to an emptiness, a numenal nothingness: "There is nothing left which can be identified as "I"; everything that is 'winks out,' ceases to be, radically stops" (Noh, 1977, p. 17).

In the practice of Insight Meditation, *Vipassana*, there are several descriptions of this winking-out stage: "Both the objects and the noting mind were abruptly cut off and stopped; ... I saw the objects and the noting mind drop away, like a heavy burden being dropped; ... Both objects and the mind that notes them suddenly stopped, like a running person thwarted by a blocked passage. ..." (Sayadaw, 2016, p. 293). In the patient's experience, this quelled the initial panic as there was no longer any conceptual evaluation possible.

The fourth stage, the peak of the experience, is where, into this void, the emptiness created by the involuntary winking out, there is a presentation of a truth, a profound reality as to the fabric of mind and existence. This is conveyed without the aid of thought, judgment, or a conceptual framework. The third and fourth stages combine to present an interlinked revelation of an underlying emptiness out of which a truth appears, both of which are not the product of a waking, cognitive ego, which has been suspended.

In the fifth stage of leaving this peak, to complete the explanation of the stages, the conscious mind immediately returns and starts making sense of what occurred. At this stage, the entire event appears as the experience of one fluid, timeless experience where the truth that was conveyed is the primary outcome, and the preliminary stages are only considered the means or mechanism for its expression.

The sixth stage, the subsequent evaluation occasioned by reading about and discussing the nature of the event, is when many aspects of the experience are intermixed with other frameworks and memories and therefore offers different emphases or characteristics to yield a cohesive meaning. This is the reason why Gershom Scholem, the Kabbalistic scholar, provides that there is no such thing as a mystical experience *per se,* "there is only the mysticism of a particular religious system, Christian, Islamic, Jewish mysticism and so on" (Scholem, 1941, pp. 5-6). This view, more recently referred to as "particularist," is that there are no unmediated mystical experiences outside of culture. This has been challenged appropriately by "perennialism," the idea that these are universal occurrences in terms of content and stages in all cultures

(Anderson, et al., 2014). Clinically, it is observable that for patients who have had these experiences, the lack of a religious or spiritual framework can weaken the impact of the occurrence providing a long-term alteration of the previous conscious position. This alteration is critical because, as Jung suggests, it is the "real therapy" as it indicates that there are dimensions of consciousness that exist beyond the ego (Jung, 1973, p. 377).

1. Noting the Experience

Whatever occurs in that winking out, the third stage, can itself be referred to as an event or experience that is *apprehended*. This noting occurs because the experience of winking out conveys an awareness that one is undergoing a change of state. The *Vipassana* explanation that insists on the presence of the conscious mind for insight, echoes this subjective moment of noting at the third stage:

> The experience of the cessation of the conditioned mental and physical phenomena does not last very long. It's as brief as a single moment of noting. Afterward, one has a recollection of the event, such as 'The cessation of objects and mind that notes them that I've just experienced must have been either something special, or path, fruition or *nibbana.*' (Sayadaw, 2016, p. 293)

The "single moment of noting" obviously occurs at the *start* of the suspension of consciousness because that is when an emerging change of state is observed. This noting is given significance by the conscious mind, as William James expresses, because the emptiness is a noticeable relief from the painful dualism of existence (James, 1902/2008, p. 127). As the patient recorded in his mystical experience, the change of state was a welcomed event because it eased the burdens created by his mind's confusion.

This apprehension or noting of emptiness may give rise, as a precursor to the emergence of that truth in the peak, to a preliminary, incipient sense of interconnectedness as the ego boundaries are being dissolved. This initial sense of unity, only a taste of harmony, was reported for all 29 mystics at this noting stage. As the noting has no other mental content besides a change of state, it does not provide a realization of the scope and dimension of what is to occur in the later peak stage. The peak stage is what ultimately defines the experience by offering a glimpse of complete unity or deeper insights into the otherwise inaccessible ground of being that is the "preconceptual foundation of all thought and existence" (Warren, 1984, p. 130).

The third stage—the winking out, emptied mind, nonduality, a void, a vacuity—is the receptacle for the emergence of the fourth stage, the peak where the truth arrives to fill it. The noting of the emptiness and the revelation of the truth are distinct in effect. One of the mystics interviewed, who had multiple mystical experiences, stated that the emptying contained a quality that was relaxing and a release from the burdens of thinking, while the truth that follows was enlivening, instructive, and of great intensity. The truth, when it arrives, is presented without the process of mentation into the emptied mind. It is not until the fifth stage, leaving the peak, and then the sixth stage of interpretation, that it is given meaning.

In the Theravada canon, the *Visuddhimagga*, it is explained that it is attention to the noting of the *combined state*: the emptiness and then the revelation of the truth, that together bring transformation as they reveal the direct, "non-teleological nature of reality." The noting of the emptiness and then the revelation of the truth indicate that the truth is not the product of the conscious self, reinforcing that the whole experience has come from elsewhere, such as an inward, impersonal nature of mind (Carpenter, 2018) or through another force.

In analyzing the revelations of the Sufi mystic, Ibn' al-Arabi, Michael Sells refers to the winking out providing what he calls an "identity shift," as well as a "meaning event." In these Sufi teachings, the divine witnesses itself and its creation through the agency of an individual who has polished the mirror of the ego by his or her own purification to allow the divine, "To reveal to it(self) through it(self) its mystery" (Sells, 1994, p. 89). In this form, the identity shift occurs by one's noting of the winking out that indicates that they are no longer just a separate ego identity but have a new identity as one that participates in the process of union with the divine. The "semantic reenactment," as Sells refers to the later explanation that will be given to the event in the fifth and sixth stages, reenacts that transition, and this is what he refers to as the "meaning event." The identity shift occurs, he states, by the "art of apprehension" (ibid., p.88), where "the dualisms of self-other, time, and space are temporarily fused through the collapse of the semantic structures that reflect them" (ibid.). In this view, the sudden collapse of dualism in the winking out yields the apprehension of the end of one identity to create another.

It is interesting that Sells suggests that, in consideration of the question of Who reveals the mystery, it can be framed after the event as a double possibility, where "we should say it is both the divine and the human at the moment of polishing the mirror" (ibid. p. 87). This is a conclusion derived from Sells's "meaning event," the semantic reenactment, the subsequent framing that takes place upon exiting the experience, the fifth and sixth stages. In the reenactment, the winking out will not be as important as the explanation of the truth that is more profound in that subsequent framing. If this is the likely case, it is because nothingness is not capable of conveying any message, other than it exists from the noting and, at most, there is a consequent loosening of boundaries.

However, the building blocks of the framing that establish a meaning event do embrace the noting of a change of state during the winking out, as well to the revelation of the truth. It is this miraculous combination that suggests a wider author than the mere ego. It is the noting stage that, in evaluation, raises the question of the nature of the experience as it is, for many who have had a mystical experience, an awareness that there are other dimensions than just the waking mind.

The attribution to the source of the truth as a Who or What, as Sells suggests, is framed upon exiting the experience and thereafter by further elaboration. The attribution may therefore be influenced by the *force* of the contrast between states, the earlier premature hypothesis in the second stage, the purpose of the revelation in the orientation of the individual, and even the urgency of the message that is conveyed in the truth. It therefore makes sense to assert that the attribution is not able to be understood by logic: "It is noted that ramifications may enter into the descriptions either because of the intentional nature of the experience or through reflection upon it" (Smart, 1965, p. 79).

It is not useful to stop too long on the precise content of a state of nonduality in the winking out, nor to try to explain it by the esoteric teachings of the East or West, or even to make a refined distinction between nothingness and emptiness (Favre, 2022). If the winking out needs to be given qualities, they can be explained as either that of the preexistent, eternal ground of being before consciousness: the *Unus Mundus*, the *Pleroma*, or, instead, what is created by a mind fully conditioned for its suspension, expressed as the merging of the mind with the Self as described in discourses on Samadhi, Nibbāna, Satori, Fana or Jnana. These positions, no matter their theoretical nuances, are all the result of a switching off the old cognitive configuration, a form of "decreation," as the philosopher Simone Weil refers to it (Weil, 1956, p. 124), by either an aspect of mind or by something else.

Noting of a change of state from emptiness to revelation has a critical role in all religious and spiritual traditions, so its proof lies in its necessity. The theological doctrine of *creatio ex nihilo* is not a starting point as it does not mirror the stages of a mystical experience and was developed as a philosophical underpinning. As an example, the work *Periphyseon* by Eriugena the Christian Neoplatonist, is not a mystical text, but rather a philosophical and theological exposition (Sells, 1994, p. 59). However, theological importance can be seen more critically in the Christian idea of kenosis, emptying oneself, creating a nothingness: (Jesus) "emptied Himself" (Philippians 2:7). Kenosis mirrors the doctrine of achieving emptiness as a precondition to religious revelation. This is consistent with the neurobiological finding that injury to the frontal lobe causing inhibition of the executive cognitive functions, yields a greater chance of a revelatory mystical experience (Critofori, et al., 2016). The emptying of the conscious mind is, in addition, reflected in those experiences that occur in psilocybin usage where the sense of self is eradicated before the emergence of insight (Barrett & Griffiths, 2018).

2. Psychological Apprehension: The Who

For Jung, psychological change requires the impact of an experience that has sufficient psychic energy to render it capable of altering consciousness, for without that alteration it has no therapeutic relevance. Accordingly, a noting of winking out or revelation of a truth cannot be faint or weak but must somehow strike consciousness with sufficient force to contribute to the alteration of one's existing conscious position. This applies even if the noting is only the dramatic sense of a change of state but not a revelation of a profound truth, as the importance lies in its psychological effect: "Only through the specific vital activity of psyche does the sense-impression attain that intensity, and the idea of that effective force, which are the two constituents of living reality" (Jung, 1921, § 77). For the experience of noting to have any capacity to alter the existing conscious position, it must contain sufficient intensity to draw to it the attention of consciousness, so that "Emptiness in this sense doesn't mean 'absence' or 'vacancy' but something unknowable which is endowed with the highest intensity" (Jung 1953, Vol 2, p. 258).

The intensity created by the nothingness is noted by all of those who have had a mystical experience as the momentary, unbidden loss of a previously held conscious position prior to or coterminous with the arrival of the truth. It may not be understood at the time as having significant intensity, but will become patent when the experience is analyzed. The source of this intensity arises by nature of what occurs in the noting, as the mystical writing of Jorge Luis Borges suggests: There is a fusing of subject and object, so that the former remains but changes form as "something else" because "there is no distance between 'I' and 'other.'" (Giskin, 1990, p. 79). The noting is then a fusing of some form of awareness with a bare, untainted loss of an "I" that suggests the possibility of the "other:" a That. The noting takes this diminished or alternative form to be effective, or otherwise it would be obscured by memory and past experiences that will distort the oncoming truth; as Borges suggests in his work *The Aleph,* the expression he uses for that which contains all things at once: "Truth will not penetrate a recalcitrant understanding" (Borges, 1998, p. 127).

Sri Aurobindo, whose subtlety of approach encompasses this issue, suggests that there are different levels of mind. The gross level is that intertwined with matter, the Little Mind, and the highest is that in contact with the divine, the Greater Mind. The Little Mind has three parts: that dominated by the body and matter, that under the power of drives and desires, and the third is that dominated by reason. The Greater Mind also has three levels: that which is refined in intellect, such as knowledge held by a professional, although still close to materiality, leading by levels to the "Ideal Mind," which is behind our life, but remains "Unseen, unguessed by the blind suffering world" (Aurobindo, 1997, Vol 33, Book Two, Cantos X, XI, XII). In his worldview, it is perhaps the Ideal Mind, the "wide and witness Self," and not the Little Mind that is carrying out the noting or apprehension. Its elevation as Ideal Mind gives it sufficient intensity to be of psychological importance and to carry weight in the later evaluation of the experience.

There are many other possibilities as to what aspect of mind can witness a change of state. For Nietzsche, the senses are the perceptive instruments of the body (Nietzsche, 1961, p. 62), and thus mystical occurrences are often accompanied by bodily reactions, such as goosebumps; for Kant, the experience of a unity occurs by a "transcendental apperception" arising from an "inner sense" (Ameriks, 1997, p. 57). These ideas indicate that psychological awareness is inclusive of the ability to have a noting in all experiences, even with a damaged frontal cortex, through the senses of the body, through intuition, by a higher or Ideal mind, or any transcendent, genetic, and instinctual promptings that can be asserted to aid in the formation of the knowledge of one's existence.

There must, however, be cognitive assessment of what is noted, even when it is merely sensed or intuited. This is consistent with research that indicates that the intensity of these types of experiences permit mentation to always be present, so that every religious experience can be said to be cognitively mediated (Azari, 2005). It is therefore not possible to speak of psychological growth or religious or mystical attainment from the point of view of a completely noncognitive noting of nothingness. Carl Jung completely accepted the possibility of a state of nothingness but asserts it would have no psychological function unless it has the potential to change waking consciousness through its consideration. Thus, Jung calls the winking out a dreamlike state, "logically identical with unconsciousness" (Jung, 1939, § 520). He was forced to also assert that it can be made the subject of cognition even if there is an "infinitesimal ego" (Jung, 1935/19a, § 817). In his acceptance that there are indeed experiences such as Satori, a state that suggests an immersion into emptiness, he attempts to solve the issue of by claiming that the experience is "practically impossible for the European to appreciate" (Jung, 1939a, § 877). Accordingly, he states: "Our knowledge of physical nature gives us no *point d'appui* that would allow us to put the experience on any generally valid basis" (Jung, 1955-56, § 177). From a psychological position encouraging mental well-being, there can be no experience of nothingness unless there is an opportunity at the time or even in later states of reason.

The noting may indeed depend on rationality by consideration after the fact and the bare noticing of a change of state may not be accurate. How is it possible to have a moment of mentation when the winking-out process has begun unless there is a clear gap? If there is no gap, then there is no noting at that time, as Sri Nisargadatta Maharaj, a profound spiritual teacher of nondualism, explains: "In that nothingness, we are also nothingness. So who is to go anywhere? For whom are there any more questions left? In that nothingness, anything is nothingness. You are also nothingness" (Nisargadatta, 1996, p.88).

One of the 29 mystics who resided in a Buddhist Monastery, who has had multiple periods of mental cessation and long states of absorption into emptiness, explained it as a possible clear noting for those who are aware of the state before being overwhelmed. In that case, he explained, it was more like the administration of propofol, the anesthetic, that starts to flood the mind before there is a loss of consciousness: You can sense the coming emptiness that is indeed a change of state.

Accepting that noting can occur, there must be some other observer or a lesser or higher form of mind that is not what we know of as the day-to-day conscious mind. Returning to the idea of Borges, where subject and object fuse and produce a different form of subject, it is one without ego, so there is no longer an intellectual mind, yet in the fusing, reality is still known. This occurs, Borges speculates, because in intellectual, cognitive awareness, there is selective attention, but with mystical intuiting, nothing is selected, "but rather the whole is seen in its infinite complexity *sub specie aeternitatis* and instantly" (Giskin, 1990, p. 73). There is, therefore, a noting by that which has a universal perspective arising out of the nothingness itself, unrelated to the cognitive mind.

The conundrum can be solved in one of two ways: by finding a lesser form of ego that is not rational, but yet has a higher perspective that would accommodate a loss of thinking, or an attribution to the witnessing of the change of state and the truth by a higher consciousness found as an indwelling aspect of being, or that is transcendent and exists outside ourselves, often referred to as "That."

3. The Lesser Ego in Dreams

Some assistance as to the form of the observer, considered as a lesser form of ego, can be found in an analysis of the dream ego, the experience of oneself in a dream. The normal waking ego, or the ego-complex, as Jung referred to it, is, by definition, the center of consciousness, that "possesses a high degree of continuity and identity" (Jung, 1921a, § 706). This solipsistic, solid seeming, waking ego is responsible for all mentation and attention, so it cannot be an observer when it has been suspended or winks out; this is the point being made by Sri Nisargadatta and is indisputable. The form of ego that is responsible for noting nothingness is, therefore, not merely the waking ego, somehow suppressed or lessened in the winking out, but rather it is an observer *without* its normal cohesive, operative form of mind.

A starting point as to the nature of that ego structure in a dream came to me in my psychoanalytic practice. A male patient, a computer programmer in his 40s, who did not meditate or have any mystical, spiritual, or religious interests, presented this narrative:

> I was on a high wire between two platforms, about 200 feet apart. To my right, appeared to be a university— there was a neon sign above it written in mathematical equations. To my left was a quarry. I looked down and realized that there was no high wire but understood that the two were somehow interconnected. I then found myself suspended in a space that was pitch black and absolutely empty. I wasn't scared but instead felt at complete peace because I understood that this was the place where there was a lesson that will come to me. But then I woke up.

This is a mystical experience delivered in a dream where the empty space is noted by an observer that cannot be the waking ego. The profound nature of this dream illustrates the primal duality represented by the university (mind), and the quarry (matter), the essential dualistic structure of our world. Such overwhelming symbolism is enhanced by the realization of that interconnectedness, a coming together in a virtual *conjunctio* leading to a suspension beyond dualities. The realization of the *coincidentia oppositorum* of spirit and matter opened a third space of a union with no thought and no materiality. The truth that may come will then arise out of a nothing brought about by that *conjunctio*, the uniting of opposites. This is what Jung considers the *res simplex* of psychoanalysis, the *Unus Mundus,* the underlying primordial one world beyond duality

(Jung, 1955-56a, § 760) that contains all opposites *in potentia*—even fullness and nothingness as undifferentiated clouds that he analyzes in his essay *Septem Sermones ad Mortuos* (Jung, 1989, Appendix V; Stein, 2015). This essay bestows the essential task on humanity as *Creatura*, to differentiate the opposites out of the *Pleroma* to make them conscious. Such a powerful statement in a dream is far beyond the conscious width and breath of the dreamer and is presenting the manner in which nothingness is created.

At this primordial level, is it he who is experiencing the nothingness? He is, unlike a person in a waking mystical experience, a part of the dream, no more material than the nothingness, but he is also the center of an undifferentiated void that contains all things that Jung attributed in the *Septem Sermones* to the old Gnostic god *Abraxas*. At this level, it certainly cannot be said to be "the first-person experience of a subject in the usual sense, dualistically split off from its object of experience" (Atmanspacher & Rickles, 2022, p. 79). The first-person experience carries with it multilayered processes through which the individual participates in cognition, creating his or her world, the process of which has always been the subject of phenomenological speculation (Depraz, 1999). There are, therefore, two possible subjects in the dream: that which produces the primordial event of a *conjunctio* and resultant nothingness; and that which observes the event. What produces the event cannot be the conscious ego that would not have knowledge of the symbolism and cannot produce a mystical nothingness, and therefore attribution is forced to exist elsewhere. As well, the dream ego is not merely a passive observer here but is a god at the center of the *Pleroma* that contains all things *in potentia* and will be presented with a truth.

Jung recalls a patient's dream of a man riddled with resistances, but his dream evoked the number 4, the quintessence of wholeness. Jung comments that this revelation does not come from him: "The thing which is meant in the dream has nothing to do with the problem of his consciousness. It has to do with the centre outside consciousness" (Jung, 1984, p. 107). The outside source is what Jung refers to as the Self, the center of psyche, but also the possibility of totality. The psyche is all that is conscious and unconscious and the source of wholeness (Stein, 2022). What is noteworthy for Jung is that the first-person experience of cognition, the processes of mentation, the ego, cannot produce the symbolism. This means that the dream ego, no matter what position it is given, is an observer of the contents of the dream, but not "That" which is responsible for the dream. As applied to mystical experiences, the nothingness and the unfolding truth may therefore be seen as coming from elsewhere, from outside, from "That," yet still is necessarily experienced by the mental apparatus of some form of consciousness.

Freud's idea was that the observer in a dream is a subordinate function of the ego; it is the conscious mind operating in a reduced form, as it has fewer dimensions than when it is awake, as it lacks a reflective function. This lesser form lacks the consistency of the waking ego but cannot be categorically described, so it is best seen as a chimera with no psychic existence that is only the ego projected onto the dream (de Monchaux, 1993, pp. 200-201; 207). Jung describes that "In most dreams, for instance, there is still some consciousness of the ego, although it is a very limited and curiously distorted ego known as the dream ego. It is a mere fragment or shadow of the waking ego." So, he suggests, "the activity of the ego-complex seldom ceases entirely; its activity is as a rule only restricted by sleep" (Jung, 1920/1948, § 580).

There is something very elusive about these lesser forms of ego as "very limited and curiously distorted." Its presence could be said to be recognized, as it has no psychic substance, as "the dreamer's actual and felt sense of identity" (Whitmont & Perera, 1989, pp. 18-19), that is, truly "wholly imaginal," reflecting the situation of the ego responding to the demands of the contents of the dream (Hillman, 1979, p. 102). Thus, in an unconscious dream state, a state of no cognition, there is a sense of identity that remains. In the dream, the contents provided in the patient's dream by "That," provides the circumstances to orient the dreamer to be a point of reference wherein there is this sense of identity. This is the mechanism through which the dream message is given a purpose in the process of living. It is therefore the observer on behalf and at the service of that higher mind and the evolution of consciousness. This explains Jung suggesting that higher order or numinous dreams come from outside the dreamer's own consciousness, yet the observer is there in dreams as a limited and distorted form of ego for the dream to convey a message.

4. The Lesser Ego and Nothingness

The observer in a dream or that which perceives nothingness in a mystical experience is certainly not the complicated activity of the waking ego. This is clear, as it lacks the power of that conscious mind in terms of reason and agency. However, it has too important a role in mystical experiences by the noting of a change of state and the truth provided to just be a mere remnant, a projection of identity, or a weakened or distorted version.

When Freud describes the existence of an unconscious censor that inhibits dreams that may be too disturbing, this is not portrayed by him as a first-person ego or a brain function but, as he expresses it, it derives usefulness as a means to describe a dynamic relationship within psyche during sleep: "I hope you do not take the term (censorship) too anthropomorphically, and do not picture the 'censor of dreams' as a severe little manikin or a spirit living in a closet in the brain and there discharging his office. ... For the time being it is nothing more than a serviceable term for describing a dynamic relation" (Freud, 1916-17, p. 140). The debate that has followed over the last century as to the nature of this censor has doubted that it has agency and draws, instead, on its role in the wider, intertwined processes of psyche. In Freudian terms, the observer is what emerges as an aspect of a dynamic process that operates in the interrelationship between motivation and repression, rather than it containing any superior, transcendental agency or solidity within the realm of the waking ego (Boag, 2006).

The dynamic process in a dream state involves the unconscious projection of images, as, for example, the imago of parents long after adulthood is reached, so that: "... the projected image goes on working as though it were a spirit existing on its own" (Jung, 1928, § 294). The imago of the observer, the sense of identity in the context and process of the mystical experience is thus present as the legacy of ego formation and is not a consciously acting first-person ego. This explains the presence of the observer as only the mere projection of a conscious attitude, and accordingly it easily can become "That," the image of the other, as it appears alien to waking ego consciousness (Kugler, 1993, p. 134).

Relating this to the noting of the start of nothingness on the path to a higher realization, it is part of complex, subtle, unconscious processes that have an ontological, teleological basis. However, this does not suffice as an answer for the realization of the truth that arises out of the emptiness where the ego has been categorically dissolved. This answer, different from the projected attitude in the noting of the winking out, may depend on other factors, such as the nature of the experiencer and the basis of the ego dissolution. A Western unconditioned mind that has an unexpected, overwhelming experience of that truth observed by that identity projection will be different in kind from an experience that occurs to a mystic where consciousness has ceased because of purification and ego relativization, and one then rests in that absolute nondual existence. There is, in that later instance, no personal imago that can be projected or a limited ego that is possible and the noting can *only* depend on a nonpersonal observer, the "That," as Sri Aurobindo explains of his realization:

> I did not become aware of any pure 'I' nor even of any self, impersonal or other, there was an awareness of That as the sole Reality, it was a nameless consciousness which was not other than That; one could perhaps say this, though hardly even so much as this, since there was no mental concept of it, but not more. ... Mark that I did not think these things, there were no thoughts or concepts nor did they present themselves like that to any Me; it simply just was so or was self apparently so... (Aurobindo, 2011, Vol. 35, p. 257)

It can be said that there is always an experience of nothingness, a noting, but it is not that which is associated with the activity of the waking ego or a variant of that ego. The change of state from the winking out is noted in a mystical experience most likely from a sense of identity conjured at that time that is participating dynamically in a particular process to bring the unconscious to consciousness. Noting of the truth, the reality of being, must come from a That, as well described by the sage Meher Baba:

> It is true that the real aim of all this imaginary striving is to become perfectly conscious of unconsciousness. To achieve this, instead of bringing about a return to the original state of Existence, the Qutub (the center) gives the entire universe a tremendous push towards conscious Unconsciousness, imparts God-realization to a few, and brings his own circle members to his own level of perfect Perfection. (Meher Baba, 2022, p. 97)

It is clear, to bring home the point again, that the ego at either moment of noting is not the same as the waking ego, nor does it have any of the characteristics of that form of ego that has the capacity for reason and association and is the subject of memory and experience. Sri Aurobindo in his epic poem *Savitri* explains: "In that absolute stillness bare and formidable, there was *glimpsed* an all-negating Void Supreme; the 'known-unknown'" (Aurobindo, 1997, Book VII, Canto VII, emphasis added). The dynamic process, to have its *required effect* of bringing the mystery to consciousness, must provide for that glimpse that creates an observer to make the unknown a known-unknown.

5. The Experience of That

The shift from a personal noting of nothingness to the idea that the witness is "That," arises for several cogent reasons. The overwhelming process of an unbidden mystical experience requires a teleological explanation. It raises the possibility of a grand prime mover or an "other," a something that creates the experience (as Jung assumed for the center point of psyche: the Self) that holds all truths, standing behind the experience as its instigator and its witness. It is a natural conclusion and the purpose that the powerful revelation is beyond the capacity of a limited, flawed individual, as explained succinctly in a Zen parable:"The wondrous secret of the enlightened ones should not be placed in a little heart" (Cleary, trans. 2001, Vol. Four, p. 199).

It is a small step from noting nothingness to say "That" is the witness of the nothingness. It becomes the only logical explanation due to the magnitude of the revelation consisting of emptiness and cosmic truth. Since it is indeed noted, nothingness must always be an object, and therefore attribution to That as the subject gives substance to what is otherwise ineffable. Naming its derivation, "That," as coterminous with the experience, as Sri Aurobindo does, allows a complete mystery to have an explanation, making that explanation and the universality of the source more important than the experience.

The realization of "That" as the source of the experience may have the effect of superseding the importance of the stages of the experience. Attribution to a prime mover confers upon it agency, and thus it naturally becomes an entity behind or the observer of the experience; it answers the What that experiences nothingness and explains all stages as part of its plan. To have an effect on consciousness, however, the existence of "That" requires constant reinforcement as a matter of belief, faith, or ideation.

Pierre Bourdieu explains that named interpsychic objects such as the That can become "camouflage through form…(and) remain misrecognized in practice; though present as substance they are absent as form; like a face hidden in a bush" (Bourdieu, 1991, p. 142-3).

This says nothing, of course, about the theological veracity and importance of That. However, it indicates how the transition from a personal, subjective experience, the Who, to the idea of a prime mover, the What, occurs by giving a name to that which is otherwise inexplicable. A quest to experience the prime mover is the formation of spiritual traditions, although its experience is always limited except, as Meher Baba explains, for rare individuals who become absorbed in the experience of That.

The noting of nothingness is part of a larger process where the dynamics require the eventual realization of That. In Buddhist terms, all experiences are part of a process leading to the two forms of realization expressed by Buddha: the peacefulness of no suffering but with remaining experiences of pleasure and pain, and the second form of a state beyond agreeable and disagreeable: "For him, here in this very life, all that is experienced, not be delighted in, will be extinguished" (Ireland, 1997, pp.139-140).

There appears, accordingly, to be two reasons for the noting of nothingness by the Who and the necessary attribution to the What. The first is that the noting of nothingness is part of a process where it is necessary that there be a perception of that emptiness for the relativization and purification of the ego to alter consciousness. The second is that the "something else" being present, as it was for the patient, is a natural consequence of an overpowering, nonconceptual experience. This joining of the inside experience with the attribution outside is explained by Jung as arising from the experience feeling alien, absolutely other, and thus "wholeness is thus an objective factor that confronts the subject independently of him" (Jung, 1951, § 59). This psychological and ontological reason for the realization of That, which is alien to the ego, is that it will "create a wider personality whose center of gravity does not necessarily coincide with the ego" (Jung, 1951a, § 297). When the emphasis shifts to the outside or an objective factor, it is then necessary to include, as Jung did, that this is the operation of the "God within us" (Jung, 1928, § 399).

The revelation of wholeness, unity or nothingness in spiritual traditions will create the imperative to find an observer that is beyond our conscious mind that is then made the progenitor of the experience. It then, to bring it closer to our conscious mind, which becomes an object that is within us that is manifesting and is a witnessing subject. The creation of the Self by Jung as having this dual character is the reason that Jung cleaved to the Hindu Atman as a parallel of the Self, as it is characterized by an inward dwelling aspect of the divine within our hearts to unite the inside with Brahman, the impersonal Absolute "That," said to be devoid of qualities (see Corbett, 2022).

6. The Why of Nothingness

In the case of a mystical experience or attainment to the final stage of enlightenment, the force of the overwhelming, alien nature of the intrusion, leads to the characterization of an objective That. Even though in the noting of nothingness the "mind now *seemed* like a vast empty room" (Aurobindo, 1997, p. 543, emphasis added), there must be some form of attribution or, instead, some means to describe *why* that has occurred.

This explains the paradox of attribution to Who *and* What that arises because of the true, transforming nature of the experience of nothingness. Nothingness is more than a moment of displacement of the conscious ego, where there is a softening of ego boundaries and the potential revelation of a nondual unity. Its qualities are vaster and are transformative in themselves, prompting closer connection with "That." Nothingness is a unique state that may arise infrequently at best, and when it does, it brings a crystalline stillness, as it quiets the mind. This stillness is not just a calming of the mind but rather a bizarre, rare occurrence where the habitual, conscious mind has been momentarily overcome. Nothingness, therefore, creates the human, innate desire for *conjunctio,* the potential uniting of all opposites, evoking a forever longing for that peace.

The longing is not conceptual or existential and is the primordial, innate instinct of evolution. It is always in the background and cannot be refused when it offers up nothingness, giving it a dimension that is at the core of all human development. It is the force of creation, what Schelling refers to as primal will, *"Wille est Ursein,"* the innate movement of being.

Thus, Jung was able to express that the energy that draws everything around it to the central point, the Self, "is manifested in the almost irresistible compulsion to *become what one is*, just as every organism is driven to assume the form that is characteristic of its nature, not matter what the circumstances" (Jung, 1950, § 634, emphasis supplied). Freud and Jung repeatedly explained that this longing activates the psyche "in the face of an incomprehensible origin and destiny" (Henderson, 2011, p. 200).

The passage from nothingness to truth is considered a miracle of emerging from the darkness of nothingness into the light, as a long night giving way to dawn. Thus, the truth emerging from nothingness is referred to as the "light of wisdom," the "torch of wisdom" (Sayadaw, 2016, p. 464), so that the contrast becomes essential to the human purpose when the light appears:

> Clement [the second-century Christian theologian] tells us that this light is that essential – that is, real in the Platonic sense and not a mere sensory phenomenon. It is without shadow, but above the opposition of light and dark. It was first, prior to this dualism. It conveys adequate insight; it is comprehensive vision viewed as an act, and, as a result of this act, pure intuition. (Pulver, 1985, p. 252)

Accordingly, light has become the symbolic contrast of the truth arising out of dark nothingness that conveys the greatest impact where one's longing is answered by a new revelation, uncluttered by points of view or affected in any way by dualism. This requires that there is a noting when entering a state of nonbeing, evoking the longing for that unique peace, that then is satisfied or substantiated in the moment of contrast when the truth arrives. The two combine to create a new space, a mystical space, that resonates in the body, and is of significance as it momentarily defies death and any form of oblivion. In fact, the truth extinguishes the longing as it is no longer necessary, as if lifted above the thousands of ways one can suffer.

This serves, as best language can do, to express the magnitude of the experience that Sri Aurobindo calls "worlds of deathless bliss, perfections home, Magical unfoldings of the Eternal's smile" (Aurobindo,

1997, Book 11, Canto 1, p. 671). Such bliss is outside the conscious experience of individuals, and thus this feeling of a miracle is present at the deepest, unconscious level. My observations of mystical experiences suggest, therefore, two forms of noting: the instant consciousness is lost accompanied by the longing that arises to always partake of that nondual peace, and the instant that the truth arrives as an answer to that longing. This is noted by an individual and is too momentous for there not to be an "other." This is consistent with psychoanalytic ideas that the experience of a change of state is accompanied by the surfacing of unconscious contents: "from the a priori inherited foundations of the unconscious" (Jung, 1921b, § 659), which are the archetypes. However expressed, the overwhelming immersion in nothingness, and the presence of a truth is what causes the individual to "discern a spiritual dimension in secular phenomena" (Ross, 1992, p. 90).

It is therefore "That," which is behind the experience, the prime mover at the instinctual, evolutionary level that, by the revelatory nature of the truth, is both the observer and the observed. It may be given one of many theological frames as the experience ends, some that even exclude the possibility of a That. However, an individual, the Who has, on reflection, as Sells puts it, a meaning event, by understanding that they are the vehicle through which this higher consciousness is expressed. An individual is not only the observer of the nothingness, but also an observer of the barest power of That which is behind the experience.

7. Conclusion

The analysis of the states of the mystics, my experiences, those of patients, the apocryphal stories so easily available, and the propositions here advanced, cannot make such an experience bend to reality. Sri Nisargadatta makes the Nothingness, the That, as the only reality because it is a dimension that exists outside the noise of the mind. This same theme is prevalent in Sufism and Hinduism, although fine distinctions are made, and the power of the experience can be also drawn in explicating different notions and levels of the Soul. The nothingness in any formulation is what Jung understood as the *Pleroma*, pure potentiality beyond time and space as the basis for all that emerges. It is also the Buddhist idea of *śūnyatā,* a reference to what is inconceivable or unnamable, but, like the *Pleroma*, it contains a sense of possibility (Pickering, 2022, p. 265).

A mystical experience, once it has been discussed and become part of an individual's identity, will emerge as one narrative among others. What has occurred is, however, the opportunity for the experience of a moment of nonduality, the rising of a longing for the possibility of that peace, and a partial answer to the longing that is always expressed as more than the ego.

The eternal truth, however cast, that which brings peace by a unity through dissolution of the ego, occurs from the nothingness. The miracle of nothingness is essential to create the expansion of consciousness as Sri Aurobindo explains in his poem *Savitri*: "In infinite Nothingness was the ultimate sign, Or else the Real was unknowable, A lonely Absolute negated all: It effaced the ignorant world from its solitude, And drowned the soul in its everlasting peace" (Aurobindo, 1997, p. 550).

This struggle for an objective reality formed out of nothingness makes "That" a living concept to which the conscious mind can relate. This then allows the subject to contain "That," as well as it being the object, the complete merging. This is because the external object changes the subject's view of agency, so the individual gives over its decisions to "That."

All these elements—duality, a union detected from glimpses of nothingness and attribution—create a logical path for attainment of that truth. As the experience is entirely internally focused, the bridge is created by the concept in Tantra that "what appears *without* only so appears *because* it is exists *within*" (Woodroffe, 2019, p. 177, emphasis supplied). Thus, the Who and What are merged and are one.

References

Atmanspacher, H., & Rickles, D. (2022) *Dual Aspect Monism and the Deep Structure of Meaning.* London: Routledge.

Ameriks, K. (1997) Kant and the self: A retrospective. In Klemm, D.E. & Zoller, G. (eds.) *Figuring the Self: Subject, Absolute and Others in Classical German Philosophy.* London: Routledge.

Andersen, M., Shjoedt, U., Nielbo, K.L, & Sørenson, J. (2014) Mystical Experience in the Lab. *Method & theory in the study of religion,* 26 (3), pp. 217-245.

Aurobindo, Sri, (1997) *Savitri: A Legend and a Symbol, Parts Two and Three.* In *The Complete Works of Sri Aurobindo, Vol. 33.* Pondicherry, India: Sri Aurobindo Ashram Publication Department.

Aurobindo, Sri (2011) *Letters on Himself and the Ashram. In The Complete Works of Sri Aurobindo, Vol. 35.* Pondicherry, India: Sri Aurobindo Ashram Publication Department.

Azari, N.P., Messimer, J., & Rudiger, S.J. (2005) Religious Experience and Emotion: Evidence for Distinctive Cognitive Neural Patterns. *The International Journal for the Psychology of Religion,* 15 (4), pp. 263-281.

Barrett, F.S, Griffiths, R.R. (2018) Classic Hallucinogens and Mystical Experiences: Phenomenology and Neural Correlates. *Current Topics in Behavioral Neuroscience, 36,* pp. 393-430.

Boag, S. (2006) Freudian Dream Theory, Dream Bizareness, and the Disguise-Censor Controversy. *Neuropsychoanalysis, 8,* pp. 5-16.

Borges, J.L. (1998) *The Aleph.* A. Hurley, trans. London: Penguin.

Bourdieu, P. (1991) Censorship and the imposition of form. In Thompson, J. (Ed.) *Language and Symbolic Power,* pp. 142-143. Cambridge, MA: Harvard University Press.

Carpenter, A.D. (2018) Attention as a means of self-dissolution and reformation. *Ratio, 31,* pp. 276-388.

Clearly, T. (trans. 2001) *Classics of Buddhism and Zen.* Vol Four. Boston, Shambhala.

Corbett, L. (2022) Jung's Self and the Atman of the Upanishads. In Stein, L., ed., *Eastern Practices and Individuation: Essays by Jungian Analysts.* Ashville, NC: Chiron Publications.

Cristofori, I., Bulbulia, J., Shaver, J.H., Wilson, M., Krueger, F., Grafman, J. (2016) Neural correlates of mystical experience. *Neuropsychologia,* 80, pp. 212-220.

De Monchaux, C. (1993) Dreaming and the organizing function of the ego. In Flanders, S. (ed.) *The Dream Discourse Today.* London: Routledge.

Depraz, N. (1999) The phenomenology reduction as *praxis.* In Varela, F.J. & Shear, J. (eds.), *The View from Within: First-person approaches to the study of consciousness.* Thoverton, UK: Imprint Academic.

Favre, D. (2022) The potential of emptiness. *Jung Journal,* 16 (2), pp. 47-61.

Freud, S. (1916-17) *Introductory Lectures on Psycho-Analysis.* Standard Edition, 15/16.

Giskin, H. (1990) The Mystical Experience in Borges: A Problem of Perception. *Hispanófila,* 98, pp. 71-85.

Henderson, D. (2011) Aspects of negation in Freud and Jung. *Psychoanalytic Practice,* 17 (2), pp. 199-205.

Hillman, J. (1979) *The Dream and the Underworld.* New York: HarperCollins.

Ireland, J. (trans. 1997) *The Udana and the Itivuttaka: Two Classics from the Pali Canon.* Kandy, Sri Lanka: Buddhist Publication Society.

James, W. (1902/2008) *Varieties of Religious Experience: A Study in Human Nature.* Rockville, MD: Arc Manor.

Jung, C.G. (1929/1948) The psychological foundations of the belief in spirits. *The Structure and Dynamics of the Psyche,* CW 8. (*The Collected Works of C.G. Jung*; Princeton: Princeton University Press).

Jung, C.G. (1921) The type problem in Classical and Medieval thought. *Psychological Types,* CW 6. (*The Collected Works of C.G. Jung*; Princeton: Princeton University Press).

Jung, C.G. (1921a) Definitions. *Psychological Types,* CW 6. (*The Collected Works of C.G. Jung*; Princeton: Princeton University Press).

Jung, C.G. (1921b) General description of types. *Psychological Types,* CW 6. (*The Collected Works of C.G. Jung*; Princeton: Princeton University Press).

Jung, C.G. (1928) The relations between the ego and the unconscious. *Two Essays on Analytical Psychology,* CW 7. (*The Collected Works of C.G. Jung*; Princeton: Princeton University Press).

Jung, C.G. (1939) Conscious, unconscious, and individuation. *The Archetypes and the Collective Unconscious.* CW 9i. (*The Collected Works of C.G. Jung*; Princeton: Princeton University Press).

Jung, C.G. (1939a) Psychological Commentaries on "The Tibetan Book of the Great Liberation." *Psychology East and Religion: East and West,* CW 11. (*The Collected Works of C.G. Jung*; Princeton: Princeton University Press).

Jung, C.G. (1950) Concerning mandala symbolism. *The Archetypes and the Collective Unconscious,* CW 9i. (*The Collected Works of C.G. Jung*; Princeton: Princeton University Press).

Jung, C.G. (1951) The Self. *Aion,* CW 9ii. (*The Collected Works of C.G. Jung*; Princeton: Princeton University Press).

Jung, C.G. (1951a) Gnostic Symbols of the Self. *Aion,* CW 9ii. (*The Collected Works of C.G. Jung*; Princeton: Princeton University Press).

Jung, C.G. (1955-56) The personification of the opposites. *Mysterium Coniuntionis,* CW 14. (*The Collected Works of C.G. Jung*; Princeton: Princeton University Press).

Jung, C.G. (1955-56a) The conjunction. *Mysterium Coniunctionis,* CW 14. (*The Collected Works of C.G. Jung*; Princeton: Princeton University Press).

Jung, C.G. (1973) *C.G. Jung Letters.* Adler, G. & Jaffe, A. (Eds.). Vol. 1. Princeton, NJ: Princeton University Press.

Jung, C.G. (1984) *Dream Analysis: Notes on the Seminar given in 1928-1930.* W. McGuire, (ed.) Princeton, NJ: Princeton University Press.

Jung, C.G. (1989) *Memories, Dreams, Reflections.* A. Jaffe, ed. New York: Vintage Books.

Kugler, P. (1993) The "subject" of dreams. *Dreaming,* 3 (2), pp. 123-136.

Meher Baba. (2022) *Creation and its Causes: Meher Baba's lectures to the Meher Ashram Boys in 1927-28.* Myrtle Beach, SC: Sherier Foundation.

Nietzsche, F. (1961) *Thus Spoke Zarathustra.* R. J. Hollingdale, trans. Harmondsworth, England: Penguin.

Nisargadatta, Sri. (1996) *The Experience of Nothingness: Sri Nisargadda Mahara's Talks on Realizing the Infinite.* R. Powell (Ed.). San Diego: Blue Dove Press.

Noh, J.J. (1977) *Do You See What I See?* Wheaton, IL: Quest.

Otto, R. (1923) *Idea of the Holy, an Inquiry into the Non-rational Factor in the Idea of the Divine and its Relation to the Rational.* London: Oxford University Press.

Pickering, J. (2022) The cuckoo's call of instant presence: Self and non-self in Jung, Buddhism and Dzogchen. In Stein, L., (ed.) *Eastern Practices and Individuation: Essays by Jungian Analysts.* Asheville, NC: Chiron Publications.

Pulver, M. (1960) The experience of Light in the Gospel of St. John, in the Corpus hermeticum. In Gnosticism, and in the Eastern Church. In Campbell, J. (ed.) *Spiritual Disciplines: Papers from the Eranos Yearbooks.* Princeton, NJ: Princeton University Press.

Ross, C.F.J. (1992) The intuitive function and religious orientation. *Journal of Analytical Psychology,* 37, pp. 83-103.

Sayadaw, M. (2016) *Manual of Insight.* Vipassana Metta Foundation Translation Committee (trans.). Somerville, MA: Wisdom Publications.

Sells, M.A. (1994) *Mystical Languages of Unsaying.* Chicago: University of Chicago Press.

Scholem, G. (1941) *Major Trends in Jewish Mysticism.* 3rd edn. New York: Schocken Books.

Smart, N. (1965) Interpretation and Mystical Experiences. *Religious Studies,* 1 (1), pp. 75-87.

Stein, L. (2012) *Becoming Whole: Jung's Equation for Realizing God.* New York: Helios Press.

Stein, L. (2015) Jung and Divine Self-Reflection. *Jung Journal,* 9 (1), p. 18.

Stein, L. (2019) *Working with Mystical Experiences in Psychoanalysis: Opening to the Numinous.* London: Routledge.

Stein, L. (2022) *The Self in Jungian Psychology: Theory and Clinical Practice.* Asheville, NC: Chiron Publications.

Stein, L. (2022a) Archetypal forces and the ego structure of Eastern practices. In Stein, L. (ed.) *Eastern Practices and Individuation: Essays by Jungian Analysts.* Asheville, NC: Chiron Publications.

Warren S. (1984) *The Emergence of Dialectical Theory: Philosophy and Political Inquiry.* Chicago: University of Chicago Press.

Weil, S. (1956) *The Notebooks of Simone Weil.* A. Will (trans.) Volume 1, New York: G.P. Putnam's Sons.

Whitmont, E.C., & Perera, S.B. (1989) *Dreams, A Portal to the Source.* London: Routledge.

Woodroffe, J. (2010) *S'akti and S'akta.* Madras. India: Ganesh & Co.

5
Nothingness in Meditation:
Making Sense of Emptiness and Cessation

Vismay Agrawal & Ruben E. Laukkonen

"For the one who sees, there is no thing."
— The Buddha, Udana 8.2 (Burbea, 2014)

Contemplative practices have been shown to elicit a range of experiences and insights often referred to as "nothingness." However, these encounters are frequently conflated and remain undifferentiated. Here we address this ambiguity and provide a nuanced understanding of two such events: 1) emptiness (lack of inherent existence in experience, i.e., no-thingness) and 2) cessation ("cut" or absence in the stream of consciousness, i.e., nothingness). We synthesize insights from Buddhist literature and empirical research, investigating the relationship between these "nothingness" phenomena, their transformative effects, and neural correlates. We also examine multiple pathways that may lead to cessation and consider potential cognitive models underlying these experiences using the active inference framework. Finally, we discuss the relationship between "nothingness" events and cessation of suffering, setting the stage for further development in this field. Our unique contributions involve juxtaposing various experiences of "void, oneness, non-dual awareness, pure consciousness" with insights into "emptiness and cessation," and analyzing their potential implications for alleviating suffering.

1. Introduction

Twenty-first century developments in physics and biology challenge the notion of our existence as isolated, solid entities truly separate from the rest of the world and each other. Intriguingly, these scientific developments align with first-person subjective realizations or "insights" reported by meditators, as documented throughout history. For example, advanced practitioners have reported insights wherein they discover the absence of any concrete existence or substantial essence in their phenomenological reality. This chapter explores varieties of such experiences and early empirical findings about their consequences on the mind and brain.

This chapter focuses on two specific insight events, which we term as no-thingness and nothingness. We define no-thingness as an experiential understanding of the nature of the personal self and objects of experience as merely mental fabrications. In Mahayana Buddhism, this is known as emptiness (Sanskrit: śūnyatā, Pāli: suññatā), meaning all things are empty of intrinsic, separate, existence. In contrast, we refer to nothingness as the cessation of consciousness and experience, known as *nirodha* in Pāli. Notably, this differs from "nothingness" in the context of the 7th *jhāna*, which still involves some subtle phenomenal content, e.g., "...awareness dwells on the absence of any object," "perception of no-thing-ness is still perception" (Gunaratana, 2009). The cessation event may be experienced as a brief "cut" in the stream of consciousness, lasting only milliseconds or seconds, and often followed by a sense of clarity and openness (Laukkonen, Sacchet, et al., 2023). We will address both of these states in detail in the coming sections.

Note that our inquiry turns away from abstract ontological and philosophical debates about the nature of reality. We are not concerned with the absolute reality of nothingness or no-thingness. Instead, we explore how they are subjectively experienced in the context of meditation and how they may impact the mind and brain. In other words, we prioritize epistemology and phenomenology over ontology, grounding our investigation in recent empirical research. We draw inspiration from computational cognitive neuroscience, contemplative science, and Buddhist literature, enabling us to distinguish between these experiences phenomenologically and empirically. We also begin to make progress in understanding how the two influence, or perhaps even give rise, to one another.

We have structured this chapter into distinct sections. Initially, we discuss multiple accounts of emptiness (no-thingness) and cessation (nothingness), their relationship, and common misconceptions. We then examine their influences on the mind and brain. We go on to explore the temporal sequence that culminates in cessation. Finally, we provide a computational framework to study these accounts and discuss future directions and potential applications. Our unique contributions to the field involve differentiating various accounts of nothingness to ascertain whether they point to the same phenomenon by drawing distinctions and commonalities among them. Returning to the big picture, we explore how these insights fit into the context of alleviating suffering and cultivating enduring equanimity.

2. Accounts of No-thingness and Nothingness

> "Form is emptiness, emptiness is form." — Heart Sūtra
> (Pine, 2005)

In this section, we will consider different accounts of nothingness and no-thingness, and the relationship between them. Additionally, we discuss the accounts that may sound similar to these experiences but may in fact be different.

2.1 Accounts of no-thingness: Emptiness and the interdependence of phenomena

No-thingness, or emptiness, as conceived within the context of Buddhist philosophy and as defined in this chapter, is the nature of all phenomena as interdependent and lacking substantial, consistent identity (i.e., thingness). No-thingness is prominently associated with the *Madhyamaka* school of Mahayana Buddhism, notably expounded by the philosopher Nāgārjuna (Garfield, 1994). Nāgārjuna's teachings emphasize that all things are empty of intrinsic nature (Sanskrit: *svabhāva*, Pāli: *sabhāva*), and our perception of inherent existence is an illusion. In the words of Nāgārjuna: "Whatever arises dependent on something, that is empty of intrinsic existence, and that itself is the middle way" (Nāgārjuna, 1995). In sutras, emptiness has a twofold meaning: a mode of perception in which nothing is added or subtracted from the perception; and the lack of self in six sense fields and their objects. In summary, no-thingness can be both—a mode of perception and an attribute of the objects perceived (Robinson & Johnson, 1997).

Note that many other Eastern schools of contemplative practice and philosophy also emphasize emptiness or related notions. For instance, a central text in Mahayana Buddhism is the Heart Sūtra, which points to the empty nature of all phenomena and asserts that in emptiness, none of the conventional notions apply (Pine, 2005). In Zen Buddhism, "mu," or "emptiness," is often presented as a koan—a paradoxical statement or question used in meditation to provoke contemplation and insight (Kubose, 1973). Practitioners are encouraged to meditate on questions like "What is the sound of one hand clapping?" to break down the mind's conceptual assumptions. In Taoism, the idea of Wu Wei, often translated as "nonaction" or "effortless action," echoes the theme of letting go of fixed notions and allowing things to unfold naturally, relating to the emptiness teachings in Buddhism (Watts & Huang, 1975). Advaita Vedānta, a school of thought within Hinduism, explores the principle of "a-dvaita," or "not-two," positing that subject and object are interconnected whole (Nisargadatta, 1999). Note that all these pointers may not exactly align with emptiness in the way we have defined it. The subtle nuances are addressed in more detail later in this chapter.

The empty quality of all phenomena can be recognized through different meditative practices, resulting in a cognitive shift or "insight" into emptiness (Burbea, 2014). These insights can be said to progress from gross to subtle. At a more intellectual or psychological level, one may realize that many conceptions are mere constructs (Van Gordon et al., 2017). For example, in an inquiry into the nature of countries and the boundaries dividing them, it becomes obvious that these things are human-made divisions with no inherent existence and hence, empty (Burbea, 2014). At subtler levels, one may realize that the sense of self is not a fixed, unchanging reality but a dynamic, ever-evolving construct. This may lead to an experiential understanding that the self is empty of any permanent, independent existence. Deeper insights are said to lead to the realization that all the five aggregates (a Buddhist formalization of different contents of experience)—form, valence, perception, mental activity, and consciousness—arise co-dependently, and the entire experience is constructed or fabricated out of these building blocks. Taking a step further, one can realize that even emptiness is empty, revealing that no-thingness is not a self-existent void as the ultimate truth beneath the veil of illusion, but itself an aspect of conventional reality (Garfield,

1994). Thus, it signifies the conditioned nature of all phenomena and rather than their non-existence (Anālayo, 2015).

To help understand no-thingness, we can draw an analogy with a dictionary. Each word in a dictionary derives its meaning in relation to other words. Any word in itself has no independent meaning (i.e., cannot be defined without using other words) and hence, is not an independently existing thing. Furthermore, the existence of a dictionary is defined by the words contained within it. Without those words, there is no such thing as a dictionary. Similarly, all experiences are thought to be a kind of "abstraction" that is constructed based on past learning, associations, and conditioning (like the words in a dictionary), without inherent nature, and hence, empty (Laukkonen & Slagter, 2021). But this does not render the independent existence of emptiness. Continuing the analogy, the existence of a dictionary is defined by the words contained within it, and without those words, there is no such thing as a dictionary. Similarly, emptiness, like a dictionary, is not an independently existing entity, instead, it finds meaning and definition through the interconnected and co-dependent nature of experiences.

2.2 Accounts of nothingness: Cessation and the absence of consciousness

In this chapter, we define nothingness as a "gap" or "cessation" (*nirodha*) in the stream of consciousness. The significance of nothingness or cessation is particularly pronounced in Theravada Buddhism, where some deem it a necessary and significant milestone in the practitioner's journey toward complete freedom from suffering (Johnson, 2017; Sayadaw, 2016). During cessation, all perceptions and feelings cease (including space, time, and awareness), resulting in a state of absence. These moments of cessation are typically short-lived, lasting only a few seconds, and often followed by a recognition of the cessation event itself (Laukkonen, Sacchet, et al., 2023). What follows is akin to a "reboot" of consciousness and is said to bring about deep insights upon re-emergence, transforming the way the mind works. Cessation can be said to be both an "insight" and a "state" (Sayadaw, 2016). It is called a state because it can be attained and last for a period of time. Additionally, it represents an important insight phase and may be equated with stages of insight known as path (*magga*) or realization and fruition (*phala*) depending on the teacher (Berkovich-Ohana, 2017; Laukkonen, Sacchet, et al., 2023).

As one practices insight meditation (*vipassanā*), it is said that certain predictable stages of insight unfold and lead meditators through various cognitive and perceptual transformations, culminating in the event of cessation (Sayadaw, 2016). Recent research suggests that adept meditators may be able to swiftly traverse these stages, creating the conditions for a cessation event (Chowdhury et al., 2023; Yang et al., 2023). Furthermore, advanced meditators who have experience with *nirodha* claim to be able to train themselves to intentionally enter longer periods (up to seven days) of cessation, known as *nirodha samāpatti*, which literally translates to the cessation attainment (Laukkonen, Sacchet, et al., 2023). Achieving this requires a substantial degree of intentional training, involving progression through absorption stages until the last stage, followed by the deliberate creation of conditions for it to manifest. It is crucial to note that, in this chapter, when we refer to *nirodha* and *nirodha samāpatti*, we are specifically referring to different forms of "cessation of consciousness" and not the ultimate goal of Theravada Buddhism, which pertains to the complete and permanent "cessation of suffering" in all facets of experience (Ñāṇamoli & Bodhi, 2009).

2.3 Relationship between no-thingness, nothingness, and other insights

No-thingness and nothingness are distinct yet closely intertwined concepts. Their significance and emphasis may vary based on tradition, individual preferences, and didactic motivations. The intricate link between no-thingness and nothingness can be understood by drawing connections with other insight knowledge in *vipassanā* practice. As briefly discussed above, a key concept in Buddhism is that one's entire experience is constructed from five aggregates. These five aggregates are viewed through the lens of (or characterized by) three characteristics: impermanence (*anicca*), suffering (*dukkha*), and not-self (*anatta*) (Ñāṇamoli & Bodhi, 2009). When the contemplation of these three characteristics is fully developed, all the other insight knowledge, like emptiness and cessation, may also be established (Sayadaw, 2016). Specifically, the contemplation of not-self nature reveals that phenomena lack inherent self, concurrently establishing contemplation of emptiness. In fact, both are said to be one in meaning, differing only in terminology (Sayadaw, 2016). Additionally, the mature insight into not-self is said to generate equanimity toward all experiences, leading to non-grasping and letting go, ultimately culminating in cessation (Yates et al., 2017). The cessation may further intensify the momentum of letting go, setting the stage for deeper layers of insight. Thus, the interplay between emptiness and cessation can be described as a spiral or a chicken-and-egg relationship. The realization of emptiness may lead to cessation, and cessation may, in turn, deepen the understanding of emptiness. As this process of deepening understanding unfolds, it is said to support letting go and the cessation of suffering.

2.4 Clarifying misconceptions about no-thingness and nothingness

Normally, human subjective experience flows between waking, dreaming, and deep sleep. In certain conditions, this flow can significantly deviate from its typical states, leading to a qualitative alteration in the conscious experience known as an altered state of consciousness (ASC). These alterations can be induced by various means, such as meditation, psychoactive substances, breathing techniques, hypnosis, sensory deprivation, or pathological conditions (Revonsuo, 2009).

Take psychedelics, for example. Substances like psilocybin, LSD, and Ayahuasca produce short-term dramatic changes in consciousness (Millière et al., 2018). It can lead to a phenomenon known as drug-induced ego dissolution, wherein the person loses one's sense of self and self-world boundaries, and experiences a state of oneness (Letheby & Gerrans, 2017). 5-Meo-DMT, a psychedelic compound found in the toxin of the toad Bufo alvarius, may lead to a pure consciousness experience, a state characterized by emptying out of all experiential content and phenomenological qualities (Ermakova et al., 2022). The experience is frequently described as pure consciousness, emptiness, nothingness, or void (Millière et al., 2018). There are also parallels in Buddhist meditation; for example, the Dzogchen tradition in Indo-Tibetan Buddhism mentions a state of "clear light," or "luminosity," that can be reached during dreamless sleep through highly skilled meditative practices, such as *yoga nidrā* or luminosity yoga (Alcaraz-Sánchez et al., 2022). In Advaita Vedānta, this state is known as *"sushupti,"* or "witnessing-sleep" (Nikhilananda, 2006). Such a state seems to lack object-directed awareness and is described as an experience of nothingness (Alcaraz-Sánchez et al., 2022). But, are these states truly contentless (nothingness)? Or do they necessarily dispel the illusion of inherent existence (no-thingness) in all phenomena?

The most common approaches to quantitatively evaluate the phenomenology of ASC involve retrospective assessment using standardized and validated questionnaires, subjective reports and micro-phenomenological interviews (Schmidt & Berkemeyer, 2018). By utilizing various standardized measures, researchers have been able to gather quantitative data on the various dimensions of ASC, allowing for a clearer understanding of the subjective experiences individuals undergo. The phenomenological analysis of peak experiences reveals that, while many are often classically described as contentless, not all reported states are truly devoid of content (cessation) and the reports can involve considerable variation (Alcaraz-Sánchez et al., 2022; Woods et al., 2022). Moreover, not all altered states of consciousness give insight into reality's fabricated nature.

Nonetheless, it is not uncommon for researchers and philosophers to use similar terms, which may conflate cessation of consciousness (nothingness) and the realization of emptiness (no-thingness) with fabricated or altered states described as experiences of non-dual awareness, pure consciousness, or brief moments of "blanking out," or experiences of "presence," "light," "silence," or "stillness." For instance, nondual awareness—a state of consciousness said to rest in the background of all conscious experiencing, akin to the "ground of being" can be misunderstood as *śūnyatā* (i.e., emptiness, though emptiness insights may co-occur with the experience). While experiences of nondual awareness often assert awareness as an ontological entity, emptiness and cessation seem to direct the mind toward an epistemic observation of how the mind operates, undermining any "ground" of experience (Attwood, 2022). Furthermore, transcendental states of mystical oneness, where subject and objects seem to dissolve, can be mislabeled as *nirodha* (Smith, 2011). Thus, such experiences of voidness, oneness, nondual awareness, pure consciousness, and similar phenomena may not be identical to or lead to nothingness (cessation) or the understanding of no-thingness (emptiness).

Note that our aim here is not to imply that one is more important than the other, just that there are nuanced differences that may help serve ongoing research into these topics and avoid further conflations currently common in the scientific literature. In fact, the experiential states labeled as "emptiness," "pure presence," "stillness," "silence," "thoughtless awareness," and so on (Berkovich-Ohana et al., 2013; Hinterberger et al., 2014), might point to transitionary states between insights into emptiness and subsequent cessations of consciousness. Though caution needs to be maintained as these experiential states may even strengthen one's belief in another reality, separate from their current experience (McGovern et al., 2023). More broadly, all manner of intense insight experiences are possible in the course of altered states of consciousness, including those induced by meditation (Tulver et al., 2023). However, that does not make them necessarily true, or even adaptive, as recent research shows that false insight experiences can be induced in the lab (Grimmer et al., 2023; Grimmer, Laukkonen, Freydenzon, et al., 2022; Grimmer, Laukkonen, Tangen, et al., 2022) and even misattributed to make false information feel true (Laukkonen et al., 2020, 2022; Laukkonen, Webb, et al., 2023).

3. Influences on the Mind and Brain

> "Theoretical understanding wears out like patches. Experiences fade away like haze. But realization remains unchanging like space." — saying in Tibetan Buddhism (Śāntideva et al., 2004).

This section explores how recognizing nothingness and/or no-thingness can influence the mind and brain from the perspective of classical Buddhist texts and scientific literature. Additionally, we examine potential adverse effects associated with these contemplative states.

3.1 Psychological effects of no-thingness and nothingness

Through the realization of no-thingness and nothingness, one may directly experience that disturbing thoughts and emotions are baseless or without any foundation. Consequently, individuals can withdraw their attentional fuel from those grosser disturbances and find inner peace (Tirado, 2008). But it is said that one may go even deeper and understand the causal mechanics of the mind at the level of the five aggregates through which these afflictions arise, potentially letting go of their root cause and leading to permanent freedom from them. From the perspective of Theravada Buddhism, these defilements are manifestations of ten fetters or *Samyojana* in Pāli, which literally means "bonds fine and coarse" (Mahatthanadull, 2016). In contemporary language, these fetters can be defined as latent tendencies (*anusaya*) that are deeply embedded in our minds, repeated and strengthened over evolutionary ages. Under their influence, the mind autonomously reacts to feeling tone or valence (*vedanā*)—pleasant, unpleasant, and neutral—with craving, aversion, and indifference, respectively, but only realizes this in hindsight (Anālayo, 2018). As the valence triggers these algorithms, the reaction is completely automated and habituated, driven by a causal process known as dependent arising (*paticcasamuppāda*) (Armstrong, 2021; Johnson, 2017). Thus, these tendencies "fetter" or "bind" the mind to make decisions in relation to a hedonic tone. At extremes, fetters can be seen as seizing control over higher-level cognitive functions, compelling the mind into a state of compulsive emotional turmoil. Note that these compulsions cause suffering regardless of whether they are expressed outwardly as a behavioral trait or not. Moreover, this kind of "co-opting" of the mind by craving and aversion to experience can be subtle and not explicitly feel like suffering if one is not aware of it (indeed, becoming aware of suffering is one of the practices that is said to allow the mind to "let go" of these habits).

According to the four-path model in Theravada Buddhism, practitioners progressively eliminate fetters in four stages by deepening their letting go, facilitated by the realization of nothingness and no-thingness. The first path, known as stream-entry, or *sotāpatti,* is said to be attained when consciousness ceases for the first time (Armstrong, 2021; Buddhaghosa, 1998; Upatissa, 1995). It eliminates the first three fetters: identity view, doubt in practice, and belief in purification by external observance like precepts and vows (Anālayo, 2021). Identity view means belief in the notion of an abiding self within aggregates, and it is self-explanatory how cessation becomes the entry point to break it. As all the views regarding self are fettering, even the view that one has "no self" is abandoned upon stream-entry. Thus, the mind does not slide into a detached nihilistic perspective where nothing holds value. Instead, it embodies the middle way or emptiness of all views as elucidated by Nāgārjuna, i.e., dropping away of self as something: real, unreal, both, or neither (Burbea,

2014). Thereby, the mind frees itself from the affliction that arises in regard to any identity views. Similarly, the falling of other fetters happens at higher path attainments, freeing the mind from even more afflictions and ultimately culminating in freedom from suffering (fourth path). Fascinatingly, the removal of fetters is not a temporary absence like that may happen in an altered state of consciousness. Instead, it is claimed to be abandoned permanently due to insight into the empty nature of underlying tendencies, which otherwise operate outside awareness (Anālayo, 2018). This contrasts with most contemporary scientific approaches to mental health and well-being, which often require prolonged symptom management or ongoing pharmaceutical or psychological interventions.

Note that it is no straightforward task to translate all these ideas into contemporary terms, and experimental evidence is required to test whether these ancient hypotheses pan out. However, it is notable that practices from these traditions such as mindfulness now boast a tremendous amount of research, interest, and application throughout the Western world and modern medicine (Van Dam et al., 2018), making the deeper roots of these practices seem worth the effort of investigation. Having said this, to the best of our knowledge, there is no contemporary scientific research on the irreversibility of path attainments, and the psychological and behavioral changes they induce, and highlights an essential area for future investigation. Similarly, research is scarce into the psychological effects of no-thingness (emptiness). A study by Van Gordon et al. (2019), analyzed psychometric measures of advanced Buddhist practitioners meditating on emptiness by investigating the empty nature of self and reality. They found meditation on emptiness to be significantly more effective in increasing non-attachment, compassion, and positive affect and decreasing negative affect as compared to mindfulness meditation. Participants described dwelling in emptiness with words such as "letting go of any emotional or conceptual baggage," "recharging," and "replenishing." The positive effects may arise as emptiness removes the locus upon which emotional and conceptual baggage accumulates and reduces ontological addiction, i.e., impaired functionality that stems from the addictive belief in inherent existence (Van Gordon et al., 2017). Hence, meditation on no-thingness may bring about a sense of psychological well-being and emotional balance.

3.2 Neurophysiological correlates of no-thingness and nothingness

Neuroscientific research on the impact of nothingness and no-thingness is still in its early stages. To the best of our knowledge, there is no research exclusive to the neurophysiological correlates of emptiness in the way we have defined it (but see Berkovich-Ohana et al., 2013; Hinterberger et al., 2014). Unlike altered states of consciousness, emptiness is purely an insight attainment and poses many challenges to be studied in a controlled setting. Some of the challenges in studying insight events include difficulty in time-locking the insight events, hypothesis testing, capturing them in an embodied way, defining reference states, and understanding insight triggers (Laukkonen et al., 2021; Laukkonen & Tangen, 2018; Luo et al., 2009; Tulver et al., 2023). Moreover, these challenges are magnified when we deal with relatively rare and advanced meditative insights like emptiness. This may be a reason for the lack of neurophysiological research on emptiness.

To speculate the potential neurophysiological correlates of meditative insights into no-thingness, we can draw parallels with psychedelic insights. While the insight into the emptiness of the five aggregates appears unique to meditation, psychedelics can induce profound insights into personality, relationships, behavioral patterns, or emotions (Davis et al., 2021; McGovern et al., 2023; Peill et al., 2022; Tulver et al., 2023). The descriptions of these insights often align with what could be termed as psychological insight into no-thingness and interdependence. Note that psychedelics can also induce metaphysical insight into the nature of the world or consciousness, and though it may sound like "waking up," it might as well lead to the reification of woken-up reality—akin to replacing one dream for another, and claiming another is real and the former is false. Hence, drawing correlations between meditative and psychedelic insights needs to be approached with caution. Nevertheless, psychedelics appear to inhibit the function of the default mode network (DMN) and salience network (SLN) in the brain (Lebedev et al., 2015). DMN activity is associated with a sense of cognitive self, mental time travel, judgment, planning, and goals. Studies suggest that downregulation in DMN correlates with the dissolution of the cognitive self, including personality traits, personal history, goals, and the sense of owning one's thoughts (ibid). Additionally, the SLN is linked to a sense of embodied self and emotional feeling. When the SLN is downregulated, it correlates with the dissolution of the embodied self, leading to changes in body boundaries, spatial self-location, and the personal significance of emotional feelings (Lebedev et al., 2015).

In contrast to emptiness (no-thingness), several recent neuro-imaging studies have investigated the cessation of consciousness (nothingness); which, although rare, is comparatively easier to study. An investigation into spectral analyses of EEG data surrounding cessation events in advanced meditators uncovered a reduction in large-scale alpha-power approximately 40 seconds prior to the cessation event, with the lowest alpha-power recorded immediately following cessation (Chowdhury et al., 2023). Furthermore, when examining specific regions-of-interest (ROIs), it was observed that this alpha suppression showed a linear decrease in the occipital and parietal regions of the brain leading up to cessation. During the pre-cessation period, there were also modest increases in theta power in the central, parietal, and right temporal ROIs. Notably, the Delta and Beta frequency bands did not exhibit significant differences in power levels surrounding cessation events. Another study by (Laukkonen, Sacchet, et al., 2023) contains a preliminary analysis of the EEG data of two adept meditators with results replicated across separate labs. For both practitioners, cessation led to a substantial decline in large-scale functional neural interactions (or brain synchrony) in the alpha frequency band. Interestingly, they found that this modulation of network integration was only specific to the alpha frequency band, with no significant differences observed in functional neural interactions in the delta, theta, or beta frequency bands. A separate study by Berkovich-Ohana (2017) analyzed the EEG data of two adept meditators, and their findings indicated an increase in global long-range gamma (25–45Hz) synchronization during cessations. The authors interpret this increase as a possible mechanism for the unlearning of habitual conditioning. Clearly, research into cessation is still young, but the possibilities for understanding consciousness and the top-down control of cognitive processes is intriguing. Some researchers have even suggested that the cessation state may be a residual skill associated with hibernation capacities going back to the early ancestors of homo sapiens (Laukkonen, Sacchet, et al., 2023).

3.3 Adverse effects of no-thingness and nothingness

Many adverse effects claimed to arise from insights into emptiness and cessation may be misattributions with no genuine connection to such practices, but it is still worth considering potential negative experiences. Particularly, the "insight into emptiness" might be conflated with the "experience of void." This void may manifest when one's sense of self is compromised and fragmented, resulting in an unusual disruption in the phenomenological perception of personal being (e.g., similar to dissociation or derealization, Ciaunica et al., 2021). Subsequently, the individual may be overtaken by feelings of unreality, and the self may lack subjective perspectives (Apter, 1992). Such fragmentation can occur due to various reasons, including conditions like schizophrenia, narcissistic personality disorder, and dissociation. For instance, certain individuals grappling with schizophrenia may find themselves in a nothingness-like experience due to the fragmentation of egoic processes, giving the impression that the person is "nowhere to be found" (Ellonen-Jéquier, 2009). Moreover, narcissists can have an inflated view of themselves, making it hard for them to disentangle the genuine aspects of their identity from the unrealistic image they have constructed, which may contribute to a pervasive feeling of emptiness created through the constant devaluation of others (Epstein, 1989).

Even specific kinds of brain injury may seem to dissolve the notion of self as a stable "thing." Athymhormia, for instance, is a condition wherein individuals lose mental self-activation, allowing them to sit idly in a fully conscious state for extended periods without a sense of self that motivates them to perform a task (Verstichel & Larrouy, 2005). Remarkably, their mind remains empty of thoughts, and they do not perceive extreme pain as problematic even when they feel it intensely (Young, 2016). While such conditions might be tempting to view as enlightenment, a careful comparison with descriptions of path attainments suggests otherwise. Buddhist insights aim to alleviate subjective suffering while simultaneously fostering the development of a compassionate and functional human being, rather than pathological states.

Nevertheless, insight meditation can destabilize the mind, leading to challenging experiences (Britton et al., 2021; Tulver et al., 2023). Such challenges may involve unresolved psychological material and may not necessarily be attributed to insights into no-thingness or nothingness in and of itself. Moreover, within Buddhism, there are descriptions of seemingly negative experiences expected to arise at certain stages of practice. For example, as individuals progress through the stages of insight during intensive meditation, they may reach the "knowledge of suffering" (*dukkha ñanas*) phase (Buddhaghosa, 1998). This phase begins at the "dissolution" stage, whereby one starts to notice "no solid ground" and "no-thingness" in all the experiences, which can be severely disruptive to existing belief structures. It conflicts with a person's sense of meaning and purpose, which is habitually rooted in the belief in the existence of mind-independent reality. Even though one might be comfortable with the idea of no-thingness at an intellectual level, the direct experience of it may create turmoil in deeper layers of the mind (Yates et al., 2017). Some meditators argue that these unconscious components reorganize the internal model as insight matures, constructing a new worldview based on no-thingness, resulting in greater ease irrespective of external conditions (Yates et al., 2017). In rare cases, intensive meditation can also lead to psychosis and dissociation (Lindahl & Britton, 2019; Tulver et al., 2023). To avoid these states, some have suggested that susceptible individuals should approach meditation with an emphasis on relaxed concentration to create ontological security and relinquish the feeling of lack before proceeding to insight practices (Epstein, 1989). Relaxed concentration practices are said to lead to a state of calm and tranquility (*samatha*) (Brasington, 2015), serving as a "lubrication" against the internal friction created by insight practices, thereby reducing the likelihood of adverse effects (Yates et al., 2017). However, empirical research on preventative features of practice has not been conducted to our knowledge and is an important path for future work.

4. The Journey to Nothingness

"When this is, that is; because this arises, that arises.
When this is not, that is not; because this ceases, that ceases."— The Buddha, Idappaccayatā or specific conditionality, AN 10.92 (Quoted in Kearney, 2002)

Cessation (nothingness), with its well-defined entry and exit points, can mark a significant moment in the meditative journey. In this section, we use cessation as a reference point to examine the temporal sequence of experiences and insights that lead to its occurrence. This understanding provides valuable insights for empirical investigations into the influence of cessation on the mind and behavior.

There is growing evidence that the mind and brain are organized hierarchically in "levels of abstraction," where the early or lower levels involve less processed sensorial input, and higher levels are more abstract and temporally thick (Friston, 2008; Laukkonen & Slagter, 2021; Taylor et al., 2015). This hierarchical process of abstraction can be deconstructed through different practices until the mind reaches complete phenomenological absence, i.e., *nirodha* (Laukkonen, Sacchet, et al., 2023). It also logically makes sense that for the mind to construct a new mental model—akin to updating software on a computer—the old one needs to stop, leading to a distinct cut in the stream of consciousness— akin to turning the software on and off again—where there is no conscious processing at all. The question is: How does meditation allow for this process of de-abstraction to unfold?

Meditation can be viewed as a series of mental exercises that modulate different attributes of the mind through processes such as mindfulness, decentering, and metacognitive awareness (Dunne et al., 2019; Slagter et al., 2011). According to Buddhist philosophy, a practitioner needs to cultivate seven attributes, known as factors of awakening (*bojjhaṅga*): mindfulness, investigation, balanced effort, joy, tranquility, unification, and equanimity. These factors theoretically permit the practitioner to attain insight into the nature of abstractions and facilitate deconstruction (Yates et al., 2017). Multiple methods establish these mental attributes, like *samatha* (calm and tranquility) preceded by *vipassanā* (insight), *vipassanā* preceded by *samatha*, and *samatha* in tandem with *vipassanā* (Thanissaro, 2013). The subsequent paragraphs explore three such methods (out of many possibilities): the first involving *jhāna* practice leading to *nirodha samāpatti*, the second from "dry" or "bare" insight meditation traditions like Mahasi noting leading to *nirodha*, and the third from contemporary science.

In the first method, the cultivation of calm and tranquility is given preference over the investigation of phenomena, but it requires mastery in both. Here, the mind goes through a series of progressively refined states of unification or concentration, known as *samatha jhānas*, before ultimately reaching *nirodha samāpatti*. Indeed, these *jhānas* could be said to represent decreasing levels of abstraction in the mind. They are achieved by the training of stabilizing attention and peripheral awareness using a meditation object, like the breath (Yates et al., 2017) As the mind stabilizes on the meditation object with growing effortlessness, and all the meditative hindrances (*nīvaraṇa*)—craving, aversion, restlessness, dullness, and doubt—are temporarily pacified, the mind enters into access concentration (*upacāra-samādhi*) (Brasington, 2015), a state which gives "access" to *jhānas*. The first *jhāna* has the characteristic quality of pleasurable sensations, second *jhāna* has mental happiness, third *jhāna* has contentment, and fourth *jhāna* is a state of pure equanimity. The next four *jhānas* are known as formless *jhānas* because they no longer have any sensory experience. The fifth *jhāna* is described as a state of "boundless space," sixth as "boundless consciousness," seventh as "nothingness," and finally, eighth as "neither perception nor non-perception." Note that many different translations and conceptions of *jhāna* exist, so our introduction here is illustrative and simplified. Moreover, the semantics of terms describing *jhānas* in classical Buddhist texts tend to differ from contemporary scientific interpretations, and the eighth *jhāna* still has some subtle phenomenal content (Laukkonen, Sacchet, et al., 2023). In terms of the reduction of levels of abstractions, the path from first to fourth *jhānas* can be said to shut off the part of the mind that recognizes pleasantness and unpleasantness, and the next four *jhānas* to shut off remaining abstractions of the mind, like space, perception of consciousness and perception of no-consciousness (Brahm, 2003). Finally, the mind may let go of knowing or awareness itself, possibly passing through the signless state (a state primarily characterized by emptiness) and then into *nirodha samāpatti*. A master in *nirodha samāpatti* is said to traverse these stages at will and abide in cessation of perception and feelings for predetermined extended periods.

In the second method, the investigation of phenomena is given priority over the cultivation of calm and tranquility and does not require mastery in *samatha jhānas*. Here, the mind goes through a series of insight knowledges (*vipassanā-ñāṇas*), including the cessation insight. While these stages slightly differ across commentaries and Pāli canon, a commonly used "progress of insight" map contains 16 stages of insight (Sayadaw, 2016). According to (Sayadaw, 2016), the progress of insight starts with the 1st stage as knowledge of discernment between mental and physical states. The 2nd stage involves understanding the cause-and-effect relationship between mental and physical states, which may provide an initial taste of no-thingness. In the 3rd insight, knowledge, the mind begins to notice the three characteristics of all phenomena, discussed previously in this chapter. As mindfulness increases, in the 4th stage, the mind gains knowledge of the arising and passing away of phenomena, which matures into the 5th stage, knowledge of dissolution. The stages from the 5th to 10th are known as "knowledge of suffering" (*dukkha ñanas*), whereby, after dissolution, the mind goes through stages: 6th fear; 7th misery; 8th disgust; 9th desire for deliverance ("get me out of here"); and 10th re-observation (a possible decision to practice further). At the 11th stage, the mind becomes equanimous toward all formations, followed by the 12th stage of adaptation knowledge. The 13th stage is known as change-of-lineage because the mind abandons arising and rushes into cessation of conditioned phenomena (initial entry into cessation). Immediately after the change-of-lineage, the mind enters the 14th stage, knowledge of the path, or *magga ñana*, which is the short moment of cessation. The final stage of cessation after path knowledge is called knowledge of fruition (*phala ñana*, 15th stage), where the mind comes to understand what had happened, and the defilements that have been abandoned are prevented from re-arising. All three forms of knowledge—change-of-lineage (entry into cessation), path (short moment of cessation), and fruition (final stage of cessation)—last only for a few moments, and therefore are usually not recognized as distinct by the meditator, though they can happen at different points in time, for some practitioners (Thera, 1965). The last/16th stage is knowledge of reviewing, where there is contemplation of the path, fruition, *nirodha*, and defilements that have been abandoned and that still remain.

In addition to the specific *jhāna* and *vipassanā* pathways described above, there is a third model of how the mind can be deconstructed based on umbrella categories of meditation drawn from contemplative science. This model aims to take into account various shared qualities of practices from many traditions in order to group them in meaningful ways. These groupings of practices seem different at face-value but are also increasingly found to be empirically differentiated (see for example Dahl et al., 2015; Fox et al., 2016; Lutz et al., 2015; Slagter et al., 2007). In brief, the three categories of practices are focused: attention meditation (e.g., directing attention to the breath or mantra, similar to *jhāna* practice); open monitoring (e.g., a relaxed witnessing of all arising experiences, similar to *vipassanā*); and nondual (e.g., a deep letting go or recognition of the awareness that underlies all experience, prior to subject-object distinctions). These practices are linked together in a gradual meditative journey because each progressive stage (FA, to OM, to ND), appears to reduce abstract, counterfactual, and temporally deep cognition (though, as noted above, any practice taken to the extreme may deconstruct the mind). Each practice, in other words, brings the meditator closer to the true here and now (Laukkonen & Slagter, 2021). However, the true here and now—i.e., where no information is integrated over time—would logically result in either a phenomenal state with no content other than awareness itself or cessation. Indeed, even perception is impossible except through the lens of past learning, and prediction is impossible without simulating one's self in future moments beyond the now (Friston, 2018).

5. Computational Directions

> "In fact, we're all hallucinating all the time, including right now.
> It's just that when we agree about our hallucinations, we call that reality."
>
> — Anil Seth (Seth, 2017)

In this section, we seek to briefly conceptualize insights into emptiness and cessation through the lens of predictive processing or active inference, an overarching theory of mind and brain that is showing promise for making sense of deep contemplative experiences such as those discussed here (Clark, 2013; Friston, 2009; Hohwy, 2013). The predictive processing (or active inference) framework posits that our brains must use inference to perceive because it has no direct access to the outside world, which aligns with the concept of no-thingness (i.e., all experiential phenomena are constructed and therefore without independent nature). The brain's input is restricted to sensory activation converted into electrical signals by the senses. Therefore, to build a complex, coherent experience, it is proposed that the brain continuously generates predictions about the causes of sensory inputs and aims to minimize errors in those predictions based on incoming information (reducing error here represents getting a closer fit between one's model and the world, though error is also just an inference). These prediction errors—the discrepancies between predicted and actual inputs—can be minimized either through updating the model to fit the sensory input (perceptual inference) or by generating the expected sensory input through action (active inference). Moreover, the brain also infers the precision of its inferences (second-order predictions), which aims to account for attention and selection processes. This hierarchical arrangement allows the brain not only to predict what sensory inputs to anticipate but also to evaluate the degree of confidence (precision weighting) associated with those predictions, prediction errors, and priors, which permits a kind of insight into one's own modeling (Friston et al., 2017; Laukkonen, Webb, et al., 2023). Furthermore, the brain also refines its generative model without active inference or novel sensory input by "chipping away" at prior knowledge (i.e., finding simple explanations for known data), known as fact-free learning (Friston et al., 2017). All these processes, when taken together, permit the mind to construct a hierarchy of predictions from temporally shallow processes like sensory experience, to temporally deep, counterfactual and abstract processes like thinking, prospection, and decision-making in order to make sense of a world in time and space where adaptive action is required (Corcoran et al., 2020; Kiebel et al., 2008; Metzinger, 2017).

According to one predictive processing account of meditation (Laukkonen & Slagter, 2021), the practice of *samatha* (relaxed concentration or stable attention) gradually reduces the temporal depth (abstraction) of predictive processing by assigning higher precision to sensory experiences like the breath, which automatically reduces the precision assigned to other temporally deeper events like mind wandering or thinking (Laukkonen & Slagter, 2021; Lutz et al., 2019). Progression through each *jhāna* can be seen as "letting go" or "releasing" the precision of temporally deeper mental process, and increasing the precision of a relatively shallower, less abstract, mental process. For instance, moving from first to second *jhāna* can be seen as releasing the expectations of pleasant physical sensation and assigning more weight to the quality of mental happiness. The experience eventually reaches eighth *jhāna* as structures of cognition fall away one by one. Finally, the subtlest expectation to be aware or alert can be released (i.e., awareness and all self-models including subjectivity), leading to *nirodha,* or cessation (Laukkonen, Sacchet, et al., 2023). The practice of "dry" insight meditation may follow a different mechanism toward cessation, since it does not involve the *jhānic* way of de-fabrication of temporal hierarchy of predictions. It is unknown how the 16 stages of insight can be modeled with predictive processing, but one hypothesis is that "desynchronizing" neural activity—as occurs in general anesthesia or high doses of ketamine—via deconstruction of one's field of experience could lead to cessation (Laukkonen, Sacchet, et al., 2023). Nevertheless, there seems to be no pre-existing computational theory about insights into no-thingness (i.e., emptiness) or processes that reduce "clinging" or reification, which is central to most meditative paths. Moreover, we also need a theoretical understanding of how these insights permanently eliminate so-called mental fetters, if this is indeed the case. Diving into all these is beyond the scope of this chapter, but we begin to offer some ideas below.

6. Future Directions

"When things dissolve, there's nothing left to say." —
Nāgārjuna (Batchelor & Nāgārjuna, 2001)

In formulating a comprehensive theory of the mind, finding meaningful alignment between subjective experiences and objective measures is imperative. Throughout this chapter, we have begun this task in the context of unusual subjective events known as cessation (nothingness) and emptiness (no-thingness) that can arise in the context of deep meditative practice. Both of these insights were discovered by the Buddha in his pursuit of finding the end of suffering and are crucial elements of the Four Noble Truths (suffering, its cause, its cessation, and the path). Indeed, without these realizations (according to Buddhist theory), a mind would forever remain in an internal battle against its own projection—a self-sabotaging loop perpetuating ceaseless suffering (i.e., *samsāra*). To our knowledge, no computational theory explains suffering and its relation to cessation and emptiness. In this section, we will discuss some preliminary ideas for theoretical and empirical future development in this field and possibly its relation to artificial intelligence (AI).

The Pāli term *dukkha* (Sanskrit: *Duḥkha*) can be translated as unease, stress, dissatisfaction, or suffering. It is sometimes regarded as an inherent characteristic of the phenomena. However, *dukkha* may not be an inherent property of experience. According to some meditation teachers, it arises from the relationship (of clinging) to experience (Burbea, 2014; Teasdale & Chaskalson, 2011). Expanding upon this definition, *dukkha* can be experienced as the unease that arises as one craves or resists experience, or even more precisely, craves pleasantness or resists unpleasantness (we are not considering neutral valence to keep things simple). Put differently, the mind is not at ease with the experience as it already is and seeks a better model or a more perfect (perceived) equilibrium with a more pleasant hedonic tone. Therefore, there is a constant struggle to reduce the gap between actual experience (what is) and envisioned experience (what ought to be). Notice that this sounds similar to the act of minimizing prediction error. To make this link explicit: Suffering may be quantified as a function of the intention to minimize the divergence between actual sensory input and its predicted state, i.e., a function of the motivation to reduce (perceived) error. Moreover, the subjective experience of "resisting unpleasantness and craving pleasantness" may be equivalent to "resisting perceived disorder and wanting an envisioned dynamic equilibrium (or homeostatic control)," respectively. One can already see how the very act of meditation involving stillness in body and mind begins to fight against this habitual tendency to predict future moments and seek their realization through action.

The next question arises: How can suffering be alleviated? In the previous paragraph, we have carefully used words like "function of" and "resisting/wanting" to point toward the idea that suffering can be eased without necessarily ending prediction errors. To illustrate this point, it is useful to distinguish between fabrication and reification. Fabrication refers to creating something (i.e., an experience) that is not a concrete, tangible thing with real, independent existence (i.e., an inference); whereas reification refers to the process of treating a fabrication (an inference) as if it were a concrete, tangible thing with real, independent existence. De-fabrication can occur in an altered state of consciousness (including during deep sleep or general anesthesia), whereas de-reification (similar to emptiness) is tied explicitly to insight attainments or cognitive shifts in how one relates to experience. Though logically suffering can be ended by ceasing all fabrications (e.g., death, coma, *nirodha samāpatti*, etc.), resulting in cessation of consciousness and no (consciously experienced impact of) prediction error, it renders one unable to function in the world. Moreover, even extended cessation is subject to change as one always emerges from it, unless one dies.

The other way to find freedom from *dukkha* may be through dereification, i.e., understanding the empty or fabricated nature of experience, while retaining the ability to generate an adaptive model of the causes of sensory experience (Burbea, 2014; Yates et al., 2017). Experientially, the mind may realize that actual experience (what is), envisioned experience (what ought to be), and the gap between them, are all mental projections. Consequently, the mind may take an equanimous stance toward all phenomena (including deliberate thinking and planning), and refrain from adding or subtracting anything from experience to enhance pleasantness or diminish unpleasantness. A plausible computational theory to explain emptiness insight and associated dereification may be the relaxing of hyperpriors on precision, i.e., prior beliefs about the precision of beliefs about the state of the world, or beliefs about uncertainty in general (Friston et al., 2013; Laukkonen, Sacchet, et al., 2023). Dereification may uncover that sensory inputs and predictions are fabricated inferences, inherently containing some uncertainty and incapable of accurately mapping the external world. Continual influxes of new sensory input and subsequent prediction errors are inevitable parts of biological existence, and it is impossible to fully model the external world to maintain equilibrium. Consequently, the system may cease resisting uncertainty and craving certainty, recognizing "uncertainty/certainty" as internal computations (i.e., dereify them).

This perspective also aligns with a biological imperative. An organism can be understood as a physical system driven to preserve and propagate itself. Through millions of years of evolutionary training, it has acquired strategies to fulfill this fundamental aim. However, a single situation may evoke multiple solutions based on diverse historical approaches, preventing the brain from acting as a unified entity and resulting in unresolved contradictions (part of *dukkha*). This may lead to a kind of tug-of-war involving (contradictory) proliferations or counterfactual thinking, whereby each viewpoint competes for attention (precision weighting) and strives to establish equilibrium independently (almost as if each organism is made of many smaller organisms). Such dynamics may manifest as increased stress in the body, ironically heightening instability in the system. The process is analogous to binocular rivalry, i.e., an altering of perception when each eye is presented with different stimuli. According to Hohwy et al. (2008), in binocular rivalry, as one stimulus dominates perception, the other stimulus generates an unexplained prediction error. The prediction error is resolved by switching the perception, but this increases error in the previously dominating stimulus, setting the stage for the next transition, and perpetual rivalry ensues. Similarly, in the mind, hundreds of potential options can quickly overwhelm and cloud the decision-making process, each perspective battling for dominance driven by relative prediction-error propagation. Dereification or emptiness reveals that all viewpoints are past conditionings that stem from specific causes and conditions. Not only do they not necessarily lead to equilibrium, but they also contribute to the incessant activity in the system. Consequently, the nervous system may not be easily "shocked" or enter into a fight, flight, or freeze mode in uncertain situations, and instead, maintain some tranquility and equanimity in such cases. In other words, the nervous system may become resilient to uncertainty. An extreme example of such a transformation is forever marked in history, when on 11th June, 1963, a Vietnamese monk (Thích Quảng Đức) committed "self-immolation" (i.e., intentionally setting himself on fire) as a form of protest against the persecution of Buddhists by the South Vietnamese Catholic government. Remarkably, he carried out this act, which is deeply heart-wrenching even to hear, while maintaining complete stillness, silence, and (apparent) equanimity throughout (Manno, 2019).

Empirical verification of this radical attainment is an important direction for consciousness research. Specifically, we need to unveil distinctions and relationships between "grasping" and "equanimity" at the computational and neurophysiological levels. A preliminary start can be conducting a study to quantify the duration a process is retained in the nervous system following a trigger and comparing this retention time between an ordinary mind and a dereified mind. For instance, a cohort of experienced insight meditators and a control group can be exposed to positive, negative, and neutral stimuli—like words of praise, criticism, and simple facts—while recording corresponding neural activities. We anticipate that, compared to the control group, experienced insight meditators will demonstrate specific abilities, such as the capacity to effortlessly "let go" of emergent phenomena, resulting in less sticky abstract processing. Consequently, the associated neural activity for all the inputs, irrespective of the type, is expected to diminish faster, and should be reflected in the temporal generalization method, which, for example, could show that electrophysiological responses associated with emotionally charged stimulus representation appear but relatively quickly disappear (King & Dehaene, 2014). This experiment would also enable us to contrast between the "indifference" observed in pathological states and the "equanimity" associated with genuine insights. Moreover, it might help us understand the mind-brain connection at subtler levels and design novel interventions to mimic "dereification" (e.g., neurofeedback).

These insights regarding emptiness and cessation may also contribute to the advancement of current AI systems. The prediction error minimization process governing mental processes can be viewed as analogous to cost function minimization in AI. The cost function or loss function in AI systems quantifies the cost associated with the difference between the predicted output of a model and the actual observed output. Minimizing this function optimizes the model to accurately predict the observed data, similar to how the brain minimizes prediction error to model the external reality. To draw an analogy, one may certainly question if AIs are conscious like humans. But one may also question whether AI systems possess or can possess genuine epistemic capacity—the ability to not only accumulate data but also understand the nature of knowledge, evidence, and the limitations of its own understanding. Similar to the human mind gaining an understanding of its causal processes, can an AI with epistemic capacity track how its core mechanisms function when subjected to variations? Is it possible for an artificial system to understand the fabricated and empty nature of its predictions? Additionally, can such a system alter its fundamental code by rebooting its generative model akin to a human mind undergoing cessation? What might happen if AI did possess such abilities and insights? Such questions might help us design an AI with meta-awareness of its own processes and an ability to self-regulate, and self-regenerate, with potential broad implications.

To conclude, this chapter makes several novel contributions to the field of consciousness research. We studied two key phenomena in meditation—cessation and emptiness—and disentangled their experiential, physical, and computational aspects, by drawing insights from multiple disciplines like Buddhist literature, psychology, contemplative science, and cognitive neuroscience. Moreover, we juxtaposed altered states of consciousness (associated with fabrication/de-fabrication) and cognitive insights (associated with reification/dereification) and considered potential negative effects therein. To the best of our knowledge, no previous scientific study has made such a distinction in regard to understanding the neural underpinnings of "cessation of suffering" or enduring "equanimity." We hope this study evokes curiosity and stimulates further development in understanding the exact mechanism of how the mind relates to the experience, and in turn, constructs it.

Acknowledgements

We would like to thank Professor Jakob Hohwy for his thorough comments on the manuscript. Additionally, we would like to thank Toby Woods for his valuable suggestions.

References

Alcaraz-Sánchez, A., Demšar, E., Campillo-Ferrer, T., & Torres-Platas, S. G. (2022) Nothingness is all there is: An exploration of objectless awareness during sleep. *Frontiers in Psychology*, *13*, 901031.

Anālayo, B. (2015) *Compassion and emptiness in early Buddhist meditation*. Cambridge: Windhorse Publications Limited.

Anālayo, B. (2018) The underlying tendencies. *Insight Journal*, *44*.

Anālayo, B. (2021) The four levels of awakening. *Mindfulness*, *12*(4), 831–840.

Apter, A. (1992) Depersonalization, the experience of prosthesis, and our cosmic insignificance: The experimental phenomenology of an altered state. *Philosophical Psychology*, *5*(3), 257–285.

Armstrong, D. (2021) *A Mind Without Craving*. Suttavāda Foundation.

Attwood, J. (2022) The cessation of sensory experience and Prajñāpāramitā philosophy. *International Journal of Buddhist Thought and Culture*, *32*(1), 111–148.

Batchelor, S. & Nāgārjuna. (2001) *Verses from the Center: A Buddhist Vision of the Sublime*. New York: Riverhead Books.

Berkovich-Ohana, A. (2017) A case study of a meditation-induced altered state: Increased overall gamma synchronization. *Phenomenology and the Cognitive Sciences*, *16*(1), 91–106.

Berkovich-Ohana, A., Dor-Ziderman, Y., Glicksohn, J., & Goldstein, A. (2013) Alterations in the sense of time, space, and body in the mindfulness-trained brain: A neurophenomenologically-guided MEG study. *Frontiers in Psychology*, *4*. https://www.frontiersin.org/articles/10.3389/fpsyg.2013.00912.

Brahm, A. (2003) *The Jhanas*. Buddhist Society of Western Australia. Singapore: https://bswa.org/teaching/jhanas-e-book/.

Brasington, L. (2015) *Right Concentration: A Practical Guide to the Jhanas*. Boston, MA: Shambhala.

Britton, W. B., Lindahl, J. R., Cooper, D. J., Canby, N. K., & Palitsky, R. (2021) Defining and measuring meditation-related adverse effects in mindfulness-based programs. *Clinical Psychological Science: A Journal of the Association for Psychological Science*, 9(6), 1185–1204.

Buddhaghosa, B. (1998) *The Path of Purification: Visuddhimagga* (B. Nanamoli, Trans.; New edition). Kandy, Sri Lanka: Buddhist Publication Society.

Burbea, R. (2014) *Seeing That Frees: Meditations on Emptiness and Dependent Arising*. West Ogwell, Devon : Hermes Amāra Publications.

Chowdhury, A., van Lutterveld, R., Laukkonen, R. E., Slagter, H. A., Ingram, D. M., & Sacchet, M. D. (2023) Investigation of advanced mindfulness meditation "cessation" experiences using EEG spectral analysis in an intensively sampled case study. *Neuropsychologia, 190*.

Ciaunica, A., Charlton, J., & Farmer, H. (2021) When the window cracks: Transparency and the fractured self in depersonalisation. *Phenomenology and the Cognitive Sciences, 20*(1), 1–19.

Clark, A. (2013) Whatever next? Predictive brains, situated agents, and the future of cognitive science. *The Behavioral and Brain Sciences, 36*(3), 181–204.

Corcoran, A. W., Pezzulo, G., & Hohwy, J. (2020) From allostatic agents to counterfactual cognisers: Active inference, biological regulation, and the origins of cognition. *Biology & Philosophy, 35*(3), 32.

Dahl, C. J., Lutz, A., & Davidson, R. J. (2015) Reconstructing and deconstructing the self: Cognitive mechanisms in meditation practice. *Trends in Cognitive Sciences, 19*.

Davis, A. K., Barrett, F. S., So, S., Gukasyan, N., Swift, T. C., & Griffiths, R. R. (2021) Development of the Psychological Insight Questionnaire among a sample of people who have consumed psilocybin or LSD. *Journal of Psychopharmacology, 35*(4), 437–446.

Dunne, J. D., Thompson, E., & Schooler, J. (2019) Mindful meta-awareness: Sustained and non-propositional. *Current Opinion in Psychology, 28*, 307–311.

Ellonen-Jéquier, M. (2009) Analysis of the creation of 'emptiness,' of 'nothingness,' in certain types of psychosis. *The International Journal of Psychoanalysis, 90*.

Epstein, M. (1989) Forms of emptiness: Psychodynamic, meditative and clinical perspectives. *The Journal of Transpersonal Psychology, 21.*

Ermakova, A. O., Dunbar, F., Rucker, J., & Johnson, M. W. (2022) A narrative synthesis of research with 5-MeO-DMT. *Journal of Psychopharmacology, 36.*

Fox, K. C. R., Dixon, M. L., Nijeboer, S., Girn, M., Floman, J. L., Lifshitz, M., Ellamil, M., Sedlmeier, P., & Christoff, K. (2016) Functional neuroanatomy of meditation: A review and meta-analysis of 78 functional neuroimaging investigations. *Neuroscience and Biobehavioral Reviews, 65,* 208–228.

Friston, K. J. (2008) Hierarchical models in the brain. *PLoS Computational Biology, 4*(11), e1000211.

Friston, K. J. (2009) The free-energy principle: A rough guide to the brain? *Trends in Cognitive Sciences, 13*(7), 293–301.

Friston, K. J. (2018) Am I self-conscious? (Or does self-organization entail self-consciousness?). *Frontiers in Psychology, 9.* https://www.frontiersin.org/articles/10.3389/fpsyg.2018.00579.

Friston, K. J., Lawson, R., & Frith, C. D. (2013) On hyperpriors and hypopriors: Comment on Pellicano and Burr. *Trends in Cognitive Sciences, 17*(1), 1.

Friston, K. J., Lin, M., Frith, C. D., Pezzulo, G., Hobson, J. A., & Ondobaka, S. (2017) Active inference, curiosity and insight. *Neural Computation, 29*(10), 2633–2683.

Garfield, J. L. (1994) Dependent arising and the emptiness of emptiness: Why did Nāgārjuna start with causation? *Philosophy East and West, 44*(2), 219–250.

Grimmer, H. J., Laukkonen, R. E., Freydenzon, A., von Hippel, W., & Tangen, J. M. (2022) Thinking style and psychosis proneness do not predict false insights. *Consciousness and Cognition, 104,* 103384.

Grimmer, H. J., Laukkonen, R. E., Tangen, J., & von Hippel, W. (2022) Eliciting false insights with semantic priming. *Psychonomic Bulletin & Review, 29*(3), 954–970.

Grimmer, H. J., Tangen, J. M., Freydenzon, A., & Laukkonen, R. E. (2023) The illusion of insight: Detailed warnings reduce but do not prevent false "Aha!" moments. *Cognition and Emotion, 37*(2), 329–338.

Gunaratana, B. H. (2009) The Taste of Liberation: The Jhanas. Lion's Roar. https://www.lionsroar.com/the-taste-of-liberation/.

Hinterberger, T., Schmidt, S., Kamei, T., & Walach, H. (2014) Decreased electrophysiological activity represents the conscious state of emptiness in meditation. *Frontiers in Psychology*, *5*, 99.

Hohwy, J. (2013) *The Predictive Mind*. Oxford University Press.

Hohwy, J., Roepstorff, A., & Friston, K. J. (2008) Predictive coding explains binocular rivalry: An epistemological review. *Cognition*, *108*(3), 687–701.

Johnson, D. C. (2017) *The Path to Nibbana: How Mindfulness of Loving-Kindness Progresses Through the Tranquil Aware Jhanas to Awakening*. CreateSpace Independent Publishing Platform.

Kearney, P. (2002) *Introducing Dependent Arising*. Retrieved from: https://patrickkearney.net/wp-content/uploads/2020/07/01_Introduction.pdf.

Kiebel, S. J., Daunizeau, J., & Friston, K. J. (2008) A hierarchy of time-scales and the brain. *PLOS Computational Biology*, *4*(11), e1000209. https://doi.org/10.1371/journal.pcbi.1000209.

King, J.-R., & Dehaene, S. (2014) Characterizing the dynamics of mental representations: The temporal generalization method. *Trends in Cognitive Sciences*, *18*.

Kubose, G. M. (1973) *Zen Koans* (1st edition). Contemporary Books.

Laukkonen, R. E., Ingledew, D. J., Grimmer, H. J., Schooler, J. W., & Tangen, J. M. (2021) Getting a grip on insight: Real-time and embodied Aha experiences predict correct solutions. *Cognition & Emotion*, *35*(5), 918–935.

Laukkonen, R. E., Kaveladze, B. T., Protzko, J., Tangen, J. M., von Hippel, W., & Schooler, J. W. (2022) Irrelevant insights make worldviews ring true. *Scientific Reports*, *12*(1), Article 1.

Laukkonen, R. E., Kaveladze, B. T., Tangen, J. M., & Schooler, J. W. (2020) The dark side of Eureka: Artificially induced Aha moments make facts feel true. *Cognition*, *196*, 104122.

Laukkonen, R. E., Sacchet, M. D., Barendregt, H., Devaney, K. J., Chowdhury, A., & Slagter, H. A. (2023) *Cessations of consciousness in meditation: Advancing a scientific understanding of nirodha samāpatti*. https://doi.org/10.1016/bs.pbr.2022.12.007.

Laukkonen, R. E., & Slagter, H. A. (2021) From many to (n)one: Meditation and the plasticity of the predictive mind. *Neuroscience and Biobehavioral Reviews, 128.* https://doi.org/10.1016/j.neubiorev.2021.06.021

Laukkonen, R. E., & Tangen, J. M. (2018) How to detect insight moments in problem solving experiments. *Frontiers in Psychology, 9.* https://www.frontiersin.org/articles/10.3389/fpsyg.2018.00282

Laukkonen, R. E., Webb, M., Salvi, C., Tangen, J. M., Slagter, H. A., & Schooler, J. W. (2023) Insight and the selection of ideas. *Neuroscience and Biobehavioral Reviews, 153,* 105363.

Lebedev, A. V., Lövdén, M., Rosenthal, G., Feilding, A., Nutt, D. J., & Carhart-Harris, R. L. (2015) Finding the self by losing the self: Neural correlates of ego-dissolution under psilocybin: Finding the Self by Losing the Self. *Human Brain Mapping, 36*(8), 3137–3153.

Letheby, C., & Gerrans, P. (2017) Self unbound: Ego dissolution in psychedelic experience. *Neuroscience of Consciousness, 2017*(1)

Lindahl, J. R., & Britton, W. B. (2019) "I have this feeling of not really being here": Buddhist meditation and Changes in sense of self. *Journal of Consciousness Studies, 26*c.

Luo, J., Knoblich, G., & Lin, C. (2009) Neural correlates of insight phenomena. In E. Kraft, B. Gulyás, & E. Pöppel (Eds.), *Neural Correlates of Thinking* (pp. 253–267). Springer.

Lutz, A., Jha, A. P., Dunne, J. D., & Saron, C. D. (2015) Investigating the phenomenological matrix of mindfulness-related practices from a neurocognitive perspective. *The American Psychologist, 70*(7), 632–658.

Lutz, A., Mattout, J., & Pagnoni, G. (2019) The epistemic and pragmatic value of non-action: A predictive coding perspective on meditation. *Current Opinion in Psychology, 28,* 166–171.

Mahatthanadull, S. (2016) Examining Saṃyojana (Fetters) in Theravāda Buddhist Scriptures. *Journal of Graduate Studies Review, Vol. 12 No. 2 (May-August 2016),* 1–17.

Manno, F. A. M. (2019) Monk on fire: The meditative mind of a burning monk. *Cogent Psychology, 6*(1), 1678556.

McGovern, H. T., Grimmer, H., Doss, M., Hutchinson, B., Timmermann, C., Lyon, A., Corlett, P. R., & Laukkonen, R. E. (2023) The power of insight: Psychedelics and the emergence of false beliefs. *PsyArXiv.* https://doi.org/10.31234/osf.io/97gjw.

Metzinger, T. (2017) The problem of mental action. In T. Metzinger & W. Wiese (Eds.), *Philosophy and Predictive Processing*. Frankfurt am Main, Germany.

Millière, R., Carhart-Harris, R. L., Roseman, L., Trautwein, F.-M., & Berkovich-Ohana, A. (2018) Psychedelics, meditation, and self-consciousness. *Frontiers in Psychology*, *9*, 1475. https://doi.org/10.3389/fpsyg.2018.01475.

Nāgārjuna. (1995) *The Fundamental Wisdom of the Middle Way: Nagarjuna's Mulamadhyamakakarika*. New York: Oxford University Press.

Ñāṇamoli, B., & Bodhi, B. (2009) *The middle length discourses of the Buddha: A [new] translation of the Majjhima Nikāya ; translated from the Pali* (4. ed). Somerville, MA: Wisdom Publ.

Nikhilananda, S. (2006) *Mandukya Upanishad With Gaudapada's Karika and Shankara's Commentary* (Sixth edition, 11th reprint). Hollywood, CA: Advaita Ashrama.

Nisargadatta, M. (1999) *I Am That* (First Edition). Chetana Pvt.Ltd.

Peill, J. M., Trinci, K. E., Kettner, H., Mertens, L. J., Roseman, L., Timmermann, C., Rosas, F. E., Lyons, T., & Carhart-Harris, R. L. (2022) Validation of the psychological insight scale: A new scale to assess psychological insight following a psychedelic experience. *Journal of Psychopharmacology*, *36*(1), 31–45.

Pine, R. (2005) *The Heart Sutra*. Berkeley, CA: Catapult.

Revonsuo, A. (2009) Altered and exceptional states of consciousness. In W. P. Banks (Ed.), *Encyclopedia of Consciousness* (pp. 9–21). London: Academic Press.

Robinson, R. H., & Johnson, W. L. (1997) *The Buddhist religion: A Historical Introduction* (4th ed). Belmont, CA: Wadsworth Publishing Company.

Śāntideva, Kunpal, K., & Chöga, K. (2004) *Śāntideva's Bodhisattva-caryāvatāra* (J. S. Amtzis, Ed.; A. Kretschmar, Trans.; Vol. 2). Tibetan Computer Company. https://pktc.org/wp-content/themes/bb-theme-child/downloads/bca2comm.pdf.

Sayadaw, M. (2016) *Manual of Insight*. Somerville, MA: Simon and Schuster.

Schmidt, T. T., & Berkemeyer, H. (2018) The altered states database: Psychometric data of altered states of consciousness. *Frontiers in Psychology*, *9*, 1028. https://doi.org/10.3389/fpsyg.2018.01028.

Seth, A. (2017, April) *Your brain hallucinates your conscious reality* | *TED Talk.* https://www.ted.com/talks/anil_seth_your_brain_ hallucinates_your_conscious_reality.

Slagter, H. A., Davidson, R. J., & Lutz, A. (2011) Mental training as a tool in the neuroscientific study of brain and cognitive plasticity. *Frontiers in Human Neuroscience, 5,* 17. https://doi.org/10.3389/ fnhum.2011.00017.

Slagter, H. A., Lutz, A., Greischar, L. L., Francis, A. D., Nieuwenhuis, S., Davis, J. M., & Davidson, R. J. (2007) Mental training affects distribution of limited brain resources. *PLoS Biology, 5*(6), e138.

Smith, D. W. (2011) Nibbanic (or pure) consciousness and beyond. *Philosophia, 39.*

Taylor, P., Hobbs, J. N., Burroni, J., & Siegelmann, H. T. (2015) The global landscape of cognition: Hierarchical aggregation as an organizational principle of human cortical networks and functions. *Scientific Reports, 5*(1), Article 1. https://doi.org/10.1038/ srep18112.Teasdale, J. D., & Chaskalson, M. (2011). How does mindfulness transform suffering? I: the nature and origins of dukkha. Contemporary Buddhism, 12(1), 89–102. https://doi.or g/10.1080/14639947.2011.564824.

Teasdale, J. D., & Chaskalson, M. (2011). How does mindfulness transform suff ering? I: the nature and origins of dukkha. Contemporary Buddhism, 12(1), 89–102. https://doi.org/10.1080/14639947.20 11.564824.

Thanissaro, B. (2013, November 30) *Yuganaddha Sutta: In Tandem.* Access to Insight (BCBS Edition). https://www.accesstoinsight. org/tipitaka/an/an04/an04.170.than.html.

Thera, K. (1965) *Path Fruit and Nibbana.* Colombo: Weerasuria.

Tirado, J. M. (2008) The Buddhist notion of emptiness and its potential contribution to psychology and psychotherapy. *International Journal of Transpersonal Studies, 27*(1), 74–79.

Tulver, K., Kaup, K. K., Laukkonen, R. E., & Aru, J. (2023) Restructuring insight: An integrative review of insight in problem-solving, meditation, psychotherapy, delusions and psychedelics. *Consciousness and Cognition, 110,* 103494.

Upatissa. (1995) *The path of freedom: Vimuttimagga* (N. R. M. Ehara, S. Thera, & K. Thera, Trans.; Reprint). Kandy, Ceylon: Buddhist Publication Society.

Van Dam, N. T., van Vugt, M. K., Vago, D. R., Schmalzl, L., Saron, C. D., Olendzki, A., Meissner, T., Lazar, S. W., Kerr, C. E., Gorchov, J., Fox, K. C. R., Field, B. A., Britton, W. B., Brefczynski-Lewis, J. A., & Meyer, D. E. (2018) Mind the hype: A critical evaluation and prescriptive agenda for research on mindfulness and meditation. *Perspectives on Psychological Science: A Journal of the Association for Psychological Science, 13*(1), 36–61.

Van Gordon, W., Shonin, E., Dunn, T. J., Sapthiang, S., Kotera, Y., Garcia-Campayo, J., & Sheffield, D. (2019) Exploring emptiness and its effects on non-attachment, mystical experiences, and psycho-spiritual wellbeing: A quantitative and qualitative study of advanced meditators. *EXPLORE, 15*(4), 261–272.

Van Gordon, W., Shonin, E., & Griffiths, M. D. (2017) Buddhist emptiness theory: Implications for psychology. *Psychology of Religion and Spirituality, 9*(4), 309–318.

Verstichel, P., & Larrouy, P. (2005) Drowning Mr. M. *Scientific American Mind, 16*(1), 38–41. https://doi.org/10.1038/scientificamericanmind0405-38.

Watts, A., & Huang, A. C. (1975) *Tao: The watercourse way.* New York: Pantheon Books.

Woods, T. J., Windt, J. M., & Carter, O. (2022) Evidence synthesis indicates contentless experiences in meditation are neither truly contentless nor identical. *Phenomenology and the Cognitive Sciences.* https://doi.org/10.1007/s11097-022-09811-z.

Yang, W. F. Z., Chowdhury, A., Bianciardi, M., Van Lutterveld, R., Sparby, T., & Sacchet, M. D. (2023) Intensive whole-brain 7T MRI case study of volitional control of brain activity in deep absorptive meditation states. *Cerebral Cortex,* bhad408. https://doi.org/10.1093/cercor/bhad408.

Yates, J., Immergut, M., & Graves, J. (2017) *The Mind Illuminated: A Complete Meditation Guide Integrating Buddhist Wisdom and Brain Science for Greater Mindfulness.* New York: Simon and Schuster.

Young, S. (2016) *The Science of Enlightenment: How Meditation Works.* Sounds True.

Logico-Philosophical Forms

6

Ex Nihilo Omnis Fit

Graham Priest

My title tweaks the well-known supposed platitude—*ex nihilo nihil fit* (nothing comes from nothing)—and means that everything comes from nothing. The view was held by (among others) the Christian mystic Meister Eckhart (1260-1328) who said (according to my book of quotations): "All things were created out of nothingness, and thus their true origin is the 'Not'" (ES, p.184). Since Eckhart identifies God with nothingness, this is a way of putting the Christian doctrine that God created the world (everything). Well, I think that Eckhart was right—not in supposing that God is nothingness, but in supposing that everything comes from nothingness. In what follows, I'll explain why.

Of course, there is a question of what exactly it means to say that everything comes from nothing: It is hardly transparent. For a start, what is to be made of the word *fit*? We will get there in due course, but there is a bigger hurdle to be cleared first. What are we to make of the *nihil*? What exactly is nothingness? That is a tantalizing question. It is what God, according to more orthodox Christians, created the world out of. It plays a central role in the thought of philosophers such as Hegel, Heidegger, and Sartre. And it is easy enough to explain to a child. It is what is left, so to speak, when you take everything away.

Yet as soon as one starts to think about it, one finds oneself in tangles and paradoxes. If it is what remains when everything is removed, then nothing is, well, nothing. But it *must* be something; after all, maybe you can't experience it (though some have thought otherwise), but you can certainly talk about it (I have been) and think about it (you are now). So, it would seem to be both something and nothing. The puzzle is ancient, driving, as it does, Plato's dialogue the *Sophist*. We first need to address this matter.

Let's start with a bit of clarification. The word "nothing" can play two roles in English. First, it can be what logicians call a *quantifier*, like *something* or *everything*. These are not nouns and do not refer to anything: Their function is quite different. Quantifier phrases are used to say that something/nothing/everything satisfies some condition or other. Thus, if I ask Mary a question and then report, "She said nothing," my remark means that she remained silent. As logicians might put it: For no x, did she say x.

But "nothing" can be a noun too. Thus, if one says (truly) that Heidegger wrote about nothing, one does not mean that for no x did he write about x (which would certainly be false!); one means that he wrote about the thing nothingness. One might say (again truly) that Heidegger and Hegel wrote about nothing but said quite different things about *it*.

The ambiguity between quantifier and noun is the source of many good jokes and puns. Thus, in *Through the Looking Glass*, the White King asks Alice if she can see a messenger coming down the road. When Alice says that she can see nobody, the King compliments her on her eyesight: He can only see real people. Alice is using "nobody" as a quantifier. The King takes her to be using it as a noun.

The ambiguity can be a source not only of humor, but of much confusion; so to avoid this in what follows, when I use the word as a noun, I will boldface it, thus: **nothing**. Without the boldfacing it is the quantifier.

The next thing that needs to be clarified is this: We are talking about whether **nothing** is something or nothing—that is, whether it is a thing, an object, or not. But what does it mean to say that something is an object, some thing? To say that x is some thing is to say that, for some y, x is y. We might argue about what the "is" means here—the word is ambiguous both syntactically and semantically in English—but the simplest understanding is that it is the "is" of identity (as in: $2 + 2$ is 4). So, to say that x is an object is to say that, for some y, $x = y$.

Now, if x is anything at all, it is self-identical, $x = x$. It follows that for some y, $x = y$. (x itself will do.) Hence, everything is an object—hardly Earth-shattering news. Perhaps more interesting is this: If x is not an object, then it is not the case that for some y, $x = y$. That is, for no y, $x = y$. In particular, it is not the case that $x = x$ (or as mathematicians write it, $x \neq x$). So, things that are not objects are not self-identical.

Given these matters of clarification, we can now look at our paradox more closely. It is constituted by two contradictory statements, to the effect that **nothing** is both something and nothing. That is:

• **nothing** is something: for some y, y = **nothing**

• **nothing** is nothing (i.e., not something): it is not the case that for some y, y = **nothing**

The first statement seems unremarkable. As observed, it is a simple fact of logic that everything is something. So, **nothing** is something. If you want an extra argument, here is one: If you are thinking about the Eiffel Tower, you are thinking about something. If you are thinking about Sherlock Holmes, you are also thinking about something (though it may not exist). Your thoughts are not contentless, and those objects are their contents. But you can think about **nothing**—you are now. So, **nothing** is something. It is the content of the thought you are having. The claim that **nothing** is something is genuinely paradoxical. Yet despite this, we seem to be forced to accept this contradictory conclusion.

The exact ground for the other limb of the paradox is less obvious. To see what it is, we need to get clearer about what, exactly, **nothing** is. As I said, it is what remains after everything is removed. That's fine, but somewhat metaphorical. We can do better than this with the help of mereology—the theory of parts and wholes.

Lots of things (in fact, most things) have parts. Countries have states, provinces, or counties; symphonies have movements; I have a head, feet, hands, etc. Moreover, if you take the parts of something and meld them together, you get the thing in question. Logicians call the result a *mereological fusion,* or *sum*. Thus, the mereological fusion of my parts is me; the mereological fusion of the four movements of Beethoven's Ninth Symphony is the symphony itself.

Now, take any set of objects, X, and throw away its members, one at a time. When you have removed the last one, what remains is the set with no members, the empty set, Ø. So, the fusion of its members is the fusion of no things. And that is exactly what **nothing** would seem to be. Hence, we may take **nothing** to be the fusion of the members of the empty set.

It might be objected that the objects in the empty set do not have a fusion. After all, it may be suggested, some bunches of things do not have a fusion. Thus, consider the set containing: New Zealand, Donald Trump, and the Hanging Gardens of Babylon. If these things have a fusion, it is an object with parts of radically different kinds and spread over space and time. Better to hold that for the members of a set of objects to have a fusion, they cannot be disparate in this way: They must "cohere" in some sense. It is not clear how, exactly, to understand this notion of coherence. However, whatever it means, the objection is irrelevant. Since the empty set has no members, it has no members that fail to cohere with each other! (As logicians might say: All the members of Ø cohere with each other because there aren't any.)

Given all this, we now know not only that **nothing** is something, but we also know exactly what it is. And we can explain why the second limb of our paradox holds: that **nothing** is nothing. **Nothing** is the fusion of the things in the empty set, and there are no things in the empty set. You can fuse no things together as many times as you like; you will never get anything! And it's no good saying that we have got the definition of "**nothing**" wrong. Perhaps nothingness in some other sense is not paradoxical. That doesn't show that nothingness in this sense is not. It's just changing the subject!

In other words, the claim that **nothing** is something is genuinely paradoxical. Yet despite this, we seem to be forced to accept this contradictory conclusion.

That conclusion may jar for some, for a rather obvious reason: It flies in the face of the principle according to which no contradictions are true—the Principle of Non-Contradiction (PNC). So let me say a few brief words about this here.

The PNC was set into orthodoxy in Western philosophy by Aristotle. (Eastern philosophy is another story). Orthodoxy and truth are, of course, quite different things. And the relevant question is why one should endorse the Principle. Aristotle's arguments were, frankly, pretty terrible, as most modern scholars now agree. (They are either tortured and opaque, or establish—if anything—something else.) Moreover, the history of Western philosophy since Aristotle has not been very successful in producing better arguments.

If one asks modern logicians why one should suppose the PNC to be true, they are likely to appeal to a principle of inference called *Explosion*—or, to give it its Medieval name, *ex contradictione quodlibet sequitur*: From a contradiction everything follows. According to this, given any contradiction, one can legitimately conclude anything. (It is called *Explosion* because, according to it, contradictory information explodes, delivering everything.) Clearly, many such conclusions, such as that $1 + 1 = 73$, that you are a frog, and that Donald Trump is Julius Caesar, are crazy. So, you can't accept a contradiction.

Since there is absolutely no connection between the premises of an inference by Explosion and these arbitrary consequences, it may come as a surprise to those who have never studied modern logic to learn that the inference is now endorsed by many—maybe most—logicians (though this has not generally been the case in the history of logic). The reason, briefly, is that an inference is valid if it is impossible for the premises to be true and the conclusion to be false. The PNC tells us that it is impossible for a contradiction to be true. So, it is impossible for a contradiction to be true *and* an arbitrary conclusion to be false. So, the inference is valid (vacuously, as logicians say).

Given this, the ground for the validity of this inference fails if the PNC does. And it is precisely the PNC which is challenged by our paradox about **nothing** (and, incidentally, many other things). To reject the truth of the paradox because of this principle therefore begs the question. Indeed, there are now many well-worked-out accounts of validity according to which Explosion is not a valid inference. They are called *paraconsistent logics*, but this is not the place to go into them.

Having cleaned up the *nihil*, we can now come to the *fit*. It is standard Christian theology that God created everything else at a certain time. Thus, all creatures depend on the creator because of God's act in time. But again in orthodox Christian theology, God's creatures depend on God in a much more profound sense (called causation *per se*). God maintains the world from moment to moment, in the way that the motion of a locomotive maintains the motion of a carriage that it is pulling. In other words, there is a continued ontological dependence of God's creatures on God. Things are (and continue to be) what they are because of a dependence of this kind on God. The notion of ontological dependence, or *grounding* as it has come to be called, has been much discussed in recent Western philosophy. This is not the place to go into it. Some simple examples will suffice for our purposes.

Suppose that something, s, is the shadow of a tree. It depends for being what it is on the thing of which it is a shadow, t, being a tree. If t had not been a tree, s would not have been the shadow of a tree. The reverse is not the case. If s ceased to be the shadow of a tree—if, for example, the sun goes in—t would still be a tree.

Similarly, m being a molecule of water (H_2O) depends on the fact that it contains an atom of oxygen, a. Had a not had an atom of oxygen, it would not have been a molecule of water. Again, the reverse is not the case. Had m not been a molecule of water, it does not follow that it would not have contained a; m could have been a molecule of alcohol (C_2H_5OH).

Next, some things are what they are by virtue of being *distinct from* other things. Thus, s being the spouse of some person, p, depends on their being distinct from p: if s were the same (person) as p, s would not be the spouse of p. The reverse does not hold. If s were not the spouse of p, it does not follow that s would be the same person as p.

Or again, being a hill depends on being distinct from the surrounding plane, p. If h were the same (height) as p, then h would not be a hill. As usual, the reverse does not hold. If h were not the same height as p, it does not follow that h would be a hill: it might be a ravine.

We are now in a position to see in exactly what sense **nothing** is the ground of reality. An object, g, being something, that is, being an object, depends on its being distinct from **nothing**. For by our paradoxical fact about **nothing**, we know that **nothing** is not an object. So, if g were the same (in ontological status) as **nothing**, it would not be an object. And the dependence does not go the other way. If g were not an object, it would not follow that it is identical with **nothing**—at least for all we have seen so far: There may be nonobjects other than **nothing**.

Indeed, one may say that what it is to be an object is to "stand out" against the background of nothingness, in just the way that a hill is what it is because it stands out against the background of the surrounding plain. One could picture it thus:

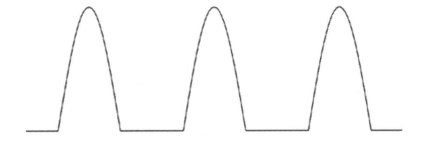

The peaks might represent hills standing out against the surrounding plane; or they might represent objects standing out against the background of **nothing**. Hence, **nothing** is the ground of reality in the sense that every object depends for being what it is (an object) on its relationship to **nothing**.

Indeed, if there were no **nothing**, there could be no objects at all. For if **nothing** were not something, there would be nothing for any object, g, to be distinct from; so, g could not be an object, something. In this sense, Eckhart got it right. Heidegger, too, got it right when he said in "What is Metaphysics?" —and in his own distinctive way:

> **Nothing** is neither an object nor any being at all. **Nothing** comes forward neither for itself nor next to beings, to which it would, as it were, adhere. For human existence **nothing** makes possible the openedness of beings as such. **Nothing** does not merely serve as the counterconcept of beings; rather it originally belongs to their essential unfoldings as such. (WM, p. 104).

(I have translated Heidegger's "das Nichts" as "**nothing**." Translators often translate it as "the nothing," but this is hardly even grammatical in English, while using the definite article with abstract nouns is standard German grammar.)

Of course, Eckhart was a mystic, and there are mystical strands in Heidegger too; but there is nothing mystical about how *we* got to our conclusion. It was straight logic! Nor is there any reason to identify **nothing** with God, as Eckhart does. **Nothing** is certainly a strange object, but that hardly means that one should worship it!

One way in which **nothing** is strange, as we have seen, is that it is paradoxical. It is both an object and not an object. And since it is the ground of all objects, it is the ground of itself as well. Moreover, to be an object, as we have seen, it must be distinct from **nothing**. But we should have expected this. As we have already seen, if x is not an object, $x \neq x$. So **nothing** $\neq$ **nothing**: **nothing** is distinct from itself —even though it is identical with itself as well!

Eckhart (and Heidegger) were, then, right—*ex nihil omnis fit*. **Nothing** is the ground of reality, that on which all objects depend for their very objecthood. Moreover, this ground, this *nihil*, is indeed a strange (non-)object. At the ground of reality lies paradox.

References

Carroll, L. (1899) *Through the Looking-Glass and What Alice Found There*. New York: G.H. McKibbin.

Eckhart, M. (1981) *The Essential Sermons, Commentaries, Treaties, and Defense* (trans.by Edmund Colledge, O.S.A., and Bernard McGinn). New York: Paulist Press.

Heidegger, M. (2008) "What Is Metaphysics?" in David Farrell Krell (ed.), *Martin Heidegger Basic Writing*. HarperCollins: New York.

7

Hegel on Nothing (in particular): A Greek Alternative to the Problem of Infinitesimals

Paul Redding

On the topic of nothingness, Hegel is best-known for the enigmatic way he commences *The Science of Logic*. Starting with the concept "being," a concept whose application to anything is seemingly presupposed by all other concepts, he declares that because of its "indeterminateness and emptiness," *being* is "in fact *nothing*, and neither more nor less than nothing" (Hegel, 2010, 59). The difficulty is that the same can be said *about* nothing itself: "Nothing is therefore the same determination or rather absence of determination, and thus altogether the same as what pure being is" (ibid.). This claim to the *identity* of such obviously opposed concepts as being and nothing is an intolerable situation, however, and thought resolves this contradiction by grasping the truth of both concepts in the further concept of *becoming*: "The truth is neither being nor nothing, but rather that being has passed over into nothing and nothing into being—'has passed over' not passes over. But the truth is just as much that they are not without distinction; it is rather that they are not the same, that they are absolutely distinct yet equally unseparated and inseparable, and that each immediately vanishes in its opposite" (ibid, 59-60). To commence our exploration of the status of nothingness in Hegel's thought, I will start by orienting Hegel in relation to a diagnosis of the West's problematic relation to the notion of nothing recently offered by Sudip Bhattacharyya in a paper "Zero—a Tangible Representation of Nonexistence: Implications for Modern Science and the Fundamental" (Bhattacharyya, 2021).

There, Bhattacharyya discusses European culture's negative attitude toward the concept of nothingness—what we might call Western "nullophobia"—an attitude that, he claims, is rooted in ancient Greek culture and expressed in the absence of the number zero in Greek mathematics. The situation pertaining in ancient Greece contrasts with the philosophical environment and mathematical achievements of India, in which a "concept of *existence originating from nonexistence*" (ibid, p. 661) had provided no philosophical impediments to the type of abstraction required to think of zero as a number. While zero was introduced into Europe in the 13th century by Leonardo of Pisa from Arab mathematical practices ultimately rooted in Indian sources, it would be still centuries before it was to become widely accepted. In contrast, already by 628 C.E., a complete system of arithmetic containing both zero and negative numbers had been presented in the work, *Brahmasphutasiddhanta* ("Correctly Established Doctrine of Brahma"), by the Indian mathematician-astronomer Brahmagupta, and the Indian use of zero is thought to have probably been around for centuries before that.

Despite this initial resistance, the adoption of the number zero would by the 16th and 17th centuries become crucial for the appropriation of the discipline of algebra in the West, again from Arabic sources. It is because of this *need* for, and yet *reluctance* toward, the use of zero that Bhattacharyya posits a deep contradiction within modern European culture between its inherited nullophobic attitudes and its embrace of the modern scientific worldview.

As a generalization about the comparative dispositions of Eastern and Western cultures, Bhattacharyya's thesis may have much plausibility, nevertheless, I suggest that Hegel's attitude toward ancient Greek mathematics and philosophy in its contrasts with both oriental approaches on the one hand and *modern* European ones on the other, considerably complicates this dichotomous picture. Here, I develop some of the *particular* features of that general attitude to nothingness found at the opening of *The Science of Logic* by exploring Hegel's engagement in a dispute over the reality of so-called "infinitesimals"—infinitesimally small but nevertheless nonzero magnitudes—that had accompanied the development of calculus in the 17th and 18th centuries. In this context, Hegel shows his clear preference for aspects of ancient Greek over modern approaches to both mathematics and physics, but it is not at the expense of relinquishing a place for the role of nothingness at a fundamental ontological level, that is, within what Bhattacharyya calls "the fundamental." While Hegel's account of numbers in Greek mathematics does not differ significantly from Bhattacharyya's, his "Greek" solution to the problem of infinitesimals reveals a role for nothingness that is perhaps even deeper than that which might be provided by the number zero. Moreover, while Bhattacharyya takes Parmenides and Aristotle as exemplars of Greek nullophobic thought, Hegel will turn to Plato, perhaps pushing back against the doctrines of Parmenides, as holding the key to an alternate Greek conception of nothingness.

1. The Concept of Nothing as "Aufgehoben" in Hegel's Triadically Articulated Categorial Structure

From the conceptual triad being-nothing-becoming with which *The Science of Logic* commences, we get a sense of the way that the conceptual system structuring that work, and indeed the rest of his philosophical system, will unfold. Concepts that on the face of it appear to be meaningful by themselves ("categoremic" ones) will be shown not only to presuppose concepts other than themselves but concepts to which they are clearly opposed, in the way that being and nothing were initially shown to be both opposed and yet identical. Thus, when being and nothing are replaced by this new internally structured concept of becoming, the new concept in turn will be shown to generate the same contradictory features that had befallen the initial concept, being. Indeed, this triadic structure seems to operate at all levels in *The Science of Logic*, as it becomes apparent to even a casual examination of its table of contents.[1]

Of the categories being, nothing, and becoming, while the first and the last were meant to be comparatively concrete, the second is clearly abstract. While one might think one can point to that something *that is* or that *is in the process of becoming*, it would seem that one cannot point to anything that *is not*. Greek nullophobia, according to Bhattacharyya, had manifested itself in a disinclination toward the abstract conceptions

---

[1] Thus, *The Science of Logic* is presented in three *books*, the doctrines of Being, Essence, and the Concept, each of which is divided first into three sections (*Abschnitten*): Quality, Quantity, and Measure, for the Doctrine of Being: Essence, Appearance, and Actuality for the Doctrine of Essence; the Subjective Concept, the Object, and the Idea, for the Doctrine of the Concept. In turn, these sections are themselves divided triadically into chapters (*Kapiteln*), the section on Quality, for example, dividing into the triad of Being, Being-there, and Being-for Itself.

of numbers that would be found in India, the Greeks tending to identify numbers with visualizable geometric shapes (Bhattacharyya 2021, 660). This, indeed, had been a well-known feature of the Pythagorean mathematics that had dominated Greek attitudes around the time of Plato, and Hegel too treats numbers as meaningless when totally abstracted from their relation to the *continuous* magnitudes of lengths, areas, and volumes represented in the diagrams of geometry.[2] This attitude to abstraction is present also in his categorial triads as abstract negative determinations always come to be replaced by comparatively more concrete ones, just as nothing gets replaced by becoming. In Hegel's rubric, the negation of the second category of a triad is itself always *negated*. But in this and similarly mediated transitions from one substantive determination to another, the intervening abstract negative "moment" is productive in that it is required for the *redetermination* of the original concrete category into some new one. In Hegelian terms, the negative, abstract phase of the cycle is negated but does not thereby disappear. It is somehow incorporated in negative form (*aufgehoben*) into the very substance of the new positive category that replaces it. Nothingness, as it were, becomes built into the further specifications of being in deeper and deeper ways.

Understood in the context of the overall structure of *The Science of Logic* itself, the triad of being-nothing-becoming with which we started is shown to lie at the lowest level of a hierarchy of triadic structures that reveals itself at the highest level by the fact that *The Science of Logic* itself is divided into three "books," which are themselves divided into three "sections," each of which is divided into three chapters, which in turn have their own internal triadic structure.[3] One might imagine that this process of conceptual division from the top down as possibly going on endlessly, but, of course, to be presented in a finite book, such subdivisions must stop *somewhere*, and Hegel's generally stop somewhere around this fourth layer. This can give the impression that Hegel's categories can be laid out in some definitive finite table, but I suggest that this is misleading. That Hegel's *linguistic representations*

---

[2] "What is overlooked in the ordinary representations of continuous and discrete magnitude is that each of these magnitudes has both moments in it, continuity as well as discreteness, and that the distinction between them depends solely on which of the two is the posited determinateness and which is only implicit" (Hegel, 2010, 166–167).

[3] That Hegel did *not* employ the terminology of "Thesis," "Antithesis," and "Synthesis," as popular lore has it, does not speak against the fact of an all-pervasive triadic structure conveyed by those terms.

of categories—the linguistic items "being," "nothing," "becoming," "determinate existence," "finitude," "infinitude," and so on—might be so arranged does not entail that the concepts or categories referred to can also be. An indication of this, I suggest, can be found in a diagram that had been unearthed among unpublished pages after Hegel's death by his biographer, Karl Rosenkrantz, and labeled the "triangle of triangles."

2. Hegel's "Triangle of Triangles"

The triangle of triangles (Figure 1, a) is supposed to have been drawn by Hegel sometime around 1800-1801, a period in which he is known to have researched extensively into ancient Greek geometry, centrally as presented in Euclid's *Elements* but, apparently, aided by the commentary of the late Neoplatonist, Proclus (Paterson, 2005). This was at a time when Hegel's approach to philosophy seemed close to that of his former roommate at the Tübingen seminary, Friedrich Schelling. Schelling was becoming known for a "nature philosophy" that had developed from his earlier reading of Plato's dialogue *Timaeus*, Schelling discussing the world in terms of the "world-soul" that gives it rational structure. Hegel's own diagram is supposed to have been intended to give a type of representation to such a Platonically conceived cosmos (Schneider, 1975).

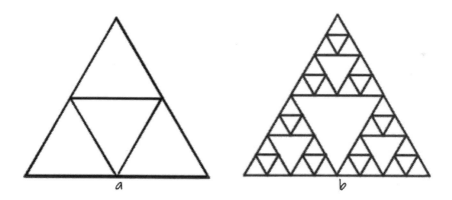

Figure 1: a, Hegel's triangle of triangles; b, a Sierpiński triangle.

Such an interest that Hegel shared with Schelling and others such as the Catholic thinker Franz von Baader certainly seems to have had a "mystical" or "theosophical" dimension.[4] The triangle had been extensively used as a symbol of the Christian doctrine of the Holy Trinity, and it seems clear that the division of Hegel's outer triangle by the inverted inner one creating three subtriangles similarly aligned to the outer triangle carries such trinitarian connotations. But it is obvious that these three new triangles could be further subdivided in a similar way into a pattern studied by the early-20th-century Polish mathematician Wacław Sierpiński and known as the "Sierpiński triangle" that can be found in tiling patterns in medieval cathedrals (Conversano & Tedeschini Lalli, 2011). Presumably these had been employed to induce in the viewer a sense of God's infinity, one's gaze, as it were, being drawn into this potentially infinitely reiterating pattern. In fact, a variant of this type of figure, the Sierpiński gasket, would be given as an example of an endlessly repeating "fractal" pattern by Benois Mandelbrot, who popularized this mathematical idea in the 1970s (Mandelbrot, 1977, pp. 56-57; Stewart, 1995, p. 54).

While Hegel's triangle of triangles may have had for him mystical connotations, it would seem that its significance at this time was not *limited* to such contexts. Both Gyorgy Lukács and Henry Harris have argued that around this time Hegel was *moving beyond* his earlier "mystical" (Lukács, 1975, pp. 121–123) or "theosophical" (Harris, 1983, p. 184) interests. Similarly, in his study of this figure, Helmut Schneider relates it to what he describes as Hegel's interest in a type of "geometric logic" (Schneider, 1975, p. 139). But the "mystical" and "philosophical" dimensions of this diagram may not have been as antithetical as Lukács, for example, suggests.[5] We will see that such self-similar diagrams were to be found in ancient Greek geometry in relation to a major concern that had affected both mathematicians and philosophers around the time of Plato—that of the discovery of the "irrationality" of certain magnitudes, such as the magnitude that in our modern number system we represent by the symbol $\sqrt{2}$—that is, the purported "real" number that, when multiplied by itself, would produce the natural number 2. Numerical techniques for

---

[4] Baader had employed a suggestively similar diagram linking the Trinity to ancient Pythagoreanism in Baader, 1798, with which Hegel was clearly familiar.

[5] E.g., "Presentiments of the dialectical interconnections occur from time to time and are then lost in the mystical haze of religion" (Lukács, 1975, p. 122).

finding *approximate* numerical values for such "square roots" had been used in Mesopotamia since sometime in the second millennium B.C.E. and seem to have been adopted by both Greek and Indian mathematicians (Zellini, 2020, ch. 2). However, the Greeks alone seem to have developed a *proof* in relation to the nature of such magnitudes—that is, a proof that such a magnitude consisting of the ratio of the lengths of a diagonal of a square to its side, for example, was *impossible* to represent in numbers.[6] Some have argued that this discovery had produced a veritable cultural crisis at the time (Klein, 1968, p. 76), but at the very least it left its mark on both mathematical and philosophical work being carried out in the early years of Plato's Academy. To bring this history to bear on Hegel's conception of nothingness, however, we must first examine the problem of infinitesimals within calculus and the links that the techniques of calculus had to earlier mathematical procedures established by the Greeks.

3. Analytic Geometry, Calculus, and Ancient Geometry

Euclid's *Elements* seems to have been composed around 300 B.C.E., almost a century after Plato had founded his "Academy" in Athens in 387. While very little is known about Euclid, it is clear that in many ways he acted as compiler and systematizer of earlier Greek work done in geometry (Knorr, 1975). Some books of the *Elements*, such as Books 7, 8, and 9, seem to reflect the more arithmetical approach of early Pythagorean mathematicians who had clearly taken on ideas from earlier Mesopotamian and Egyptian mathematics. Other crucial books, however, are attributed to the work of mathematicians who were associated with Plato's Academy in its early decades, especially Theaetetus (Books X and XIII) and Eudoxus of Cnidus (Book V).

While the *Elements* may testify to the greatness of Greek geometry, Greek arithmetic and algebra had remained comparatively undeveloped when compared to what had been achieved in Mesopotamia and Egypt. Thus, it has been argued that this made the Greeks render problems in a geometrical way that in other cultures were approached in more arithmetical and algebraic ways—the fact alluded to by

---

[6] It is not true that non-Greek mathematical traditions had developed *no* proofs. A proof for Pythagoras's theorem, for example, is to be found in ancient Chinese mathematics. Needham, 1959, pp. 22-23.

Bhattacharyya in his thesis of the Greek reluctance toward the degrees of abstraction pursued by Indian mathematics, for example. Thus, it is said that the Greeks had created a type of "geometric algebra" in which diagrams were used to represent *general* magnitudes analogous to the way generality was represented elsewhere algebraically (Høyrup, 2017). In the 17th century, European mathematics would be revolutionized by the independent inventions by Pierre de Fermat and Rene Descartes of "analytic" or "coordinate" geometry that synthesized the traditions of Euclidean geometry from the Greeks and Hindu/Arabic arithmetic and algebra. With the use of coordinates (still called "Cartesian" coordinates) geometric figures could be equated with the abstract *equations* of algebra, as when a circle, for example, is represented by an equation such as Analytic geometry had in turn provided a platform for the development of calculus by Newton and Leibniz, allowing them to address problems that arose in relation to geometric *curves* that could be understood as equivalent to algebraic equations involving squares and higher exponential powers. It was in this context that infinitesimals were posited in relation to the type of mathematics required by developments in the science of mechanics.

A typical problem facing 17th-century mechanics concerned accelerating bodies, such as freely falling ones. For a body moving at a *constant* velocity, the relation of velocity, time, and distance traveled can be expressed by a *linear* equation (velocity = distance / time)—so named because, plotted on Cartesian coordinates, this function can be represented by a straight line, the slope of which shows the velocity. In cases of acceleration, however, one needs to measure the *change* in velocity with time. Here, acceleration = velocity/time, which is equivalent to the distance traveled / time / time, or distance / time^2, the equation now involving a variable to the power of 2. Represented diagrammatically, an accelerating body will be plotted by a curve, a parabola. But unlike the idea of *distance*—that is, change in *location*—over time, the more abstract idea of change in *velocity* over time is far from intuitive. It might be asked: Exactly what does it mean to speak of the velocity of an accelerating body *at some point in time*? Can a body considered at a momentary point be thought to be *moving*?[7] Intuitively, the velocity represented at some point on a curve representing acceleration might be

---

[7] C.f. the opinion of Bertrand Russell in 1903: "Weierstrass, by strictly banning infinitesimals, has at last shown that we live in an unchanging world, and that the arrow, at every moment of its flight, is truly at rest" (Russell, 1903, 347).

conceived as the *slope* of the tangent touching the curve at that point, and the development of differential calculus involved the task of building on this idea.

The idea underlying this solution is simple. One can calculate the *average* velocity of an accelerating body over a stretch of time by drawing a straight line (a "chord") between two points on the curve A and B. One might then repeat the process for a further chord BC, such that the difference in x values, representing time, between B and C is the same as between A and B. The difference between the slopes of the lines AB and BC will represent the difference in average velocities over these times. If one then makes a succession of such time slices AB, BC, CD, etc., *smaller and smaller*, the changes in velocity will be less abrupt, and the different chords will come closer and closer to forming a single straight line. At some point, when the represented time slices become zero, the set of chords will have transformed into a single straight line which is tangent to the curve. The difficulty is that at that limit point there can be *no ratios* of distance traveled to time taken for the sequence, as such values are now zero.[8] Hegel expresses this problem in *The Science of Logic* thusly: "It may be objected that vanishing magnitudes do not have a final ratio, because any ratio before the magnitudes vanish cannot be the last, and, once vanished, there is no ratio any more" (Hegel, 2010, p. 217). Earlier, Bishop George Berkeley had summed up the ontological problem posed by these infinitesimal magnitudes by referring to them as the "ghosts of departed quantities" (Berkeley, 1996, p. 81).

Of course, differential and integral calculus did not appear from nowhere. They were, as mentioned, predicated upon the introduction of coordinate geometry by Fermat and Descartes. Newton, in particular, seems to have drawn on Fermat's conceptualization of tangents by means of sequences of chords of decreasing size (Simmons, 1996, pp. 20-21). But the appeal to a succession of shrinking finite magnitudes in order to find their limit also resembled a method used in ancient Greece by Archimedes called the "method of exhaustion." In "On the Measurement

---

[8] In some intuitive sense, the *point* arrived at between two shrinking time intervals was thought of as the "limit" of this process, but it took until the work of Cauchy and Weierstrass in the 19th century to make this notion clear. While their work has *generally* been accepted as finally ridding calculus of the problem of infinitesimals, not all contemporary mathematicians are convinced by this solution. For Hegel, "limits" are always rational *bounds* of some continuous magnitude.

of a Circle" (Archimedes, 1897), Archimedes had employed this technique to estimate the ratio of the circumference of a circle to its diameter (the ratio now represented by the symbol 'π' (*pi*)) by inscribing a six-sided regular polygon (a hexagon) inside a circle, and another hexagon outside the circle, such that the circumference of the circle was touched by the vertices of the inner polygon and by the sides of the outer (Figure 2 below). The circumference of the circle was clearly greater than the sum of the sides of the inner hexagon and less than the sum of the sides of the outer, with both these values able to be computed. Moreover, by doubling the number of sides of both polygons from six to 12, a narrower range of upper and lower limits, and hence a more accurate estimation of the value of π, could be achieved. Archimedes went from a six-sided polygon to a 96-sided one, narrowing the range of the value of π to between and , in modern terms between 3.14285 and 3.14084. The value of π to five decimal places is now given as 3.14256, so it can be appreciated how the method of exhaustion establishes a reasonably accurate range of approximations.[9]

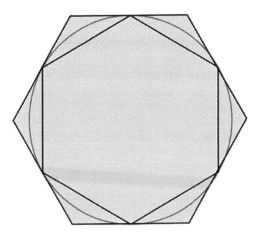

Figure 2. Archimedes's polygons

---

[9] The method of exhaustion remained the fundamental way of calculating the value of π up to the time of Newton, when he introduced a more easily applied algebraic method. It must be emphasized, however, that *all values* given for π to this day remain, and such values will always remain, approximations. Represented as a real number, π has an *infinite* and nonrepeating decimal expansion. The value of π to 1 million decimal places is given at One Million Digits of Pi On One Page!- [Plus Guides And Information] | Pi Day, but of course this, like *any* finite representation of the number, is still an approximation.

There is a crucial difference between the ways in which Archimedes had applied this method and the way it was applied by Newton and others in the 17th century. As pointed out by Thomas Heath, Archimedes "followed the cautious method to which the Greeks always adhered; he never says that a given curve or surface is the limiting form of the inscribed or circumscribed figure; all that he asserts is that we can approach the curve or surface as nearly as we please" (Heath, 1920, 27). By the time of Archimedes, the Greeks were well familiar with the idea that certain magnitudes were incommensurable, and it was assumed that such incommensurability held between the lengths of the diameter and circumference of a circle (although this would not be *proved* until the 18th century). But the Greeks did not have our concept of an "irrational" *number*, which could be understood as the "limit" *on which* a sequence of ratios including the ratios were converging. The Greek concept of number was effectively limited to the positive integers, conceived as multiples of the unit, or "monas," and ratios of such integers, and the sorts of situation we express by referring to the irrationality of a "number" such as π had been expressed in terms of the *incommensurability* of the two geometric magnitudes involved—here, the circumference and diagonal of a circle.

This difference between Greek and modern approaches is insisted upon by Hegel when discussing the development of calculus in the late 18th century by Jean-Louis Lagrange:

> Lagrange's exposition of the rectification of curves, since it proceeds from the principle of Archimedes, involves the *translation* of the Archimedean method into the principle of modern analysis .... But Archimedes' principle, that the arc of a curve is greater than its chord and smaller than the sum of the two tangents drawn at the endpoints of the arc and contained between these two points and the point of their intersection, does not yield any direct equation. Its translation into modern analytical form consists in the invention of an expression which is *per se* a simple fundamental equation, whereas in the earlier form the principle simply *demands* an endless alternation between terms each time determined as too great and too small, the successive advance only yielding new terms which are still too great and too small, albeit between always narrowing limits. (Hegel, 2010, 257)

Lagrange, with all other "analysts" dating back to Descartes, had simply assumed that there *was* a number at the "limit" of the converging sequences of rational numbers—an "irrational" number that could find a place on the continuum of "real" numbers, somewhere between rational numbers such as 22/7 and 223/71. Such a number is thought to be "irrational" in that it cannot be represented by a ratio of natural numbers nor completely specified by a decimal expansion, as such an expansion would go on infinitely with no repeating pattern. But from the modern point of view, it is a *number* nevertheless.

On this issue, Hegel clearly sided with the Greeks. Nevertheless, the value of π could still be *approximated* with a ratio—not a ratio "before or after they vanish, but the ratio with which they vanish" (Hegel, 2010, p. 217). Earlier in *The Science of Logic*, Hegel had used a similar expression for the same phenomenon: "These magnitudes are so determined that they *are in their vanishing*—not *before* this vanishing, for they would then be finite magnitudes; not *after* it, for then they would be nothing" (ibid, p. 79). I suggest that Hegel is here alluding to techniques for approximating other irrational magnitudes, in particular, the "square roots" of *nonsquare* numbers, such as 2, 3, and 5—techniques that were known to the Greeks but that had probably originated in Mesopotamia and had also spread to other non-Greek civilizations.[10]

In these calculations, the irrational magnitudes in question typically involved the ratio of sides of regular polygons to their diagonals—ratios discussed in Chapter 13 of Euclid's *Elements*, that is attributed to Theaetetus—and these ratios were numerically approximated *via* the generation of sequences of numbers by the application of simple algorithms, a technique alluded to in *Elements* Chapter 10, also attributed to Theaetetus. Probably the most widely known one was that used for calculating the ratio of the side and diagonal of a square, a ratio that is very likely to have been the first to be grasped by the Greeks as an *incommensurable* one.[11] Thus, in a work from the second century C.E., Theon of Smyrna's, *Mathematics Useful for Understanding Plato* (Theon of Smyrna ,1979, pp. 29-30;143 note VII), can be found a technique used by earlier Pythagoreans for approximating the value of the ratio of the

---

[10] In fact, Archimedes application of the method of exhaustion for giving an approximation of π *presupposed* a technique for finding values for the square root of 3 and some other nonsquare numbers, which he apparently had. (Stein, 1999, p. 104).

[11] The connection to Archimedes's technique for the calculation of π becomes clear when it is kept in mind that the regular polygons can themselves all be inscribed within a circle.

diagonal to the side of a square, the value we now know as √2. It involves the construction of a table consisting of rows of "side and diagonal numbers," the columns of which would, in the modern understanding, converge on √2 understood as the *limit* of the sequence. The importance of these for us is that in the case of the Greeks these techniques would come to be linked to the existence of *proofs* for the (for us) irrationality of the numbers that were being approximated.

4. Side and Diagonal Numbers

The technique Theon cites consists of forming two number columns labeled "sides" and "diagonals" with the aid of a simple formula for generating values for each row. To start, in the first row, the number 1 is inscribed as the first entry for *both* side and diagonal. The side in the next row is now given the value of the *sum* of the side and diagonal values of the row above, hence the second "side" entry will have the value of 2 (1+1). The *diagonal* in the second row is now given the value of *twice* the side in the row above when added to the diagonal number of that row. Hence in the second row, the side and diagonal values will be andrespectively. In turn, the third row will now be given the value 5 for side (i.e., 2+3) and 7 for diagonal. This simple procedure can, of course, be continued indefinitely as in Table 4, generating a series of pairs of numbers that approximate with increasing precision the value of √2 by giving its upper and lower bounds, respectively, the gap becoming smaller and smaller with each step.

Sides	Diagonals	Ratio of diagonal to side
1	1	1:1 = 1
2	3	3:2 = 1.5
5	7	7:5 = 1.4
12	17	17:12 = 1.41666…
29	41	41:29 = 1.41379…
70	99	99:70 = 1.41428…
169	239	239:169 = 1.41420…
…	…	…

Table 1: The side and diagonal numbers used for approximating the value of √2.

The type of electronic calculator found in every modern computer, tablet, or smartphone uses an algorithm related to this ancient way of generating number sequences, and of course *no* human procedure or computational process can give a complete specification of the value of √2, as that would involve a table with an *infinite* number of rows. The storage of the most massive *possible* computer is, of course, still finite, as are the screens, sheets of paper, and so on upon which such numbers could ever be displayed. However, applied, say, in the solution of practical problems of engineering, these values only need to be *accurate enough*. For example, it is said that for the purposes of interplanetary travel, NASA engineers need to calculate π to no more than 15 decimal places (NASA/JPL 2022), and clearly most practical applications would require far fewer. As can be seen from Table 1, the method of side and diagonal numbers can generate comparatively accurate estimates of √2 in a manageably small number of steps.

As noted above, the incommensurability of certain continuous magnitudes had become known within Greek mathematics, it generally being thought that a proof for the incommensurability of the side and diagonal of a square had been discovered during the fifth century.[12] From Plato's dialogue *Theaetetus*, we can estimate that such proofs were being discussed in Athens around 399 B.C.E., the year of Socrates's death. The dialogue *Theaetetus* is actually set around 369, on the occasion of Theaetetus's death, his having been wounded in a battle fought at Corinth. In it, Euclides relates a story told to him by Socrates and so set at least 30 years earlier, in which a young Theaetetus tells Socrates of a geometry lesson by his teacher, Theodorus. Traditionally, commentary on this dialogue has focused on the *definition* of knowledge pursued by Socrates—effectively, knowledge considered as "justified true belief"— but more recently, the specific *instance* of knowledge being discussed in the dialogue has become a primary object of concern (e.g., Brown, 1968, Burnyeat, 1978, Fowler, 1999). This knowledge involved *proofs* for the incommensurability of different pairs of geometric magnitudes.

The mathematician Theodorus is portrayed as demonstrating to Theaetetus and his companion the incommensurability of the sides of squares with a range of different areas—effectively from squares of three

---

[12] According to legend, the Pythagorean, Hippasus of Metapontum had been drowned at sea for making this discovery known beyond the Pythagorean cult.

square units up to 17 square units—when measured in relation to a square of one square unit (Plato, *Theaetetus*, 147a-148b). As noted above, the incommensurability of the side and diagonal for a square of *two square units* (in modern terms, the irrationality of √2) had been discovered earlier, but that proof involving a type of *reductio ad absurdum* is specific for the value of √2 and cannot be simply generalized to further square roots.[13] Although not much is known about Theodorus's proofs, it seems that he had a series of separate proofs involving the use of diagrams (ibid., 147d) and lacked a *general* proof of the "irrationality" of the roots of nonsquare (or "diagonal") numbers larger than 17. In contrast, his student, Theaetetus, is said to have come up with a form of proof generalizable to *all* such nonsquare numbers (Brown, 1968; David, 2011).

One interpretation that has attracted support among Plato scholars since the early 20th century is that Theaetetus had discovered a technique that is called *anthyphairesis*—the technique of "successive subtraction"—that is referred to by Euclid in *Elements* Book X (Euclid 1956, Book X, Proposition 2), a book whose contents are largely attributed to Theaetetus. While it is hardly usual for this notion to be mentioned as having any relevance *for Hegel*, a link has recently been postulated by two different authors. In a discussion of Hegel's concept of infinity, Vojtěch Kolman has linked *anthyphairesis* to Hegel's alternative to the modern use of calculus with its problems of infinitesimals (Kolman, 2016, pp. 261-264). In a quite differently directed work on the history of mathematics, Paolo Zellini, in a seemingly off-the-cuff remark, links the idea of *antanairesis*, a term he, like most historians of Greek mathematics, takes to be the same as that of *anthyphairesis*,[14] to be "cognate with the German *aufheben*, the Latin *tollere*, with which Hegel would go on to unite the two complementary moments of dialectic, the taking away and the keeping" (Zellini, 2020, p. 37). With these connections Kolman and Zellini bring Hegel into contact with the ongoing reassessment of Plato's

---

[13] That particular proof is given as the example of a proof by contradiction (or "*reductio ad absurdum*") given by Aristotle in *Prior Analytics* Book 1 (Aristotle, 1984, *Prior Analytics* 41a20-37). On the assumption that the side and diagonal of a square are commensurable, it is deduced that the length of the side must be both even and odd. Therefore, the initial assumption must be false.
[14] The notion "*antanairesis*" is found in Aristotle's *Topics*, where it is employed in the *definition* of sameness of ratio applying to continuous magnitudes (Aristotle, 1984, *Topics*, 158b33-35). The terms "*antanairesis*" and "*anthyphairesis*" were taken to be synonymous in antiquity by the interpreter of Aristotle, Alexander of Aphrodisias, and this understanding has been followed by most subsequent scholars (Fowler, 1999, 31).

late theory of ideas seen as influenced by Theaetetus's mathematics (e.g., David 2011; Negropontis, 2018). The present work proceeds within the broad spirit shared by all these authors.

In *Elements* Book X, *anthyphairesis* is portrayed as a technique for deciding the commensurability or incommensurability of two *continuous* magnitudes: "If when the less of two unequal magnitudes is continually subtracted in turn from the greater, that which is left never measures the one before it, the magnitudes will be incommensurable."[15] This is now commonly thought to be a specifically *geometric* form of the so-called "Euclidean algorithm" for numbers found in Book VII (Euclid, 1956, Book VII, Propositions 1 and 2). In Proposition 1, this is given as a mechanically applied procedure for finding whether or not two numbers are *relative primes*—that is, like 4 and 7, having no common divisor other than 1.[16] In Proposition 2, it is extended to a technique for finding the "greatest common measure" of any two positive integers that are *not* relative primes—that is, for finding the largest integer that will divide both *without remainder*. In short, the Euclidean algorithm seems to belong to those similarly "algorithmic" procedures for mechanically generating sequences of approximations to irrational numbers like those of the "side and diagonal numbers" that the Greeks are thought to have adopted from Mesopotamian mathematicians. Here, the procedure runs roughly as follows:[17]

To find the greatest common measure of two natural numbers, a and b, first subtract the smaller (say b) from the larger a sufficient number of times (let's say n_1 times) until a remainder c is obtained that is itself smaller than the "subtrahend," b. Now, subtract c from b (the former subtrahend), again, a sufficient number of times (say, n_2 times), such that a new remainder, d, is obtained that is smaller than c. The process is repeated in this way and will terminate after a finite number of steps when *no* remainder is left. The *last* number to be subtracted

---

[15] Where *numbers* are concerned, sameness of ratio will be defined simply by the ratios having the same "exponent," as with, say, 3 : 4 and 6 : 8. Ratios among continuous magnitudes can be between incommensurables, however, and so sameness of ratio needed to be defined differently.
[16] That 4 and 7 are only *relative* primes is shown by the fact that 4 is not itself a prime.
[17] The summary below is largely paraphrase of the description given in Knorr, 1975, 29.

leaving no remainder is the greatest common measure of the original two numbers, and the ratio can be defined in terms of a sequence of "*anthyphairetic coefficients*," the number of times each successive subtrahend had needed to be subtracted.

Such is the Euclidean algorithm as applied to *numbers*, that is, *discrete* magnitudes, but when applied to *continuous* magnitudes, such as line segments, as in the geometric *anthyphairesis* of Book X, a new dimension of this process is revealed. Pythagorean numbers were, by definition, all commensurable, but continuous magnitudes had, of course, been discovered to be possibly *incommensurable.* The presentation in Book X has it that if these magnitudes *are* commensurable, the series of subtractions will, as in the arithmetical procedure, terminate after a finite number, with the last subtracted length being the greatest common measure of the original two magnitudes. Were those magnitudes to be *incommensurable,* however, the process will not terminate. It will reiterate indefinitely, and the series of *anthyphairetic* coefficients will simply repeat in a periodic fashion. Such is thought to have been the discovery of Theaetetus.

Book 7 is typically seen as reflecting an earlier, more "arithmetical" phase of Pythagorean mathematics and in its arithmetical form, and like those similar procedures such as the use of side and diagonal sequences for computing $\sqrt{2}$, is thought to have been adopted from earlier non-Greek sources.[18] However, it would seem to have been *only* in Greece that the geometric version given in *Elements* Book 10 had become interpreted as a *proof* for the incommensurability of certain continuous magnitudes and the diagrammatic presentation of this proof involves the sorts of "self-similar" diagrams that had attracted Hegel around 1800. This is perhaps most easily appreciated in diagrams associated with *another* incommensurable side-diagonal ratio analogous to that of the square— that found in a regular *five-sided* polygon, or *pentagon*. This is surely the most familiar of ratios from ancient Greece, known as the "golden ratio," having an irrational numerical value of $(1 + \sqrt{5})/2$, and linked to an algorithmic process similar to that involving side and diagonal numbers called the "Fibonacci series."

---

[18] The algorithm itself seems to have been independently discovered in both China and India in distinctly algebraic contexts (Stillwell 2010, ch. 5), suggesting a common source in pre-Greek mathematics.

5. The Golden Ratio, φ, the Golden Rectangle, and the Pythagorean Pentagram

The golden ratio, claimed by enthusiasts to underlie instances of aesthetic perfection ranging from the proportions of the façade of the Parthenon on the Athenian Acropolis to the faces of iconic screen goddesses, is a proportion discussed by Euclid in the *Elements* as the "Division in Extreme and Mean Ratio."[19] It is constructed by dividing a line, *AB*, at a point *C*, such that the ratio of the smaller to the larger segment (*AB* to *BC*), is the same as the ratio of the larger segment to the line itself (*BC* to *AB*). Thus, *AB: BC :: BC : AC*. Or, if extending *AC* to point *D* such that *AC = CD*, we could write this as *AB : BC :: BC : CD*, as in Figure 3 below.

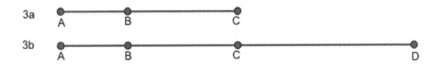

Figure 3, The Golden Ratio
3a, B divides *AC* such that *AB:BC=BC:AC*.
In 3b, with *AC=CD*, the ratio *AB:BC* can be seen as being equal to *BC:CD*.

Exemplifying this double ratio in the latter of these two ways allows us to appreciate how the golden ratio can be thought of as constructed from the first two of the *three* double ratios structuring Pythagorean music theory—the geometric, arithmetic, and harmonic proportions. Dividing *AC* at point *B* means that the segment *BC* is the *geometric mean* of *AB* and *AC* or equivalently *AB* and *CD* as for three quantities, *x*, *y*, and *z* (either discrete or continuous), *y* is the geometric mean of *x* and *z*

---

[19] This division is discussed in a number of places in *Elements* (Euclid, 1956, Book II, Prop. 11; Book IV, Prop. 11; Book VI, Prop 30; Book XIII, Prop. 5). The term "golden ratio" seems to have been coined in the 19th century during a wave of enthusiasm over this proportion. Earlier, in the Renaissance, a similar period of enthusiasm had seen the proportion referred to as "the divine proportion." For an exhaustive account of this mathematical object and its history, see Herz-Fischler, 1998. For a sober separation of its genuine mathematical properties from variously attributed properties see Markowski, 1992.

if or, equivalently.[20] But as defined by Archytas in Greece in the fourth century B.C.E. (Barker 1989, 42), C divides AD as its *arithmetic mean* if C is equidistant from A and D (or, in terms of numerical values, the arithmetic mean of a and b is calculated as $\frac{a+b}{2}$). The third, slightly more complicated "harmonic mean," which can be ignored for the moment, is actually the *inverse* of the arithmetic mean—a feature, the importance of which, will be seen below.[21] Thus, by examining the lines in Figure 3b, it can be readily appreciated that both geometric and arithmetic means are involved in the golden ratio.

From an algebraic perspective, we can regard the golden ratio as constrained by two equations:[22] (that of the geometric mean) and (that of the arithmetic mean). Solving these equations reveals the numerical equivalent of the golden ratio, standardly represented by the Greek letter φ (pronounced "phi"), to be $(1 + \sqrt{5})/2$, which, like $\sqrt{2}$, is an irrational number. Moreover, just as $\sqrt{2}$ had been associated with the generated sequence of pairs of numbers we have seen above as the columns of sides and diagonals, so too is φ associated with a similarly generated sequence known as the "Fibonacci series."[22] The Fibonacci series is typically attributed to Hindu mathematics, and whether or not the Greeks were familiar with it is irrelevant for our purposes. What is crucial for us concerns the diagrammatic presentation of the golden ratio that, using the technique of *anthyphairesis*, can serve as a proof for the irrationality of φ.

To this end we might consider the so-called "golden rectangle," the sides of which stand in the golden ratio such that if the shorter side is equal to 1 unit, then the longer side will be equal to φ units. It can be shown that *subtracting* a square of side 1 from the original rectangle, a new rectangle will be produced that is *similar*, although differently oriented, to

---

[20] For the Greeks, with their predominantly *geometrical* approach, the geometric proportion was thought to hold if the *area of a square* built on the side BC is equal to the *area of a rectangle* constructed from the sides AB and CD.

[21] The *harmonic* mean is calculated as 1 divided by the arithmetic mean of $\frac{1}{a}$ and $\frac{1}{b}$, or $(\frac{a^{-1}+b^{-1}}{2})^{-1}$, which can be reduced to the simpler formula, $2ab/(a+b)$. The inverse relation between the arithmetic and harmonic means is reflected in the peculiarities of the scale, in that counting *down* a *perfect fourth* from a note, say from C to G below reaches the same note that results from counting *up* a *perfect fifth* from the C below.

[22] The Fibonacci series is commenced by writing down the pair of terms 1 and 1, with the next term being determined by the sum of these two terms, hence, 2. For the rest of the sequence, as with the third term, 2, each subsequent integer will be the sum of its two immediate antecedents, the series thus proceeding as 1, 1, 2, 3, 5, 8, 13, 21, 34, 55, 89 …. It turns out that each contiguous pair of this advancing sequence becomes closer and closer to the numerical value of φ as, the ratio of sides and diagonals converge on $\sqrt{2}$.

the original. As in Figure 4 below, the rectangle *EBCG* left as remainder after subtraction of the square *AEGD* from the large rectangle *ABCD* will have its longer side equal to 1 unit and its shorter side equal to $\varphi - 1$ units. That this ratio between its sides, $1:\varphi - 1$, is the *same ratio* as that holding for the original rectangle, $\varphi:1$, and hence is the golden ratio, can be shown in a few simple steps.[23] In short, the ratio of the sides of the smaller rectangle is the same as that holding between the sides of the original rectangle, i.e., the "golden ratio." Alternatively, this could be expressed in terms of the idea of these two ratios having the same "*anthyphairesis,*" since, as Aristotle had pointed out, having *the same anthyphairesis* (or *antanairesis*) is what makes two ratios the same.

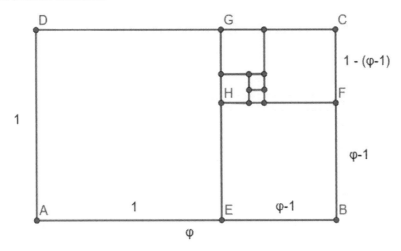

Figure 4. The Golden Rectangle

From contemplating the figure of the golden rectangle, it can be easily appreciated why this repeating *anthyphairesis* cannot terminate and hence why the golden ratio is irrational. Each subtraction will apply exactly once and will leave a remainder that is in the same ratio to the *subtrahend* that produced it as the previous remainder was to the *subtrahend* that produced *it*. Here the *anthyphairesis* can be represented

---

[23] Multiplying both sides of the ratio $1 : \varphi - 1$ by $\varphi + 1$ shows $1 : \varphi - 1$ as equal to $\varphi + 1 : \varphi^2 - 1$. We know, however, from the definition of the golden ratio that $\varphi^2 = \varphi + 1$ (expressed above as AB x CD = BC^2). This allows the left-hand side of the new ratio to be replaced by φ^2, giving the ratio $\varphi^2 : \varphi^2 - 1$. It also allows the φ^2 on the *right-hand side* to be replaced by $\varphi + 1$, resulting in the ratio $\varphi^2 : \varphi$, or $\varphi : 1$.

by an infinite and periodic sequence of "*anthyphairetic* coefficients," 1, 1, 1, 1, …. Just as in Hegel's triangle of triangles, further divisions of the golden rectangle in this manner must continue forever. Moreover, just as Hegel's *Archimedean* application of the method of exhaustion involved a sequence of approximations to π which, in contrast with its modern "analytic" version, could not be seen as bearing down on some "limit," here, too, any "convergence" cannot be seen as having some *real number* as its telos—a number that would only become fully determinate at the purported "end" of an infinite process. From Hegel's *Greek* perspective, there *are* no such limits, there are only such infinite sequences of converging pairs of rational magnitudes. As with the value of π, the value of φ can be *approximated* by a ratio, but this is not a ratio that holds "before or after" the approximating upper and lower limits "vanish." It is the ratio "with which they vanish" (Hegel, 2010, 217)—a ratio that forever "becomes"— and that is determined by the particular *anthyphairesis* involved.

The golden rectangle is often portrayed with an infinite spiral passing through points *D*, *E*, *F*, *H*, and so on, a spiral sometimes contestably said to apply to shapes found in nature from galaxies to flowers, but for the Pythagoreans perhaps the best-known diagram that shows the infinitely repeating *anthyphairesis* for the golden ratio is the *pentagram*, formed by the diagonals of a regular five-sided polygon, the pentagon (Kolman, 2016, 262-263), as in Figure 5.

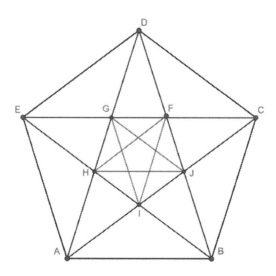

Figure 5. The Pentagon with Pentangle

In *Elements* Book XIII, Proposition 8, Euclid, presumably following Theaetetus, shows how the diagonals of the pentagon divide each other in the golden ratio. As can be seen from Figure 5, the larger segment of a divided diagonal is actually equal to the *side* of the pentagon, the line *EF*, for example, being equal to *ED*. It is known that the Pythagoreans used the pentagram as a symbol of recognition and associated it with *health* (Heath 1921, vol 1, 162), and Heath and others have speculated that observations of the properties of the pentagon may have led to the discovery of the golden ratio. The pentangle also provides a nice illustration of the unending *anthyphairesis* of the golden ratio, as it can be seen how the diagonals of the pentagon *ABCDE* enclose a further pentagon *FGHIJ*, now inverted in relation to the original. If we subtract the side of the original pentagon from its diagonal, such as subtracting *EF* (= *ED*) from *EC*, the remainder will be a segment the size of *FC*. This remainder can now be subtracted from the former subtrahend *EF* (= *CG*) to give the remainder *GF*. But *GF*, being the side of a *new* pentagon, similar to the outer pentagon, can now be subtracted from the diagonal of the inner pentagon, repeating the pattern that was commenced with the outer pentagon. Once more, the *anthyphairesis* will continue infinitely.

From these types of consideration, Kolman has suggested "the figure of the pentagon with its inscribed diagonals" as providing a more appropriate representation than the circle for Hegel's "closed and completed infinity" (Kolman, 2016, 263). I suggest that it is essentially for the same reason that Hegel could have thought of his triangle of triangles as an appropriate diagrammatic presentation of Timaeus's cosmic animal, a precursor to the Hegelian absolute.

6. The Relevance of Anthyphairesis for Hegel's Logic and Metaphysics

The golden ratio discussed above is the best-known of the complex double ratios with which Greek mathematicians experimented, but it was not the only one. In a neo-Platonic treatise on Greek arithmetic which Hegel had in his library (Mense, 1993, 673), Nicomachus of Gerasa had posited that what was responsible for the binding of the cosmos into a whole in Timeaus's account was a double ratio of four numbers, 6, 8, 9, and 12 (Nicomachus of Gerasa, 1926, 284-286). This sequence, also found in Plato's *Epinomis* (Plato 1997, *Epinomis* 991a-b), was known as the "musical *tetractys*," or "*harmonia*," because it instantiated the mathematical relations holding between the three harmonious musical intervals recognized by the Pythagoreans—in modern terms, the octave itself and the intervals dividing the octave into the "perfect fourth" and "perfect fifth."

In Archytas's system, the arithmetic mean between the numbers 1 and 2 is determined as the ratio 3 is to 2 and the harmonic mean as 4 is to 3, resulting in the sequence, 1, 4:3, 3:2, 2, signifying the Pythagorean scale of what is, in modern musical theory, equivalent to the sequence of tonic note, perfect fourth, perfect fifth and octave (Barbera, 1984). Multiplying each term by 6, gives Nicomachus's sequence 6, 8, 9, 12, with 6 and 12 representing the extremes of an octave and 8 and 9 represented the fourth and fifth intervals, respectively. In fact, buried within this whole structure can be found Theaetetus's infinitely repeating *anthyphairetic* process. Briefly, this works as follows.

The Greeks clearly esteemed the geometrically based relation between ratios, as in $a : b :: b : c$, as a structure responsible for the harmony of the world and, appropriately, it marked the fundamental musically harmonious interval, that between two notes an octave apart. But peculiarly, when an octave itself is divided geometrically in this way—that is, when the *geometric mean* of the octaval extremes is calculated—the note that is *most dissonant* in relation to the extremes (the modern "tritone," six semitones above the tonic) results. In contrast, the perfect fourth is one semitone below the tritone, and the perfect fifth, one semitone above it. That is, in the context of a number sequence that itself increases geometrically, a geometric interval can be divided by three means, the harmonic, the geometric and the arithmetic, with the harmonic and the arithmetic *bounding* the geometric from below and above.

Remember that *anthyphairesis* had become identified with a technique for finding the greatest common measure of two numbers, but when applied to continuous magnitudes, it can turn out that two such magnitudes have no such common measure. It can only be approximated. For two numbers in a geometric sequence, such as 6 and 12, there is no "number" in the Greek sense that forms their geometric mean. In modern terms, $\sqrt{(6 \times 12)}$ (or $\sqrt{72}$ or $6 \times \sqrt{2}$) is "irrational." My pocket calculator spits out the value 8.48528137423857... for the $\sqrt{72}$, but in so doing *it* is performing an algorithm not unlike that found in *anthyphairesis*, and the musical *tetraktys* provides us with a good first approximation for this value in that the geometric mean of the extremes 6 and 12 falls somewhere between the harmonic and arithmetic means, and so has a value greater than 8 and less than 9. But, because of the inverse relation between arithmetic and harmonic means, it turns out that the geometric mean of 6 and 12 is the same as the geometric mean of 8 and 9—in both cases, $\sqrt{72}$—and so we can find a more narrowly specified approximation of this magnitude by asking for the harmonic and arithmetic means of the pair 8 and 9. This reveals a new pair of lower and upper bounds for $\sqrt{72}$, 8.47 and 8.5, respectively, and of course, the same process can be repeated again and again in a "recursive" process.[24] This is all enabled by the peculiar relation between the three means such that the geometric mean of any interval is the same as the *geometric mean of the harmonic and arithmetic means* of that interval. At some point the sequence of upper and lower bounds *must* "vanish" in the sense that the iterative processes carried out by finite individuals must end somewhere—but Hegel was interested in the *ratio* "with which" such sequences vanish (Hegel, 2010, 217). This is surely their *anthyphairetically* defined ratio.

There *may* have been a strongly nullophobic dimension to aspects of Greek culture, as Bhattacharyya describes, a dimension perhaps manifested in the thought of Aristotle and, especially, Parmenides. However, Hegel's alternative to the modern "analytic" approach of calculus, an approach which had adopted the Indian numerical representation of nothingness with the number 0, was to appeal to a phase of Greek thought that some current interpreters see as central to Plato's response to the problems that Parmenides had posed to Plato's *own* earlier theory of ideas, a response influenced by Theaetetus's redefinition of *measure*. In this revised form of Platonism, carried on by later neo-Platonic followers, Plato's ideas would be no longer conceived as otherworldly analogs of worldly things—that is, things existing in a type of transcendent Platonic heaven. On the alternate reading, Plato's ideas become more tightly tied to their worldly instantiations, but not as found in Aristotle, for whom the actual bed, say, "contains" in some way, the "idea" or "essence" of which it *is* an instantiation. In the revised Platonic picture, "ideas" are still *not* to be found directly in the actual world, but

---

[24] A recursive process involves the step-wise application of a formula to a term or terms. One or multiple first terms is (are) defined, providing the initial input for the formula, with the subsequent output(s) then being used as the next input(s) to the same formula.

their existence is nevertheless tied to the worldly approximations in a new way, somewhat like the way an "irrational number" is tied to a converging series of rational numbers providing better or worse approximations. Kolman expresses a similar idea as follows: "There are no circles, justice or numbers beyond this world but only their satisfactory realizations, their here's and now's, consisting in a different usage or attitude to the same worldly phenomena such as pictures (as representing the circle), particular people (as representing eternal justice and law) or objects (such as the Parisian meter representing the measuring etalon)" (Kolman, 2016, 264).

Of course, the model of instantiable numbers coming to closer and closer approximate some "ideal" nonnumerically instantiable magnitude is *only* a model. For neither Plato nor Hegel were ideas identifiable with or reducible to numbers. But the new model conveys a new and profound sense of a void or a nothingness—a nonmetrical space into which the sequences of actual numbers vanish. This is the type of infinite nonmetrical Platonic space into which we are drawn when contemplating Sierpiński triangles, infinitely iterating pentagons, or sequences of iterating pairs of arithmetic and harmonic means of geometrically related extremes. Moreover, it is a void that depends upon, rather than exists in spite of, the lack of the number zero within Greek arithmetic.

References

Archimedes. (1897) *The Works of Archimedes*, edited and translated by T. L. Heath. Cambridge: Cambridge University Press.

Aristotle. (1984) *The Complete Works of Aristotle: The Revised Oxford Translation*, edited by Jonathan Barnes, Princeton: Princeton University Press.

Baader, F. (1798) *Über das pythagoräische Quadrat in der Natur oder die vier Weltgegenden*. Tübingen, Germany: Cotta.

Barbera, A. (1984) The consonant eleventh and the expansion of the musical tetractys: A study of ancient Pythagoreanism, *Journal of Music Theory*, 28, no. 2 (Autumn): 191–223.

Barker, A. ed. (1989) *Greek Musical Writings. Vol. 2, Harmonic and Acoustic Theory*. Cambridge: Cambridge University Press.

Berkeley, G. (1996) The analyst. In Ewald, W. (ed.) *From Kant to Hilbert: A Source Book in the Foundations of Mathematics*. Oxford: Oxford University Press, pp. 60–92.

Bhattacharyya, S. (2021) Zero—a tangible representation of nonexistence: Implications for modern science and the fundamental. *Sophia,* 60, pp. 655-676.

Borzacchini, L. (2007) Incommensurability, music, and continuum: A cognitive approach. *Archive for the History of Exact Sciences*, 61 (3), pp. 273–302.

Brown, M. (1968) *Theaetetus*: Knowledge as continued learning. *Journal of the History of Philosophy*, 7, pp. 359-379.

Burnyeat, M. (1978) The philosophical sense of Theaetetus' mathematics. *Isis*, 69 (4), pp. 489-513.

Conversano, E. & Tedeschini Lalli, L. (2011) Sierpiński triangles in stone, on medieval floors in Rome. *Aplimat: Journal of Applied Mathematics,* (4), pp. 113-122.

David, A. P. (2011) *Plato's New Measure: The Indeterminate Dyad*. Austin, Texas: Mother Pacha, Inc.

Euclid. (1956) *The Thirteen Books of the Elements*. Translated with introduction and commentary by Sir Thomas L. Heath. New York: Dover Publications.

Fowler, D. (1999) *The Mathematics of Plato's Academy: A New Reconstruction*. Oxford: Oxford University Press.

Heath, Thomas L. (1920) *Archimedes*. New York: Macmillan.

Heath, Thomas L. (1921) *A History of Greek Mathematics*, two volumes. Oxford: Clarendon Press.

Hegel, G. W. F. (2010) *The Science of Logic*. Translated and edited by George di Giovanni. Cambridge: Cambridge University Press.

Herz-Fischler, R. (1998) *A Mathematical History of the Golden Number*. Mineola, N.Y.: Dover.

Høyrup, J. (2017) What is 'Geometric Algebra,' and what has it been in historiography? *AIMS Mathematics*, 2(1), pp. 128–160.

Klein, J. (1968) *Greek Mathematical Thought and the Origin of Algebra*, translated by Eva Brann. Cambridge, MA: MIT Press.

Knorr, W. R. (1975) *The Evolution of Euclidean Elements*. Dordrecht, Netherlands: Reidel.

Kolman, V. (2016) Hegel's 'Bad Infinity' as a logical problem. *Hegel Bulletin*, 37 (2), pp 258-280.

Mandelbrot, B. B. (1977) *Fractals: Form, Chance, and Dimension*. San Francisco: W. Freeman and Co.

Markowsky, G. (1992) Misconceptions about the Golden Ratio. *College Mathematics Journal,* 23 (1), pp. 2–19.

Mense, A. (1993) Hegel's library: The works on mathematics, mechanics, optics, and chemistry. In Perry, M. J. (ed.) *Hegel and Newtonianism*. Dordrecht, Netherlands: Kluwer, pp. 669–709.

NASA/JPL, (2022) How many decimals of pi do we really need? *EDU NEWS*, October, 24.

Needham, J. (1959) *Science and Civilisation in China. Volume 3, Mathematics and the Sciences of the Heavens and the Earth*, with the collaboration of Wang Ling. Cambridge: Cambridge University Press.

Negrepontis, S. (2018) The anthyphairetic revolutions of the Platonic ideas. In Sialaros, M. (ed) *Revolutions and Continuity in Greek Mathematics*. Berlin: Walter de Gruyter.

Nicomachus of Gerasa. (1926) *Introduction to Arithmetic*. Translated by Martin Luther D'Ooge; with studies in Greek arithmetic by

Frank Egleston Robins and Louis Charles Karpinski. New York: Macmillan Co.

Paterson, Alan L. T. (2005) Hegel's early geometry, *Hegel-Studien*, 39/40, pp. 61–124.

Plato, (1997) *Complete Works*. Edited with Introduction and Notes by John M. Cooper. Indianapolis: Hackett.

Russell, B. (1903) *The Principles of Mathematics*. Cambridge: Cambridge University Press.

Simmons, G. F. (1996) *Calculus with Analytic Geometry*. 2nd Edition. New York: McGraw-Hill.

Stein, S. (1999) *Archimedes: What Did He Do Besides Cry Eureka?* Washington, DC: The Mathematical Association of America.

Stewart, I. (1995) Four encounters with Sierpiński's gasket. *The Mathematical Intelligencer,* 17 (1), pp. 52-64.

Stillwell, J. (2010) *Mathematics and Its History*. New York.: Springer Science+Business Media.

Theon of Smyrna. (1979) *Mathematics Useful for Understanding Plato*. Translated by Robert Lawlor and Deborah Lawlor, edited and annotated by Christos Toulis. San Diego: Wizards Bookshelf.

Zellini, P. (2020) *The Mathematics of the Gods and the Algorithms of Men: A Cultural History*. Translated by Simon Carnell and Erica Segre. London: Allen Lane. First published in Italian as *La Matematica degli dèi e gli algoritmi degli uomini*. Milano: Adelphi Edizioni, 2016.

8

Nothingness: Martin Heidegger and Georges Perec

Inja Stracenski and Daniela K. Helbig

The question of nothing puts us, the questioners, in question.
— Heidegger, *Was ist Metaphysik?*

To write: trying meticulously to retain something, to make something survive.
— Perec, *Espèces d'Espaces*

The enigma of *Nothingness* regained and retained urgency during the 20th century. It was the meaning of the world, or of *Being*, and its crushing narrowness that was being questioned by the two very different thinkers we are juxtaposing here. Both looked back on Europe's past during the middle decades of the 20th century: Martin Heidegger on the history of its metaphysics; Georges Perec on the history of its murderous agony. Heidegger's work has affected the philosophies of those who followed his path as well as many of those who opposed it. Perec rewrote the future of the novel as he turned personal experience into collective times and spaces, the meaning of absence into the tenor of our existence. In his thinking, Heidegger brought the long history of philosophical anti-Judaism in Europe to its apex. Perec's writing, born out of the memories of an orphaned child who survived the Shoah in hiding, brought those memories to sparks illuminating human life, measuring its breath like a chronograph. Rarely have these two towering figures in philosophy and literature been gauged together as we do in this paper. They have *nothing* in common.

Nothingness was one of the overt themes of Heidegger's thought, and it continues to animate histories of 20th-century philosophy as a marker of diverging paths between metaphysics and logical analysis of language, paths commonly traced back to Rudolf Carnap's analysis of Heidegger's pronouncement that "The Nothing itself noths." [*Das Nichts selbst nichtet.*] as his most prominent example of a meaningless sentence (Carnap, 1931, p. 230). But any engagement with Heidegger's thought is also an engagement with a thinker who played an active role in transforming the institutional landscape of German academic philosophy as a supporter of National Socialism and whose philosophy—from his earlier writings through the history of Being developed during his later years—is grounded in and develops an anti-Judaism that Heidegger both inherited from the German philosophical tradition and sought to take radically further (Cohen and Zagury-Orly, 2021).

We are among those who think that the problems with, and articulated in, Heidegger's thought cannot be sidestepped by ceasing all explicit engagement with it. But we also want to work against Heidegger's claims to singularity, manifested above all in his idiosyncratic idiom that renders his work difficult to read at best in his native German and close to untranslatable into other languages. If we point, in what follows, to analogies between Heidegger's thinking on nothingness with Perec's as well as to these analogies' limits, it is also to resist the absurdity imposed by Heidegger's portrayal of his thinking as so unique that it ultimately escapes conversation and the exchange of thoughts enabled by linguistic and formal conventions.

Let us first give a brief introduction to Georges Perec, whose name might come as more of a surprise in an exploration of nothingness than Martin Heidegger's. Perec was born in Paris on 7 March 1936 to Polish-Jewish immigrants to France. His father, Icek Judko Peretz (the sound of whose last name changed with its spelling, *Perec*, in his new French identity papers), died on 16 June 1940 as a member of the French military's foreign legion during the attempt to defend Paris against the advancing German army. His mother, Cyrla Szulewicz ("Cécile" once in France), was arrested on 23 January 1943 and deported to Auschwitz. The exact date of her death there is unknown. Georges survived with relatives in France (Bellos, 1995).

Georges Perec chose to become a writer, not an academic philosopher. An experimenter with words, he made a living as *documentaliste*, or scientific archivist for medical research—a job he performed with information management skills that turned out to be as remarkable as his humor. In 1967, he joined the group of mathematician-writers that has become renowned under the name of *OuLiPo* (*Ouvroir de littérature potentielle*, or "Workshop of Potential Literature"), and whose members investigated and used a variety of constraints as productive of literary composition. For example, Perec's 1969 novel, *La Disparition* (translated into English as *A Void*), is a lipogram, a text composed without using a given letter of the alphabet, here the letter "e." His first novel, *Les Choses* (*Things*) had received the prestigious Renaudot literary prize; his masterpiece of playing with compositional rules and constraints, the 1978 *La vie mode d'emploi* (*Life A User's Manual*), brought him the *Prix Médicis* and with that, the financial independence he longed for as a writer who also considered it essential to earn his living outside literature.

Although Perec's texts could hardly be more different from Heidegger's in their playfulness and tongue-in-cheek-ness, both writers converge—as we will see—in probing the everyday experience of Being as "nothingness" and in their emphasis on the demands on language to voice "nothingness." It is hard to overstress the difference in points of departure for Heidegger's and Perec's respective reflections, though. While Heidegger's attempt to rethink Western metaphysics rested on the exclusion of Judaism from his history of Being (Cohen & Zagury-Orly, 2021), Perec, as a secular, French-Jewish writer, grappled with the specific, historical reality of Europe after the Shoah. His lipogram-novel *La Disparation* started out as a game and drew in countless friends and acquaintances challenged by Perec to come up with e-less phrases. But the detective story of a series of disappearing protagonists is also an experiment with a language of storytelling without glossing over absences. Read out loud, the letter "e" sounds like *eux*, "them," designating the absence of human beings—of Perec's parents and much of European Jewry after the Second World War. Without describing that concrete absence explicitly, Perec's text attempts to apprehend its reality by turning it into a constitutive part of the language of storytelling.[1]

---

[1] We should note that Perec, not one to be pinned down by others' attempts at interpretation even if he planted the seeds for those interpretative attempts himself, followed up with a text containing no other vowel than e a few years later, *Les Revenentes* (1972).

Perec is writing against a dissolution of time, places, and memory by introducing *absence* or *nothingness* into their very composition. Durability and fragility enter and simultaneously establish the fabric of time, the composition of places, and the web of memories. Hence, the meaning of that which occurred in time appears in places, and it is conjured up in memories conveyed by absence and nothingness. For both Perec and Heidegger, nothingness and time are dimensions of being, not external or opposed to it, as is a simple negation or an operational tool in logic and epistemology[2]. Both sought to transgress the limits of a philosophy or literature respectively that could, in their eyes, not or no longer account for the meaning of being, time, and nothingness.

I. Knowing what to say: Heidegger

It is a matter of urgency, Heidegger maintains, to elaborate new possibilities for thought, to open a new horizon that can "overcome" (not overthrow); in Nietzsche's words, "oh friends, even the Greeks!" (Nietzsche, 1988, pp. 569-70)[3]. Leaving aside the validity of this judgment, one thing is certain: *not* to draw along the patterns of philosophy, in its traditional or contemporary forms, appears more difficult than we are usually ready to admit. And Heidegger's own, lifelong struggle to develop first steps toward something different, together with a novel language for saying it, is the best case in point.

Hence, to read Heidegger, one needs to be, another word from Nietzsche, "friends of the lento. ... what will drive to despair everyone who is 'in a hurry'" (ibid., p. 17)[4]. Two things are central to Heidegger, and central to understanding his notion of nothingness: firstly, that thinking begins with Being; secondly, the role of language. Let us take a moment to consider the former before we return to the latter.

---

[2] On *Nothingness* in Hermann Cohen's *Logic of Pure Knowledge* and Franz Rosenzweig's *Star of Redemption*, see Gordon (2005) pp. 47-54.

[3] "Oh friends! We need to overcome even the Greeks!" (*"Ach Freunde! Wir müssen auch die Griechen überwinden!"*). Translations throughout this essay are the authors' unless otherwise noted.

[4] "Such a book, such a problem has no hurry; besides, we are both friends of the lento, me as much as my book. I have not been a philologist in vain, perhaps I still am, which means, a teacher of slow reading: - I finally also came to write slowly. Now it belongs not only to my habit, but also to my taste – a malicious taste perhaps? – To write nothing but what will drive to despair everyone who is in 'a hurry.'"

Thinking, for Heidegger, begins with Being as opposed to beings, i.e., single entities of which we say that they *are* and *what* they are. This beginning is altogether different from the European philosophical tradition he was educated in but also sought to distance himself from. In early modern philosophy, the notions of the "infinite" and of the "first cause" define what being *is* in relation to human knowledge. On this early modern model, the cognition of finite entities is possible against the background of being's infinite actual activity (gr. *entelecheia*) and power (gr. *energeia*), the motion (gr. *kinesis*) and force (gr. *dyname*) of modern physics and the sciences.

But for Heidegger, this understanding of being encapsulates "the inability to address the fundamental problem of Being" in philosophy (Heidegger, 1993, p. 94).[5] The problem is not that philosophy cannot solve its age-old questions or remains riddled with contradictions as old as those questions, but that being, in the tradition he critiques, is drawn in analogy to other (finite) entities. Conceived in such eminently contrasting terms as absolute, infinite, independent, actual in its power, being nevertheless remains a "thing" (lat. *ens*), given in intellection, posited in simple opposition to the finite as the nonfinite or infinitum.

In other words, no matter how groundbreaking the early modern notion of being might have been, it is for Heidegger just the latest result of a long yet misguided development in the history of metaphysics, another *Vor-Stellung* (representation). "Representing could even be the all-prevailing basic feature of previous thinking" (Heidegger, 2002, p. 59). Hence, the standard distinctions in philosophy between intellect and sense perception, subject and object, cause and effect, body and mind, being and nothing, contingency and necessity, and other pairs of opposites, are mere re-presentations for Heidegger. And representations do not concern thinking but imagining, do not attend to what *is*. They are, then, to be "overcome." Why? Not least because the contrasting notions are "preventing the essential oneness of the human being" (ibid., p. 73).[6]

---

[5] We are following the spelling of Heidegger's "Being" with a capital B that is conventional in English translations as a reminder of Heidegger's insistence on having introduced a fundamentally new understanding of *Sein*, being. We are not, however, following Heidegger's distinction of his earlier notion of *Sein* from the *Seyn* of his later history of Being.

[6] In this text passage, Heidegger criticizes the definition of the human being as a "rational animal" (lat. *homo animal rationale*), a definition which brings two conflicting qualities (lat. *proprium*), animality and rationality, together, creating a discord, contradiction, or

In fact every philosophy, traditional or contemporary, undertaking to determine the nature and conception of being is inevitably at the same time determining the nature and the conception of the human being. Or as Heidegger puts it: "Each doctrine of Being is *in itself already* a doctrine about the essence of the human being" (ibid., p. 85).

Heidegger's question about the "meaning of Being," initially raised in *Being and Time* (1927) and worked through in all of his subsequent writings, is a simple question of massive proportions. Being concerns everything that *is* and the consequences of putting it in question are therefore great. Being has always been (mis)understood as atemporal, eternal, timeless *presence*, or so Heidegger alleges. But, he insists in contrast, Being is inherently tied to time. This understanding of Being, he claims, is entirely novel: "This connection, namely that in the determination of Being there is also a determination of Time, has never been considered before" (Heidegger, 1993, p. 68). The most important feature of this Heideggerian connection between Being and Time is that the basic tenses of Being are past and future—with no present.[7] Being is consequently spoken of in terms of "event" and "occurrence." It moves, as it were, and "withdraws" itself, is "concealed." Put in (Heidegger's) Greek terms, Being is no longer *parousia* (presence) but *apousia,* or *absence.*

We can now reverse the perspective and say that, indeed, to human experience (in the everyday as well as in the sciences) Being *is* nothing. Not a thing among other things that we could in any way pin down. And obviously, when we try to heed Heidegger's warning and not represent, but rather *turn* to Being—which is to say, away from that which we perceive through the senses (entities of our sense perception) and as far as possible away from that which has already been thought and

---

dichotomy within that (human) "being" who is supposed to be "one" out of two essentially conflicting sides (of body and mind): "This dichotomy is preventing the essential oneness of the human being and thus the ability to become free for what we usually call reality."

[7] In the "Task of a Destruction of the History of Ontology," Heidegger writes: "[T]he simple apprehension of something objectively present in its sheer objective presence [*Vorhandenheit*], which Parmenides already used as a guide for interpreting being—has the temporal structure of a pure 'making present' of something. Beings [single finite entities], which show themselves in and for this making present and which are understood as genuine beings, are accordingly interpreted with regard to the present, that is to say, they are conceived as presence (*ousia*). However, this Greek interpretation of being comes about without [...] understanding the fundamental ontological function of time, without insight into the ground of the possibility of this function. [...] On the contrary, time itself is taken to be one being [single entity] among others [...], a naïve way [of understanding time]" (Heidegger, 2010, pp. 22-23).

conceived (ideas and conceptions of the mind)—we first have, see, think, or hear *nothing*.

This *nothing* (*not a thing* among other things, not an *ens*), however, is not a mere abstraction or mental exercise but corresponds to the nature or essence of Being for Heidegger. Put differently, it is not emptiness or a void. The "place" of Being's absence is a place cleared of anything we could represent, namely what Heidegger calls a "clearing" (*Lichtung*). It is our own human place, where we "dwell" into the open, where *Dasein* (human existence) exists.[8] Only the human being can, in this view, be called a *Dasein* (in Heidegger's reading of the word as a compound noun, a being that is here, *da*; a being that *is* the *here*[9], but never Being itself (whose *absence* is the *place* of single beings). Heidegger could not have asked, as Kant or Fichte still did, the question of God's presence (*Dasein Gottes*), but only of God's absence. That is, of that *nothing* which, in this specific sense, belongs to the very essence of Being.

Hence, when we turn to Being and are left with *nothing*, we remember that which we normally do not consider or think much about, precisely because we experience it as nothing. This explains the importance Heidegger attributes to the acts of remembering (*die Gedächtnis*),[10] thinking of, thinking toward (*An-denken, Be-denken*) what we usually "forget": These acts are, to Heidegger, the (re-turning) move of all genuine thinking. Clearly, such re-turning is not characterized by a chronology of any kind (e.g., returning to an imagined golden age) and can happen at any time and at any place of human life. This understanding of turning to "nothing" as the move to genuine thinking brings us to the second element of thought that is central for Heidegger, in addition to his insistence that thinking begins with Being: the role of language beyond a means of representation.

We have seen that representation merely creates a set of contrasting images in philosophy, which we then take to be "real"— the reason why Heidegger could say that "we are still not thinking"

---

[8] i.e., "ex-sist" (from Latin *sisto, sistere*). The word "Dasein," introduced into the German language by Leibniz as a translation of the Latin *existentia*, is difficult to translate. It has since acquired a complex web of meanings and connotations that cannot be reverted into *existentia*. Heidegger's use of the German word *Dasein* has commonly been either left untranslated or rendered literally as being-there.

[9] As Heidegger explains in his *Letter on Humanism* (1978).

[10] "*Die* Gedächtnis" is a process as opposed to the neuter German noun "das Gedächtnis," a process which Heidegger relates to the Greek "Mnemosyne," the goddess of memory.

(Heidegger, 2002, p. 7). He asks us to abandon the "seeing" or representing for the sake of *listening*. This priority of hearing over seeing in Heidegger, which stands in contrast to Greek philosophy from Plato and most of the Western philosophical tradition since, is well known. Often understood as a challenge to Cartesian perspectivalism (Jay, 1994, p. 81), Heidegger's priority of hearing over seeing could also be read as borrowing one of the oldest and most important tenets of Judaism, which attributes to hearing an exceptional role in human comprehension and understanding. Hegel knew this well, educated as he was in Christian theology like many other German Idealist philosophers, but preferred the Greek approach. Heidegger—himself also educated in Christian theology—aligned himself instead with Judaism's preference of hearing over seeing. Yet, and ironically perhaps, he turned this alignment into the most radical anti-Judaism in German philosophy. His debt to the Judaic tradition, in this and other respects, remains "unthought," as the title of Marlène Zarader's fine book on Heidegger suggests (Zarader, 1990).

Back to Heidegger's insistence: why listen? Even if we do listen, we also at first hear nothing. But the act of listening—or so Heidegger claims—can recall what has usually been forgotten. Within the place of Being's absence, we can voice its silence, articulating what we call a word. To describe these genuine acts of verbal thinking, Heidegger chooses a whole family of terms related to music. Thinking itself, he writes, "demands its own mode (*Weise*) of being, which should be understood more like a melody" (*mehr im Sinne von einer Melodie*) (Heidegger, 1994, p. 134). The key terms in this musical vocabulary play on the German words *Stimmung* (translated as mood, disposition, tuning) and *Stimme* (the voice).[11]

Language's centrality to Heidegger's thinking rests upon his claim that concealed and absent Being *needs* human language in order to be "revealed" or to come to the fore. In this sense, we can say that language is what human beings are "called for." Or as Heidegger emphasizes in his later writings, human language is "needed and used"

---

[11] On translating Heidegger's "*Stimmung* family," see the entry on "Stimmung" in Cassin (2014, p. 1064). Other family members are *stimmen* (to attune, tune, also being correct or true), *Gestimmtsein* (being attuned), *Ungestimmtheit* (being incorrect, not attuned) *Verstimmung* (detuning, malaise), *Bestimmung* (determination, calling), *bestimmen* (to determine, decide, having a say, voice), *übereinstimmen* (to be of one voice: to agree or correspond).

(*gebraucht*) for that very purpose. We, human beings, are essentially within (*eingelassen*) this need or use. This is for Heidegger who (rather than what) we are. Namely, a being capable of its own "saying," or what Heidegger calls *die Sage*.

Such saying is, for Heidegger, creative: It can only occur once we have "let go of the actuality [...] so as to enter that free realm in which the creative (gr. *poesis*) resides" (Heidegger, 1978, p. 185). Saying is never *about* something, but rather it is creative in that it responds to, like a singing voice in tune with another, something that is: the *silence* and the *nothing* of Being. Precisely because it is not empty and void, this silence can be voiced and thereby reveals some truth of what is. Such acts, each of them a "plunge" (*Sprung*) into Being's *silence* according to Heidegger, are rare. But whenever they occur, and silence is voiced into what Heidegger calls a saying, each time this saying is *new*. For the one who listens and for the one who is saying it.

Among Heidegger's contemporaries, Paul Celan—despite his strong misgivings about Heidegger (Lyon 2006)—is an important, and well-known example of someone who saw the distinctive underlying difference between *saying* a truth and speaking "about" the same truth, and someone whose poetry enacted such saying. Celan's poem "The Death Fugue," for example, does not speak about the Shoah, as does a history book (to maintain the same level of concreteness, say, Timothy Snyder's *Bloodlands*). The poem is saying *it*. Celan's voice houses, so to speak, the ashes of those murdered, provides a site for their burial in his poem. The dark mood (*Stimmung*) of Celan's own experiences during the Shoah corresponds to truth, is forming his own inimitable voice (*Stimme*). In this sense there is no void or emptiness: We are not arbitrarily inventing themes that speak to us, compelling us into a *saying*. Rather, it is the temporal dimension of Being itself, experienced by Dasein, by a human being at a certain time and place, that is being *said*, or "brought to the fore" and thus "protected."

In this way, we can protect a single truth with words. In fact, we have *nothing* else. But "language itself is raised into the clearing of Being" (Heidegger, 1977, p. 263), and 'holds' it. The truth *remains* in this "protective heed" (ibid., p. 262). Perhaps we can now better understand what it means that "language is at once the house of Being and the home of human beings," "an open house" ("*Die Sprache: das* offene *Haus*)" (Heidegger, 2020, p. 143). In contrast to Nietzsche, there is no eternal recurrence in Heidegger; each occurrence, and "Saying is an occurrence of Being" (ibid., p. 155), is a unique event.

History, for Heidegger, is unfolding along the rhythm of such unique occurrences, that is, in the rhythm of our capacity or incapacity to question, or which is the same in his view, to think. In turn, human beings only have a presence insofar as we have and cultivate this capacity.[12] Where acts of thinking succeed is when language speaks to us and we are able to hear it and respond into the future, into what Heidegger calls the "World-Play-Joint" that playfully holds the world together through human presence or the creativity of *saying* truths. Thus, when "time is out of joint," it is a time in which we are losing our presence, not being playful enough, no longer knowing what to say.

Learning how to ask a good question might, then, be more decisive than a good answer. How to do this? Not in the form of a new philosophical discourse, in Heidegger's view. There are no rules for the act of *saying*, no deductive structures organized along a common concern. There is no strategy for a new group of statements. The islands of occurrences of *saying*, giving a rhythm to human historical as well as personal time, resemble eruptions in which a word is "heard" or "spoken" whose truths need no proof or analysis, only listening and understanding. The voicing of silence is a wandering figure, never conclusive in its saying, at any time open to other voices.

II. Speaking, not speaking about: Perec's *Espèces d'espaces*

Georges Perec took pride in all his published texts (novels, but also radio plays and film scripts) being very different from one another. *Espèces d'espaces* from 1974, our focus here, speaks directly to the question of nothingness through a roaming exploration of the structure of spaces, exploiting the full range of ambiguity between a variety of colloquial occurrences of the word *rien,* or "nothing," and nothingness

---

[12] Without reconstructing Heidegger's argument for this claim here, it results from the temporality of Being. Since Being has no present, human beings too—as part of what is—are contained only within the past and the future as well. The meaning of *Da-sein* as a human presence is, similarly, one of constantly becoming; in turn, this becoming is determined by our ability, or failure, to respond to Being's absence, i.e., by the ability to voice its silence.

as a concept.[13] The book's first page shows a large, empty square with the caption "Figure 1. Map of the ocean (extract from Lewis Carroll, *The Hunting of the Snark*)." Perec explains in his foreword (Perec, 1974/2000, p. 13):

> This book's subject is not exactly the void but rather what is around, or inside the void (cf. fig. 1). Yet after all, initially there isn't a lot: nothing, the impalpable, practically immaterial: extension, the exterior, that which is exterior to us, that in the middle of which we move about, the surroundings, the adjacent space.

The text is divided into 13 chapters carrying as their title spatial units of increasing size from "Page" to "Bed," "Bedroom" and outward from there all the way to "World" and, finally, "Space." (The only proper noun in the chapter table is "Europe," but that chapter consists of a single line: "One of the five parts of the world.") The theme to be unfolded over the book's chapters is the contingency of the spaces of human life. The physical spaces we move in, and the ways they are circumscribed and separated from one another, make sense to us—as turns out to be Perec's premise—only in virtue of coordinates that are constituted by layers of inscriptions. Spaces come into existence out of "nothing, or almost nothing," and end up "multiple, in pieces, diversified" (ibid., p. 15).

This unruly exploration of nothingness, an exploration full of detours and tangents, is framed by an opening and closing gesture at the memory of the Second World War. "To live," Perec's foreword continues after his characterization of spaces as being brought into existence out of nothingness, "is to pass from one space to another, trying as hard as possible not to bump into anything. Or, if you prefer"—and what follows is a one-page script for a stage play in three acts. The first act, four lines long, has a voice from the off observe:

> "To the north, nothing. To the south, nothing.
> To the east, nothing.
> To the west, nothing.
> In the centre, nothing."

---

[13] There is an English translation under the title *Species of Spaces*. Perec's word play does not readily translate into English; the title can also be read in a much more colloquial rather than zoological register as "kinds" or "sorts" of spaces.

The second act leaves the first three lines unchanged, and replaces the fourth: "In the centre, a tent." The third and last act expands:

> "In the centre, a tent,
> And,
> In front of the tent,
> A military aid busy
> Waxing a pair of boots
> With *Lion Noir* wax!*"

Without further comment or explication, the attribution reads: "Unknown author. Learned around 1947, re-memorized in 1973" (ibid., pp. 16-17).

The penultimate section of the book, followed only by two brief pages of conclusion ("Space (continued and end)"), is a less oblique historical reference. Titled "The Uninhabitable," the section consists solely of a letter which Perec quotes from *Le pitre ne rit pas* [The clown isn't laughing], a collection of documents of National Socialism published by the French writer and resistance member David Rousset in 1948. Written on 6 November 1943, the letter is signed by Rudolf Höss, commandant of the Auschwitz concentration camp. It's strictly on topic for Perec, concerning as it does the creation and demarcation of spaces. It requests the requisition of 200 deciduous trees, 3 to 5 meters high, of 100 tree shoots between a meter and half and 4 meters high, and of 1,000 shrubs between 1 meter and 2.5 meters high, to plant around the camp's crematories as a "green band to designate the camp's natural limit" (ibid., p. 178.)

Let us turn from Perec's historical point of departure to his conceptual point of departure, the connection he draws between nothingness and writing. "The page," the opening chapter of *Espèces d'espaces*, stages writing as a genuine act of creation, but not in the sense of making things up or inventing fictional realities. Rather, the act of writing generates visual distinctions and thereby coordinates, spatial as well as temporal, that make orientation possible—the first step toward the "terrestrial writing," geo-graphy, that Perec traces across *Espèces d'espaces*. In the beginning, for Perec, is not the word but writing. Semantic content is not what matters; in fact, it suffices to reproduce in writing the act of writing: "I write… I write: I write. I write: 'I write.' I write that I am writing. Etc. …" The process of writing, writing anything at all, generates a set of coordinates as the written lines blacken and thereby "vectorise the virgin space" (ibid., pp. 21-22):

> Before, there was nothing, or almost nothing; afterwards there isn't a lot, just a few signs, but that is enough for there to now be an up and a down, a beginning and an end, a right and a left, a recto and a verso.[14]

The void that is the blank page is not the same as "nothing." Rather, that nothingness is the lack of the possibility of orientation before anything at all is on the page. "A few signs" structure the void, not in virtue of signifying or being descriptive of anything in particular but in virtue of providing spatial coordinates that can morph into temporal ones.

"Space," Perec insists, "begins thus, with words alone, signs traced on the white page" (ibid., p. 26). This claim follows a very long list (contained in a two-page sentence) of various pieces of paper that can harbor the traces of the events of human life, moving seamlessly from metro tickets, requests for automatic bill payments, shopping lists and crossword puzzles into the "works" of literature (with their own, parenthetical, list of elements of the labor of writing: e.g., typing day and night, or "trying to tear from what will always seem to be an inconsistent scrawling something else that resembles a text, succeeding, failing, smiling (sometimes)") and work in the sense of a day job like Perec's writing as a lab *documentaliste*. As this list illustrates, Perec's interest is in the mundane, in deciphering how the seemingly most banal of written signs generate the coordinates that render meaningful the spaces of human life.

This interest in the quotidian, the ordinary, and indeed infraordinary (Perec, 1989) as that which escapes our problematization because we fail to perceive it even as a potential object of questioning was a long-standing one for Perec. It was partly inspired by anthropologist Marcel Mauss, by Henri Lefèbvre as a theoretician of the everyday, and by Lefèbvre's student Guy Debord's situationalism. But just as Perec resisted readings of his first, prize-winning novel, *Things,* as a

---

[14] The jump from basic spatial and narrative-temporal distinctions to the reliance on book production techniques and conventions is not left hanging in the air: Right away, Perec proceeds to discussing international paper format norms and calculates how many words are required to fill a book, an entire library, an island.

sociological critique of consumer culture along Lefèbvrian lines, his insistence in *Espèces d'espaces* to look anew at familiar objects is not a matter of expecting us to become simply more attentive to what we usually overlook. Rather, it asks what makes it possible for a scrap of paper to hold a life's traces and yet not be seen as such. It dramatizes the contingency of what we take for granted.

Never one to take too seriously any "idea,"[15] Perec's way of showing the absurdity of attempts to clarify "nothingness" (*le rien*) as a concept on a par with others is to try and think of a useless space, "absolutely and deliberately useless"—and he finds that experiment impossible (ibid., p. 66). "Language itself, it seems to me, turns out to be inept at describing that nothing, that emptiness, as if one could only speak about what is useful and functional." The unthinkable parallels the unsayable for him: He might succeed at thinking of nothing, *à rien* (or so it must be when suddenly one finds oneself having arrived at one metro station without even having noticed leaving the previous one), but not at turning nothingness into a direct object of thought, *penser le rien*. "How to think nothing? How to think nothing without automatically putting something around this nothing, which makes a hole of it, into which one will hurry to put something: a practice, a function, a fate, a look, a need, something that is missing, a surplus?" (ibid., p. 67). Perec claims to have pursued "with docility the infirm [*molle*] idea" of thinking nothingness, only never to arrive anywhere satisfactory (ibid., pp. 68-69).

In contrast, the actually interesting exercise[16] for getting at nothingness, for Perec, is to observe and describe how "nothing happens" (ibid., p. 104)—for example, in a given street and indeed "perhaps with a little systematic attention." His instructions are to note down place, time, date of observation, and the weather too (e.g., the terrace of a café in Saint-Germain, around 7 p.m. on May 15, 1973, stable sunny weather), and then to note what we see, what strikes us. But here is the problem: "Nothing strikes us. We don't know how to see" (ibid., p. 100).

From there, Perec unfolds an exercise of description that renders visible, in a first step, what escapes our attention—or more precisely,

---

[15] One of Perec's examples of the written traces of life is that of "notes taken at some talk, scrawling down something that might come in handy one day (a word play [*jeu de mots*], a stream of words [*jet de mots*], a game of letters, or what one commonly calls an 'idea')" (Perec, 1974/2000, p. 25).

[16] The relevant section in the chapter 'La Rue' is titled *Travaux pratiques*, like the lab session in a science course.

that makes it possible to articulate it, since learning how to "see" is inextricably bound up for him with the process of writing. Through this process, layers of contingency of our lived reality become apparent and, as such, open in principle to transformation. How to do this? "Must proceed more slowly, almost stupidly so. Forcing oneself to write what isn't of interest, what is the most evident, the most common, the dullest" (ibid., p. 100). What are people doing. The many steps involved in parking, locking, double-checking a car. What is and isn't sold in the shops. Bus numbers. Rhythms of cars (squeezed into batches: They are the effect of traffic lights), pedestrians (some careful: They have brought raincoats). "Don't say, don't write 'etc.' Exhaust the subject, even if it seems grotesque, or futile, or stupid. We haven't even looked yet..." (ibid., p. 101).

The exercise is to be continued, continued "until the place becomes improbable," begins to feel not just strange but incomprehensible (ibid., p. 105). To use Perec's opening image of coordinates spanned by writing on a blank page, the act of describing, of listing the literal and metaphorical inscriptions of the street scene removes their semantic function of structuring life and makes the taken for granted appear as such. Perec makes us look anew. Just like the page gains a new meaning as the site of an originary creative act when it is no longer seen merely as void, i.e., the potential the carrier of referential meaning, it becomes possible to imagine the site of observation differently: "make torrential rains rain down, smash everything, make the grass grow," make King Kong appear or Tex Avery's haunted mouse. Or better still, conjure up what is there but out of eyesight—gutters, underground networks of electricity lines or telephone cables—or what was once there. "Resuscitate the Eocene," its layers of limestone and marl, of sand and clay, and of chalk (ibid., p. 106).

A single, unbound page "to be inserted" accompanies the bound pages that constitute *Espèces d'espaces*. In the sentences printed on this little material play with the book format, Perec explains his problem: not to invent space, but to "interrogate it, or even more simply, read it; because what we call ordinariness [*quotidienneté*] is not evidence but opacity: a form of blindness, a form of anaesthesia." If language cannot, as Perec claims, capture nothingness as a concept, it can bring out how we see and hear nothing, and therefore become responsive to that kind of nothingness, turn it into a new kind of potential. Perec's sprawling and exuberant exercise of reading space lays bare coordinates for orientation whose very existence we have forgotten. And it reminds "us," the joint authors over time of what Perec calls "terrestrial writing" (ibid., 156), of another thing we have forgotten, namely that we are its authors.

Much of *Espèces d'espaces* can and has been read as an autobiographical project, brimming as the text is with references to sites of Georges Perec's life, and with the denial of others, such as "The Countryside"—about which he claims "not to have a lot to say... It is an illusion" (ibid., 135), casually disregarding the many events of his life that occurred in places in the countryside, and that would commonly be read as biographically significant (say, his stay in the Vercors during the German occupation of France, or a long love affair mostly lived out at Andé in Normandy). The last two pages in particular lend themselves to being taken to be an author's personal confession, as an articulation of Perec's own search for "stable, immobile, untouchable spaces," spaces such as "the attic of my childhood years, filled with intact memories" when such spaces to do not exist for him, when his spaces are "fragile," to be destroyed by time just like the author will be betrayed by his memories (Perec, 1974/2000, p. 179-180).

But against the background of having read *Espèces d'espaces* as an exploration of nothingness as we have done here, Perec's concluding paragraph in particular appears to have a different emphasis, an emphasis on writing not as an act of remembering or conjuring up imagined memories in the place of those forgotten or never had, but of drawing out elements of reality that hold up—and making the effort, physical and concerted, to perform the transformative act that creates new spaces and transcends the apparently given, to set up the page to say something new. Perec ends *Espèces d'espaces* by reinvoking the *quelques signes*, a few signs, that made all the difference to the "Page" that opened his text by providing coordinates to the "nothing, or almost nothing:" "To write: to try meticulously to retain something, to make something survive: to tear a few precise scraps from the hollowing void, to leave, somewhere, a furrow, a trace, a mark, or a few signs" (ibid., 180).

III There is no "given," but *nothing* there is.

The world in its crushing narrowness examined through the theme of nothingness by both authors, Perec and Heidegger, reclaims in their writings a wider, more open horizon. Both examine human experience through the composite of three elements, language, time and being, but they come at it from poles apart: Heidegger positions the question of the meaning of Being as the "fundamental question of philosophy" (Heidegger 1993, p. 27); Perec explores the quotidian in all its concreteness as the historically generated result of specific human acts. Neither leaves us with a depiction of reality saturated with things where there is no blank space or gaps; both dismantle any notion of a reliable givenness of entities in space and time. Their shared initial move isn't unusual: It is to look for endurance within the contingencies of things. But they are both, and this is unusual in philosophy as well as literature, reversing the picture by finding endurance not through plenitude but through the initial experience of nothingness. As we have seen, what sounds paradoxical at first is the result of elaborate reflection on existential concerns.

Human knowing and experience begins, for both authors, with *nothing* permanent. Heidegger makes this clear through his investigation of the temporality of Being, Perec through his examination of the processes of the construction and deconstruction of the apparently given in its minutest details. The transitory nature of things within the passage of time is not an illusion; the given is not an illusion because it does not exist, but because what exists is not a given. If, with Heidegger, we accept that time is a dimension of Being, there is no atemporal realm in which truths are safeguarded or simply remain. Nevertheless, and this makes the whole difference for both authors, there is something which, according to them, endures. But this something looks far more perishable than we are used to thinking of, a light breeze in the passage of time, the echoing of a sound in space: the human voice. That which is enduring through, and which responds to the experience of nothingness is writing for Perec and the "saying" for Heidegger.

The word alone, written or spoken, would not introduce any endurance if it didn't correspond to a truth. Put differently, words alone do not "have," but introduce endurance only for their specific meaning, a meaning which corresponds to a being in its temporality. The language both Perec and Heidegger are after, in so very different ways, is not a means of representation but a means to articulate what is by echoing what remains. Thus, both are invested in responsive *acts*. They are not trying to solidify what is transitory, but rather to learn how to respond to, or comply with, the contingent nature of the world. For Heidegger, that means to learn how to listen and to transform the experience of silence into a "saying" that reveals some truth of what is. For Perec, it means to learn how to see in every respect different from representing, and to transform what comes into view into writing; such writing draws out elements of reality that transcend the transitory nature of the given.

The kind of knowing that results from the experience of nothingness is therefore not characterized by the "given." Contingencies, rather than a realm of permanent positivity, are sustaining what endures, opening a wide horizon of human creativity each time voicing anew that which remains at any moment. In this sense there is no given, nothing permanent that we could perceive in its immediacy, but nothingness there is. Heidegger's and Perec's "nothing" is not a nihilistic void; rather, the nothingness to which they direct our attention is full of meaning— an abundance rather than privation. Heidegger's nothingness of Being withdrawn and concealed, and Perec's nothingness of coordinates to be written and to be noticed as such, both use and need human language to become audible, perceptible, intelligible. The acts of response to that abundant nothingness are genuine thinking for Heidegger and the true purpose of literature for Perec.

References

Bellos, D. (1995) *Georges Perec: A Life in Words*. London: The Harvill Press.

Carnap, R. (1931) 'Überwindung der Metaphysik durch logische Analyse der Sprache' in *Erkenntnis* 2, 219–241. https://doi.org/10.1007/ BF02028153.

Cassin, B. (2014), ed. *Dictionary of Untranslatables: A Philosophical Lexicon*. Princeton, NJ, and Oxford: Princeton University Press.

Cohen, J. and Zagury-Orly, R. (2021) *L'adversaire privilégié*. Paris: Éditions Galilée.

Gordon, E. P. (2005) *Rosenzweig and Heidegger: Between Judaism and German Philosophy*. Berkeley and Los Angeles, CA: University of California Press.

Heidegger, M. (1959) *Unterwegs zur Sprache*. Stuttgart, Germany: Neske.

Heidegger, M. (1978) *Wegmarken*. Frankfurt am Main, Germany: Vittorio Klostermann.

Heidegger, M. (1993) *Sein und Zeit*. Tübingen, Germany: Max Niemeyer Verlag.

Heidegger, M. (1994) *Bremer und Freiburger Vorträge* Frankfurt am Main, Germany: Vittorio Klostermann. Vol. 79.

Heidegger, M. (2002) *Was heißt Denken?* Frankfurt am Main, Germany: Vittorio Klostermann. Vol. 8.

Heidegger, M. (2003) *Holzwege*. Frankfurt am Main, Germany: Vittorio Klostermann.

Heidegger, M. (2004) *Die Grundbegriffe der antiken Philosophie*. Frankfurt am Main, Germany: Vittorio Klostermann. Vol. 22.

Heidegger, M. (2010) *Being and Time,* transl. J. Stambaugh. New York: State University of New York Press.

Heidegger, M. (2012) *Die Geschichte des Seyns*. Frankfurt am Main, Germany: Vittorio Klostermann. Vol. 69.

Heidegger, M. (2014) *Überlegungen XII-XV (Schwarze Hefte 1939-1941)*. Vol. 96.

Heidegger, M. (2019) *Vier Hefte I und II (Schwarze Hefte 1947-1950)* Vol. 99.

Heidegger, M. (2020) *Winke I und II (Schwarze Hefte 1957-1959)* Vol. 101.

Heidegger, M. (2022) *Vorläufiges I-IV (Schwarze Hefte 1963-1970)* Vol. 102.

Jay, M. (1994) *Downcast Eyes. The Denigration of Vision in Twentieth-Century French Thought.* Berkeley, CA, Los Angeles, London: University of California Press.

Kundera, M. (1988) *The Art of the Novel,* transl. L. Asher. London and Boston: Faber and Faber.

Lyon, J. K. (2006) *Paul Celan and Martin Heidegger. An Unresolved Conversation, 1951-1970.* Baltimore: Johns Hopkins University Press.

Nietzsche, F. (1988) *Idyllen aus Messina. Morgenröte. Die fröhliche Wissenschaft.* Munich: Deutscher Taschenbuch Verlag.

Perec, G. (1974/2000) *Espèces d'Espaces.* Paris: Éditions Gallimard.

Perec, G. (1989) *L'Infra-ordinaire.* Paris: Éditions du Seuil.

Zarader, M. (1990) *The Unthought Debt. Heidegger and the Hebraic Heritage.* transl. Bergo, B., Stanford: Stanford University Press.

Artistic and
Cultural Forms

9

The Vitality of Nothingness in Jing Hao's *Notes on the Art of the Brush*

David Chai

Jing Hao 荊浩 (ca. 850-911) lived at a time of tremendous change in the history of Chinese art. Having briefly served as a minor official, he abandoned his political career in favor of a life of seclusion in the Taihang mountains of his native Shanxi province. Prior to the seventh century, landscape painting in China lacked technical sophistication and was persistently eclipsed by portraiture. In the Tang dynasty (618-907), several factors would see landscape painting become an independent genre of art, spawning essays on its contribution to human creativity and spiritual flourishment: the cursive script of calligraphy, the vitality and movement of the artist's brush, the merits of monochrome ink wash over color, and the notion that nature contains the principles of Buddhism and Daoism. The first art historian of China, Zhang Yanyuan 張彦遠 (815-907), had this to say of ink wash painting:

> Now Yin and Yang fashion and form all things, and the myriad phenomena are strewn and spread far and wide. The mysterious evolution of things goes on without speaking and the divine work of nature operates by itself...For this reason, one may be said to have fulfilled one's aim if one can furnish a painting with all the five colors by the management of ink alone. But if one's mind dwells on the five colors only then the shapes of things will go wrong. Now in painting any subject the things which one should especially avoid are a methodical completeness in delineation and coloring, as well as

extreme carefulness, extreme detail and the display of skill and finish. From this it follows that one should not deplore lack of completeness but rather that completeness is deplorable (Acker, 1954: 185-186).

From the above we can say that landscape painting in the early Tang had already begun to abandon the characteristics of pre-Tang artworks—verisimilitude of ink and completeness in brushstrokes—in favor of monochrome ink wash and incompleteness in brushstrokes, both of which were now associated with visually conveying an object's inner spirit. In his *Notes on the Art of the Brush* (*Bifa ji* 筆法記),[1] Jing Hao argues that a landscape painting can only embody the genuine spirit of nature when it conveys the vital breath (*qi* 氣) of both the painter and natural scene. The question of how a thing's inner state bears upon its outward appearance was not new to the literati of the Tang; what was wholly unexpected was Jing Hao asking this question of landscape painting. While the topic of authenticity lies at the heart of Jing Hao's text, there are other aspects deserving examination, especially its stance that a landscape painting should not be measured by the lifelikeness of its image but the transformative movement of the brushstrokes that created it.

Although Jing Hao does not explicitly mention the concept of nothingness, it grounds his aesthetic system. For example, the breath he speaks of is a vitality not beholden to physical forms but is inherent to the world at large; painters who observe nature and form an image in their mind act according to the receptiveness of nothingness; capturing the essence of nature entails grasping it on a spiritual level so as to convey its ineffability; mastering ink wash is to spontaneously flow with it as it leaves the brush; and, painting a landscape that embodies incompleteness is to balance the used and empty space of the canvass to atmospheric effect, illuminating what the eye cannot see. In addition to expounding upon these qualities, this paper will also investigate how the painter receives the breath of nature as a formless form, allowing it to gestate and transform into the pre-gestural potentiality of the brush, before actualizing it via the placement of ink on the canvas.

---

[1] Several English translations of Jing Hao's essay exist; I will be using that by Munakata, which is reproduced in Bush (2012, pp. 145-148).

Jing Hao's essay revolves around a fictional dialogue between the narrator, an amateur painter living in the Taihang mountains, and an old gentleman whom he meets on one of his excursions. The narrator begins by describing a hidden grove he discovers off the main mountain path. The language is remarkable, a painting in its own right:

> Inside there was a moss-grown path dripping with water, and along it were strange stones enveloped in a mysterious vapor. I went through the path quickly, and found an area covered solely with old pine trees. Among the trees, one had grown to occupy a huge area by itself. Its aged bark was covered with green lichen. It looked as if it were a flying dragon riding the sky, or as if it were a coiling dragon aiming at reaching the Milky Way. The trees that formed a grove looked fresh in spirit and were flourishing in their mutual sustenance. Those which could not form a group crouched by themselves as if to keep their own creeds within themselves. Some trees exposed their winding roots out of the ground; others lay directly across a wide stream; others were suspended over the cliffs and still others crouched in the middle of the ravine. Some grew tearing mosses and cracking rocks. I marveled at this curious sight and walked around admiring the scenery.[2]

It is not accidental that Jing Hao commences his text with a portrayal of the three essential elements of a landscape painting: trees, rocks, and

---

[2] Reading this passage, one cannot but think of the various portrayals of trees in the ancient Daoist classic, the *Zhuangzi* 莊子: Huizi said to Zhuangzi, "I have a big tree called a *shu*. Its trunk is too gnarled and bumpy to apply a measuring line to, its branches too bent and twisty to match up to a compass or square" (Watson, 2013, p. 6); "In the mountain forests that lash and sway, there are huge trees a hundred spans around with hollows and openings like noses, like mouths, like ears, like jugs, like cups, like mortars, like rifts, like ruts" (ibid, p. 7); "Ziqi of Nanbo was wandering around the Hill of Shang when he saw a huge tree there, different from all the rest. A thousand teams of horses could have taken shelter under it, and its shade would have covered them all...looking up, he saw that the smaller limbs were gnarled and twisted, unfit for beams or rafters, and looking down, he saw that the trunk was pitted and rotten and could not be used for coffins. He licked one of the leaves, and it blistered his mouth and made it sore." (ibid., p. 31). Is it a coincidence that Jing Hao's language resembles that of the *Zhuangzi*? Given he employs Daoist imagery throughout his essay, the answer would seem to be no.

water. The narrator's choice of words is designed to instill in the reader a sense of wonderment, movement, and vitality, which is also the essence of ink wash painting. As Jing Hao's text is about the art of brushwork, readers can envision how they would approach said scene. There are elements—the moss-grown path, the lichen-covered tree, the pine tree's bark—needing technically adept brushwork and others—the dew, mist, and stream—demanding mastery of ink, while others still—the coiling pine tree and its winding, hanging, suspended, and crouched roots—call for brushstrokes imbued with the painter's breath and spirit. We must also consider the best way to translate the variegated colors—the green moss and lichen, the white mist and dew, the brown of the pine tree and its roots, the gray rocks, and the blue water—into a palette composed of black ink.

The moss-grown path is a miniature pasture of life and as such, the water it drips must likewise be tiny in size. In contrast are the stones, large enough in size to be enveloped in mist. These stones stand freely in the world, misshapen and carved by the wind and rain, yet they are somehow not open enough to invite living creatures to shelter in their midst. This brings us to the pine trees. The central pine appears as if a living sculpture, its lichen-dressed branches resembling the wings of a dragon and its twisting trunk the dragon's body. Such a spectacle invites closer inspection, and the narrator does so, discovering the network of roots spreading out around his feet. Having such a convoluted stature, the old pine tree refuses to be defined by ruler and square; the deformedness of its circularity surpasses anything a compass can produce. The pine tree is the axel around which its roots radiate, yet this web of tentacles is itself deformed in its circularity, here rising, there sinking, here again twisting, there again turning. Taken in its entirety, the old pine tree is a formless form, a space of overlapping and intertwining tunnels and planes of emptiness. How can anyone possibly paint such an object, let alone do so without the use of color and shadow?

If Jing Hao's text is to serve as a pedagogical tool, its primary image cannot be a run-of-the-mill tree or one that is dilapidated and half-dead; on the contrary, it must be a superlative specimen. The challenge for the painter is how best to symbolize the sublime aura of the old pine tree? Since ink wash paintings do not strive to produce images of formal likeness but spiritual resonance, the painter can only paint in traces so as not to disturb the unity of what is naturally incomplete. What is incomplete about Jing Hao's opening scene? It is not that the pine tree is lacking in some way; rather, incompleteness amounts to balancing the presence of nothingness. The interstitial voids between the pine tree's branches, the nothingness that buttresses the cliff face, the ravine whose existence is fed by its own emptiness, the space enveloping the pine tree that permits the narrator to wander around it—these states of being become complete when the contribution of nothingness is recognized. Formal likeness does not convey the mutual flourishing of being and nothingness because the formlessness of the latter belongs to the realm of the imageless. Only what is imageless preserves its wholeness in that such oneness includes the becoming of formed images. To see the pine tree from the perspective of its form—a compilation of images (i.e., roots, trunk, bark, branches, and needles)—is to miss its continuous and formless shadow.

Ink wash painting in the Tang dynasty was still dependent on an artist physically visiting a natural scene in order to paint it and for observers to grasp its content. In the Song dynasty, it was no longer necessary to travel to scenic spots to witness the magnificence of nature; one could leisurely gaze at an ink wash painting from the comfort of one's home and experience the same level of resonance as if one visited that place in person. This trend would require the creation of new theoretical texts espousing how artists implant their spiritual encounter with nature into their artwork, but in Jing Hao's time, moving away from the technical perfectionism of portraiture and religious iconography was all that mattered. To see how this unfolds in the *Notes on the Art of the Brush*, let us continue reading the text.

Having outlined his discovery of the pine tree, the narrator then speaks of his return to the mountain grove the next day in order to paint this magical specimen. After countless attempts, he finally produces a painting which, he feels, faithfully resembles the old pine. He then jumps ahead in time, to the following spring, where he runs into an old gentleman who asks him what he is doing in the grove. Having answered, the old man asks the narrator if he has heard of the art of brushwork, to which the latter says:

> "Your appearance is that of an old rustic. How can you know the art of the brush?" The old man retorted: "But how can you know what I hold inside?" Hearing this, I was both ashamed and surprised. The old man said: "If

you, a young man, like to study, you can accomplish it in the end. Now, there are six essentials in painting. The first is called breath. The second is called resonance. The third is called thought. The fourth is called scene. The fifth is called brush. And the sixth is called ink."[3]

Having put aside their initial hostility, the old gentleman promptly states there are six essentials (*liu yao* 六要) to painting: breath (*qi* 氣), resonance (*yun* 韻), thought (*si* 思), scene (*jing* 景), brush (*bi* 筆), and ink (*mo* 墨).[4] Four centuries before Jing Hao, Wang Wei 王微 (415-443) penned his *Discussion of Painting* (*Xu hua* 敘畫) wherein he argued that painting should no longer be limited to formal likeness or the production of map-like representations of places:

> What is based in form is infused with the numinous, and what activates transformation is the mind. The numinous is invisible, hence what it is entrusted to does not move. Eyesight has its limits, hence what is seen is not the whole. Therefore, with one reed brush I simulate the embodiment of the great void, and with fragmentary shapes I paint the intelligence of inch-wide pupils.[5]

Closer to Jing Hao's time, Zhu Jingxuan 朱景玄 (ca. 840) had this to say of painting:

---

[3] Munakata's translation of *qi* 氣 as "spirit" is one of many possible ways of understanding this term (the others being vital energy, force, essence, etc.) but to avoid confusion with the character *shen* 神 (spirit, divine), which Jing Hao uses to describe one of four classes of painter (see section 4 below), I have replaced all instances of spirit with "breath." It should also be noted that Jing Hao has not linked painting to the spirit of the painter; Guo Xi 郭熙 (ca. 1023-1085) in the early Song dynasty would instigate this trend. For more, see Chai (2021). Finally, it must be said that Jing Hao demonstrates his familiarity with the *Zhuangzi* when he has the old gentleman respond to the narrator so brusquely—this mirrors the exchange between Zhuangzi and his friend Hui Shi in Chapter 17 of the text— and the narrator's shock at being treated so crudely by the old man, which is comparable to how Confucius felt after his encounter with Lao Laizi in Chapter 26. See Watson (2013, p. 138; p. 229) respectively.

[4] Jing Hao's six essentials are based on the "six methods" of painting established by Xie He 謝赫 (ca. 500-535?): Breath rhythm gives birth to movement, bone method in use of the brush, correspondence to a thing's image and form, following typology in applying color, arrange and plan the position and placement of things, transmission by copying and recording. For more, see Mair (2004).

[5] Bush (2004, p. 70).

I have heard that men of old said that a painter is a sage; doubtless because he searches out that which is beyond heaven and earth, and reveals that which is unillumined by the sun and moon. When he wields a fine pointed brush, an endless variety of things issues forth from his mind. When he displays his talent within a square inch, a thousand miles lie within his grasp. As for conveying the spiritual while determining the material, when the light ink falls upon white silk that which has physical appearance is established, and that which is formless is created.[6]

When Wang Wei speaks of forms infused with the numinous (*ling* 靈), this is no different from Zhu Jingxuan speaking of what lies beyond heaven and earth yet is shrouded in darkness. When Wang Wei states that human vision is limited and partial, this is no different from Zhu Jingxuan observing how ink manifests the invisible spirit, rendering forms while also creating the formless. The great void is thus brought to life in painting for Wang Wei whereas for Zhu Jingxuan, the sagacious painting employs the subtle to penetrate the ineffable. What does Jing Hao have to say of this? According to his six essentials, the breath of nature must resonate with the artist in such a way that the latter's thoughts about the scene in which he stands are not encumbered by the tools of his craft (e.g., brush and ink). Said differently, ink is the language of the painter's thoughts, yet the brush, which serves as an intermediary agent, must somehow embody the breath of nature and painter alike so as to instigate a resonance between them. Should the painter only strive for formal resemblance, the painting will appear lifeless. This is why, upon being told of the six essentials, the narrator says:

> Painting is equivalent to flower [outward appearance]. That is to say, one obtains the genuine when he devotes himself to attaining life-likeness. How could this be distorted?[7]

---

[6] Bush (2012, pp. 48-49). This passage is from Zhu Jingxuan's *On Famous Paintings of the Tang Period* (*Tangchao minghua lu* 唐朝名畫錄) which contains succinct descriptions of roughly 120 painters grouped into four categories: divine (*shen* 神), marvelous (*miao* 妙), talented (*neng* 能), and casual (*yi* 逸).

[7] When it comes to translating *zhen* 真 in the second sentence, Munakata's "reality" is inadequate insofar as *zhen* can be used to describe the internal or external state of any physical or mental object. I have thus changed all instances to "genuine."

There are two reasons for giving this view: It sets the stage for the old gentleman's rebuttal, and it announces that this orthodox approach to painting has become insipid. If Jing Hao holds that painting prior to his day is merely exterior ornamentation (*hua* 華) that strives for life-likeness or resemblance (*si* 似), wherein lies the genuine (*zhen* 真)? If the genuine cannot be obtained within a painting, it must lie outside it, in the object being painted. In the case of landscape painting, the exteriority of the genuine is the entirety of nature, thus to paint nature is to paint its genuineness. This, however, is not the case! The old gentleman explains why:

> Painting is equivalent to measuring. One examines the objects and grasps their genuineness. He must grasp the outward appearance from the outward appearance of the object, and the inner reality from the inner reality of the object. He must not take the outward appearance and call it the inner reality. If you do not know this method, you may even get life-likeness but never achieve genuineness in the painting.

Painting entails demarcating things to create an image knowable as such; however, in order to paint something, one must begin from nothingness, stir the mind from its repose in emptiness, and use the invisibility of breath to guide the brush. Furthermore, to paint a painting whose genuineness transcends the likeness of its forms is to remain vigilant against misconstruing the appearance of said forms for their reality (*shi* 實). Being a distinction of great importance, the narrator asks the old gentleman to clarify what he means by outward resemblance and inner genuineness. The response is this:

> Life-likeness means to achieve the form of the object but to leave out its breath. Genuineness means that the forces of both breath and substance are strong. Furthermore, if breath is conveyed only through the outward appearance and not through the image in its totality, the image is dead.

The tripartite system of resemblance, form, and breath is ordered from least to most important and then transformed and inverted as the genuine, breath, and appearance (*xiang* 象). Resemblance corresponds to appearance, form to breath, and breath to the genuine. Recall the old man said one must weigh or consider (*du* 度) the appearance of things to know what makes them genuine. How one does this is the subject of the next section of Jing Hao's essay, but we can get a preview by returning to Zhang Yanyuan's text:

> The painters of antiquity were sometimes able to transmit likeness of form while at the same time giving importance to bone-energy. They sought to extend their painting beyond mere formal likeness. This is something very difficult to discuss with vulgar people. But in modern paintings, even if by chance they achieve formal resemblance, a spirit resonance does not arise. If they had but used spirit resonance in their pursuit of painting, then formal resemblance would have been immanent in their work...Now the representation of things necessarily consists in formal resemblance, but this likeness of form also requires to be supplemented with bone energy. But bone energy and formal resemblance, while both have their origin in the conception formed by the painter, must finally depend on the use of the brush. (Acker, 1954, pp. 148-150)

The terminology used in this passage is echoed by Jing Hao. There is an explicit argument being made that breath and its resonance will not occur so long as the painter fixates on replicating things in as life-like a manner as possible. Though painters may conceptualize (*yi* 意)—have the intent—to paint something, the realization of this intention inevitably returns to how painters wield their brush. If they infuse it with breath, their images will appear alive; if the brush is taken to be nothing more than a technical instrument, their images will be lifeless. At this point in his essay, Jing Hao has not fully revealed why he is so displeased with earlier painters or how his six essentials will allow painters to explore the intangible side of painting by developing an aesthetic philosophy of breath. We must, therefore, return to the conversation between the narrator and old gentleman.

Having listened to the old gentleman's initial explanation of the craft of painting, the narrator asks for further clarification. Before he gives it, the old gentleman says something odd: "Limitless desire is a threat to life. This is why wise people thoroughly enjoy playing the zither (*qin* 琴), calligraphy, and painting. They replace worthless desires with those [worthy ones]." Given this is the only place where Jing Hao speaks of desire (*yu* 欲), we should be careful not to overemphasize the matter. Nevertheless, we can cite the following passages from the *Zhuangzi* as precedents for the rejection of desire by Jing Hao and others in his day:

> There are five conditions under which the inborn nature is lost. One: when the five colors confuse the eye and cause the eyesight to be unclear. Two: when the five notes confuse the ear and cause the hearing to be unclear. Three: when the five odors stimulate the nose and produce weariness and congestion in the forehead. Four: when the five flavors dull the mouth, causing the sense of taste to be impaired and lifeless. Five: when likes and dislikes unsettle the mind and cause the inborn nature to become volatile and flighty. These five all are a danger to life. (Watson, 2013, p. 96)
> If you try to fulfill all your appetites and desires and indulge your likes and dislikes, then you will bring affliction to the true form of your inborn nature and fate. And if you try to deny your appetites and desires and forcibly change your likes and dislikes, then you will bring affliction to your ears and eyes. (ibid., p. 199)

The Daoist principles of natural harmony and cosmic oneness inspired many treatises on the art of painting, but for Jing Hao it was the concepts of breath, simplicity, and genuineness that influenced him the most. With this, we come to the section of the essay containing the six essentials, four forces of brushwork (*shi* 勢), and two faults (*bing* 病) in painting. To begin, the old gentleman expounds the six essentials:

Breath is obtained when your mind moves along with the movement of the brush and does not hesitate in delineating images. Resonance is obtained when you establish forms while hiding traces of the brush, and perfect them by observing the proprieties and avoiding vulgarity. Thought is obtained when you grasp essential forms eliminating unnecessary details, and let your ideas crystallize into the forms to be represented. Scene is obtained when you study the laws of nature and the different faces of time, look for the sublime, and recreate it with reality. Brush is obtained when you handle the brush freely, applying all the varieties of strokes in accordance with your purpose, although you must follow certain basic rules of brushwork. Here you should regard brushwork neither as substance nor as form but rather as a movement, like flying or driving. Ink is obtained when you distinguish higher and lower parts of objects with a gradation of ink tones and represent clearly shallowness and depth, thus making them appear as natural as if they had not been done with a brush.

In Xie He's formulation, resonance of breath generates movement of life in a painting. Jing Hao expands this by including the heart-mind—recall Wang Wei's claim that the heart-mind initiates transformation—and the need for it to avoid self-doubt when moving the brush. Painting is equivalent to measurement, Jing Hao told us, but painting qua measuring is an activity whose target is resonance of breath and whose directionality is guided by spirit; however, breath and spirit are intangible without being ephemeral, the reason for which is they take the oneness of nothingness as their root. In the words of Zhuangzi: "All that have faces, forms, voices, colors—these are all mere things ... They are forms, colors— nothing more. But things have their creation in what has no form, and their conclusion in what has no change" (Watson, 2013, p. 146). Zhuangzi is here speaking of the Dao, the generative source of the universe, but the Dao cannot appear in a painting without the assistance of breath and spirit, hence it falls upon painters to first embody the Dao and then imbue their artwork with its presence.[8] Seeing as painters partake in the same breath as all other things in the universe, the varying degrees to which their spirit displaces this breath is what differentiates one painting from the next. Should the painter hesitate in moving the brush, this will not only disrupt the flow of breath and disperse the spirit, it will produce artificial brushstrokes. To paint a landscape painting in such a manner is to create a scene that is lifeless.

Resonance for Xie He was the establishment of a painting's structural basis by means of the brush. For Jing Hao, resonance can only occur when brushwork is traceless and harmonious. To be ornamental and hence vulgar with one's brush is to openly take outward appearance as the extent of a thing's genuineness, never for a moment considering the still and darkened spirit within. In their natural state of quietude, breath and spirit become mere traces of their visible selves, receding into the nothingness from which they emerge once the mind and/or body is stirred into action. Painting with an agitated breath or spirit, however, will translate into brushstrokes that are stuttered and jaunted, collapsing under the burden of ink. As the second most important of the six essentials, resonance is the intermediary realm between breath and the images of thinking. Unless painters can release the images in their mind in a manner befitting the atmosphere produced by their breath, resonance will not occur. In the words of Francois Jullien,

> the image ... cannot therefore be fully itself—"alive"—
> except when, far from being cut off from the worldly
> order of phenomena, it remains inhabited by the same
> flow of reactivity that, in its course, ceaselessly brings
> about and also comes about. It does so through breath-
> energy, which continuously makes the image emanate,
> just as it continually makes the world breathe. It

---

[8] Compare this to Brubaker and Wang who write: "...a painted image that is authentic and alive, because it shows objects as existing or inhering within an observable and animating field, just as objects appear in nature to the human eyewitness" hence "the painted image expresses the "inner spirit" of an object in nature authentically when it resonates with the way the landscape is observed and witnessed by the eye of the individual person who is actually within nature" (Brubaker and Wang, 2015, p.61 and p. 63). The problem with this reading is that it remains rooted in the realm of human senses and does not account for the way Jing Hao experiences the world via the non-sensory unity of spiritual harmony with the Dao.

permeates the traces of the painting just as it passes through the veining of the mountain or the arteries of the human body. (Jullien, 2009, pp. 239-240)

Corresponding to a thing's image and form—reflecting its likeness—representation is transformed by Jing Hao into a mode of thinking whereby only the essential traits of a thing are considered and incorporated into a painting. Thinking in free images as opposed to copying the models of old masters allowed ink wash painters to wield the brush in innovative and unencumbered ways. This newfound mode of expression also demonstrates the generative potentiality of nothingness. Breath moves via the emptiness of nothingness, resonating with the things it comes into contact with. The retention and releasement of breath relies on the presence, or lack thereof, of nothingness, not the thing within which breath circulates. Should the breath stimulate the mind, images form, but these are yet to be articulated and fully formed, hence they wander in and out of realization within the mind until they congeal into thought. Thought in its pre-verbalized state has yet to leave the domain of generative nothingness that is the playground of the imagination. The tripartite system of breath, image, and thought is the extent of the genuine; once a painter moves beyond them into the realized world of ink, the pulse of the genuine fades with each stroke of the brush. Genuine representation thus preserves thought of pure simplicity, images rendered ephemeral by nothingness, and the breath whose essence never departs from the oneness of the Dao.

The three remaining essentials—scene, brush, and ink—have the task of taking what is but a collection of shadows in the mind and turning them into less elusive forms. In doing so, they must also ensure that scene conforms to the laws of nature, brushwork mirrors the natural motions of the wind, and ink replicates the natural gradations of a wave coming ashore. Given scene utilizes the brush to express itself, and brush depends on ink to signify what is otherwise a beclouded form of self-expression, to produce a painting in the rote manner of our narrator is to fall into the trap of mistaking external appearance for internal reality. This is, in the words of the *Zhuangzi*, "to stare at muddy water and be misled into taking it for a clear pool" (Watson, 2013, p. 165). Staying with the theme of water, the following passage from the *Zhuangzi* can also be applied to the art of ink wash painting: "It is the nature of water that if it is not mixed with other things, it will be clear, and if nothing stirs it, it will be level. But if it is

dammed and hemmed in and not allowed to flow, then it, too, will cease
to be clear" (ibid., p. 121). Pure, clear water is analogous to the breath
that is not dispersed outside of the body; in an unagitated state, breath
empties itself of desires and thoughts, becoming one with the nothingness
facilitating its nebulous form. If, however, the breath is blocked or
neglected, it turns stagnant and becomes the catalyst for disease. When
viewed in the context of landscape painting, the resonance between the
breath of nature and that of the painter is akin to clear water; allowed to
flow uninhibitedly, this breath of the Dao is received by all things and
levels itself within them according to their physical disposition. Through
its self-leveling it remains still and clear; this is also true of the painter
whose thought is grounded in the inner reality of things and not driven
by their external form. This is why the first three of Jing Hao's essentials
carry more weight than the last three.

Before he moves on and discusses the four forces of brushwork,
the old gentleman digresses into a discussion of the four principal
categories of painting: divine (*shen* 神), sublime (*miao* 妙), distinctive
(*qi* 奇), and skillful (*qiao* 巧). To paraphrase the old gentleman, divine
paintings have no artificial elements, and their images are spontaneously
created; sublime paintings are the result of pondering the essence of all
things in the world and ensuring the brush captures this when outlining
their forms; distinctive paintings contain brushwork that is untrammeled
and unexpected, yet not enough thought has been given to matching
objects from the real scene to those on the canvas; finally, skillful
paintings might be known for their minutiae of seductive beauty, but they
heedlessly copy the outer form of things, thus diverging from true images
filled with breath. The significance of this brief overview will become
clear when Jing Hao assesses painters from previous times in the next
section of his essay.

Since the aforementioned categories are self-explanatory, let us
proceed to Jing Hao's idea that there are "four forces" (*si shi* 四勢) at
work when using the brush: muscle (*jin* 筋), flesh (*rou* 肉), bone (*gu* 骨),
and breath. The old gentleman elaborates:

> If a stroke is discontinued but its force continues, its force
> is called muscle. If a stroke with thickening and thinning
> width is filled with substantial inner force, its force is
> called flesh. If a stroke is vigorous and upright, with force

to give life to dead matter, its force is called bone. If each
stroke delineating the whole painting is undefeatable, the
total force is called breath. From this it may be understood
that a stroke with the ink of too thick and unrefined quality
loses its structural integrity, while a stroke with the ink
of weak color is defeated in the right breath. The stroke
whose force of muscle is dead cannot have the force of
flesh either. The stroke which is completely interrupted has
no muscle. The stroke with a seductive beauty has no bone.

Jing Hao spends very little time analyzing these forces; besides this paragraph,
the only other place they are mentioned is in a single sentence just before
the narrator's poem on the pine tree at the end of the essay. Nevertheless,
the four forces are related to the six essentials and add an important layer
to the aesthetic framework Jing Hao is constructing. The technical names
given to these forces of the brush might be anatomical, but each embodies a
principle of motion that takes it ever closer to the all-embracing unity of the
Dao. Muscle's movement is one of continuation, flesh's movement is one of
inner force, bone's movement is one of restoring life, while the movement
of breath is insurmountable. Said differently, muscle symbolizes the body,
flesh symbolizes the mind, bone symbolizes the will, and breath symbolizes
the spirit; moreover, the body is tied to physical sensations, the mind is tied
to emotions, the will is tied to spirit, and spirit is tied to the Dao. In this way,
the painter whose spirit is one with the Dao will have a breath that animates
bone, flesh, and muscle collectively. As necessary as these forces are, they
cannot be allowed to dominate breath, otherwise the resultant image will be
an empty work of ornamentation. Collectively,

> force in a landscape painting is the dynamic configuration
> that visually epitomizes the interaction and tension
> among various elements of the landscape. The artist
> must convey not only the breath resonance of depicted
> objects, such as trees and rocks in a landscape, but also
> the movement and flow arising in their interaction—
> namely, the dynamic configuration of the whole scene.
> (Kang, 2022, pp. 32-33)

This is why Jing Hao declares "different formations of mountains and streams are formulated by the combinations of breath and force." The ratio of breath to muscle, flesh, and bone directly determines what, if any, faults lie within a painting. According to the old gentleman, the first fault involves disproportionate or ill-placed objects, while the second fault is the absence of breath and resonance, or objects that violate the rules of nature. The first fault can be rectified with brush and ink, but the second cannot. To substantiate this claim, Jing Hao has the old gentleman lecture the narrator on the nature of different tree species before expounding the merits and faults of historically important painters. This discussion forms the longest section of the text and is where Jing Hao brings together all his arguments on why ink wash painting is the best medium for capturing the sculptural forms of nature. It is also where he reveals his most significant tenet: Painting is the realization of possibility.

Painting qua realizing possibility has one poignant precondition: Before one can paint a cloud, forest, or landscape, one must grasp their origin (*yuan* 源). It is fitting that the old gentleman uses trees to exemplify this principle of origin; not only is the tree the foundational image in the essay, conveying the spirit of a tree is one of the most challenging tasks facing a painter. As if to prove this point, the old gentleman commences his discourse with the following:

> Every tree grows according to its natural disposition. Pine trees may grow bent and crooked, but by nature they are never too crooked. They are sometimes densely and sometimes rather sparsely placed; they are neither green nor blue. They are upright from the beginning. Even as saplings their soul is not lowly, but their form is noble and solitary. Their branches may bend down and lie low, but they turn in an opposite direction and do not droop to the ground. Piling layer over layer, they resemble a fortress. Indeed, the pine trees in the forests are like the moral character of virtuous men which is like the breeze. To paint them as soaring or coiling dragons with their branches and needles in mad confusion, therefore, is not at all in harmony with the spirit and rhythm of the pines.

The pine (*song* 松) tree has been a fixture of Chinese landscape painting since the genre's inception, and its ability to retain its color year-round and survive inhospitable climates made it one of the few objects in nature to be associated with the moral norms of Confucianism. Indeed, Jing Hao appears to support this view when he says the upright nature and noble form of the pine aligns with the character of the gentleman (*junzi* 君子) whose virtue transforms society in a manner akin to wind blowing over a field of grass.[9] One should not, Jing Hao says, paint the pine as a soaring or coiling dragon because this would violate the harmony between its spirit and rhythm. Has Jing Hao forgotten his description of the old pine at the start of the essay? What are we to make of this disparity? Let us read the remainder of this paragraph on trees before making any assumptions:

> The arborvitae is by nature full of motion. It is twisted and coiled. It is vigorous; its leafage is abundant, but has no flowers. Its joints are regular, and its veins follow the course of the sun. Its leaves are like knotted threads, while the branches are like clothes of hemp. Therefore, one should paint arborvitae like a serpent or a floss of silk. To draw its soul empty and its position twisted, is not at all correct. Besides these, there are catalpas, pawlonias, camellias, oaks, elms, willows, mulberries, and pagoda trees. Each of them is different in its form and natural disposition. Even if the trees look alike in the distant view, they ought to be clearly individualized.

Arborvitae (*bai* 柏) trees are notable for their flattened, outwardly splayed branchlets. They are by nature twisted and coiled and are to be portrayed in a serpent-like pose. This idea was not unique to Jing Hao; we find it in the writings of later figures such as Han Zhuo 韓拙 (ca 1095-1125) who in his *Collective Writings on the Purity of Landscape* (*Shanshui Chun quanji* 山水純全集) says: "Trees without structure twist and wind in a confused fashion and are deficient in force. But, if only stiffness and hardness are stressed, without turns and bends, then they are deficient in

---

[9] The analogy of the gentleman and the wind is a reference to Book 12 of the *Analects* by Confucius, which says: "The virtue of the gentleman is like the wind; the virtue of the petty people like the grass. When the wind blows over the grass, surely it will bend" (Watson, 2007, p. 83).

a sense of life" (Bush 2012, p. 149). Interestingly, Han Zhuo adopts Jing Hao's image of the old pine tree reaching for the Milky Way and combines it with the above-mentioned moral virtue of the Confucian gentleman:

> Pine trees are like noblemen; they are the elders among trees. Erect in bearing, tall and superior, aloft they coil upward into the sky and their force extends to the Milky Way. Their branches spread out and hang downward, and below they welcome the common trees. Their reception of inferiors with reverence is like the virtue of the gentleman whose conduct should be "catholic and not partisan." (Bush, 2012, p. 149)

Other painters at the time, especially those in the Song dynasty, say remarkably similar things. If the notion that certain species of tree exhibit physical traits reflective of a spirit bearing the hallmarks of Confucianism, it would be reasonable to assume other species of tree personify the spirit of Daoism. Be this as it may, the point is that we cannot take the above example as indicative of all pine trees, for they clearly differ in their expression of breath and the painter must recognize this or else resonance will not arise. This is what the *Zhuangzi* calls "matching the heavenly with the heavenly."[10]

Looking at the imagery underlying the old gentleman's words, the use of movement and spatial layering is superb. The role of this imagery not only attests to the need to perfect one's brushstrokes, it enlivens the sedate, one-dimensional depiction of trees that were the norm before the Tang dynasty. Jing Hao's three-dimensional imaginings also paved the way for Guo Xi to later proclaim that to gaze upon a sublime landscape

---

[10] An expression from the story of woodcarver Qing in the *Zhuangzi*. See Watson (2013, p. 152). On this point, I cannot support Willard Peterson's criticism of Martin Powers, which reads: "Thus for Powers *xiang* [image] seem to be products, expressions of dynamic structure "in which some kind of action is implicit." ... Powers undoes his own interpretation of *xiang* by relocating it from the silk of the landscape painting to the "natural scenery." In this added sense, the *xiang* is not just "there all over the tree for all to see," which implies that *xiang* is an aspect of appearance and perception. It is also, for Powers, an attribute of the tree. As he puts it, "One suspects that, for Jing Hao, the significance, the expressive figure (i.e., the *xiang*), is 'there' in the tree, whether we see it or not, but in order for it to enter the painting, the artist has to see it first." In this sentence, *xiang* cannot be a "consequent or result of some other activity;" it is there prior to, and regardless of, anyone's perception or depiction of it." See Peterson (2000, p. 241).

painting was akin to being spiritually transformed. As sensuous as the old gentleman's imagery is, it is still the product of the force of breath. With this point in mind, the old gentleman continues to instruct the narrator by turning to the properties of the other objects comprising a landscape painting: the mountain, its streams and waterfalls, and clouds. After naming the various features of a mountain, its streams, and clouds, the old gentleman reminds the narrator of the importance of being faithful to these formal features or risk producing a work that is incorrect while at the same time bearing in mind the need to grasp their essential features while disregarding variances in their minor details. He then says this: "Realize fully what is possible and what is not, and then later one can master the brush technique."

This prompts the narrator to ask: "Who are the most perfect among the learned of ancient times?" The old gentleman's reply consists of 11 people divided into three groups: Lu Tanwei 陸探微 and Zhang Sengyao 張僧繇 form the first group; Zhang Zao 張璪, Qu Ting 麴庭, the priest Baiyun 白雲尊師, Wang Youcheng 王右丞, General Li 李將軍, the recluse Xiang Rong 項容山人, and Wu Daozi 吳道子 form the second group; Chen Yuanwai 陳員外 and the priest Dao Fen 僧道芬 form the third group. The artists of the first and third groups garnered no praise from the old gentleman. Of those from the second group, Zhang Zao's use of brush and ink was full of breath and resonance; Qu Ting and Baiyun displayed an unfathomable depth of breath and form; Wang Youcheng's brush and ink contained subtle a breath and resonance; General Li exhibited beautiful brushwork, but his use of ink was weak, Xiang Rong was a master of ink, but his brush strokes lacked bone; and Wu Daozi's brushwork was incomparable, but his use of ink was weak.[11] With this historical interlude over, the old gentleman says to the narrator: "I have revealed to you the method of painting, though it cannot be done satisfactorily with words."

Despite the concise evaluation of these esteemed masters, the old gentleman acknowledges the difficulty of conveying the intangible side of painting. Such an admission brings to mind the words of the *Zhuangzi*, firstly on the craft of making wheels—"You can get it in your hand and feel it in your mind. You cannot put it into words, and yet there is a knack to it somehow. I cannot teach it to my son, and he cannot learn it from

---

[11] For biographical details about these figures, see Munakata (1974, fn 55-70).

me" (Watson, 2013, p. 107)—and secondly on the physical attributes of things: "We can use words to talk about the coarseness of things, and we can use our minds to visualize the fineness of things. But what words cannot describe and the mind cannot succeed in visualizing—this has nothing to do with coarseness or fineness" (ibid., p. 129). Does the challenge for the old gentleman lie with the breath or its resonance? The wheelwright is neither hindered by the wood nor his tools when they are taken in isolation but is obstructed by the act of bringing them together. The painter's canvas, brush, and ink stand alone in their being yet it is on account of how well they are harmonized that the created image is imbued with spirit. This bringing together and harmonizing of things takes place in the intervals between them, but said intervals are simply the ubiquitous presence of nothingness. The method of painting the old gentleman speaks of is thus one whereby the painter abandons himself to nature and in so doing, rediscovers his genuine self.

In Daoism, the genuine self is a selfless self that forgets its selfhood so as to wander carefree in the harmonizing oneness of the Dao.[12] Forgetting the self is not a transcendental act; on the contrary, it facilitates the resonance between a painter, the act of painting, and the scene being painted.[13] The releasement of self to the oneness of the Dao uplifts it from its mundane pursuit of ornamental accoutrements such that the creative process becomes one of inversion and reversal. Conjoining with the non-self of the Dao, the authentic painter paints with and not over nothingness, breathes the unified breath of nature and not that of humanity, and manipulates brush and ink in such a way that the original purity of the canvas is not concealed. Realizing fully what is possible and what is not, the painter who is able to traverse the corporeality of nature and enter its inner sanctum is one whose selfhood changes along with the seasons and whose likes and dislikes play no part in the creative process. Landscape painting is hence a dynamic art form, and in order for the painter to convey the genuineness of nature, his breath must not betray the essence of the scene encountered at that moment in time. This means the painter should not try to sanitize the hardship of a season or glorify its abundance but capture the essence of its breath as it ebbs and flows.

---

[12] See Chai (2022b).
[13] This principle is also applicable to sculpture. See Chai (2022a).

The narrator's response to the old gentleman's pronouncements is to show him a painting he made of a strange pine tree, to which the old gentleman says: "The flesh of your brushwork lacks method; the muscles and bones are not at all in harmony. How can you paint such pine trees well? I have already taught you the method of brushwork." Feeling confident in his instruction, the old gentleman hands the narrator several blank scrolls and demands he paint something, adding: "Your hand is my mind. When I listen to your words, I shall then know your action. Can you now summarize what I have said to you?" The narrator expresses his gratitude and answers as follows: "To teach and enlighten is the task of the wise and virtuous men. Happily or unhappily, one cannot escape from such influence. Whether it be for real or woe, it will influence me. Your instruction is such that I dare not disobey you." Having declared his allegiance to the old gentleman's method of the brush, the narrator spontaneously composes a poem on the pine tree. Containing attributes that are unmistakably Confucian—the pine is chaste (*zhen* 貞), powerful (*shi* 勢) yet reverent (*gong* 恭), and takes after the gentleman (*junzi* 君子)—it also uses visual cues from Daoism, such as the shadow, the brooding (*you yin* 幽陰) and mysterious (*meng rong* 蒙茸) nature of the vines and creepers, the sound the pine makes when the wind blows, and the sound condensing into emptiness (*ning kong* 凝空) once the wind stops.[14] One would think the old gentleman would be pleased by such a poem, but he heaves a sigh and, after a long pause, tells the narrator that if he can forget brush and ink (*wang bimo* 忘筆墨), he will have a genuine scene (*zhen jing* 真景).[15] The essay thereupon concludes with the narrator lamenting how his search for the old gentleman the next day came to naught, thus he has taken the old gentleman's method of the brush as his guiding principle in painting.

Jing Hao's *Notes on the Art of the Brush* appeared at a time when landscape painting in China had only just started to be recognized as an alternative genre to portraiture or religious iconography. Although modeled after Xie He's six laws of painting, Jing Hao's six essentials

---

[14] An allusion to the following passage from the *Zhuangzi*: "The Great Clod belches out breath, and its name is wind. So long as it doesn't come forth, nothing happens. But when it does, then ten thousand hollows begin crying wildly...In a gentle breeze they answer faintly, but in a full gale the chorus is gigantic. And when the fierce wind has passed on, then all the hollows are empty again" (Watson, 2013, p. 7).

[15] Both the *Daodejing* and *Zhuangzi* subscribe to the notion that forgetting is a way to achieving authenticity in one's life.

broke new ground with its inclusion of breath. What is more, Jing Hao's argument that resonance of breath reveals the genuineness of nature paved the way for others to formulate aesthetic theories and images of nature that were more firmly rooted in a philosophical worldview, not beholden to set moral values or intellectual frameworks. Though intimated in Jing Hao's essay, we do not see the wholehearted adoption of Daoist naturalism as found, for example, in the thought of Guo Xi. Be this as it may, Jing Hao's effort to inject an element of dynamism into his artwork via the concept of breath-resonance would not have been possible without the inclusion of nothingness qua creative potentiality. As one of the earliest proponents of monochrome ink wash, Jing Hao would help transform the way the Chinese viewed and practiced painting, and for this, he is worthy of our continued attention.

References

Acker, William, trans. (1954; 1974) *Some Tang and Pre-Tang Texts on Chinese Painting*. 2 volumes. Leiden, Netherlands: Brill.

Brubaker, David and Chunchen Wang. (2015) *Jizi and His Art in Contemporary China: Unification*. Heidelberg, Germany: Springer.

Bush, Susan and Hsio-Yen Shih, eds. (2012) *Early Chinese Texts on Painting*. Hong Kong: Hong Kong University Press.

Bush, S. (2004) The Essay on Painting by Wang Wei (415-453) in Context. In Zong-Qi Cai (ed.) *Chinese Aesthetics: The Ordering of Literature, the Arts, and the Universe in the Six Dynasties*. Honolulu: University of Hawaii Press, pp. 60-80.

Chai, D. (2021) Guo Xi on Painting the Invisible Gaze of the Dao. *Journal of Chinese Literature and Culture*, 8 (2), pp. 287-306.

Chai, D. (2022a) Zhuangzi, Heidegger, and the Self-Revealing Being of Sculpture. In Chai, D. (ed.) *Daoist Resonances in Heidegger: Exploring a Forgotten Debt*. London: Bloomsbury, pp. 163-179.

Chai, D. (2022b) Zhuangzi on No Emotion. In Chong, K. (ed.) *Dao Companion to the Philosophy of the Zhuangzi*. Cham, Switzerland: Springer, pp. 199-215.

Jullien, F. (2009) *The Great Image Has No Form, On the Nonobject through Painting*. Translated by Jane M. Todd. Chicago: University of Chicago Press.

Kang, Y. (2022) *Zhen* as the Ideal of Landscape Painting in *Bifaji*. *Sungkyun Journal of East Asian Studies*, 22 (1), pp. 27-47.

Mair, Victor. (2004) Xie He's "Six Laws" of Painting and their Indian Parallels. In Zong-Qi Cai (ed.) *Chinese Aesthetics: The Ordering of Literature, the Arts, and the Universe in the Six Dynasties*. Honolulu: University of Hawaii Press, pp. 81-122.

Munakata, Kiyohiko and Yoko H. Munakata. (1974) Ching Hao's "Pi-fa-chi:" A Note on the Art of Brush. *Artibus Asiae Supplementum*, 31, pp. 1-9 and 11-56.

Peterson, W. (2000) Perspective on Readings of "The Record of the Method of the Brush." In Pauline Yu et al. (eds.) *Ways with Words: Writing about Reading Texts from Early China.* Berkeley, CA: University of California Press, pp. 236-244.

Powers, M. (2000) How to Read a Chinese Painting: Jing Hao's *Bifaji.* In Pauline Yu et al. (eds.) *Ways with Words: Writing about Reading Texts from Early China.* Berkeley, CA: University of California Press, pp. 219-236.

Watson, B. trans. (2007) *The Analects of Confucius.* New York: Columbia University Press.

Watson, B. trans. (2013) *The Complete Works of Zhuangzi.* New York: Columbia University Press.

10

Thoughts on Nothingness from Japan

James W. Heisig

The picture of nothingness I would like to lay out here is no more than a small snippet cut from a tapestry too immense and too intricately spun to take in all at once. And that is only the front side of the weave. With a bigger talent, I might have turned it over to look at the entanglements and crisscrossings of so many slender threads of ideas wound together over the course of an extended intellectual history, long ignored by Western philosophy, to produce the conceptual bundle we call "nothingness." I am tempted to pause here and own up to the limitations of my account, but all of that, together with the chronic mesh of jargon that scholars have devised in pursuit of clarity, seems out of place here. My aim is simpler: to argue that talk about nothingness, in particular as it appears in 20th-century Japanese philosophy, is nothing to take lightly.

What is the most absolute thing you can say about reality? What is the class of all classes, the universal of all universals? In other words, what is the most general concept that can be thought to embrace every thought we have about reality?

At first sight, the concept of "being" cannot fill that role because everything that is is always becoming. Insofar as beings are radically relative to time and space, no one being can represent the permanent universality of the most general of all concepts. For the scholastics, being is only real when it is tied to a particular essence, that is, when it has a substance to hold that being in place and allow it to retain its individual identity. And since essence cannot actually exist without accidents—that is, properties subject to change—to be real is to be impermanent. This suggests that perhaps it is not the fact of "being" but only the quality of being or "beingness" that can be said to be the universal of all universals, that which makes reality real.

To say beings are real because they have beingness is an empty claim, an answer that accounts to a tautology: For a being to be real is for it to possess the quality of beingness. At the same time, if "becoming" were the all-encompassing universal of reality, the class of all classes would be unstable, defeating its role as a universal.

But now, what if there were a discreet and superior being in reality whose very essence was beingness and which was not subject to change? This would mean that "that than which nothing greater can be conceived" would not be merely an idea but would actually be present among all the many beings whose reality is limited by becoming. This is how Anselm came to his notion of God as a being-without-becoming, without having to define God as simply the total beingness of all reality. Something similar is also implied in Aquinas's theory of participation in virtue of which all real beings share in the beingness of a being whose very essence it is to be without becoming.

This whole line of argument—including the Aristotelian assumption that the actual existence of everything that is real is possessed of an underlying substance—was foreign to Japanese philosophy prior to its contact with Western thought. The tradition that it was fed from India through China considered the notion of substance to be bound to a provisional but ultimately illusory view of the world. To be real was to become, and becoming was always the constellation of concrete but impermanent conditions, not the continuation of an essence which remained more or less stable as its properties underwent change. Given the central role that the concept of a Supreme Being or a Primer Mover played in Western philosophy, dialogue with that tradition made it necessary to find a place for the concept of God. Not surprisingly, they were more sympathetic to pantheistic thinkers like Spinoza or the panentheistic tendencies in German idealism. These sympathies were not so much a way of taking sides in a longstanding debate within Western philosophy as they were an attempt to absorb the whole discussion into their own very different perspective on reality.

To begin with, Japanese philosophy accepts, as a matter of definition, that to be is to become. Everything real, without exception, is caught up in the flux of coming to be and passing away. There is nothing in human experience to indicate otherwise. The class of beings exempt from becoming is a class with no members, a metaphysical fantasy that holds for all of philosophy and not just the worldviews of East Asia. But if what is is always coming to be something other than it happens to be at any given moment, the question remains: Is this the whole of reality? If not, where does the whole of reality ultimately lie? The answer—in nothingness.

Obviously, the notion of nothingness is more than simply a counterposition to philosophies of being. For one thing, prior to contact with Western philosophy, there was no universal of being in the philosophical traditions that shaped the Japanese notion of nothingness. Strictly speaking, there was not even a word for "being" in the sense of "beingness" until the need arose in connection with the translation of Western philosophical texts. The word that was chosen meant "having at hand"; and its opposite, nothingness, "not having at hand." Thus, for example, when we find translations of the *Daodejing* that read, "being is superior to non-being" or "being is generated from non-being," these are anachronisms imposed in a recent century on ancient terms that refer to the presence and absence of things.

The idea of nothingness, then, was not parasitic on an idea of being. It was not one side of a dualism distinguishing what is from what is not, or what is and what can be. It was not a privative, or any other negation of the real for that matter. That said, the varieties of nothingness in Eastern philosophy are as rich as varieties of the concept of being from Parmenides to Heidegger. Unlike notions of nothingness and nonbeing defined in opposition to the universal of being, the nothingness we are talking about here emerged from traditions of thought all their own.

To look on ultimate reality as nothingness is to affirm, in part, that that which holds the identity of individual things in place through time is impermanent, not a substantial essence but a constellation of conditions which are forever in flux and lacking a permanent center. If these constellations are manifestations of a final horizon of reality not subject to change, it could not be merely a superior, unconditioned being. It can only be a nonentity, not in the simple sense of something lacking the reality that actual entities have but as a nothingness that can never be reduced to a particular, identifiable thing among other things. Despite the feeling the work evokes, nothingness is not primarily a negation of anything, let alone a negation of the universality of being. It is a positive concept all its own. Its logical consequences entail certain negations, but it must be more than the sum of those negations.

As the most abstract of all abstractions, the universal of being is a common denominator that compresses things into unity by distracting from the specificities that make them what they actually are. It is a kind of shared identity which overrides individual identities, a principle of unity that wraps the many into a One. The universal of nothingness is less abstract. Its aim is not so much to structure reality rationally around a principle of unity as it is to protect the fragile harmony of diversity. For this reason, it would be the crassest error to think that nothingness means that nothing at all exists. To make such a claim would require a place from which to review reality and conclude that none of it is actually there—a claim that is already refuted by the very fact that it can be made at all. On the contrary, nothingness begins from our recognition that our dim rational credentials, as often as not, diminish our ability to see things just as they are.

There is no underestimating the stimulating effects that Western philosophies of being had on Japan. Among the young scholars dispatched to Europe in the 19th century were those charged with studying "philosophy," which the authorities had long supposed to be the cradle of science and the crucible of ideas that made modernization possible. Unlike the technology, industrialization, and the structuring of financing, schooling, and politics, there was never any thought of transplanting whole forests of philosophical thinking into the soil of Japanese culture. The aim was always a way to understand how the West understood itself in order better to secure Japan's place in the community of nations. It took some time to settle on a term to find the right word to translate philosophy, one that would define it as an academic discipline without having to redefine Japan's own intellectual history as a subset of the West's. It was only in the last decades of the 20th century that talk of "Japanese philosophy" came to be seen as a source of pride rather than a vestige of colonialism. The story of how that came about is inseparable from a circle of thinkers that formed around the illustrious figure of Nishida Kitarō (1870–1945), the so-called Kyoto School, and their philosophy of nothingness. Most of what I have to say here is drawn from what I have read of their work.

I have no mind to make their case for nothingness sound more familiar than it is. Not that it is more unreasonable than I make it out to be, just perhaps more disagreeable. So let us be clear: The idea of nothingness throws a sabot in the wheels of Western philosophy. If the sabotage that philosophies of being worked on the Japanese mind produced something new and unexpected, I see no reason not to expect the same from the introduction of philosophies of nothingness into worldviews by and large unprepared for them.

The idea of nothingness feeds on and broods over a long history of ideas marked by three interlocking assumptions: the idea of reality as an appearance empty of stable, accessible content; the idea that letting go and wonderment are superior to clinging and certitude; the idea of the "self" as a guiding but ultimately misguided fiction. None of these ideas, of course, is without a clear analog in the history of philosophy that traces its origins back to the Greeks, but their crystallization about the idea of nothingness gathers and directs reason into a distinctive view of the world.

I find it useful to single out four salient aspects of nothingness, each of them associated with a Japanese term that helps keep them in context: mu, engi, soku, and muga.

Mu, the absolute of nothingness

Everything that is real has its identity, a oneself, an itself, a himself, or a herself. By definition, an identity is what holds an entity in place and keeps it from disintegrating into its surroundings. To be "in place" is to have a specific locus within a defined place, which functions as its embracing "universal." Without it, it would not be possible to locate anything. The is as true of ideas as it is of the people who entertain them. Take the simple judgment, "The willows are green." The locus of that idea is mind. It is what it is because of the reasoning mind that defines it as such. And mind, in turn, is located in consciousness.

But now, clearly the mind is not identical with the judgments it makes, because judgments refer to a place outside of consciousness, a wider place that envelops consciousness and all its functions. The claim is that the willows are green, but the fact is, the willows are not green in the place where the claim is being made. They are green somewhere else. The very awareness of a thinker thinking thoughts breaks through the walls of mind to the wider landscape of a world that can be thought about. In other words, knowing is not all there is; there must also be something knowable. The mind cannot understand itself except as one element in a more embracing intelligible world, a world coming to be and passing away interminably in time and space.

The fact that mind is part of that world means that its will to know is not the final will. The mind's desire to know is located in a world which, we may say, desires to be known for the simple reason that it includes minds desiring to know. This coincidence of opposites—the mind's desire to know and the world's desire to be known—leads us to ask where the universal of will or desire itself is to be placed. The only answer is: nowhere. Will or desire as such is not a function of any higher entity; it is not located anywhere and does not belong to anything. Not surprisingly, Nishida's first intuition was to follow Hegel's lead and classify it as an "absolute." It is the final place that nothing in the world of being and becoming can embrace as a more encompassing universal. It is a universal of mu, of which it can only be said that it does not itself exist and yet it is manifest in everything that exists.

The most absolute thing you can say about reality, the universal of all universals, the place that envelops all places, is that it is not a universal idea or a place at all, that it has no identity in existence because it has no defining place, and precisely for that reason its reality is manifest in everything that has its place in existence. Conversely put, the idea that things are defined and limited and have identities only has meaning against a backdrop that is indefinite, unlimited, and unidentifiable. There can be no final place to embrace all places any more than there can be time before time, a cause of causation, or an unenclosed universe. Far from negating the world of being or minimalizing it, nothingness is its most positive affirmation. It is the one thing that cannot be negated, the one thing that everything that is bears witness to. It is not that it lacks defining qualities, but rather that no defining qualities could exist except against a background that is not limited by them. It is like a series of concentric circles, each providing a location in existence for what it envelops, until the final circle fragments and scatters into a nothingness beyond being.

My resume may make it seem that, with slight adjustments, the notion of an absolute mu would be fairly covered by the idea of a Supreme Being or an Unmoved Mover. For example, teologia negativa, the affirmation of God through the negation of anything that the human mind can affirm about a divine being, would seem to overlap handily with the reasons for introducing the idea of nothingness I have extracted from

Nishida's "logic of place." There are three main reasons for resisting this line of argument.

First, the metaphysical function of mu is different from that of a Supreme Being. Its primary question is not "Where do things come from?" but "Where are things located?" It is not a matter of the whence, which seeks to explain the present as the repository of past causes, that is dominant but rather of the where, which seeks the conditioned context within which things "take place," the landscape that allows for meaning and meaninglessness, harmony and disharmony, intimacy and isolation. Cause and effect are not denied; they are only denied primacy.

Second, mu is not apophatic. It is not understood by what it is understood not to be or by what we cannot understand. On the contrary, the word nothingness seems to grate immediately and irredeemably on our assumptions of what we value as affirmative, positive, and meaningful for human beings. Furthermore, if one cannot have direct contact with nothingness or describe its presence in concrete terms, it can hardly be expected to take the place of a loving, provident, saving deity. Indeed, when Nishida himself first came to realize the need to replace being with nothingness as the foundation of philosophy, his immediate fear was that he had simply "capitulated to mysticism." It did not take him long to realize how rich a vein of thought he had tapped into and how much more there was to say.

Finally, mu contradicts the idea that an unchanging, unmoving, transcendent being can be either ontologically or morally absolute. I will have more to say about this later.

In a word, the idea of mu comes down to a fundamental option about reality. Either there is some being that is not becoming, which would locate it in a supernatural realm other than our own or dismiss it as a delusional, imaginal nonbeing; or else there is something in reality that neither is nor becomes, something that is not at all like anything we identify as existing. This unlikeness, as Nishida says, shreds the outer limits of our most abstract ideas and scatters them in all directions, like an outermost circle drawn with dotted lines about the series of concentric circles by which mind classifies the qualities of particular beings.

The line is dotted for a reason: It is not an enclosure. Mu is misunderstood if it is assumed to be some kind of ultimate landscape, a matrix behind reality, like the deep darkness of outer space that surrounds the multitude of universes that make up the cosmos. Plato's chora has been suggested as a way to explain the basic meaning of mu without having to appeal to a transcendent being, but the comparison collapses the further it is carried.

The original idea of chora rests on a distinction between the notions of Being and becoming. If becoming were to collapse into Being, or Being into becoming, chora could no longer serve as a middle ground between the actual and the eternal, between inconstant, visible forms and the invisible, indestructible formless form of all forms. For Plato, the chora is not a backdrop to the material world but rather the crucible in which matter takes shape in things and the substratum that holds them in place. It is not merely an indeterminate place for existence to take place but the creative and structured womb of a world in the making. This generative quality of chora takes its meaning from the bond it forms between the degeneration and flux of that world and the stability of eternity. In short, insofar as the chora is seen as the locus of potentiality, the power to transform that which is not into that which might be, it belongs to a beingness superior to any sort of nothingness, and it allows meaning to emerge only in departure from the realm of nonbeing for the realm of Being. Plato's chora is a third "realm" (the original meaning of the word in Homer) in which nonbeing is transformed into being. Its meaning lies not in the *nihilum* from which it created but only in the creations it positions *extra nihilo*.

Like chora, mu stipulates the irreducible correlativity of beings and their becoming. The logical marker for this is the copulative soku, to which we shall return presently. The important point here is that together they constitute a "beingness" that stands in opposition to a "nothingness," which cannot be reduced to becoming or any other negation of Being. The more the absence of potential is seen as the presence of something more ultimate, the further the metaphor of the chora slips away from the meaning of nothingness.

For these same reasons, nothingness cannot be seen as generative. All generation is at the same time a degeneration. All causality is an abstraction of reality in the sense that something of what was is always sacrificed for what comes to be. This may be so in the actual realm of existence, but there is no coming to be or passing away for nothingness. Generation and degeneration are rather seen as manifestations of nothingness, as ciphers of a presence that hides itself by showing itself. It is not itself a power or a force or an energy field; it is only experienced as such. Nothingness is present both in the effects of force as well as in the force itself, but it is not reducible to either. If the supreme expression of being is pure happening, then nothingness cannot be said to "happen" at all. There is no conditioning, no cause, no contingency, and no necessity—nothing to take place and nowhere for it to be placed in.

Moreover, insofar as chora is imagined as "the receptable of all coming and being" (*Timaeus*, 48e), it is always full to the brim. In this sense, Plato's χώρα differs from the devouring mother of Anaximander's ἄπειρον and the tranquil void of Democritus' κενόν. Nor can it open up and overflow like an Aristotlean τόπος. Setting aside the logical question of how a container that contains everything could be considered a container at all, it is what is in the receptable that gives chora its meaning. It is a creative matrix in which Being and becoming generate the world—both the fragile world of appearances and the infrangible world of Ideas.

Metaphors of nothingness require a change in standpoint. Nothingness is not seen as a receptable for beingness but precisely the other way around: The world in its constant flux is where nothingness takes place, where it becomes visible, tangible, knowable, and meaningful. As we have seen, Nishida's idea of the ultimate basho (locus) of nothingness is not itself a basho but a manifestation of all other basho as basho. It is not any kind of a divine locus locorum but rather the point in human experience at which we recognize our basho-affected thinking as the nothingness of ultimate reality at work in being and becoming. Reality itself always overflows the receptacle of beingness. It is accessible to us only in glimpses and fleeting sentiments that interrupt the rhythms of the everyday world. Beingness is like Laotze's cup (*Daodejing,* 45). By itself, it is useless and without meaning. Its meaning and purpose begin where the cup ends, in the emptiness that it holds within it.

Engi, the interconnectedness of all beings

The guiding image of the way in which nothingness is manifested in the actual world is the connectedness of all things—not just in the mind or among human beings, but for all things. If everything that exists in reality is always coming to be and passing away, then nothing is really always and only itself. Things literally are their connections, and any thing thought to be disconnected cannot at the same time be said to be. This, simply put, is what is known as engi, the permanent affiliation of all things with one another, of which relationships among humans are only a small part.

The only thing of which it can be said is that it is always and everywhere connected to everything is not a thing at all but only the reality of connectedness itself. Each universal or each class of beings is defined by its connections, and this is what we might call the universal of all universals, the class of all classes—the absolute. It is not an absolute being but an absolute relatedness. Nothing in reality is unrelated, and relatedness itself is present throughout reality by not being attached to any single item in reality.

Engi is not an illusion. It is not nothing in the sense of being cut off from being. On the contrary, its nothingness is what allows it to be present in everything. Of course, how connections work is relative to where an entity is located. The varieties of human perspective, which are dependent on our bodily senses and the instruments that extend them, allow us to "see" connections and manage them in consciousness. Lower animals have quite different sensual perspectives that enable them to navigate the immediate connections with their surrounding world, and the farther removed this is from consciousness, the more perspective becomes associated with autonomic activity. But in all cases, everything that exists is a bundle of relations, a field of vectors that hold it in place and make it what it is. What makes nothingness real, and not a mere empty medium in which reality exists, is this absolute, unknowable, and uncontrollable connectedness. Far from a meaningless void of nonbeing, nothingness is the crucible that makes meaning possible. The ultimate mystery of meaning is less a matter of why there is being rather than nothing than of why everything that exists comes to be in relation to everything else. Engi is a name for that mystery.

Nishida's first and most notorious successor, Tanabe Hajime (1885–1962), suggested that nothingness is dynamic, a pure power or potential to mediate and be mediated—to connect. The actual bonds that give continuity to things in space and time are themselves intangible and recognizable only in the manifestation of their binding. This is as true of energy and gravity in material reality as it is to culture and society in immaterial realities like thoughts and feelings. Tanabe spoke of it as "absolute mediation," by which he meant that nothingness is not only visible in actual connections but in their binding power as well—like the interlapping petals of the dahlia that separately and together give specificity to the life that flows through the flower's stem. This binding, he insisted, requires more than an empty void for interaction among individual entities. The dynamic of nothingness cannot be reduced to a mere dialectical logic by which a thing is said to be only in virtue of what it is not. To understand the reality of mu is to identify it as a concrete force, and not just an abstract, rational potential for existence. This should be kept in mind as we turn to the final two aspects of nothingness I have chosen to discuss here: soku and muga.

Soku, the logic of nothingness

Under the influence of his lifelong friend, D. T. Suzuki, Nishida was drawn to a logic of correlativity expressed in the term soku. He needed a way to deal with the way in which contradictory elements combine to sustain the identity of individual beings. The logical status of this contradiction was not a simple synthesis of opposing elements—as was the case in Hegel's dialectical logic—but a way of preserving them. Its goal was not to harmonize a dualism of coexisting principles, but rather to rethink the binary opposition of yes/no as both-yes-and-no and at the same time neither-yes-nor-no.

This may seem to land us in a logic that is ultimately self-contradictory, or at least incapable of making up its mind about the nature of the relationship between contradictory elements. Obviously, Nishida and his circle understood logic as more than the rules of formal logic. Its task is to guide our use of language in order to make sense of the world. Logic was understood broadly to represent the basic structure of thought that aims to make the real rational, without flying off to some ideal world or abandoning rational thought. The only rational way to express the interconnected reality of the world was to refuse to affirm the identity of any individual without including its reliance on its surroundings, and at the same time without denying that ultimately reality does not cater to the demands of language and its aversion to contradiction. The mixture of sense and nonsense that is the inescapable fate of *homo loquens* needs to be reflected in logic, and this is precisely what soku aims to do.

It is not easy to find an equivalent for soku in English, just as it is difficult to find a precise way to express the copulative "is" in Japanese and Chinese, whose grammars are more fluid than Indo-European

languages when it comes to tenses and declensions and definable parts
of speech. Even with adjustments that have been made to accommodate
the translation of Western literature, Chinese and Japanese retain a native
flexibility that can be deceptive for the translator. Be that as it may, soku
is commonly rendered as sive, qua, or "as." I myself prefer "in," but
none of these terms give quite the same feel to the way soku functions
in actual use; explanatory paraphrase is poorer still. At the same time,
there is nothing particularly mysterious about the mutual entailment of
life and death, divinity and humanity, transcendence and immanence, and
so forth that the copulative soku implies. Nor is it hard to understand the
self-denial of rational clarity in the face of the unclarity of the real world.
It is just that our language does not have a simple word to carry the load.

Thus, when we say death-in-life or divine-in-human, I-in-Thou,
we mean not only to preserve the dialectical relationship of opposites as
essential to an entity's reality—like two sides of a piece of paper that need
one another to exist—but also to bend that paper into a Mobius strip so
that one side flows naturally into the other. Nishida famously captures this
in his enigmatic description of individuation as "absolutely contradictory
identity." The same pattern may be said of the soku that binds being and
nothingness. The formula "nothingness-in-being, being-in-nothingness"
is cited frequently as a shorthand for the logical axiom that the reality of
nothingness only becomes apparent in things that exist, and that being
is only real because it appears against the backdrop of nothingness. To
this we add Tanabe's corrective that the logic of soku is never a pure,
abstract relationship among ideas, a union of contradictory concepts, but
it always colored by the specific cultural conditions in which the concepts
are located. Insofar as mu can be thought, it is shaped by the specificities
that affect where and when that thinking takes place.

Muga, the experience of *mu*

There is only so far we can go in thinking about what happens when
we are thinking. Like a mirror facing a mirror, what is reflected recedes
into a smaller and smaller image that erases whatever clarity there was
without ever allowing us to grasp it as it actually is. In the end, there is no
place we can stand in the world to make the world an object unaffected
by our thinking about it. Conversely, the thinking self is like one rock

among the 15 that disappears from view no matter where you sit in the famous rock garden at Ryōan-ji temple in Kyoto. We can only think of reality in *medias res*, in the thick of it. The idea of the human subject as an unmovable point of reference for objective truth is the ultimate illusion, and the idea of nothingness is the mind's way of acknowledging the illusion. If this acknowledgement is allowed to run its course, it does not stop at a rational proposition about the limits of reason. It marks an awakening to a nothingness-self, or muga, which in turn determines the goodness of the good life amidst the irrevocable interconnectedness of the world.

At this point, the influence of Buddhist philosophy comes into clearer relief. Only late in life did Nishida begin to give Buddhist language a place in his writings, making explicit what had been there all along in the background. The same is true of Tanabe after his turn to "metanoetics," a philosophy of moral conversion occasioned by a rigorous self-examination of aspects of his thinking that had kept him from taking a stalwart stance against Japan's militaristic engagements in the Second World War.

Tanabe's successor at Kyoto University, Nishitani Keiji (1900–1990), was more forthcoming from the start. His writings offer a lodestone for Buddhist elements latent in the philosophy of mu that he had inherited from his teachers Nishida and Tanabe. This is nowhere more evident than in the idea of muga.

As an idea, muga—commonly translated as "no-self"—is a critique of anthropocentrism carried out from within the unavoidable anthropocentricism of philosophy. Nishida saw it as overcoming the subject-object dichotomy. Tanabe approached it as the rational disruption of reason; Nishitani, as a kind of self-overcoming of self-centeredness. Purely as an idea, the point is the same: Every human "perspective" on reality is a function of mind that occurs as part of the actual interconnected agency of existing beings but is not required by it. The self that thinks about the world marks the emergence within history of the world of a capacity for subjectivity that is capable not only of a high degree of consciousness but also of subjecting the nonself-conscious world to objectification, instrumentation, and representation prone to distortion—in short, anthropocentricism. Simply put, muga seeks to restore mind to its place of honor in the history of the world and at the same time to avoid its self-destruction. This begins with understanding the primordial state of the self as no-self and acting from a standpoint of soku in which the relationship of self to no-self can be realized.

Nishitani speaks of this as a standpoint of "emptiness," a term he generally prefers to "nothingness" because of its echoes in the Buddhist ideal of no-self. His muga is an "emptiness-self," a self that becomes what it truly is by emptying itself of itself. Thus, when his successor at Kyoto University, Ueda Shizuteru (1926–2019), introduces the phrase "I am I by not being I," he is speaking about more than an idea of the nature of human consciousness as a dialectic that correlates self and other. Muga is always a question of taking an actual stand in the world: I am only truly an I when I dislodge the "I" from the center of my worldview and carry that over into practice. For this reason, the connectedness of engi and the logic of soku are not meant as a metaphysic or ontology that can stand on its own; they are rather a rational foundation for the practice of no-self.

Following hints that Nishida scattered in his final essay, Nishitani took up the Christological doctrine of *kenōsis*, as a way of universalizing the idea of no-self beyond its Buddhist expression. The image of the self-emptying of a suprahistorical, supernatural being into the historical person of Jesus seemed to him to disclose the true essence of the divine and the human at once. The total and irreversible negation of the idea of a detached, disinterested, absolute, and transcendent being who creates the world, holds it in existence, and directs it back to its point of origin opens the way to an affirmation of a divinity-in-humanity as a living symbol of reality itself as nothingness-in-being.

Takeuchi Yoshinori (1913-2002), a disciple of Tanabe Hajime who followed Nishitani in the Chair of Religious Studies at Kyoto University, likened *kenōsis* to the Buddha's transcendence of the world through a transdescendence into the world. A worldview based on such an ideal of "transdescending the self" is neither theocentric nor anthropocentric but rather what he calls "anthropo-eccentric." One becomes fully human only in vacating self-centeredness, in acting for the harmony and welfare of all beings. The rejection of self-centeredness is not a rejection of the ordinary self, let alone a depreciation of humanity. On the contrary, it is confirmed at those times when the mind feels most centered in the world. If only for a fleeting moment, in the "no-self"-centeredness of mind everything, just where it is and as it, seems to be just where and as it should be: One becomes the connectedness. This is what is meant by the nothingness-mind viewing the world from the standpoint of emptiness.

Any sympathies Nishida and his circle felt toward pantheistic views of the presence of God in all things were incomplete without an understanding of that presence as self-emptying or indiscriminate love. The incorporation of theological imagery into the meaning of nothingness for the realization of true selfhood is, of course, in no way intended as a literal theism or a literal atheism. But neither is it a simple agnosticism. Rather than dislocate God from philosophy, their aim was to relocate notions of "absolute being" in the quest of a true humanness freed of any illusion of the individual self—human or divine—as a self-sufficient, self-enclosed center. In so doing, the relationship between the "absolute" and the "relative" is radically changed. Rather than contradictory attributes that cannot, in a two-valued logic, both be true at the same time, the two are linked through the soku: absolute-in-relative, relative-in-absolute. The relative is the absolute with the lining turned out. Reality is absolutely relative, with no exceptions, which is to say that it is relatively absolute. Nothing is absolutely absolute or only relatively relative. Accordingly, the most comprehensive and rational expression of reality just as it is, the all-embracing universal of all universals, is the engi of interconnectedness. An absolute "cut off" from the world by preexistence or independence, an absolute that is absolute in itself and not for others, is a rejection of reality as the being-in-nothingness, nothingness-in-being that it is.

As we have been saying, nothingness is only absolutely real in its appearance as the tangled web of relations that make up this world as it comes to be and passes away at every moment. Accordingly, muga, is not a nonexistent self but a radically conscious existing self which is most fully alive in death to the illusions of selfishness, that is to say, in the loving, compassionate, responsible, and clear-thinking mind of self-in-other. Its self-denial is not a capitulation to the meaninglessness of our nature but a fundamental conversion to acting naturally and in harmony with who we really are. Nothingness shines nowhere more brightly and positively than in a self that exists in awareness of its connectedness to others. To be in love is to exist in the original likeness of divine love. This is how Japan's philosophers of nothingness appropriate stories of God into their view of reality: as a collective image of one to whom those who are dead to the world are still alive, of one who lives most fully in the world by dying to otherworldliness.

It should be obvious that the philosophy of nothingness developed by the Kyoto School philosophers and roughly sketched above has taken the classical ideas of mu, engi, soku, and muga beyond the confines of their Asian birthplace. As I remarked earlier, if nothingness can be transplanted into foreign soil at all, it cannot be expected to produce the same fruit. But it can alert us to fugitive elements in our own tradition that have been marginalized or otherwise neglected. Again and again, the spontaneous attraction of these philosophers to esoteric, mystical, and hermetic traditions helps nudge us out of the clear orthodoxy of the mainstream and into the muddy backwaters of our own arcana. Start to finish, their writings on nothingness represent a dialogue with Western philosophy that has fractured our tidy assumptions about the role the intellectual history of the East has to play in philosophy's pursuit of a universality that does not collapse into uniformity and certitude, and the way in which this is reflected in aesthetics, morality, and religion.

The context of the idea of nothingness and the relative positioning of that context in a broader worldview is too important to extract the conceptual ingredients alone and assimilate them into one or the other variety of a *philosophia perennis*. The hubris is still more visible in attempts to treat the idea like an appendix and or a new row of patches stitched to the edges of the already motley quilt of Western philosophy. What is needed is not a mere accommodation but a disruption and restoration, similar to the one that Nishida and his circle initiated. The Japanese style of pottery known as kintsugi is a good image of the formative reconstruction already underway.

The art of *kintsugi* dates to a 15th-century art of expressing beauty through the repair of broken clay vessels. A lacquer mixed with gold dust is used to fix the pieces back together. The veins of gold show both the wounds and their healing in a way that a smooth glaze cannot. They give value to the finished composition at the same time as they highlight the fragility of its origins. What you hold in your hands is a reconnection with a broken past, an image of the temporary nature of all our handiwork intersecting with the desire that it last forever. It reconnects time, which moves from one fragmentation to the next, to the irrepressible but always uncertain longing for reparation. It is an image of the mind itself as it strains for the wisdom to restore unity to ideas disrupted by novelty, to recover a unity that never quite holds.

The philosophers of the Kyoto School have left behind an impressive record of how debate with philosophies of being can enrich philosophies of nothingness. It is still too early to conduct an audit on movements in the opposite direction. What we can say is that once the idea of nothingness has intruded into the history of the notion of being, neither tradition of thought can be the same. In that search for balance-in-imbalance lies the beauty of philosophy. And that is something we cannot afford to take lightly, not as long as we revere our native instincts to be reasonable and to live in harmony with the world that first delivered us over to them.

References

Plato, *Timaeus*, 48e.
Lao Tzu (Laozi). Chapter 45. *Tao Te Ching* (*Daodejing*).

Theological
Expression

11

"Something Formless Yet Complete": Nothing and Divine Consciousness

Gerard Guiton

From the *halākā* of Jesus of Nazareth has emerged some of the most powerful literature of all time—the central core of his teaching, the Sermons on the Mount and Plain (Mt. 5-7; Lk. 6:19-49). Along with their respective Beatitudes, they largely comprise Jesus's manifesto, the Kingdom of God.[1] We are assured that The Way—as I usually call the Kingdom to avoid gendered, noninclusive language—is within (or inside) and among *all* people. Jesus counseled putting It *first* (Mt. 6:33; Lk. 17:20-21). Today, The Way's politics are as radical and progressive as they ever were in Jesus's day. As a result, I consider The Way one of *the* means of enacting effective and lasting peace, nonviolence, truth, justice, and compassion in the world, indeed of furthering the understanding that humanity is one, that the totality of life/reality is a Unity with a sacred purpose.

Followers of The Way, which medieval mystic Johannes Tauler (1910, p. 523) described as "nothing less than God's own self," love God. Loving God means being in love with Love. For me, this love is best nurtured by contemplative silence-stillness. Long-etched into my own life, waiting and listening in silence-stillness is essential to my understanding of God as unconditional Love, Divine Consciousness, in

---

[1] For me, "God" is a code word for, *inter alia*, Ultimate Meaning, Christ (i.e., Spirit), Brāhman, Love, Presence/Omnipresence, Oneness, Inward Light, The Way and Consciousness etc. Based to a large extent on biblical Wisdom literature, the Sermons need reading with theological care if their overall message is to have direct meaning for us in the present era. Not all of their injunctions are adaptable to current settings, e.g. most obviously, those concerned with divorce.

whom and with whom I am free. In such silence I discover and rediscover a sanctum, spiritual space in which "there is no distance, no segmentation of yesterday, today and tomorrow [for] in eternal time all is now, time is presence" (O'Donohue, 1999, pp. 276-7). I hope to enter this sanctum with heart and mind prepared, not already made up, since it's important to protect God from my own ego-driven preconceptions *of* God. This allows God the silence to be "heard," and the freedom for me to breathe with integrity the aphonic air of No-thing-ness, Presence or Omnipresence, to wait attentively upon the Presence. It is also a special place where I can, momentarily at least, liberate myself from "the body," as the *Aṣṭāvakra Gītā* says, in order to "rest in Intelligence [Consciousness]" (Nityaswarupananda, 1940, p. viii).[2] All in all, during my moments of worship, meditation and prayer, I simply listen lovingly with One-der.

Such silence is without inner and outer dimension. It has also been described as a way of detachment (*Abgeschiedenheit*) by Meister Eckhart (Walshe, 2009, pp. 490-2)[3] and as emancipation or true emptiness (*śūnyatā*) by Buddhism, the latter, according to Kitarō Nishida, being "nothing less than what reaches awareness in all of us as our own absolute self-nature" (Nishitani, 1982, p. 107): "To learn the Buddha way," said Sōtō Zen master Dōgen Zenji, "is to learn one's self; to learn one's self is to forget one's self" (Kasulis, 1985, p. 92).

So, my silences are also a means of forgetting myself so that I can be open to, and know more of, who I am *vis-à-vis* God's love: "whoso knows [themselves] know [God]," wrote Ṣūfī Muḥyī al-Dīn Ibn Al-'Arabī (Weir, 1901, p. 809), and *vice-versa*. Writings such as his *Kitāb al-Ajwiba* (also *Kitāb al-Alif*, c.1215-20?) help me focus more on the nature of Consciousness which is, substantively, what I've been addressing so far. The more I undertake this task in prayerful silence-stillness, the nearer I am to the unicity that is M̲e̲ (as we'll soon see with Catherine of Genoa), that is to say, the nearer I am to No-thing-ness, The Way within, Spirit, Inward Light-Divine Consciousness who is our deep heart's core.[4] Such silences and the stillness accompanying them are not, therefore, voids or empty spaces, times of doing nothing (as we

---

[2] *Aṣṭāvakra Gītā* (= *Aṣṭāvakra Saṃhitā*); also Chpt. 1 (§4), p. 4.
[3] For Eckhart's treatise "On Detachment" see Walshe, pp. 566-575.
[4] *Kitāb al-Ajwiba* = Bk. *of Answers*. "Deep heart's core" from "The Lake Isle of Innisfree" by Irish poet W. B. Yeats. Innisfree pronounced "Inish-free."

imperfectly imagine "nothing" to be), but something that meaningfully colors the week ahead.

Further, from my silence-stillness and other moments of solitude can emerge a commitment toward, as well as much needed strength and persistence to practice, The Way's peace, justice, compassion, and Nature-care. And the desire and determination, also, to help build and enhance life-giving comm*unity* in the hope of shaping a future in which we can live regeneratively and sustainably with each other and the Earth, including *its* other creatures and things.

Therefore, in silence-stillness I have found an effective means of directly accessing the Divine. Put another way, it is through personal (small c) consciousness—which gives rise to awareness at all times while our body is alive—that I can instantaneously access Divine (capital C) Consciousness since It "and" consciousness are exactly the same, a unicity.[5] Contemplative silence-stillness is magnificently suited to the task, therefore, of not only helping us (on our choosing) to sink into what Ibn Al-'Arabi called "Oneness of Being" (*Wujud*)—whose equivalent in Indian religion is *Satcitānanda*—and *Its* meaning for our lives and the Earth, but also for bringing It to our full awareness (Yiangou, 2017, pp. 437-8).

So, in exploring possible answers to the questions, What are "nothing" and "ontological-immaterial no-thing-ness?", and Does nothing actually exist?, I will briefly delve into the cosmology of what I call the "In here" or uncreated "In here-ncy," which, in my view, nullifies the classical theistic theology of *creatio ex nihilo*: Consciousness, being All, is not outside anything; It *is* everything. And although nothing/ness has substantial literary import—take, for example, the philosophical impact of, say, Jean-Paul Sartre's *Being and Nothingness*, and/or how the immaterial is not nothing—I will highlight various objections to the existence of "physical" nothing/ness by sages past and present, but also discuss how everyone experiences plenty of something, e.g., matter, which is Consciousness by another name refracted through our finite minds. In this respect, I make use of a neologism, ConsciousnessMatter, who or which is what we, the non-human world and Nature, including the cosmos in its entirety, *are*. I will also argue that such an appreciation

---

[5] Sometimes C/consciousness is confused with "awareness" and "mind," each being "a quale" (plural: qualia) of C/consciousness.

of C/consciousness-Oneness, and thereby Not-nothing-The Way, reveals Consciousness as non-interfering in humanity's and Nature's affairs, but also "personal" (though not a person), and as Continuum whose Isness unfolds as interconnectedness *par excellence*. Finally, I hope to show how Consciousness-Love has direct, practical, and life-giving import for our daily lives—our politics, economics, and the planet's ecology—and how, as The Way, It cannot fail (if we also help It) to promote peace, justice and compassion.

*****

The preposition "with" in my phrase "listen lovingly with One-der" is important in the way it assumes cooperation with God who is not almighty except, perhaps, as the Omnipresence of Love. God needs us and all-Nature just as we and all-Nature need God; we and God, together with Nature, are one and thus inseparable. As we read in 1 Cor. 1: 12-13, Christ (for our purposes, Consciousness-Love) can never be divided. And when I say all-Nature, I mean all existence, physical *and* immaterial, i.e., that which *is* and not "out there" because there *is* no "out there" but an "In here," the In-here-ncy of all existence which is what Consciousness-Love Is. More succinctly, Is is All and there is no Is outside All because All is all there Is. I'm inclined to think, therefore, that "nothing" on the physical level is an impossibility, that something has always been. Hence, nothing exists that is not Consciousness-Love.

What I've written so far renders statements such as "nothingness is absolutely nothing: it is nothing at all" contradictory because "it" makes nothing something. Equally, when we talk of the absence of everything, we talk of *something* because nothing cannot be absent if it doesn't exist. And if we maintain nothing is not a thing, that what is *is*, what then *is* nothing? All of which means "nothing" cannot escape being something. It seems I'm a Somethingist rather than a Noneist!

Still, nothing/ness as a word/concept rather than as a so-called physical reality is of great help in understanding more of the world and the truth of humanity's place in it. This might have been an aim of artist Mark Rothko, much of whose nothingness oeuvre, appropriately untitled, can be interpreted, like much modern art, in a variety of ways. For example, when purposefully and dramatically applying yet another layer of paint over a previous layer, was he drawing attention to our human propensity to repeatedly deny the nothing beyond our death, the brutal truth (as he may have understood it) of the eternal silence of the *postmortem* void?[6]

However, outside the reasons for Rothko's repeated applications, nothingness-as-concept *can* nudge us toward a greater awareness of ourselves in relation to life (including the cosmos), as well as to the actions and motivations of people in general, including any nihilist philosophies they may hold. Such a largely apophatic approach certainly sustains a powerful charism of its own which grants nothingness specific agency, something of which mystics, artists in their own way, have made good use down the years. Examples can be found, for instance, in the *Kena Upaniṣad* where we read, "[They] who think it not think it, [they] who think it know it not; it is not understood by those who know and known by those who do not know" (1900, pp. 2-4, 11).[7] In the older *Bṛhadāraṇyaka Upaniṣad*, Brāhman is ultimately characterized as *neti, neti* (not this, not this). The *neti* here of the sage Yājñavalkya (Mādhavānanda, 1950, p. 336) reminds me of the *nescio* of Bernard of Clairvaux, and Jan van Ruysbroeck's "dark silence [the Abyss, i.e., no-thing-ness of Being] where all lovers lose themselves" (Ruysbroeck, 1916, p. 178). We encounter apophasis in the various teachings of Angela of Foligno, who focussed on God as Unknown Nothingness. Out of pure love, she said, God undergoes annihilation by self-abasement (she may have had the Atonement in mind) so that the spiritually dead can have life, an *annihilatio* confounding the "pride" of human *nihilitas*. God, now reduced to nothing, deflates the nothingness which had imagined it was something (Newman, 2016, pp. 608-9).

Thinking about the somethings in my own life, I've also reflected upon the impossibility of getting beyond nothing/ness as an actuality. Since we have no direct experience of its existence or nonexistence, just as we have no direct experience of matter outside our perception, it is impossible to know empirically that nothing exists.[8] Yet despite no one

---

[6] For Rothko's art see <https://www.nga.gov/features/mark-rothko/mark-rothko-classic-paintings.html>. (Accessed: 26/07/23).
[7] See *Kena Up.*, 1. Mantra 2, pp. 2-3; Mantra 3, p. 4.
[8] For the inability to directly experience matter outside our perception see Pandit (2004, p. 58). In his *Īśvara Pratyabhijñā Kārikā of Utpaladeva* he records the Kāśmīrī Śaivan sage, Utpaladeva (*c.*900-950) saying:

> Matter, wherever or whenever It is perceived, is essentially not a thing different or separate from one's perceptual knowing of it. Therefore, its existence outside knowing cannot be proved. Knowing

ever proving it *does* exist, nothing/ness continues to stalk our senses. And so, we are compelled to engage with it, as I've intimated, as both concept and word. This is to give it existence through imagination.

So, what else has been said down the years about "nothing?" The answer is a great deal of something of which the following is a small sample. Hence, on the cosmological level, ancient Israelite, Chinese and Greek philosophers generally believed the universe was created not from nothing so much as formless matter. Pre-Socratic philosophers (among them Thales, Democritus, Empedocles and Parmenides) strongly insisted that nothing could arise from what did not exist, a view supported by Aristotle but also the *Bhagavad Gītā*: "All around I behold thy infinity . . . Nowhere I see a beginning or middle or end of thee, O God, of all, Form Infinite" (Mascaró, 1962, p. 90).

Across the globe, and writing roughly about the same time as our pre-Socratics, Laozi (Waley, 1934, p. 174), dwelt on the possibility of

> *. . . something formless yet complete,*
> *That existed before heaven and earth;*
> *Without sound, without substance,*
> *Dependent on nothing, unchanging,*
> *All pervading, unfailing.*
> *One may think of it as the mother of all things under heaven.*
> *Its true name we do not know;*
> *'Way' is the by-name that we give it.*
> *Were I forced to say to what class of things it belongs*
> *I should call it Great.*[9]

Georg Hegel (Wong, 2011, pp. 56, 64, 75), relying entirely on the work of French Sinologist Jean-Pierre Abel-Rémusat and *his* hermeneutic of Laozi, believed he was reading "nothingness" to mean

> the absolute, the origin of all things, the last, the highest,
> . . . being in itself, [the] deprivation of all representation,
> all the objectiveness—that is, the simple, the identity

---

is a [characteristic] of Consciousness. Therefore, matter and all material phenomena have Consciousness as their essence and cannot be proved, even by inference, to be anything outside Consciousness.

[9] "Name" (line 7) = the class of things to which it belongs.

with itself, the indeterminate, the abstract unity. It is at the same time also affirmative; it is what we call essence.[10]
Our embodiment of the *Dao*, including Laozi's nameless and indefinite "nothingness," is considered a continuous psychic process of self-negation—"cut off sagacity and dispense with wisdom," "extend nothingness and preserve tranquillity." In the *Zhūangzi* (*Chuang Tzŭ*) we read, "concentrate one's spirit," "devote oneself to the fasting of the heart-mind," "sit and forget," "open one's heart-mind and release one's spirit." For emptying the psyche, the *Zhūangzi* was confident that our worldly concerns *could* be shut out during meditation: "Do not listen for it with your ears, listen for it with your heart-mind. Do not listen for it with your heart-mind, listen for it with your *Qi* [vital energy/force]" (Fan and Sullivan, 2010, p. 562). *Qi* is empty and waits for things to act. I think it's acceptable, therefore, to interpret *Qi* as Consciousness.

Fast forward to medieval times and we find a number of Jewish thinkers like Rashi, influenced by Hellenism, maintaining that the Genesis account of "creation" could mean God creating from pre-existing formlessness or unformed matter (Winston, 1971, pp. 191-2).[11] In contrast, the Christian Church has insisted, from the second century, that God created the universe from absolute nothing, *creatio ex nihilo*. God was beyond all matter, including the universe; consequently, matter was never eternal. Despite this, while Clement of Alexandria in his *Stromateis* (*Miscellanies*) agreed that God did indeed create the world from nothing—"Out of a confused heap who didst create this ordered sphere, and from the shapeless mass of matter didst the universe adorn" (Clement, 1869, p. 364)—he was convinced the world was made not from absolute nonexistence (*ex ouk ontos*) but, like our Chinese, Greek and Jewish thinkers, from unformed matter (*ek me ontos*).

Nothingness, as in a total void, was also debated by the Greek (Church) Fathers themselves and roundly rejected. Much later, John Scotus Eriugena in *Periphyseon* wrote, "I would not believe that there was another thing apart from . . . and outside [God]. For in [God] are all things and outside [God] there is nothing" (Eriugena, 1987, pp. 115-16, 308).

---

[10] Abel-Rémusat (1788-1832). I am grateful to Dr. K. Wong (Assoc. Prof., Baptist Univ. of Hong Kong) for sending me his paper.
[11] Rashi (Shlomo Yitzchaki, 1040–1105), French commentator on the Talmud, and Tanakh in general.

This statement is OK as far as it goes, but there *is* no outside of God and therefore not even nothing. However, for Eriugena nothingness (no-thing-ness) seemed to have offered possibilities for authenticity by which we could let go of any need to control Being.[12] Later still, Eckhart preached, "God is nothing, not in the sense of having no being. [God] is neither this nor that [but] Being above all being . . . Beingless Being" (Walshe, 2009, pp. 316-17).[13] That is, God as Godhead (*Gottheit*) is not absolute nothingness, but No-thing-ness beyond entity and quiddity. Arguably, his concept of the Godhead was meant to convey a sense of mystical space behind or beyond our *everyday* understanding of God, a way of communication enabling God to be God without our preconceptions.[14] For Eckhart, drawing much on Dionysius the Areopagite who himself saw God "as naught, meaning God is as incomprehensible as naught," it followed that all statements about God would always be inadequate (Walshe, 2009, pp. 40-1).[15] This *via negativa* was well-captured by the Spanish medieval Kabbalist, Joseph Gikatilla (Matt, 1990, p. 128), who understood that:

> The depth of primordial being . . . is called Boundless. It is also called *ayin* [nothing] because of its concealment from all creatures above and below . . . If one asks, 'What is it?,' the answer is, Ayin, that is, no one can understand anything about it . . . It is negated of every conception.'

Meanwhile, Marguerite Porete in her *Mirror of Simple Souls* (*c.*1295) recorded a dialogue between Reason and Dame Amour (Porete, 2010, pp. 17-18)—i.e., Soul, Love or what today we may call Consciousness—in which Amour declares that an "enfranchised or annihilated soul"

---

[12] See *Periphyseon* (= *De Divisione Naturæ*), Bk. 1, §516a-518a, pp. 115-16 and Bk. 111, §681c, p. 308. In Sermon 57, Eckhart maintains the same; see Walshe, pp. 295-299.
[13] Eckhart's idea here probably derivative of St. Dionysius's notion of *hyperousia*; see Walshe, Sermon 62, pp. 314-317; *cf*: Sermons 19 (pp. 137-142), 47 (pp. 255-257), 67 (pp. 341-346).
[14] Whether this concept works is debatable. It appears to fall victim to what French philosopher Jacques Derrida called *différence*, that is, the naming of something one brings into existence which has nothing to do with its principal reference, in this case God, the unnameable; the effect is to finitize the infinite.
[15] Pseudo Dionysius (or Dionysius the Pseudo-Areopagite) was probably a fifth- or sixth-century C.E. Syrian or Greek monk. His pseudonymous workings of St. Dionysius (the biblical Dionysius the Areopagite; see Acts 17:34) were a major influence on Eckhart.

ravished by the fulness of understanding becomes
nothing in her understanding. And such a soul who has
become nothing has everything, wills nothing and wills
everything, knows nothing and knows everything.

The Béguine communities in northern European cities, of which she was
a member, generally accepted annihilation of the soul into God to be God
as a theory of self-abnegation only (premortem), one which enormously
influenced Eckhart. According to Keiji Nishitani (1982, p. 107), Eckhart

refers to the 'essence' of God that is free of all form—
the complete 'image-free' (*bildlos*) godhead—as
'nothingness,' and considers the soul to return to itself
and acquire absolute freedom only when it becomes
totally one with the 'nothingness' of godhead.[16]

Indian philosophy took a different path. "Life eternal," said Sarvepalli
Rādhākrishnan, commenting on the *Bhagavad Gītā*, "is not dissolution
into the indefinable Absolute but attainment of a universality and freedom
of spirit, which is lifted above the empirical movement" (Rādhākrishnan,
1970, p. 314). He was speaking, of course, more for Advaita Vedāntin
Ādi Śaṅkarā rather than for Viśiṣṭādvaita Vedāntin Rāmānuja for whom
God was personal. For my part, I believe that in the postmortem state,
harmonious interaction with God, rather than exclusively total annihilation
in God, preserves *who we are* and thus our self-knowing, our personality,
our identity. It is expressed in Kāśmīrī Śaivism as *bheda-abheda*,
"difference and non-difference" or "identity-in-difference" (Godbole and
Mundra, 2022, pp. 3, 10, 13).[17]

On the whole, the medieval mystics thought the No-thing-ness that
is God was beyond all things that are and are not—i.e., classical theism.
The well-known Thomist position is typical in this respect. According to
Gaven Kerr (2012, p. 344), it states that "all creatures receive existence
from a superior cause," [so,]

---

[16] Nishitani was most likely referring to Eckhart's Sermon 7; see Walshe., pp. 72-76.
[17] *Bheda-abheda* is nowadays invariably bracketed with Kaśmīri Śaivism but has a
considerable provenance.

insofar as [God] is pure existence, God creates out of nothing; that is to say, God's creative [meonic] causality does not presuppose anything on which to work. God originates everything that exists and is thereby [ruler] over and superior to all that derives existence from [God] . . . Thus, in the creator, being naturally precedes non-being. God, as [B]eing [I]tself, is naturally prior to non-being; other than God there is nothing and it is from nothing other than [God]'s own being that God brings things into being. Creatures on the other hand do not exist of themselves; they depend on God for their being. Thus, non-being naturally precedes their being; their natures are nothing until brought into being by God.

Consequently, the universe was not even a thought in Thought before it became an actual thought and thus not nothing, but *as* nothing "it" obviously had no existence, and as a result, no beginning in time and space prior to "its" eventual appearance. The best one can say here is that this line of thinking is meonic in the sense that the universe is always *in potentia*, and mereological in its subsequent physical and ontological diversity, *and* an expression of Divine Oneness.

    I agree with Alfred North Whitehead who, while explicitly rejecting *creatio ex nihilo,* suggested there may never have been an original, material creation. Time, he believed, was/is infinite; there was no first day, no act of origination, only a continuing bringing-into-being in which past, present, and future were/are structurally similar. "God is not before all creation," he wrote, "but *with* all creation" (Whitehead, 1941, p. 521). For me, God *is and with* "creation" (*bheda-abheda*), matter and Consciousness-God being one, and that ConsciousnessMatter always was, is, and will always be indivisible. That is, matter, *aka* Consciousness, manifests in diverse forms when refracted through our finite mind.[18] And yet for ConsciousnessMatter to be in Itself indivisible, It must be actual and not nothing. We'll soon see, with a brief exegesis on Mark 8:22-26 and two personal stories—one about a religious or peak

---

[18] Does this mean my mobile phone is God? Yes, but only in the sense that consciousness is manifest within it as a quantum presence (its molecules, atoms, etc.). It is devoid of self-reflexivity (a quale of C/consciousness), the ability to know that it knows, conscious that it is conscious. Conscious and consciousness are not the same but can be mistaken as such.

experience in present-day Serbia, the other about an airport lounge—how this Not-nothing can be knowable, indeed is personal in a very real and tender way. In the meantime, in what I think is an important pantheistic statement, Whitehead concluded that God, though *not anterior* to matter and forever coextensive *with* it, was "not to be treated as an exception to all metaphysical principles, invoked to save their collapse. [God] is their chief exemplification" (Whitehead, 1941, pp. 521).

I need to add here that although pantheism can result in fatalism—which many rightly regard as a danger to human freedom—the idea that fatalism, as Friedrich Schelling noted, "is not essentially connected with [pantheism], is elucidated by the fact that so many are brought to [pantheism] through the most lively feeling of freedom" (Bruno, 2017, p. 7). This "feeling of freedom" he described as primordial, and, in my view, it is predicated squarely upon our free will and self-reflexivity (knowing that we know), as well as upon the power of memory and our vision of preferred futures, all of which contribute in no small way to our identity as free agents "within" Consciousness who/which is also Absolute Freedom.

In support of Whitehead, I believe *creatio ex nihilo* is long overdue for laying aside if only for the reason that God *is* and has always been, in my opinion, Uncreated Matter (ConsciousnessMatter) and thus forever *in potentia* (meonic, as already suggested), diverse in all manifestation (mereological) and One. A total physical void, which is undoubtedly something, is therefore impossible to imagine *with* such a God, in the same way it's impossible to think of "being" or even nothing without Consciousness. So, if we cannot image "nothing" as in "a total void," how can it be said with any confidence that the universe was created from absolute nullity (*ex ouk ontos*)? Another suspicion: If we can't imagine "physical" nothingness, is this proof it doesn't exist since everything we do, and everything ever occurring cosmologically, has depended on there being something, and nothing *but* something, and not nothing? And so, if a state of absolute nullity *were* possible, would *it* not be something?

I've stated that God is Presence; as such, God is in and as all-Existence who recognizes Itself in all things simply because, as we've seen, all things constitute Itself. Therefore, as God-Omnipresence-All, It cannot keep Itself to Itself alone since that would not be in the nature of Love which It is. And so, saying something like "God guides us" is to utter a truism but only in so far as *we* work truthfully *with* God for guidance (whatever the form it takes). Such an immediate and conscious cooperation is a natural outcome of the *bheda-abhedan* relationship which we've always had *with* God-Presence, although we so often display considerable ignorance of its promise. Our free will, which this relationship ensures, means we can choose to initiate the cooperation mentioned, or not. We are assured that working *with* Presence, *with* The Way of peace, justice and compassion, guarantees the prospect of rejoicing in whatever outcomes result, and enhancing them if need be. Unity, Not-nothing, works to sustain Its wholeness.

As *the* living Reality, this Omnipresence-Unity-Love can be construed as an incomprehensible vastness which, in its physical form, includes the universe and perhaps even an infinity of multiverses. However, It also possesses *an ontological-existential* vastness, one that never ceases to interact lovingly with Itself (which includes ourselves with all our wonders and shortcomings). It is spontaneous yet autopoietic, an ever flowing, pulsating, and involuting Continuum of Love. The Self-awareness of this Consciousness-Continuum typifies Its intrinsic, absolute freedom in the same way an eye knows *itself* through the very act of seeing.

Consequently, Love-Consciousness is *the* Reality that remains *inherently unaffected* by modifications and changes that are forever happening within It. Eckhart wrote, "God dwells in [God's] own pure essence where there is nothing that is contingent" (Walshe, 2009, p. 167).[19] In *this* sense, while Love-Consciousness is, as David Bohm (2005, p. 219) observed, "a single unbroken totality of movement," It is always *innately* still. Its stillness lies at the heart of everything and every movement. Picture a stormy ocean, and now imagine its utterly peaceful depths. In short, Consciousness *is* Stillness in which there is movement *and* repose.

With our awareness of Consciousness so far, we can now see how all-Nature, including all people, is a jewel in Indra's Net, its manifestations connected by the inter-refractions of Consciousness-Love's radiant illumination.[20] Paying homage to the interconnectedness of this all-Reality means being in dynamic and perfect unity, "perfect"

---

[19] See also Walshe, Sermon 62, p. 311.
[20] A Mahāyāna Buddhist reference from the *Avataṃsaka Sūtra* to the mythological God-King Indra and his infinite Net. Jewels were placed at each warp and weft crossing with all gems refracting each other. The Net signified the interconnectedness of all Reality (*pratītyasamutpāda*).

because anything otherwise hides or is antithetical to that who we actually are—universally-shared Consciousness, Not-nothing.

So, is "not nothing" rather than Not-nothing, meaningless? This was certainly theologian Paul Tillich's conclusion in respect to Gottfried von Leibniz's well-known question, "Why is there something and not nothing?" It was meaningless, he said, in the form Leibniz presented it because "every possible answer would be subject to the same question in an infinite regression" (Tillich, 1975, p. 163). However, "something" cannot be denied and "physical" nothing cannot exist. Anyway, I got the impression on first reading Leibniz that, being also a mystic, his aim was to emphasize something over nothing out of a sense of gratitude and that if we did the same, then we, too, would look upon life with gratitude; the more gratitude—solid down-to-Earth sort, not the wistful kind—the less anxiety and fear. He might have known that the Gospels address fear well over 300 times. As in his day, many people nowadays do tend to swim around in a sea of anxiety, nihilism, and disconnection, and for this reason alone Leibniz's seemingly innocent inquiry performs a great healing service by nudging us toward Something, and so doing maintains a timeless potency (Leibniz, 1890, p. 101).

That said, is Consciousness-God outside the scope of our human conceptual systems, as philosopher-theologian John Hick (1995, p. 28) supposed? To answer Hick, at least in part, I offer two personal experiences of God, of Divine Something. The first occurred in 1971 when a friend and I were traveling through present-day Serbia to Belgrade. After crossing the mighty Danube, we boarded an old, blue, rickety bus which soon wended its way along narrow and unmetaled roads in the alarmingly vertiginous Carpathians, a karst mountain region on the now Serbian-Română border. After negotiating one particularly sharp bend, an utterly magnificent sight suddenly came into view—the majestic Iron Gates Gorge. Far below us, the waters of the great river glistened in the midday sun, a wonderful, breathtaking spectacle in itself. I quickly took a photo after which, without warning, I was instantly in another place, dimension, existence—call it what you will—but I also knew I was me and that "me" encompassed, and was connected to, everyone and everything around my person in that moment, a moment that seemed eternal in its "nowness," Something that nothing can go beyond.

Looking back, the timelessness I experienced, and the fact that nothing else mattered, was somehow linked to not-actually-thinking but to just-being, and not being outside anything but rather being a conscious part of a greater, assuring Wholeness in which subject-object dichotomies disappear. It was as if a portal had opened in dimension-time through which I could experience an amazing, meaningful oneness, what seemed to be a Reality, which I now can only describe as Universal Mind, Divine Consciousness, No-thing-ness, God. Which is why I agree that this sort of realization "is the direct apprehension of the existence of a pre-existing dimension that is . . . characterised by a non-logical but certain knowing" (Stein, 2019, p. 10). The "certain knowing" was, I wish to emphasize, definitive and based on a pure loving; and without suggesting Stein inferred otherwise, there was nothing hostile about it in any way whatsoever.

My second experience is much less dramatic but no less important to me. It occurred in an airport lounge. Near where I was sitting, a young mother was playing with her newborn baby. After a while, the infant began to cry, and mother responded by discreetly breastfeeding. As we know, there was a time, and not all that long ago, when people would have registered embarrassment, shock, or even anger at the sight of this very natural and loving human interaction. Thankfully, Australia had moved on and, sure enough, that day was very different. Far from being uncomfortable, it was clear that those of us around mother and child were holding both in our affection, quietness, and smiles. It was as if we had all left the world behind to share a moment of sabbath and benediction, a moment that was gentle, loving and *together*, a moment full of the wonder of Love who was "right there" with us all, indeed a moment when within this Presence we all shared connections of One-der.

These experiences remind me of how, in the anonymous medieval text *The Cloud of Unknowing* (1973, p. 23), this Something or Presence cannot be known empirically but needs experiencing and embracing by our insight and love, tacitly one might say.[21] "God's face" (Consciousness) was in and all around us that day, Its effectiveness dependent upon our responses to the beauty, caring, tenderness, and truth of the moment of which we were all partakers. It was a moment that opened me to a deeper feet-on-the-ground appreciation of Love in the ordinary comings and goings of daily life, and what is meant by "God is personal." And a moment, too,

---

[21] See later for *die Wirklichkeit*; and see also Michael Polanyi's very helpful works, *Personal Knowledge* and *The Tacit Dimension*.

of learning *how* "Personal" is realizable through Consciousness-Love by those in attendance in any one situation. In our airport experience Love's response was "requested" *through our goodwill and love to which Love cannot fail to respond,* after all, our love is Its love. And Love can only love, nothing else.

Though outwardly unremarkable, my airport experience is also an example of how religion and spirituality are not the exclusive domain of any élite; they are very much the commonweal. The life and ministry of Jesus, like other sages I've mentioned, stands as a One-derful demonstration of this fact—a life of simplicity, and of respect and empathy for everybody else no matter what they were like, what they did in life, or whatever situation they found themselves in any one moment. His life remains a testimony to a great deal of something rather than nothing since he walked among and healed the broken, marginalised, saddened and diseased; his love was available and near (Mt. 3:2). We need not take his miracles of healing literally but understand them as demonstrations of the power of Love who, as I've said, can *only* love as we see, for example, in Mark 8:22-26.

In this passage, the Greek *prósōpon* helps us appreciate in kataphatic terms Love's relational and liberating movings. Theologically, it means we can meet Love "face-to-face," Love being supremely accessible. When Jesus "cured" a blind man who had called to him, the first "face" the man "saw" was that of Love. He was "cured" because of his faith and trust in the assuring "attendingness" of Love, the personal depth of Reality that spread to him *through* Jesus. Put another way, acknowledging God as personal is to know God's "face" is turned toward us and/or others; every face that looks to God-Love, said Nicholas of Cusa, "sees nothing that is *other* than itself or *different* from itself, because it sees its own Truth" (Cusa, 1988, p. 688).[22]

If we remember that sight in the Gospels is often a sign of faith, then the man's confidence in Jesus provides him with in-sight into the Presence. Once he *really* "sees," the sickness of his distancing (rather than separation) from The Way-Love, his spiritual disfigurement, his existential nothingness, of which his blindness is symbolic, is cured.[23]

---

[22] Cusanus's emphases; see *De Visione Dei* (1453), Chapter 6, §19.

[23] Regarding "distancing," I prefer the Greek *hamartia*, whose meanings emphasize "ignorance" and "missing the mark," both of which lead to *diistémi* (setting apart but not

His "cure" involves turning his face toward Love (*prósōpon*) and, in so doing, taking full responsibility for his own sickness, i.e., his distancing, by realizing the Truth that is also within. More accurately, it involves turning his *whole being* toward Truth-Love (*metānoiā*)—from human or ego-bound thinking to Divine understanding—thus confronting the blinding, directionless state of his spiritual life (*cf.* Jn. 8:24). The stress here is not so much on Jesus but on the response to God-Love in what is a deeply religious interaction of true attentive seeing, a coming together in Divine Truth to enact a harmonious interaction *with* Divine Truth (*bheda-abheda*), something that is open to us all if we also care to "see." My use of "religious" from the Latin *religare* signifies a rebinding of that which has been damaged. The blind man's relationship (i.e., our relationship) to God-Love *had* been damaged, and his tuning into Love, Spirit-Personal, bound his wounds so that healing could take place. Herein lay *the* miracle, but a "miracle" exemplifying a resurrection of Love within the blind man, and Its continuity on the inner and outer levels of his life.

In Hebrew, presence (*pânîym*) can *also* mean "to face" or "turn toward." So, when we understand what Love can do within ourselves, our family, friends—in whomsoever, wherever and whenever—we see the "face" of Love, Spirit-Personal, and witness Its healing presence. To use more conventional religious language, this is one way in which Love enters into space-time, our reality, to speak and become real and visible to us. So, we who are often blind in our hearts can likewise welcome Love into our self for wholeness. In other words, accepting Love-God, ever-present Divine I, gives us the same *personal*-ized opportunity as the blind man for insight that is both healing and enriching. A pathway is then opened for Love to do what It naturally does—love by healing and nurturing, so providing us with a direction home to Omnipresence who is full of meaning, hope, and purpose. That is to say, a great deal of

---

separation, to create an interval) (Dawe, 1968, pp. 89-90). Distancing carries a sense of being still connected to God while separation and sin suggest, in my view, the possibility of a complete, irreversible break. As we've seen, it is impossible to be separated from Love (Rom. 8:38-39). Sin also suggests our "disobedience" to God, a traditional notion that is infantilizing. Distancing, on the other hand, acknowledges our innate goodness and possibilities for reconciliation *because we are Consciousness* (see Lk: 17:20-21). It also assumes our capacity for eventually liberating ourselves from what Julian of Norwich (Trajtelová, 2019, pp. 4, 6-8) identified as spiritual isolation, self-alienation [from Divine I], including our vulnerability and low self-worth; these accompany a lack of spiritual knowledge and discernment (both from ignorance, fear and conflicts of intention etc.).

something of lasting delight, not nothing, but a valorization instead of Not-nothing, No-thing-ness—Presence.

If we remember that Presence is indivisible then it is impossible for us to be separated from Presence since, as already noted, we *are* Presence-Love-Consciousness just as everything in all-Nature is also Presence-Love-Consciousness.[24] This is hardly nothing! But a question arises, am I being blasphemous in stating such a thing? The mainline Church certainly regards such a claim as at least presumptive, but in the writings of Ṣūfī poet Jalāl ad-Dīn Rūmī (Nicholson, 1914, p. 184) we find a different, considered and liberating understanding of *Ana 'l-Ḥaqq* (I am God):

> People imagine that it is a presumptuous claim, whereas it is really a presumptuous claim to say *Ana 'l-'abd* (I am the servant of God); and *Ana 'l-Ḥaqq* is an expression of great humility. They who say *Ana 'l-'abd* affirm two existences, their own and God's, but they who say *Ana 'l-Ḥaqq* make themselves non-existent and have given themselves up [to the extreme humility since] what this comes to is this: 'I am nothing, God is all; there is no being other than God's.'

Much earlier, medieval Kāśmīrī Śaivist sage Abhinavagupta (Williams and Woollacott, 2021, p. 127) arrived at a similar conclusion:

> There is no separate individual limited being that is me. Rather, I am the ultimate, a unified mass of luminous awareness, which is aware of both the perceiver and perceived. I am that and that alone, and nothing else.

Western medieval mystic Catherine of Genoa, too, could joyfully declare, "My Me is God. Nor do I recognise any other Me, except my God . . . God is my Being, my Me" (von Hügel, 1909, p. 265), a statement that

---

[24] According to Godbole and Mundra (2022, p. 3), Utpaladeva says in his *The Ajaḍa-Pramātṛ-Siddhiḥ* (= *Sambandha-siddhiḥ*) that all objects are nothing but Consciousness. However, he says, they appear manifold because of *māyā* (i.e., in this case, noncognition of nonduality) and that once we understand this, it is then easy to comprehend the oneness in the manifoldness of objects.

bears mystical similarity to Eckhart's "God's ground is my ground and my ground is God's ground."[25] In fact, in the same sermon (13b), he *explicitly* says that we are innately God and hence nothing in ourselves because of our inseparability from God (Walshe, 2009, p. 109).[26] For her part, Catherine was giving expression to Divine-Love within her, her acceptance of Its tenderness, wisdom, and authority—Consciousness. Like "her" Me, "our" Me is God, Consciousness. Another name for this Divine Me is, as we've seen, I, the name everyone shares the world over (hence the inverted commas around "our") but also with God as we read in Exodus 3:14—"I am that I am." Note that whenever "I" refers to the ontological It is irreducible. So, when we say, "I am," "you are," "everything is God," it is to God within me, you and *everything* or, more accurately, *as* me, you and *everything*, to whom we refer—I, you, and everything being Consciousness, and Consciousness being God.

So, as I've said, Presence has *always* been uncreated Unity, Consciousness-God, immutable and thus never provisional. Nishida said something similar with which I generally agree: "the universe is not a creation of God, but a manifestation [expression] of God [for] there is nothing that is not a manifestation of God," which means "our consciousness is one part of God's consciousness" (Nishida, 1990, pp. 158, 161). I differ a little in maintaining Consciousness-God-Love is, as I've claimed before, *exactly* the same as consciousness to which we awake each day, to that very experience which is never absent even when we sleep or are unconscious due to an accident, illness or anesthetic. In these circumstances, it is our body or finite mind that is unaware of C/consciousness, for C/consciousness can never be lost or be unaware of Itself. We pass each day in this eternally aware Omnipresence-Love, in Is-ness, in Divine Something.

Consciousness, then, though no-thing and immaterial, is real: In German, Its closest associative is *die Wirklichkeit*, the *reality* of the immaterial, rather than *die Realität*, ordinary reality experienced daily. We have seen that this Omnipresence-Love resides within us (Lk. 17:20-21) and is everywhere—where is Consciousness not? Much of It is

---

[25] Re: Consciousness, I'm cautious about using words like ground, substrate, substratum, basis, foundation, and underlying, etc.; if we're not careful, they can suggest a duality where there can be none. Being All, Consciousness is devoid of any kind of underpinning/substrate.

[26] See also Walshe, Sermon 49, p. 263.

experienced through our finite senses and through others gifted in Love. We are indeed indelibly entangled with/in Consciousness as Continuum, with/in this vast ImmateReality (*bheda-abheda*), to suggest another neologism, and there is nothing "spooky" (Einstein) here since there is no distance, not even nothing "between" us all, "between" ourselves "and" Nature, "and between" everything "and" Consciousness-God.[27] Any such distance is an illusion. Frithjof Schuon (1975, p. 76) has this to say:

> The universe comprises something of the Divine for the simple reason that by virtue of the miracle of existence it is not nothingness; being, it is unable to escape from Being. If this is a kind of pantheism, then we are obliged to admit that pantheism is not entirely without justification when it is considered from a particular standpoint, namely that of metaphysical homogeneity or solidarity of not-nothingness, non-unreality, or non-impossibility. In a certain sense all that is not nothing is God, not in its particularity, but in and through ontological Substance.

We've seen that nobody knows if matter in the form of, say, the universe came from nothing. But what if the universe has interiority, as Jesuit mystic Pierre Teilhard de Chardin suggested (1959, pp. 56-57)? In discussing this briefly, we can start with physicist Andrei Linde (2014, p. 12) who asks, "If space-time did not exist for times less than zero, how could everything appear from nothing?" In effect, he's saying there may never have been actual absolute nothing prior to any "Big Bang," as the ancients came to understand for themselves. Theologian and philosopher Keith Ward (1999, p. 7) reminds us that scientists like Linde now theorize about the existence of a

> very full and complex [yet evanescent] set of [relativistic] quantum fields [prior to the possible Big Bang] constantly fluctuating in regular and systematic ways—so that every possibility is realised in time.

---

[27] For reference to Albert Einstein's (1935) famous observation of quantum entanglement as "spooky action at a distance," see Muller, A. (2022) "What is Quantum Entanglement?" at: <https://theconversation.com/what-is-quantum-entanglement-a-physicist-explains-the-science-of-einsteins-spooky-action-at-a-distance-191927>. (Accessed: 26 July 2023).

Such "energy" is, of course, not nothing. In short, we can confirm the lack of any evidence for "physical" nothingness, and if there *were* nothing/ness it would be something, as we've seen. We are reminded that if we wish to inquire of "nothing," metaphysics needs to posit "nothing" in advance as an object of reference, but that any objectification of nothing transforms it into something, and so the question subverts itself. We might add here Hegel's observation that they who hypothesize that nothing can produce something have already implicitly infused being into nothing, and that this nothing, therefore, is no longer pure nothing but already becoming. If nothing produces nothing, nothing remains the same, and there is no becoming that can occur (Wong, 2018, p. 580). Shades here of Laozi, Parmenides, and a host of similar thinkers. Indeed, in what I think is a stunning affirmation of something over nothing—actually Something— Parmenides (Kirk and Raven, 1971, p. 273) wrote:

> One way only is left to be spoken of, that it [Existent = Reality, Oneness] is; and on this way are full many signs that what is, is uncreated and imperishable, for it is entire, immovable and without end. It was not in the past, nor shall it be, since it is now, all at once, one, continuous; for what creation wilt thou seek for it? how and whence did it grow? Nor shall I allow thee to say or to think, 'from that which is not'; for it is not to be said or thought that it is not. And what need would have driven it on to grow, starting from nothing, at a later time rather than an earlier? Thus it must either completely be or be not.

Comparing this statement with the *Parātrīśikā-vivaraṇa* of Abhinavagupta reveals a remarkable similarity; here I quote Indologist André Padoux (1990, p. 79):

> Tantric thought, indeed, and not only non-dualistic Śaivism, seems averse (like any mythic thought probably) to the idea of an ex nihilo creation, of an absolute fiat, of a shift from the state of nothingness or pure being to that of the phenomenal world. Accordingly, the universe is not considered as created but as emanated, projected, by the primary principle which is able to manifest it only

insofar as it was already implicit within himself: what
is not inside the primary principle cannot exist outside
thereof. [28]

Such a meonic character for matter is also found in Teilhard (1959, pp.
56-7) for whom matter was not inanimate, as it *does* seem to be. For
him, it certainly possessed Consciousness (as we saw) being "more than
the particulate swarming, so marvellously analysed by modern physics."
Thus, ConsciousnessMatter-God appears to us as C/consciousness
noumenally and as matter phenomenally.

Up to this point, I've referred to human love and Divine Love
63 times. Obviously, we can't physically see "both types" (which are the
same) or, like Consciousness which is what Love is, define "them" to our
full satisfaction. Nevertheless, when I say I love my partner, children,
and grandson, this love *is* a reality (*die Wirklichkeit*). It's something *very
real* to me and to my partner, son, grandson and his respective parents. Or
when I say I love waterfalls, roses, or remember wondrous times, nobody
can see my feelings and memories, but they *are* beautiful *somethings*
nevertheless. Without *die Wirklichkeit* we'd wander aimlessly in a void;
thankfully, "physical" nothingness just cannot be.

So, immutable Love-Consciousness is always "there," everywhere, as Presence even though, as mentioned before, some deny
It outright, a stance vociferously and entertainingly criticized by
philosopher Galen Strawson, a warrior for consciousness. Frankly, I
don't think we'll ever be able to define C/consciousness (like love) to
our full satisfaction. However, with so many different beings and things
inhabiting this planet—leaving aside the universe for a moment—we *do*
know that Consciousness is unbelievably varied, complex, and protean,
indeed ever potentially so, but also that It is a unicity in the same way
the atmosphere can't be cut with a knife although it, too, contains a host
of things, particles, and gases, etc. The rose window, a unity of parts, is
another good analogy. Equally, to say there's "that of God" in each person
does not mean "a bit of," "a part of," or "a spark of" God; rather, it is a
way of pointing to the totality of Consciousness-God-The Way in each

[28] Tantric = relating to, or involving the doctrines or principles of, the Hindu or Buddhist
tantras, particularly the use of mantras, meditation, yoga, and ritual.

person, Its sheer reality *as Wholeness*, as All. The great big mereological world and universe around us simply defy nothing.

With all this in mind, I've never read anything that convincingly refutes Baruch Spinoza's contention that Nature is indivisible, self-caused, *the only* substantial whole. Clearly, he wasn't pointing to the physical, outward difference between, say, an elephant and a spinach leaf, but the very life they have—their shared Consciousness. For Spinoza, this unified, interrelated, unique, productive, necessary Being that is all-Nature, *is* what's *also* meant by God or, as one might say today, Ultimate Reality, Completeness of Existence, Presence, Consciousness. He insisted God was *the* Substance, "the immanent and not the transient cause of all things" who did cause all things *but not* by standing outside God's effects; rather, these effects resided in God. Which is why he could say, "Whatsoever is, is in God" to mean all existence *is* God yet possessing many diverse forms, one element of which we call "I" or "our life." God, therefore, being the universe (and everything else), could not transcend it (Spinoza, 1941, p. 11). Nothing can possibly transcend Consciousness-Reality: not even Consciousness can transcend Itself just as a candle cannot light itself.

According to Canadian philosopher Eliza Ritchie (1902, p. 14), Spinoza rejected any notion of an anthropomorphized Deity but was equally certain that the Divine

> is consciousness, eternal, all-embracing, and self-sufficient; and that consciousness is cognizable by our reason, which, pertains to it, though it cannot be pictured by our imagination, which misleads us when it represents it as analogous to our own, since the latter being only a 'mode' is finite, transitory and dependent.

So, being a unity, Consciousness is the same in all people and all-Nature. Go to Buenos Aires and sit on a tram. The person next to you will be the very same Consciousness as you although manifest differently. Experiences such as these can be replicable anywhere. Everybody, and everything, experiences the one Consciousness because, I repeat, It is indivisible; there is no other, or outside to, All-Consciousness as Spinoza said. Nor are there levels, varieties, stages, or states of Consciousness.

This might be true of Its qualia, but Oneness cannot be Twoness or Threeness, just Consciousness.

And because we all are, along with all-Nature, the same one Consciousness, it makes no sense to be racist, misogynist, sexist, ageist, classist, ableist, homophobic, transphobic, physically and verbally violent, and manipulative etc. Such damage reverberates far and wide—again, Indra's Net. And because we're addressing All-Consciousness, Indra's Net obviously applies to the *natural* world, a refraction through our finite minds, to be sure, but nonetheless actual, tangible. Our commodification of Nature results from the sort of binary/dualist thinking just listed, and it is clearly ruinous; each day we see evidence of its frightening retribution which hardly augers well for the planet's future, or ours with it. We had better change our ways, and quickly, by making real to ourselves the shared experience that is Consciousness, Not-nothing.

In the noncanonical Gospel of Thomas, Jesus is made to lament how The Way (Consciousness) covers the Earth without people realizing it. It's not difficult to see this today, one reason being our continuing mesmerization by consumerism, that dazzling child of the materialist hegemon but which is, in my view, an insidious cultural disease.[29] Jesus's lamentation is also ours, particularly in the way it accounts for a sizeable number of existential voids, the current significant example being, as I've said, the ongoing destruction of our planet home. It is a lamentation that highlights the critical need to advance The Way's peace, justice and compassion for humanity and the Earth, and the promise of a One-derfully fulfilling future if The Way-Consciousness is validated at all levels of our political, social, cultural, and economic life.

This is the globalization I support, and, in my view, there are two effective ways of putting it into practice, viz. by studying the spiritual nature of Consciousness, and doing our utmost to *be* The Way, to *be autobasileia* as early Church theologian Origen described Jesus (1903, p. 498).[30] Saying this reminds me of the community development workers I once met in Khayelitsha, a South African township (slum) near Cape Town, who demonstrated how *autobasileia* can be actualized (Guiton, 2016, p. 99).[31] Under very challenging conditions, they applied practical skills, understanding, and hope to the needs of those in their care. Hugely

---

[29] Gospel of *Thomas*, Logion 113.
[30] See Mk. 1:14; 1 Cor. 13:6; Jm. 1:27.
[31] Khayelitsha, pron: 'Kigh-ya-leesh-ah.'

impressive was the depth of their compassion for everybody in an area gripped by violence and poverty, and, of course, the despair these create. The inner power and humility that went with this presence of heart and mind was much more than efficacious. Here were truly inspiring people, prophets on the margin, who were indeed The Way-in-action. Also interesting for me was how their orthopraxis was secured by their prayerful silence-stillness.

In sum, I have long felt that the most grounded way of establishing lasting peace, justice and compassion for everyone today, and for future generations and the planet, is for each of us to dwell on C/consciousness along with Its "other" form, The Way, as best we can with the aim of becoming *autobasiliea*.

In so dwelling on C/consciousness we'll discover that It's not a thing we *have* but *are*, and an experience we all share just as we all share the same DNA and the name "I," the latter forever reminding us of the Oneness who is C/consciousness, and indeed the Oneness we also are. This Consciousness-God is within, not "out there" beyond the universe because, as we found, there *is* no "out there" or a beyond All. Instead, everything, including ourselves, partakes of what I called the "In here" or "In-here-ncy," Continuum. Which is one reason among many why there is no nothing, as opposed to the Not-nothing that is Consciousness.

Linguistically, "nothing" does have considerable cachet depending on the way it's used in various contexts. Despite this, it is always preferable and fruitful to address *Something*, the shared Not-nothing that is "closer to us than breathing, and nearer than [our] hands and feet," to quote poet Lord Alfred Tennyson (Buckley, 1958, p. 352). This Something is Presence-Love whom everyone experiences every nanosecond of their lives, at every incidence of the Eternal *Now* in which everything finds itself.

Finally, to know more of Consciousness is to know more of ourselves and *vice versa*. This is essential for a deep and healthy spirituality, a spirituality with compassion as its foundation. We can do this best by studying and, as I say, consciously living Consciousness whose tones of felicity have always reverberated with Divine plenitude.

References

Anon. (1973) *The Cloud of Unknowing*. Garden City, NY: Doubleday.

Bohm, D. (2005) *Wholeness and the Implicate Order*. London: Routledge.

Bruno, G. A. (2017) "Schelling on the Possibility of Evil." *SATS-Northern European Journal of Philosophy,* 18(1), pp. 1-18.

Buckley, J. (1958) *Poems of Tennyson*. Boston: Houghton Mifflin.

Clement of Alexandria. (1869) *Miscellanies* (*Stromateis*). Translated from the ancient Greek by W. Wilson. Edinburgh: T. & T. Clark.

Dawe, R. (1968) "Some Reflections on Ate and Hamartia." *Harvard Studies in Classical Philology,* 72.

Fan, M. and Sullivan, I. (2010) "The Significance of Xuwu 虚无 (Nothingness) in Chinese Aesthetics." *Frontiers of Philosophy in China,* 5(4), pp. 560-574.

Godbole, M. and Mundra, A. (2022) *The Ajaḍa-Pramātṛ-Siddhiḥ of Utpaladeva*. Available at: <https://www.academia.edu/69537313/ The_Aja%E1%B8%8Da_Pram%C4%81t%E1%B9%9B_ Siddhi%E1%B8%A5_of_Utpaladeva_A_Translation_Proof_of_ the_Conscious_Knower_>. (Accessed: 26 July 2023).

Gospel of Thomas. (2017) Available at: <https://www.newworld-encyclopedia.org/entry/Gospel_of_Thomas>. (Accessed: 26 July 2023).

Guiton, G. (2016) *What Love Can Do*. Melbourne, Australia: Morning Star (Wilpf & Stock) Publications.

Hick, J. (1995). *The Rainbow of Faiths*. London: SCM.

John Scotus Eriugena. (1987) *Periphyseon* (*De Divisione Naturæ*). Translated from the Latin by I. Sheldon-Williams and J. O'Meara. Montreal: Bellarmin.

Kasulis, T. (1985) "The Incomparable Philosopher" in LaFleur, W. (ed.). *Dōgen Studies*. Honolulu: University of Hawaii Press, pp. 83-98.

Kena-Upanishad. (1900) Translated from Saṃskṛt by G. Prasadji. Delhi: Sarvadeshik Arya Pratinidhi.

Kerr, G. (2012) "A Thomistic Metaphysics of Creation." *Religious Studies,* 48(3), pp. 337-356.

Kirk, G. and Raven, J. (1971) *The Presocratic Philosophers.* London: Cambridge University Press.

Leibniz, G. (1890) "On the Ultimate Origin of Things [1697]" in *The Philosophical Works of Leibniz.* Translated from the Latin and French by G. Duncan. New Haven, CT: Tuttle, Morehouse & Taylor, pp. 100-106.

Linde, A. (2014) "Universe, Life, Consciousness." Available at: <http://www.andrei-linde.com/articles/universe-life-consciousness-pdf>. (Accessed: 26 July 2023).

Mādhavānanda. (1950) *Br̥hadāraṇyaka Upaniṣad.* Mayawati, India: Advaita Ashrama Mayavati.

Mascaró, J. (1962) *The Bhagavad Gita.* Harmondsworth, England: Penguin.

Matt, D. (1990) "Ayin: The Concept of Nothingness in Jewish Mysticism" in Forman, R. (ed.) *The Problem of Pure Consciousness.* Oxford: Oxford University Press, pp. 121-159.

Meister Eckhart. (2009) *The Complete Mystical Works.* Translated from the Middle German by M. O'C Walshe. New York: Crossroads.

Newman, B. (2016) "Annihilation and authorship: Three Women Mystics of the 1290s." *Speculum,* 91(3), pp. 591-630.

Nicholas of Cusa (Cusanus). (1988) *De Visione Dei.* Translated from the Latin by J. Hopkins. Minneapolis, MN: A. J. Banning. 2nd. edn.

Nicholson, R. (1914) *The Mystics of Islam.* London: Bell.

Nishida, K. (1990) *Inquiry into the Good.* New Haven, CT: Yale University Press.

Nishitani, K. (1982) *Religion and Nothingness.* Berkeley, CA: University of California Press.

Nityaswarupananda. (1940) *Ashtavakra Samhita* [= *Aṣṭāvakra Gītā*]. Mayawati, India: Advaita Ashrama Mayavati.

O'Donohue, J. (1999) *Anam Ćara.* London: Bantam.

Origen. (1903) "Commentary on the Gospel According to Matthew" in *Ante-Nicene Christian Library* [Orig. Supp. to the American edn.]. New York: Charles Scribner's Sons: Vol. 9, Bk. XIV.

Padoux, A. (1990). *Vāc: The Concept of the Word in Selected Hindu Tantras.* New York: State University of New York Press.

Polanyi, M. (1964) *Personal Knowledge.* New York: Harper and Row.

_____, (1966) *The Tacit Dimension*. New York: Doubleday.

Porete, M. (2010) *The Mirror of Simple Souls*. Translated from the French by E. Colledge. Notre Dame, IN: University of Notre Dame Press.

Rādhākrishnan, S. (1970) *The Bhagavadgītā*. Bombay: Blackie & Son. 2nd.edn.

Ritchie, E. (1902) "Notes on Spinoza's Conception of God." *The Philosophical Review*, 11(1), pp. 1-15.

Sartre, J-P. (1984 [1943]) *Being and Nothingness*. New York: Washington Square Press.

Schuon, F. (1975) *Logic and Transcendence*. Translated from the German by P. Townsend. New York: Harper Torchbooks.

Spinoza, B. (1941) *Ethics*. London: Dent.

Stein, L. (2019) *Working with Mystical Experiences in Psychoanalysis*. Oxford: Routledge.

Strawson, G. (2019) "A Full-on Defence" in *The Guardian Review* 102(16), p. 16.

Tauler, J. (1910) *The Sermons and Conferences of John Tauler*. Washington, DC: Apostolic Mission House.

Teilhard de Chardin, P. (1959). *The Phenomenon of Man* (now *The Human Phenomenon*). New York: Harper.

Tillich, P. (1975) *Systematic Theology*. Chicago: University of Chicago Press: Vol. 1.

Trajtelová, J. (2019): "'All Shall Be Well': Several Phenomenological and Metaphysical Insights into a Spiritual Experience of Julian of Norwich." *Spirituality Studies*, 5(1).

van Ruysbroeck, J. (1916) *The Adornment of the Spiritual Marriage*. Translated from the Flemish by C. Wynschenk. London: Dent.

von Hügel, F. (1909) *The Mystical Element of Religion in St. Catherine of Genoa*. London: Dent, Vol. 1.

Waley, A. (1934) *The Way and Its Power: A Study of the Tao Tê Ching*. London: Geo. Allen & Unwin.

Ward, K. (1999) "Why God Must Exist." *Science and Christian Belief*, 11(1), pp. 5-13.

Weir, T. (1901). "Translation of an Arabic Manuscript." *Journal of the Royal Asiatic Society*. Art. 29, pp. 809-825.

Whitehead, A. N. (1941) *Process and Reality*. New York. The Humanities Press.

Williams, B. and Wollacott, M. (2021) "Conceptual Cognition and Awakening: Insights from Non-dual Śaivism and Neuroscience." *The Journal of Transpersonal Psychology,* 53(2), pp. 56-79.

Winston, D. (1971) "The Book of Wisdom's Theory of Cosmogony." *History of Religions,* 11, pp. 191-192.

Wong, K. K. (2011) "Hegel's Criticism of Laozi and its Implications." *Philosophy East & West,* 61(1), pp. 56-79.

_____, (2018) "Hegel, Schelling and Laozi on Nothingness." *Frontiers of Philosophy in China,* 13(4), pp. 574-584.

Yiangou, N. (2017) "Is a New Consciousness Emerging? Reflections on the Thought of Ibn 'Arabi." *World Futures,* 73(7), pp. 427-441.

12

Apophaticism and Deification in Meister Eckhart and Nicholas of Cusa

Ken Parry

I have selected two themes to examine in Meister Eckhart and Nicholas of Cusa, apophaticism or negation, and deification or godlikeness. It is not my intention to suggest these themes exhaust the depth of thought in these two authors, but rather to highlight them in the broader context of understanding their contribution to this volume's topic. Besides, in this presentation I can only scratch the surface. The two themes are characteristic of both theologians but are not always discussed together, with apophaticism taking the lion's share of the commentary. While apophaticism is an essential element of their theological thinking, it needs to be discussed and understood in relation to that of deification (Russell, 2004; Ortiz, 2019), which for our thinkers is the ultimate destination of the apophatic way (Mortley, 1986; Carabine, 1995). The terminology of both ideas originates in the ancient world with passages from the Judaeo-Christian scriptures quoted to endorse them. The traditional pairing of the two emerges in the writings of several early Christian authors, with apophaticism, mediated through later Platonism, having a lasting impact on all three Abrahamic faiths (Kars, 2019; Fagenblat, 2017). We will begin with some general remarks related to apophaticism and deification.

Before we do that, however, we should say something about the term Neoplatonism, which is often mentioned in relation to our two thinkers. When we refer to this term, we have in mind those philosophers who from the third to the sixth century C.E., developed a particular form of Platonism that became pervasive during this period. The term Neoplatonism is a modern term applied to the philosophy of Plotinus in the third century, who developed a far-reaching metaphysical and religious interpretation of Plato's works. He was followed by his pupil Porphyry, who in turn was followed by a succession of other thinkers, notably Proclus in the fifth century.[1] Although we might call them Neoplatonists or new Platonists, a title they would have repudiated, they were not simply Platonistic but took ideas from other schools of philosophy. One of the characteristics of the later Neoplatonists was writing commentaries on the works of Aristotle as well as those of Plato. This was often done with the intention of harmonizing them (Karamanolis, 2006; Hadot, 2015).

By the time we come to the 14th and 15th centuries in the West, so-called "Christian Platonism" had filtered through into mainstream theology (Moran, 2014; Hampton & Kenney, 2020). It was characterized by emphasis on the One, the ultimate Being, the transcendent but unknowable source of all things. The Neoplatonic triad of the One, Intellect, and Soul might be seen in parallel with the Christian trinity of Father, Son, and Holy Spirit.[2] Although Eckhart and Cusa were aware of the wave of Aristotelianism that had swept through the medieval schools mediated by the Arabs, they adhered on the whole to the Christian Platonism initiated by the ninth century Irishman, John Scotus Eriugena, and his promotion of the Christian Neoplatonist, Dionysius the Areopagite (Albertson, 2020). Having said that, however, we should not imagine that Aristotle was the leading archenemy when we have observed that it was a Neoplatonic enterprise to establish harmony between the Academy and the Lyceum. In fact, a recent volume of studies has brought out the Aristotelianism inherent in Cusa's writings (Vimercate & Zaffino, 2020), but I am not aware of a similar volume dedicated to Eckhart's engagement with the Stagirite.

1. Apophaticism

I will say something first about the Greek background to the idea of apophaticism. At its most basic apophasis is the use of the alpha privative to negate a positive word in Greek. The following from John of Damascus in the eighth century is a good example of this rudimentary method. John

---

[1] Justinian I's closing of the Academy at Athens in 529 was not the end of philosophy in Byzantium (see Trizio and Bydén: forthcoming 2026).
[2] Cusa is said to have claimed the doctrine of the Trinity originated with Pythagoras (Cornelli, 2013: 29).

gives a list of negative affirmations descriptive of God, each beginning with the alpha privative:

> God is without beginning (ἄναρχος), without end (ἀτελε-
> ύτητος), uncreated (ἄκιστος), immutable (ἄτρεπτοσ), un-
> changeable (ἀναλλοίωτος), non-composite (ἀσύνθετος),
> incorporeal (ἀσώματος), invisible (ἀόρατος), uncircum-
> scribed (ἀπερίγραπτος), ungraspable (ἀπερίληπτος), incom-
> prehensible (ἀκατάληπτος), unfathomable (ἀπερινόητος) …
> (Russell, 2022, pp. 60–61)

In English we apply a variety of prefixes to negate a word, but in Greek, the alpha private will generally do this. In addition to its grammatical usage, the idea of using negation to explore abstract and metaphysical ideas is to be found in the writings of Plato, notably in his *Parmenides,* in which the notions of what "is" and "is not" are discussed.[3] Apophaticism in Eckhart and Cusa relates primarily to its theological function in denying we can know the ultimate essence of God.

It is with the Middle Platonists of the first and second centuries C.E., that apophaticism became an intellectual tool in Greek metaphysics and theology (Dillion, 1996, pp. 184–185). It was particularly influential at that time on Christians of the Alexandrian school, notably Clement and Origen of Alexandria, as well as the Jewish thinker Philo of Alexandria (Wolfson, 1948; pp. 94–164; Hägg, 2006; Ramelli, 2019). Plato is said to have promoted "Socratic ignorance," a state of philosophical being based on a remark attributed to Socrates: "I know only one thing—that I know nothing," although the exact phase is not found in Plato (*Apology*, 23b). Here, ignorance is made the beginning of wisdom, the wisdom of unknowing, which is probably where the phrase "learned ignorance" (*docta ignorantia*) comes from in Augustine (*Letter to Proba*, 30.28) and later in Nicholas of Cusa (Dubbelman, 2020), especially in his work with that title published in 1440.

---

[3] There is ambiguity in Parmenides's ἔστιν ἦ οὐκ ἔστιν (Kirk & Raven, 1979; Chap. 10).

2. Dionysius the Areopagite

The main representative of the apophatic way for our thinkers is Dionysius the Areopagite, the late fifth/early sixth century author known today as Pseudo-Dionysius, whose name is mentioned by Paul in Acts 17:34. This was when the apostle was in Athens discussing with philosophers the dedication of an altar to the "unknown god" (Ἄγνωστος Θεός), indicating divine unknowability but appropriated by Paul for the Christian God. His toponym refers to the Areopagus outcrop on the Acropolis, where the law council assembled.[4] Dionysius is called Pseudo-Dionysius because the unknown author hid his identity behind this first century name. This was undoubtedly done to give his work apostolic prestige.

The *Corpus Dionysiacum* consists of a selection of letters and four theological works of which the shortest, *The Mystical Theology,* is probably the most famous (Coakley & Stang, 2009; Perczel, 2015). It was written in Greek in a Syrian environment and translated into several Eastern Christian languages, notably Syriac and Armenian,[5] before it was translated into Latin. It was the translation of John Scotus Eriugena, along with his translation of the seventh-century Greek theologian Maximos the Confessor that brought Dionysius and the apophatic tradition to the attention of the West. John Scotus himself wrote a work entitled *Periphyseon* or *On the Division of Nature*, which is a precursor to the Christian Neoplatonism of our authors, particularly Cusa, who annotated his manuscript copy of this work (Watanabe, Christianson & Izbicki, 2011; 72, Kobusch, 2022). We can see the tone set by Eriugena from the following quotation:

> Hence, when we say that God is, we do not say that He is after some manner; [and] therefore we use the words "is" and "was" in Him simply and infinitely and absolutely. For the Divine is incomprehensible to all reason and all intellect, and therefore when we predicate being of Him, we do not say that He is; for being is from Him but He is not Himself being. (*Periphyseon,* Sheldon–Williams, 1987, p. 73)

---

[4] According to tradition, Dionysius is said to have been a lawyer and the first bishop of Athens, who subsequently became patron saint of the city.
[5] An Arabic translation also exists (Treiger, 2007).

Although the authenticity of the Dionysian corpus was questioned at
Constantinople as early as 535, on the grounds that there were no previous
citations of a Christian author by this name, ultimately it did not matter
that the corpus was not what it pretended to be. Indeed, Maximos the
Confessor was prepared to ignore the anachronisms and to accept the
corpus as the inspired writings of an author utilizing both apophaticism
and deification, referring to him as "divinely inspired" and "godlike"
(Constas, 2022, p. 223). Dionysius is the most quoted authority by Thomas
Aquinas after Augustine and the inspiration for the anonymous Middle
English author of the 14th-century work, *The Cloud of Unknowing*.[6] In
the West Lorenzo Valla's remarks of 1457 concerning the pseudonymity
of the corpus were rather late in the day, with Cusa himself having already
expressed his doubts about its dating (Robichaud, 2022), perhaps through
his discussions with Greeks during his sojourn in Constantinople in 1437.

Such was the interest in authenticating Dionysius as a true
Christian voice that it was claimed his Neoplatonic contemporary and
successor (*diadachos*) at the school at Athens, Proclus, had stolen his
ideas from Dionysius (Parry, 2006).[7] This reversal of the historical
chronology was a neat piece of Christian propaganda intended to allay
suspicions surrounding the identity and dating of the corpus. This can be
seen in a scholion attached to the *Corpus Dionysiacum*:

> It should be known that some of the pagan philosophers,
> and above all Proclus, make frequent use of the doctrines
> of the blessed Dionysius and often literally with his own
> words. This justifies the belief that the older philosophers
> of Athens had appropriated Dionysius' works, as the author
> relates in the book here, and held them hidden in order to
> appear themselves as the fathers of the divine discourse of
> Dionysius. (Quoted by Lankila, 2011, pp.18–19)

It was through Dionysius via Proclus that Neoplatonic thought found its
way into Christian speculative theology in a lasting and meaningful way.

---

[6] The author cautions his student not to divulge its contents (*The Cloud of Unknowing*,
Spearing, 2001, pp. 44–45).

[7] The Middle Platonist Numenius had claimed Plato was an Atticizing Moses, an idea
adopted by several early Christian authors (Ridings, 1995).

By the time we come to Eckhart and Cusa, they are reading the Areopagite through various translations and layers of historical exegesis.

Anticipating Dionysius is several ways, Gregory of Nyssa in the fourth century says that the mind needs to leave behind all sense perceptions and intellectual concepts in seeking the unseen and incomprehensible God:

> This is the true knowledge of what is sought; this is the seeing that consists in not seeing, because that which is sought transcends all knowledge, being separated on all sides by incomprehensibility as by a kind of darkness. (Malherbe & Ferguson, 1978, p. 95)

The mention of darkness refers to Exod. 24:15, where Moses enters a cloud to speak with the unseen God. The cloud became a common metaphor for the unknowability of God, hence the title *The Cloud of Unknowing* mentioned above.[8] In his *Mystical Theology*, Dionysius discusses what can be affirmed about the cause of all beings, suggesting that it is more appropriate to negate all affirmations, since it surpasses all being:

> Now we should not conclude that the negations are simply the opposite of the affirmations, but rather that the cause of all is considerably prior to this, beyond privations, beyond every denial, beyond every assertion. (Luibheid, 1987, p. 136)

What lies beyond every denial and every assertion is what Eckhart, following Dionysius, calls the "negation beyond negation" (*negatio negationis*), that is, the hypernegation, or superessential God. The resulting silence, unknowing, and ignorance, must be recognized as the ultimate state in which to contemplate the divine.

We can see the role Dionysius played in Cusa's thinking in the opening section of his treatise *On God as Not-Other* (*De li non aliud*). It begins with three of his students telling him what they are studying. The first is studying Plato's *Parmenides* and Proclus's commentary on it;

---

[8] Cusa remarks on the necessity to enter the cloud to acknowledge the coincidence of opposites (*De visione Dei*, Bond, 1997, p. 251).

the second is studying Proclus' *Platonic Theology* and translating it into Latin; the third is studying Aristotle, while Nicholas himself is studying Dionysius the Areopagite. This sets the scene for a conversation in which Nicholas praises Proclus and Aristotle but describes Dionysius as taking things a stage further (Hopkins, 1987, p. 1). Dionysius's promotion of a baptized Platonism provides Cusa with an intellectual bridge between Neoplatonism and Christianity.

3. Deification

We discuss next the Greek background to the idea of deification and its adoption in Christian thought. On several occasions Plato defines philosophy as "becoming godlike as far as is possible," for example in the *Theaetetus* (176a). Among the Neoplatonists this became one of the standard six definitions of philosophy, along with another definition "a preparation for death" (Elias and David, 2018, pp. 27, 106). This was adopted by Christians as a monastic virtue stemming from a voluntary purification of the senses. Defining philosophy "as a preparation for death" was related to "becoming godlike as far as is possible," because without self-denial and asceticism there was no achieving godlikeness, whether by means of divine grace or without it. Although grace is not commonly associated with Neoplatonism, there is a sense of divine benevolence activating the philosopher (Dillon, 2014). For Iamblichus in the fourth century contemplation and prayer would seem to be means by which we move toward divinization:

> The consciousness of own nothingness, if one judges it in comparison with the gods, make us naturally turn to supplications; and by the practice of supplication, we are raised gradually to the level of the object of our supplication, and we gain likeness to it by virtue of our constant consorting with it, and, starting from our own imperfection, we gradually take on the perfection of the divine. (Clarke et al, 2003, pp. 58–61)

Iamblichus takes this a stage further when speaking about the participation of matter and created things in divinity because of the divine nature of the Demiurge:

> And let there be no astonishment if in this connection we speak of a pure and divine form of matter; for matter also issues from the Father and Creator of all and thus gains its perfection, which is suitable to the reception of gods. And at the same time nothing hinders the superior beings from being able to illuminate their inferiors …for since it was proper not even for terrestrial things to be utterly deprived of participation in the divine, earth also has received from such participation a share in divinity …
> (Clarke et al, 2003, pp. 266–267)

In this passage the Neoplatonic notion of creation as a theophany in which the divine participates in matter, may be compared with Christian incarnational theology in which creation is transformed through divinity uniting with humanity. Both traditions treat creation as fundamentally good even though their views on the origin and purpose of creation may differ. Neither the Platonist Demiurge nor the Christian God abandons their creations because the universe continues to operate under the governance of divine providence (Parry, 2017). For both, evil is ultimately a privation that has no ontological status and for which human freedom must take responsibility.[9]

In the Roman world the idea of apotheosis applied to the transformation of a hero or emperor into a god, but in Christianity deification turns no one into a god. Justin Martyr, writing in the second century, makes this clear:

> And what shall we say of the emperors who when they die among yourselves are always deemed worthy of deification (ἀπαθανάτίσις) and you produce someone

---

[9] Plotinus's inclination to downgrade physical matter because it is at the end of the spectrum of being, and thus being furthest from the good may be considered evil, needs to be nuanced, given his anti-Gnostic treatise in the *Enneads* and the commissioning of his pupils to write against the Gnostic worldview (*Enn.* 1.8; 2.9, Gerson, 2018, pp. 110–123, 206–235).

who swears that he has seen the cremated Caesar
ascending from the funeral pyre to heaven. (Russell,
2004, p. 25)

Justin uses the same Greek term ἀπαθανάτίσις (immortalization) for
"those who have lived a holy and virtuous life close to God." It is personal
virtue, not senatorial decree that confers this status. The Christian
distinction in vocabulary from the pagan tradition emerged with the term
theosis in Greek and *deificatio* in Latin.[10] Christian deification followed
the dictum attributed to Athanasius of Alexandria in the fourth century:
"God became human so that humanity might become divine" (Russell,
2004, 169), backed by such scriptural passages as Psalm 82:6: "You are
gods and all children of the Most High" (Gen. 3:5).

Neither Neoplatonism nor Christianity suggests that deification
means total absorption of the human into the divine. Such an occurrence
would make us gods before our time. The path of virtue as a way of life
was embraced by both traditions, and for Christians being made in the
divine image and likeness was the key to understanding the deification
process. That it was a process and not an event, that is, a means to an end
ultimately unattainable in this life, was made clear by Gregory of Nyssa,
who called it "unending" (*epektasis*) (Musurillo, 1995, pp. 83–84). It was
progressive, not retrogressive, meaning it was not about restoring humanity
to its prelapsarian state, but moving forward to divine embracement. The
question hinged on what was lost because of the fall: Was it the image or
the likeness, or both? To some degree East and West saw differently the
implications for humankind. In the Greek patristic tradition, the image
was retained but the likeness was lost (Basil the Great, 2005, pp. 43–44),
while in the mainly Augustinian tradition, both were lost, resulting in each
having differing views on the need for grace and what was necessary for
salvation. Nevertheless, in both cases deification acted as a counterweight
to apophaticism, with negative theology providing the ultimate way to a
positive experience.

---

[10] Eriugena comments on the rare use of the terms *deification* and *theosis* in Latin works,
suggesting that it is too sublime and therefore not to be proclaimed openly (Dietrich &
Ducklow, 2008, p. 108).

4. Eckhart on Detachment

Eckhart applies the apophatic way in his treatise *On Detachment* (MHG *Gelâzenheit*) (Heidegger, 1966; Moore, 2019).[11] He praises detachment more than the virtues of love, humility, and mercy, yet he is not disparaging these virtues in any real sense. He places them on a lower register to that of detachment because none of them can be performed without it. Its nature is such that it becomes the instrument of all virtues. But what does he mean by detachment, especially when he says that it borders closely on nothing? He writes that "God's own and natural place is unity and purity," which come from detachment, so for us to practice detachment brings us nearer to God. For him detachment "is receptive of nothing but God," remarking that "detachment is so near nothingness that nothing is so delicate that it could remain in detachment except God alone" (Clark & Skinner, 1958, p. 157). Eckhart is not equating nothingness with God. This cannot be the case because the term nothingness no more signifies God than everythingness. It would compromise his apophaticism by attributing a nothing, that is a something, to God, while also undermining his divine transcendence. God is neither nothing nor something because both terms are inapplicable.

Detachment is a process of mind-emptying of which self-abasement and nihilism (thinking one is nothing) are part of it. For Eckhart a soul in a state of pure detachment attracts God to it. It is the nearest we come to being in a formless state. He sums it up thus:

> If a human being is to become like God, in so as far as
> a creature can possess similarity to God, it must be by
> means of detachment. (Clark & Skinner, 1963, pp. 159–
> 160)

The end of detachment is deification (*Vergöttlichung*), with the proviso "in so far as," which is a throwback to Plato's definition of philosophy as "assimilation to God as far as is humanly possible." Furthermore, this

---

[11] I have retained the translation "detachment" rather than "releasement" because it is nearest to the monastic notion of *apatheia*, or dispassion and, although taken from the Stoics, does not mean devoid of compassion. See the comprehensive study by Markus Vinzent (2011) of Eckhart's idea of detachment and the newly rediscovered *Parisian Questions*.

Apophaticism and Deification in Meister Eckhart
and Nicholas of Cusa
321

similarity or assimilation cannot happen without an experience of the divine presence, only we need to understand what is meant by that.[12] We should not expect the skies to open and the hand of divine grace to reach down to us with a supernatural blessing. Notice that in saying "to become like God" Eckhart is indicating that deification is potentiality (*in posse*); it is *becoming* godlike, never actuality (*in esse*) *being* God. The *inquantum* qualifier, which means in Latin "insofar as" or "inasmuch as," distances the creator from the creature, the intelligible from the contingent, pointing to the inequality in the relationship between God and humanity (*Meister Echkhart*, Davies, 1994, p. xxiv).

At the same time, Eckhart is rather scathing of those who lay emphasis on special dispensations to prove their closeness to the Deity. He writes:

> If a man thinks he will get more of God by meditation, by devotion, by ecstasies, or by special infusion of grace, than by the fireside or in the stable, that is nothing but taking God, wrapping a cloak round His head and shoving Him under a bench. For whoever seeks God in a special way gets the way and misses God, who remains hidden in the way. (*Sermon* 13, Walshe 1979, vol. 1, 117–118)

We may think we are being rewarded for our devotion when we experience ecstatic states, but these may get in the way of what we are really seeking. We should not desire such experiences for their own sake but should put them aside and move on to the next stage. Eckhart's warning against mistaking the sideshow for the main event echoes across the traditions.[13] Eckhart goes on to say:

> It is lamentable how some people think themselves very lofty and quite one with God … They are a long way from where they imagine themselves to be. They have

---

[12] Plotinus remarks that our comprehension of the One corresponds to a presence rather than scientific knowledge (*Enn.* 6.9.4, Gerson, 2018, p. 887).

[13] The Buddha denounced extreme forms of asceticism to find the Middle Way with his warning exemplified in images of him shown emaciated. Aristotle's path of virtue was the Golden Mean or moderation of the passions (*metriopatheia*) whereas the Stoics taught their eradication (*apatheia*).

> great notions and desires to match. I once said, "If a man
> seeks nothing, to whom should he complain if he finds
> nothing?" (*Sermon* 68, Walshe 1981, vol. II, 161)

He is critical, too, of those who boast about their spiritual achievements
and think themselves a cut above the rest:

> We should not think that holiness is based on what we do
> but rather on what we are, for it is not our works which
> sanctify us but we who sanctify our works. (Davies,
> 1994, p. 7)

It is not the outward character of our actions that should concern us but
the ground or origin of them. If our intentions are good, then it should
follow that our actions will be good as well.

There is a strong ethical dimension to Eckhart's idea of
detachment. It is not just an intellectual exercise but an act of personal
renunciation. It is an ongoing habit of introspection based on a daily
routine to examine one's actions and confess one's conscience.[14] Eckhart
makes the following observation: "You should know that no one has ever
renounced themselves so much in this life that there was nothing left of
themselves to renounce" (ibid.).

Eckhart is clear that detachment does not mean indifference or
apathy. We should remain sensitive to our surroundings no matter our
state of inner tranquility. He says it is wrong to think that in trying to
be perfect we need to overcome feelings of joy and sorrow. It is wrong
because there is no seeker who has not felt emotion while trying to find
God (Hunt, 2004). He says some claim they have progressed so far along
the path to perfection that they remain unaffected by things around them,
but remarks that he will never reach the point where a hideous noise is
as pleasing to his ears as sweetly sounding music (*German Sermon* 21,
Davies, 1994, p. 202).

---

[14] This was enjoined by Pythagoras in *The Golden Verses* and commented on by the
fifth-century Neoplatonist Hierocles (*Hierocles of Alexandria*, Schibli, 2002, pp. 267–71).
Basil the Great proposes a diurnal review of our deeds (*The Ascetic Works of Saint Basil*,
Lowther Clark, 1925, p. 139).

5. Eckhart on Deification

For Eckhart all creatures are searching to be Godlike (*Gottähnlich*) (*Sermon* 79, Walshe, 1981, Vol. II, p. 232), due to a spark of divinity in the soul which is the essence or ground which desires to be in communion with God. He uses the scholastic term *synteresis*, meaning an inner state of moral awareness or conscience, which for him is the disposition (*habitus*) of the soul to apprehend the divine. However, the soul in seeking this communion through apophatic detachment may need to be rescued. He writes:

> The soul falls into her nothingness and in that nothingness so far from the created something, that of her own power she cannot return to her created something. God with his uncreatedness upholds her nothingness and preserves it in his something. The soul has dared to become nothing and so cannot of herself return to herself, for she has departed so far from herself before God comes to the rescue. (*Sermon* 6, Walshe, 1979, vol. I, p. 59)

In wanting to become Godlike we are in fact asking to be sons of God, but how, asks Eckhart, can we be sons of God when God is not like anybody:

> Since it is God's nature not to be like anyone, we have to come to the state of being nothing in order to enter into the same nature that he is. So, when I am able to establish myself in nothing and nothing in myself, uprooting and casting out what is in me, then I can pass into the naked being of God … All that smacks of likeness must be ousted that I may be transplanted into God and become one with him; one substance, one being, one nature and the son of God. (*Sermon* 7, Walsh, 1979, vol. 1, p. 66)

He suggests that if someone *is* one with God and *is* God on the basis of that union (*unio*), then it must be on that part of the image in which we are like him and not upon the created part. He is referring here to the "image and likeness" theme with the uncreated part being the divine:

> For when we consider someone as God, we do not
> consider them according to their creatureliness, but
> when we consider them as God, we are not denying
> their creatureliness in such a way as to negate it, rather
> this is to be seen as an affirmation of God which denies
> creatureliness in him. (*German Sermon* 11, Davies, 1994,
> p. 150)

He then quotes Augustine as saying:

> We are what we love. If we love a stone, then we are a
> stone, if we love a person, then we are that person, if we
> love God – I hesitate to go on, for if I said that we would
> then be God, you might want to stone me. (*German
> Sermon* 11, Davies, 1994, pp.150–151)

At this juncture we might recall Eckhart's statement that was condemned
as article 10 in the Bull of Pope John XXII issued in 1329, not long after
Eckhart's death. It is one of 28 articles condemned of which the first 15
were declared heretical. Number 10 reads as follows:

> We are fully transformed and converted into God; in the
> same way as in the sacrament the bread is converted into
> the body of Christ, so I am converted into Him, so that
> He converts me into his being as one, not as like. By the
> living God it is true that there is no difference. (Walshe,
> 1979, vol. I, p. xlviii)[15]

We can see why this passage called his orthodoxy into question. It is quite
a claim for a Christian to make, that there is no difference between oneself
and God, that we become the same as God. It is the "not as *like*" that is
of interest here, because it is reminiscent of the "like" and "same" debate
during the Arian controversy of the fourth century. This controversy

---

[15] See also (*Sermon* 47, Walshe, *Meister Eckhart*. 1981, vol. II. p. 28). The 10th-century
Sufi al-Hallaj whose execution under the Abbasids is said to have been occasioned by a
poetic utterance that led him to claim he was one with God. "I saw my Lord with the eye
of the heart. I asked, 'Who are You?' He replied, 'You.'" There is a pun here on his name
Hallaj which means "God" (*Allah*).

centered on whether Christ was of "like" substance (*homoiousios*) to the Father or of the "same" substance (*homoousios)* as the Father. This became embedded in the Nicene Creed as Christ being "consubstantial with the Father," but here Eckhart is suggesting that humanity and divinity are *homoousios*. He seems to be taking the deification of the human nature in the person of Christ to include himself and potentially other Christians as well. The eucharistic context for this bold statement would appear to give validity to the transubstantiating effect of deification.[16]

It is of interest that Nicholas of Cusa in his apology for his work *On Learned Ignorance* writes of Eckhart as follows:

> The teacher [that is Cusa] said that he had never read that Eckhart thought that the creature was the creator and praised his talent and fervour. Yet he wished that his books would be removed from public places; for the people are not ready for what he often has to say, contrary to the custom of other learned men, even though the intelligent find in them many astute and useful things. (Klibansky,1932, pp. 15, 7–12)

6. Cusa on Learned Ignorance

Nicholas of Cusa's most famous work is his *On Learned Ignorance,* written in 1440, after his visit to Constantinople in 1437, as a member of the delegation to win Greek support for the pope's proposal for a council of union in Italy. This was to be the Council of Ferrara-Florence of 1449, which failed in its main objective, just four years before the fall of Constantinople to the Ottoman Turks in 1453. He appears to have spent his time in Constantinople looking for Greek manuscripts, including a copy of Pseudo-Dionysius and Proclus's *Platonic Theology* (Bond, 1996, p. 141). He appended a letter to *On Learned Ignorance* explaining that the inspiration for it came to him while at sea for two months returning to Venice:

---

[16] Dionysius speaks of the deifying effects of the eucharist (*Ecclesiastical Hierarchy,* Luibheid, 1987, p. 217). See also (Russell, 2004, pp. 248–288).

> Returning by sea from Greece when by what I believe was
> a celestial gift from the Father of Lights, from whom comes
> every perfect gift, I was led to embrace incomprehensibles
> incomprehensibly in learned ignorance, by transcending
> those incorruptible truths than can be humanly known.
> (Bond, 1997, p. 206)

In his apology for this work written nine years later in 1449, he notes
that his discovery of "learned ignorance" came initially as a gift, which
he then traced in earlier sources, notably Augustine, Pseudo-Dionysius
(Casarella, 2009), Bonaventure, Therry of Chartres, and Meister Eckhart.[17]
The work represents his first systematic attempt to explain the concepts
of "learned ignorance" (*docta ignorantia*) as well as "coincidence of
opposites" (*coincidentia oppositorum*), two ideas that he continued to
develop throughout his *Lebenswerk*.

The expression "learned ignorance" is Cusa's term for theological
apophaticism. It is a lack of knowledge that paradoxically must be learned,
but which is also epistemic because it is an intellectual achievement. He
sometimes refers to it as enlightened ignorance or scared ignorance,
being as much a gift as a pedagogical outcome. It is the ignorance that
comes from knowing that one will never know the absolute nature of
things, especially God. It echoes Anselm's famous ontological argument:
"For God is a being that which nothing greater can be thought." Although
affirming God's existence, Anselm's argument places God out of reach
of the human intellect and beyond anything that may be conceived in
relation to him. What is denied is perhaps more important than what can
be affirmed. Learned ignorance is knowledge that is unknown because
it is beyond being, affirming both its epistemological and ontological
significance.

On Learned Ignorance is divided into three parts: God,
Universe, and Christ. The harmonizing of opposites, the *coincidentia
oppositorium*, is a way of viewing theological and philosophical issues
from the viewpoint of eternity (*sub specie aeternitatis*) rather than from
the viewpoint of humanity (*sub specie humanitatis*). The fact of viewing
human life under the aspect of eternity does not necessarily mean it is

---

[17] Eckhart writes: "But here we must come to a *transformed* knowledge, and this
unknowing must not come from ignorance, but rather from *knowing* we must get to this
unknowing" (*Sermon* 2, Walshe, 1979, vol.1, p. 21).

without value and meaning (Landau, 2011). On the contrary, it helps us to evaluate our lives and those of others and to determine the importance we attach to ourselves and the rest of our species. Cusa finds in the idea of the coincidence of opposites what he needs to understand that everything is one in God and that God is one in everything. It brings God into the world rather than separating him from it.

7. Cusa on Divine Names

Cusa writes in his *On Seeking God*; "*Theos* is the [Greek] name of God but only as God is sought by humans in this world" (Bond 1997, p. 218). *Theos* is not itself the name of God because we do not know what name God calls himself. However, in Exod. 3:14 of the Septuagint, God calls himself by the abstract concept "the Being" (ὁ ὤν in Greek). This translation reflects the ancient Jewish reluctance to pronounce the sacred name of God by substituting the tetragrammaton, representing the four Hebrew consonants of Yaweh or Jehovah. Cusa knows and refers to this tradition must probably via Moses Maimonides when he writes:

> God's proper name, which we say is ineffable and which is a tetragrammaton, that is, consisting of four letters [YHWH in Hebrew], is proper to God, because it applies to God according to God's own essence and not through any relation to creatures. (Bond, 1997, p. 121)

The use of the Greek philosophical concept "the Being" is discussed by Pseudo-Dionysius in his *The Divine Names*, where he locates its primary position in the hierarchy of sacred nomenclature (Luibheid, 1987, pp. 59; 96). The English translation "I am that I am" of Exod. 3:14 does not convey what the Greek or Hebrew implies. Yet why should our naming be of any consequence to that which surpasses every name? Naming is all from our side and what is from our side amounts to nothing. We are beholden to our names which are only "around" God, as John of Damascus explains:

> Whatever we say about God cataphatically makes manifest not the nature but what is around the nature (ἀλλὰ τὰ περὶ τὴν φύσιν). Whether you talk about

goodness, or justice, or wisdom, or anything else, you are
talking *not* about God's nature but about what is *around*
the nature. (Russell, 2022, p. 66)[18]

The frailty of names is clear from the fact that names we give to God are
misnomers. God remains nameless and outside the category of naming.
Cusa writes in his *On Learned Ignorance* that Oneness is the only name
for God but qualifies it by saying:

> It is not the case that Oneness is the name of God in the
> way in which we either name or understand oneness; for
> just as God transcends all understanding, so a fortiori, he
> transcends every name. (Hopkins, 1985, p. 40)

If we return to the Neoplatonists for a moment, we can find many examples
of the ineffability of the One. For example, Plotinus puts it thus:

> To say that the One is a cause is not to predicate an accident
> of it, but of ourselves, because we grasp something of
> it, although it is in itself. If one is speaking precisely,
> one should not say either "that thing" or "being" of it,
> but of us. It is us, in a way circling it from the outside,
> who wish to interpret the affections we undergo, as we
> sometimes are closer to it and sometimes more distant
> from it, through the puzzles arising from it. (*Enn.* 6.9.3,
> Gerson, 2018, pp. 886–887)

Yet despite the One being ineffable its name was an enigma to decipher. It
was a pupil of Iamblichus in the fourth century, Theodorus of Asine, who
taught a doctrine of letters to explain the inner meaning of the One. The
One in Greek *hen* (τὸ Ἕν) was a triad with each member equivalent to one
of the three parts of the word in Greek, the diacritic, the epsilon, and the nu.
This led him to state: "There is no name of the One for it is even beyond
breath" (Gersh, 1978, pp. 289–304), referring to the rough breathing, the
δασὺ πνεῦμα or *spīritus asper*, of the aspirated epsilon, meaning it cannot

---

[18] On the notion that we cannot know God in himself but only from those things that
are around him, see Maximos the Confessor, *Ambiguum* 34 (Constas, 2014, vol. 2, pp.
64–67).

be spoken. The Neoplatonic, Christian, and Judaic traditions converge at
this point in pronouncing the divine name unpronounceable.

8. Cusa's Apophaticism

As we have mentioned, Cusa was familiar with the Latin works of Meister
Eckhart, which he collected and annotated, as well as those of Dionysius
the Areopagite and John Scotus. All these authors in one way or another
contributed to his Christian Neoplatonic worldview. He writes in *On
Learned Ignorance*:

> The theology of negation is so necessary to the theology
> of affirmation that without it God would not be worshiped
> as the infinite God but as creature; and such worship is
> idolatry, for it gives to an image that which belongs only
> to truth itself. (Bond, 1997, p. 126)

The idea that idolatry is the worship of creation rather than the creator
has a long history in Judaeo-Christian thought. What we affirm about
God may give a false impression, because our affirmations are merely
human projections, and so dimmish his divine glory. Even to say he is
absolute power still attempts to contain him within a human idea of what
constitutes power. For we have no idea what divine power is like, we have
only analogies that hint at it, but we must not mistake these analogies as
encompassing the truth. We need to recognize that cataphatic statements
are only one side of the coin.

For Cusa the human mind or intellect is without measure or
quantity being absolute in its capacity to comprehend and form ideas and
concepts. He writes:

> For when you attend to the fact that mind is a certain
> absolute measure that cannot be greater or smaller since
> it is not restricted to quantity, and when you attend to the
> fact that this measure is alive so that it measures by itself
> (as if a living compass were to measure by itself), then
> you grasp how it makes itself into a concept, measure, or
> exemplar so that it attains itself in everything. (Quoted
> by Miller, 2003, p. 134)

The human mind is unquantifiable and thus indicative of its nearness to infinity and ultimately to something beyond itself. This may be identified with the "ground" or "spark" spoken of by Eckhart, who treated it as the divine within us. For Cusa there is something remarkable about the human mind being immeasurable, while at the same time being limited in its capacity to grasp the ultimate truth. It represents another of the paradoxes which are for him part of the human condition. Each of us lives with our own inner infinitude, and yet we are frustrated by it as much as liberated by it. This is confirmed by Plotinus, who says:

> The soul or mind reaching towards the formless finds itself incompetent to grasp where nothing bounds it, or to take impression where the impinging reality is diffuse; in sheer dread of holding onto nothingness, it slips away. The state is painful; often it seeks relief by retreating from all this vagueness to the region of sense, there to rest on solid ground. (*Enn.* 6.9.3, MacKenna, 1991, p. 538)[19]

Cusa recognizes that the freedom the mind gives us imposes a moral obligation to act in accordance with the divine ground that underlines it.

9. Cusa on Deification

There is no doubt that Cusa was influenced by the Eastern Christian notion of deification because he often refers to it by its Greek name, *theosis*.[20] In his work *On Being a Son of God* (*De filiatione Dei*) of 1445, he makes the following remark:

> To put my view summarily: I judge that being a son of God is to be regarded as nothing other than deification, which, in Greek, is called theosis. ... I do not think that we become sons of God in such way that we will be then

---

[19] Gregory of Nyssa writes in a similar vein (*Commentary on Ecclesiastes*, Musurillo, 1995, pp. 127–128).

[20] See the excellent study by Nancy Hudson, *Becoming God: The Doctrine of Theosis in Nicholas of Cusa* (Hudson, 2007).

something [essentially] other than we are now; instead,
then we will be in another manner that which now we
are in our present manner. (Hopkins, 1994, pp. 341; 343)

For Cusa, sonship or filiation means that what we are now will be different
from what we become by deification, only in a manner we cannot envisage
or conceive. This sonship is a transformation into the likeness of God, it is
not a transubstantiation into the divine essence in the sense that Eckhart
wants to give it. Furthermore, sonship is limited in our present state:

> And since this filiation is the ultimate of all power, our
> intellectual faculty is not exhaustible this side of theosis,
> nor does it attain that which is ultimate perfection at any
> level this side of the stillness of sonship's perpetual light
> and life of eternal joy. (Hopkins, 1994, p. 342)

Yet despite relating the idea of sonship to the individual believer, Cusa
comes near to endorsing an Adoptionist position regarding the sonship
of Christ. He says Christ has a double sonship, being the Son of God
by nature and a son of God by adoption. However, this could mean
speaking of two sons, which might be misconstrued as heresy. There was
an Adoptionist controversy in the eighth century involving Alcuin of York
and another in the 12th century involving Peter of Lombard, which Cusa
would undoubtedly have been aware of. There are not two hypostases in
Christ the preexistent Logos, a divine and human, only one, the divine
(Meyendroff, 1986, pp. 151–167). This must be the case if the logic of
the trinity is to be safeguarded; otherwise there would two sons, making
it a quaternity, not a trinity. Adoption in Cusa needs to be understood in
a restricted sense.

Just as with Eckhart, we find the *inquantum* qualifier at work
in Cusa. This qualifying term shows the dependency of humanity and
creation on the divine will. The divine gaze which encompasses everything
continues to focus on the individual creature, no matter how unworthy:

> … for I exist only insomuch as (*inquantum*) you are
> with me. And since your seeing is your being, therefore,
> because you regard me, I am, and if you remove your
> face from me, I will cease to be. (Bond, 1997, p. 240)

God is not lessened or diminished by the act of creation; on the contrary, creation participates in God through his immanence. For Cusa, God is *non aliud*, that is, he is "not-other" in the created realm, which is nothing per se because it is derivative and owes everything to its creator. He struggles on occasion to maintain the distinction between transcendence and immanence, because he does not really want to separate them in his unifying vision of the coincidence of opposites. Accusations of pantheism were leveled at him by the Aristotelian Johannes Wenck (Dupré, 2006; Gaetano, 2019), who in his rebuttal of *On Learned Ignorance*, echoes Eckhart's condemned article 10 on deification as given above (Hopkins, 1988, p. 441). It was Wenck's rebuttal that gave rise to Cusa's own apology on behalf of his *On Learned Ignorance* in 1449.

10. Cusa on the Idea of Contraction

We might finish by looking at Cusa's notion of divine contraction. This is the idea that the infinite God self-contracts to make room for the finite creation. It involves God withdrawing into himself to make a space in which creation can come into being and coexist. The question centers on how the infinite can give rise to the finite, the uncreated to the created, the eternal to the temporal, and so on. For Cusa, only God being absolute is uncontracted but who nevertheless remains present in his contracted universe. The notion of divine contraction necessitates creation; otherwise it would remain latent and unrealized in infinity (Bond, 1996, pp. 148–149). It bears some resemblance to the Pythagorean notion of Limit and Unlimited by which differentiation occurs because of Limit taking an inhalation or "breath" (πνεῦμα) of emptiness or void from the Unlimited (Kirk & Raven, 1979, pp. 252–253).

The notion of divine self-contraction was already in the repository of Christian thinking. This is the idea of *kenosis*, that is, the self-emptying of Christ in taking on humanity. The topic is found in Phil. 2:7, where it says: "He emptied himself, by taking the form of a servant, being born in the likeness of humankind." It is this *kenosis,* or self-emptying, of Christ's own will to become receptive to the divine will that actualizes his incarnation. However, this act of emptying does not diminish his divinity or magnify his humanity, because he is said in the Chalcedonian Definition of 451 to be fully human and fully divine. What Cusa appears to have done is transfer the concept of *kenosis* from Christology to cosmogony. Hitherto the idea was used in relation to the person of Christ, not in relation to the formation of the world. The space for the human in the divine has now become the space for creation.

Perhaps Cusa is here pursuing a more Greek patristic approach to the idea of kenotic contraction, in which the idea of divine self-emptying can be understood in a broader sense to include the creation of the cosmos. Christ as the second person of the trinity is said to be part of creation from the beginning. The use of the first-person plural rather than the first-person singular in Gen. 1:26 ("Let *us* make ...") was given a trinitarian interpretation by Christian authors, meaning that humanity was made in the image and likeness of the Father, Son, and Holy Spirit. In Jewish thought, Divine Wisdom (*Chokmah*) was associated with God at the creation of the world, while in the Eastern Byzantine tradition, Divine Wisdom (*Sophia*) became an attribute of Christ.[21] John the Theologian gave prominence to the relation between creation and Christology when he writes: "In the beginning was the Word" (Jn. 1:1),[22] that is, Christ the pre-existent Logos was there at the world's inception, being referred to as "the firstborn of all creation" (Col. 1:15).

Another and earlier witness to the idea of a cosmic contraction is Moderatus of Gades, modern Cadiz in Spain. He was a Neopythagorean of the first century C.E., who conceived of a triadic One, or Monad, as a self-contracting deity. He is said to have taught that this self-contraction gave rise to quantity that is itself shapeless, undifferentiated, and formless, much like Plato's empty receptacle (*Chora)* in the *Timaeus* (49a), but which is receptive of form, shape, and differentiation. By withdrawing into himself, the One creates the necessary conditions under which the paradigms of form, shape, distinction, and the rest can operate (Dillon, 1996, 344–351; Boys-Stones, 2018, pp. 117–118). The theory is reported by some Neoplatonists but does not appear to have gained much traction (Merlan, 1967).

Now much of this is reminiscent of Isaac Luria's *tzimtzum*, or divine contraction, an idea developed by him in his study of the Kabbalah

---

[21] The Great Church of Constantinople was dedicated to Divine Wisdom (*Hagia Sophia*) as were other churches in the Eastern Orthodox world, but not in the Western tradition.
[22] Basil the Great remarks that the profundity of this first line was incorporated by pagan philosophers into their own works (Basil the Great, 2012, p. 250).

in the 16th century.[23] As taught by Luria, God contracts into himself to make room for the creation of the world. He begins the process of creation by contracting his infinity to allow finite things to exist, this contraction forming a "vacant space," like the formlessness and void (Hebrew: *tohu-va-bohu*) before the creation of light in Gen.1:2. Without this restrictive space, nothing would exist, the world being the contracted likeness of God (Bielik-Robson & Weiss, 2020). It is a way of explaining how the world exists if the creator is infinite, but his creation is finite. The Lurianic and Cusanian contractions allow for distinctions, for opposites to exist, limited as opposed to unlimited, imperfect to perfect, immanent to transcendent, and so on, but which being in God are ultimately reconcilable, hence Cusa's *coincidentia oppositorum*. Although the universe may appear infinite, it is in fact confined in a limited space so long as the creator intends it.

11. Conclusion

What I have tried to show in this paper is that the twin pillars of speculative theology in Eckhart and Cusa, apophaticism and deification, are essential elements of their approach to understanding the nature of the divine. Although I have referred to these terms as two sides of the same coin, we might venture to identify apophaticism with "nothingness" and deification with "being," but the implications of saying this will need to be investigated further. I have deliberately avoided the term "mysticism" because I think the modern connotations attached to this word detract from our appreciation of their writings. Not that I think deep religious experience is absent from their lives; on the contrary, it is essential to the development of their thought, but I think the term misses the essential nature of their contribution, which is highly speculative, both metaphysically and theologically. Both sailed close to the wind as far as the ecclesiastical authorities of the time were concerned, but thankfully the rich legacy of their thought remains for us to explore.

---

[23] The idea was taken up by the Protestant theologian Jürgen Moltmann in his *God in Creation: An Ecological Doctrine of Creation* (Moltmann, 1985).

References

Primary sources

Anonymous. (2001) *The Cloud of Unknowing and Other Works.* Translated by A. C. Spearing. Harmonsworth, England: Penguin.

Augustine of Hippo. (1886) Letter 130, To Proba. In P. Schaff (ed.), *Nicene and Post-Nicene Fathers, Letters of St Augustine, Vol. 1,* pp. 455–459.

Basil the Great. (2012) Homily on the beginning of the Gospel of John. In St. Basil the Great, *On Christian Doctrine and Practice,* Translated by M. DelCogliano. New York: St. Vladimir's Seminary Press, pp. 241–257.

Basil the Great. (2005) Homily on that which is according to the image, 16. In St. Basil the Great, *On the Human Condition.* Translated by V. Harrison. New York: St. Vladimir's Seminary Press, pp. 31–48.

Basil the Great. (1925) *The Ascetic Works of Saint Basil.* Translated by W. K. Lowther Clarke. London: SPCK.

Elias and David. (2018) *Elias and David: Introductions to Philosophy, with Olympiodorus Introduction to Logic.* Translated by S. Gertz. London: Bloomsbury.

Gregory of Nyssa. (1978) *The Life of Moses.* Translated by A. Malherbe and E. Ferguson. Mahwah, NJ: Paulist Press.

Gregory of Nyssa. (1995) On Perfection. In *From Glory to Glory: Texts from Gregory of Nyssa's Mystical Writings.* New York: St. Vladimir's Seminary Press.

Hierocles of Alexandria. (2002) *Commentary on the Golden Verses of the Pythagoreans.* Translated by H. S. Schibli. Oxford: Oxford University Press, pp. 165–325.

Iamblichus. (2003) *On the Mysteries.* Translated by E. Clarke, J. Dillon, & J. Hershbell. Atlanta Society of Biblical Literature.

John of Damascus. (2022) *On the Orthodox Faith*. Translated by N. Russell. New York: St. Vladimir's Seminary Press.

John Scotus Eriugena. (1987) *Periphyseon*. Translated by I. P. Sheldon–Williams, revised by J. O'Meara. Montréal: Editions Bellarmin.

Johannes Wenck. (1981) *On Unknown Learning*. Translated by J. Hopkins. Minneapolis: Banning Press.

Maximos the Confessor. (2014) *On the Difficulties in the Church Fathers: The Ambigua. 2 vols*. Translated by N. Constas. Cambridge, MA: Harvard University Press.

Meister Eckhart. (1979, 1981) *Sermons & Treatises. 2 vols*. Translated by M. O'C Walshe. London: Watkins.

Meister Eckhart. (1994) *Selected Writings*. Translated by O. Davies. London: Penguin.

Meister Eckhart. (1963) *Selected Treaties and Sermons*. Translated by J. M. Clark & J. V. Skinner. London: Collins.

Meister Eckhart. (1981) *The Essential Sermons, Commentaries, Treatises, and Defense*. Translated by E. College & B. McGinn. Mahwah. NJ: Paulist Press.

Nicholas of Cusa. (1997) *Selected Spiritual Writings*. Translated by H. Lawrence Bond. Mahwah. NJ: Paulist Press.

Nicholas of Cusa. (1985) *On Learned Ignorance*. Translated by J. Hopkins. Minneapolis: Banning Press.

Nicholas of Cusa. (1987) *On God as Not-Other*. Translated by J. Hopkins. Minneapolis: Banning Press.

Nicholas of Cusa. (1994) *On Being a Son of God*. Translated by J. Hopkins. Minneapolis: Banning Press.

Nicholas of Cusa. (1932) *Apologia doctae ignorantiae*. Translated by R. Klibansky. Leipzig, Germany: Meiner.

Plotinus. (1991) *The Enneads*. Translated by S. MacKenna. London: Penguin.

Plotinus. (2018) *The Enneads*. Edited by L Gerson. Cambridge: Cambridge University Press.

Pseudo-Dionysius. (1987) *Pseudo–Dionysius: The Complete Works*. Translated by C. Luibheid. Mahwah, NJ: Paulist Press.

Secondary Sources

Albertson, D. (2020) Echoes of Eriugena in Renaissance Philosophy: Negation, Theophany, Anthropology. In Guiu, A. (ed) *A Companion to John Scottus Eriugena*. Leiden, Netherlands: Brill. pp. 387–418.

Bielik-Robson, A. & Weiss, D. H. (eds.) (2020) *Tsimtsum and Modernity: Lurianic Heritage in Modern Philosophy and Theology*. Berlin: De Gruyter.

Bond, H. L., (1996) Nicholas of Cusa from Constantinople to "Learned Ignorance": The Historical Matrix for the Formation of the De docta ignorantia. In G. Christianson & T. M.

Izbicki (eds), *Nicholas of Cusa on Christ and the Church: Essays in Memory of Chandler McCuskey Brooks for the American Cusanus Society*. Leiden, Netherlands: Brill. pp. 135-165.

Boys-Stones, G. (2018) *Platonist Philosophy 80 BC to AD 250: An Introduction and Collection of Sources in Translation*. Cambridge: Cambridge University Press.

Carabine, D. (1995) *The Unknown God: Negative Theology in the Platonic Tradition: Plato to Eriugena*. Grand Rapids, MI: Eerdmans.

Casarella, P. (2009) Cusanus on Dionysius: The turn to speculative theology. In S. Coakley, S. & Stang, C.M. (eds.) *Re-Thinking Dionysius the Areopagite*. Chichester, England: Wiley Blackwell. pp. 137-148.

Coakley, S. & Stang, C. (eds.) (2009) *Re-Thinking Dionysius the Areopagite*. Chichester, England: Wiley Blackwell.

Constas, M. (2022) Maximus the Confessor and the Reception of Dionysius the Areopagite. In Edwards, M., Pallis, D. & Steiris, G. (eds) *The Oxford Handbook of Dionysius the Areopagite*. Oxford: Oxford University Press. pp. 222–240.

Cornelli, G. (2013) *In Search of Pythagoreanism: Pythagoreanism as a Historiographical Category*. Berlin: De Gruyter.

Dillon, J. (1996) *The Middle Platonists*. London: Duckworth.

Dillon, J. (2014) Signs and Tokens: Do the Gods of Neoplatonism Really Care? In D'Hoine, P. & Van Riel, G (eds.) *Fate, Providence and Moral Responsibility in Ancient, Medieval and Early Modern Thought: Studies in Honour of Carlos Steel*. Leuven, Belgium: Leuven University Press. pp. 227-238.

Dubbelman, S. J. (2020) I know that I do not know: Nicholas of Cusa's Augustine. *Harvard Theological Review*, 113 (4), pp. 460–482.

Dupré, L. (2006) The Question of Pantheism from Eckhart to Cusanus. In Casarella P. (ed) *The Legacy of Learned Ignorance*. Washington, DC: Catholic University of America Press. pp. 74–88.

Fagenblat, M. (ed.) (2017) *Negative Theology as Jewish Modernity*. Bloomington, IN: Indiana University Press.

Franke, W. (ed.) (2007) *On What Cannot Be Said: Apophatic Discourses in Philosophy, Religion, Literature, and the Arts, 2 vols*. Notre Dame, IN: University of Notre Dame Press.

Gaetano, M. T. (2019) Nicholas of Cusa and Pantheism in Early Modern Catholic Theology. In Burton, S., Hollmann, J. & Parker, E. (eds) *Nicholas of Cusa and the Making of the Early Modern World*. Leiden, Netherlands: Brill. pp. 199–228.

Gersh, S. (1978) Excursus, The Linguist Doctrine of Theodorus of Asine and its Background in Philosophy and Magic. In his *Iamblichus to Eriugena: An Investigation of the Prehistory and Evolution of the Pseudo-Dionysian Tradition*. Leiden, Netherlands: Brill. pp. 289–304.

Hadot, I. (2015) *Athenian and Alexandrian Neoplatonism and the Harmonization of Aristotle and Plato*. Leiden, Netherlands: Brill.

Hägg, H. F. (2006) *Clement of Alexandria and the Beginnings of Christian Apophaticism*. Oxford: Oxford University Press.

Hampton, A. & Kenney, J. (eds) (2020) *Christian Platonism: A History*. Cambridge: Cambridge University Press.

Heidegger, M. (1966) *Discourse on Thinking: A Translation of Gelassenheit*. New York: Harper & Row.

Hudson, N. J. (2007) *Becoming God: The Doctrine of Theosis in Nicholas of Cusa*. Washington, DC: University of America Press.

Hunt, H. (2004) *Joy-Bearing Grief: Tears of Contrition in the Early Syrian and Byzantine Fathers*. Leiden, Netherlands: Brill.

Karamanolis, G. (2006) *Plato and Aristotle in Agreement? Platonists on Aristotle from Antiochus to Porphyry*. Oxford: Oxford University Press.

Kars, A. (2019) *Unsaying God: Negative Theology in Medieval Islam*. New York: Oxford University Press.

Kirk, G. S. & Raven, J. E. (1979) *The Presocratic Philosophers: A Critical History and Selection of Texts*. Cambridge: Cambridge University Press.

Kobusch, T. (2022) Dionysius the Areopagite and Nicholas of Cusa. In Edwards, M., Pallis, D. & Steiris, G. (eds), *The Oxford Handbook of Dionysius the Areopagite*. Oxford: Oxford University Press. pp. 454–475.

Landau, I. (2011) The meaning of life sub specie aeternitatis. *Australasian Journal of Philosophy*, 89 (4), pp. 727–734.

Lankila, T. (2011) The Corpus Dionysiacum as a crypto-pagan project. *Journal of Late Antique Religion and Culture*, vol. 5, pp. 14-40.

Merlan, P. (1967) Moderatus and Nicomachus. In Armstrong, A. H. (ed.) *The Cambridge History of Later Greek and Early Medieval Philosophy*. Cambridge: Cambridge University Press. pp. 90–96.

Meyendorff, J. (1983) *Byzantine Theology: Historical Trends and Doctrinal Themes*. New York: Fordham University Press.

Miller, C. L. (2003) *Reading Cusanus: Metaphor and Dialectic in a Conjectural Universe*. Washington, DC: Catholic University of America Press.

Moltmann, J. (1985) *God in Creation. An Ecological Doctrine of Creation*. London: SCM Press.

Moore, I. A. (2019) *Eckhart, Heidegger, and the Imperative of Releasement*. Albany, NY: SUNY Press.

Moran, D. (2014) Neoplatonism and Christianity in the West. In Remes, P. & Slaveva-Griffin, S. (eds), *The Routledge Handbook of Neoplatonism*, Routledge: London. pp. 508–524.

Mortley, R. (1986) *From Word to Silence, 2 vols*. Bonn: Hanstein.

Ortiz, J. (ed.) (2019) *The Doctrine of Deification in the Latin Patristic Tradition*. Washington, DC: Catholic University of America Press.

Parry, K. (2006) Reading Proclus Diadochus in Byzantium. In Tarrant, H. & Baltzly, D. (eds.), *Reading Plato in Antiquity*. London: Duckworth. pp. 223-235.

Parry, K. (2017) Fate, Free Choice, and Divine Providence from the Neoplatonists to John of Damascus. In Kaldellis, A. & Siniossoglou, N. (eds.) *The Cambridge Intellectual History of Byzantium*. Cambridge: Cambridge University Press, pp. 341-360.

Perczel, I. (2015) Dionysius the Areopagite. In Parry, K. (ed) *The Wiley Blackwell Companion to Patristics*. Chichester, England: Wiley Blackwell, pp. 211-225.

Ramelli, I. (2019) Philo's dialectics of apophatic theology, his strategy of differentiation and his impact on patristic exegesis and theology. *Filosofiya Zhurnal Vysshey Shkoly Ekonomiki*, 3 (1), pp. 36–92.

Ridings, D. (1995) *The Dependency Theme in Some Early Christian Writers*. Göteborg, Sweden: Acta Universitatis Gothoburgensis.

Robichaud, D. (2022) Valla and Erasmus on the Dionysian Question. In Edwards, M., Pallis, D. & Steiris, G. (eds.) *The Oxford Handbook of Dionysius the Areopagite*. Oxford: Oxford University Press. pp. 491–515.

Russell, N. (2004) *The Doctrine of Deification in the Greek Patristic Tradition*. Oxford: Oxford University Press.

Treiger, A. (2007) The Arabic version of Pseudo–Dionysius the Areopagite's mystical theology, Chapter I: Introduction, Critical Edition and Translation. *Le Muséon*, 120 (3-4), pp. 365–393.

Trizio, M. & Bydén, B. (eds.) (forthcoming, 2026) *Brill's Companion to Byzantine Philosophy*. Leiden, Netherlands: Brill.

Vimercate, E. & Zaffino, V. (eds.) (2020) *Nicholas of Cusa and the Aristotelian Tradition: A Philosophical and Theological Survey*. Berlin: De Gruyter.

Vinzent, M. (2011) *The Art of Detachment, Eckhart: Texts and Studies, vol. 1*. Louven, Belgium: Peeters.

Watanabe, M., Christianson, G. & Izbicki, T. (eds.) (2011) *Nicholas of Cusa, A Companion to His Life and Times*. Farnham, England: Ashgate.

Wolfson, H. (1948) *Philo: Foundations of Religious Philosophy in Judaism, Christianity, and Islam, vol. II*. Cambridge, MA: Harvard University Press.

13

Nothingness and the Desire for Being: Der Nister's Modernist Zoharic Theogony

Nathan Wolski

> The gate of heaven is non-being hence the myriad things emerge from non-being. Being cannot be born from being hence it must emerge from non-being. However, non-being is itself nothingness. This is where the sage hides himself.
>
> *Zhuangzi,* chapter 23

Jews discovered the divine nothingness quite late. Although the idea of creation from nothing first appeared categorically in Jewish texts from the third and fourth centuries (Niehoff, 2006; Kister, 2007)—Genesis 1 assumes a primordial preexistent chaos—it was only in the 13th century that kabbalists began speculating on the nature of this nothing (Scholem, 1987, pp. 422-27; Matt, 1997, 2000; Wolfson, 2019). Even *Sefer Yetsirah* (The Book of Creation), the enigmatic eighth-ninth (possibly sixth-seventh)[1] century work, which speaks of numerals of nothingness (*sefirot belimah*) as agents of creation, has little to say of the nothing aside from God's having "made what is not into what is" (*SY* 2:6). By the end of the 13th century, though, *Ayin*, Nothingness, had assumed its place as the very apex of the godhead. From the *Zohar*, the immense and influential 13th century kabbalistic anthology, on to Hasidic texts of the 18th and 19th centuries, nothingness assumed a key role in the mystical quest, be it as ascent through the sefirotic realm to the highest reaches of divinity, or

---

[1] The dating of this work is notoriously contested (see Wasserstrom, 1993, 2002; Langerman, 2002; Weiss, 2018).

through the practice of self-annihilation—making oneself nothing—as a mode of fully realized worship.

At the beginning of the 20th century, the kabbalistic *Ayin* and its relationship with *Yesh*, being, was the focus of a Yiddish myth penned by one of the luminaries of modern Yiddish literature, Pinkhas Kahanovitch, known by his pen name, Der Nister, The Hidden One. Published in 1910 in Warsaw, "Der Kadmen," *The Primordium*, is at once a stunning modern meditation on the dialectics of being and nothingness, and one of the boldest experiments in writing Jewish myth in modernity. As Der Nister's tale draws directly on the *Zohar*, I shall begin with a brief overview of kabbalistic and zoharic conceptions of nothingness, after which I shall attempt to decipher his complex and at times bewildering tale. As I hope to make clear, Der Nister offers a view of nothing as ontologically superior to being, though working in harmony with being to establish the created order. As the pregnant realm of no-thing-ness beyond being and longing for manifestation in being, Der Nister's nothing challenges the Parmenidean aporia of thinking nothing and instead brings to mind Daoist understandings on the impossibility of the nonbeing of nothingness.

1. A Brief History of Jewish Nothing

There are two different, though more or less simultaneous sources for the Jewish discovery of nothing. On the one hand, we can point to the Castilian kabbalists Moses de León and Joseph Gikatilla with their mystical appropriation of Maimonidean negative theology. From the core medieval Aristotelian position that negation is the only path to knowledge of God—one cannot say or know what God is but only what God is not—a direct path can be traced from "God is not x" to "God is not" or "God is the Not." (In Hebrew, the relationship between the particle for negation אֵין / *ein*, not, and the noun אַיִן / *ayin*, nothing, is also immediately apparent.) The following two passages make the connection between divine unknowability and God's nothingness clear:

> The depth of primordial being ... is called *ein gevul*,
> Boundless. Because of its concealment from all creatures
> above and below, it is also called *Ayin*, Nothingness.... If
> one asks, "What is it?" the answer is, "*Ayin* (Nothing),"

meaning: "No one can understand anything about it." It is
negated of every conception. No one can know anything
about it—except the belief that it exists. Its existence
cannot be grasped by anyone other than it. Therefore, its
name is *Ehyeh, I am / I will be*. (Exodus 3:14). (Gikatilla,
1883, folios 44a-b)

[The first sefirah] is ... the sum of all existence, and all
have wearied in their search for it.... The belt of the
wise is burst by this mysterious cause of causes. Arouse
yourself to contemplate, to focus thought, for God is
the annihilation of all thoughts, uncontainable by any
concept. Indeed, since no one can contain God at all, it
is called *Ayin* (Nothingness). (de León, 1911, pp. 23-24)

As indispensable as these sources are, both de León and Gikatilla owe
their understanding of God as nothingness, and the identification of the
most recondite aspect of divinity, the first *sefirah* in the theosophical
kabbalistic system of divine emanations, with *Ayin*, to an earlier kabbalist.
As Gershom Scholem (1987, pp. 423-25) demonstrated nearly a century
ago, it is to Azriel of Gerona that medieval Kabbalah owes the discovery of
nothingness as the deepest aspect of the godhead. Consider the following
well-known passage in which we encounter a decisive reinterpretation of
a phrase from *Sefer Yetsirah*: עשה אינו וישנו / *asah eino yeshno*, He made
nothing into something:

If someone asks you: What is the creator?
Answer: He who is in no way deficient.
If they ask: Does anything exist outside of Him?
Answer: Nothing exists outside of Him.
If they ask: How did He bring forth being from
nothingness? Is there not an immense difference between
being and nothingness?
Answer: He who brings forth being from nothingness
is not deficient, for being is in nothingness in the mode
of nothingness, and nothingness is in being in the mode
of being. Concerning this they have said (*Sefer Yetsirah*
2:6): "He made *eino* (His nothingness) into *yeshno*
(His being)" and not "He made *yesh* (being) from *ayin*

(nothingness)," to indicate that nothingness is being and being is nothingness. ... And the place of the attachment of being as it begins to emerge from nothingness into existence is called faith. For faith neither applies to being that is seen and comprehended, nor to nothingness that is neither seen nor comprehended, but only to the place of the adherence of nothingness and being....
(Azriel of Gerona, 1942, p. 207; see also Pachter, 2004, pp.13-51; Kaplan, 2013, pp. 278-30)

As Scholem noted, Azriel seems to have developed this idea at least in part through his encounter with the thought of John Scotus Eriugena. Through Eriugena, the Neoplatonic and pseudo-Dionysian, nothing thoroughly penetrated Jewish thought, and so, like Eriugena, who understood creation ex nihilo to signify the emergence of being from God's *nihil*, the kabbalists reinterpreted the notion of יש מאין, *yesh-me-ayin*, creation from nothing, to mean the transformation of God's nothingness into God's being.

2. Being from Nothingness in the Zohar

The coming to being of divinity from its own hidden recesses within infinity and nothingness on to full manifestation occupies a central place in the *Zohar*. Where the Bible and the Rabbis eschewed theogonic speculations,[2] the *Zohar* delighted in them. While these theogonies differ in tone—from the abstract to the mythical—they all explore the breakthrough of divine being from divine nothingness. Consider the following passage, notable for its use of human psychological processes to convey the emergence from unknowability:

> Come and see: Thought is beginning of all, and being
> Thought, it is within, concealed and unknowable. As
> this Thought expands further, it approaches the place

---

[2] Unlike all other Ancient Near Eastern myths, the Bible, famously, contains no theogony and begins with the uncreated *Elohim*. As for the Rabbis, see BT *Ḥagigah* 11b: "Whoever speculates on four things, it would be better for him had he not come into the world: what is above, what is below, what was before, what will be after."

where spirit dwells, and when it reaches that place it is
called *Binah*, Understanding, for it is not as concealed
as at first, although it is concealed. This spirit expands
and generates a voice blended of fire, water, and spirit—
namely, north, south, and east. This voice is totality of
all others. This voice conducts speech, conveying a word
refinedly; for voice is released from the place of spirit
and proceeds to conduct a word, issuing true words.
When you contemplate rungs—it is Thought, is *Binah*,
is voice, is speech, all is one. This itself is Thought,
beginning of all; there is no division—rather, all is one.
And this cluster—genuine Thought—is linked with *Ayin*
/ Nothingness, eternally inseparable. This is: *YHVH is
one and His name One* (Zechariah 14:9). (Zohar 1:246b)[3]

We need not focus on all the complex symbolism to appreciate what the
Zohar is doing here. What is crucial, though, and of direct relevance to
Der Nister's tale, is the picture of the becoming of God as the expansion
or externalization from hidden thought (the second *sefirah*, *Ḥokhmah*)
through to speech (the final *sefirah*, *Malkhut*). Importantly, the arrayal of
divine being does not begin with hidden thought, but with nothingness,
Ayin, the first *sefirah Keter*, coeternal with *Ein Sof*, Infinity, and the
ultimate source of being. Note, too, that the oneness of divinity here is
precisely the continuous chain from nothingness through to manifestation
and expression.

The following passage also presents *Ayin* as the source of divine
edifice, the source of the breakthrough to the divine beginning, the point
of thought—the second *sefirah Ḥokhmah*, from which the divine being
unfolds. Significantly, of all the *sefirot*, only *Ayin*, the divine nothingness,
the first *sefirah Keter*, is capable of grasping infinity:

Infinity [*Ein Sof*] is not susceptible to being known,
nor does it produce end or anything, as primordial
Ayin generates beginning and end. Who is beginning?
Supernal point, beginning of all, concealed one abiding
in thought. And it produces end, called *end of the matter*

---

[3] All *Zohar* translations from *The Zohar: Pritzker Edition.*

(Ecclesiastes 12:13). But there, *ein sof*, no end—no wills, no lights, no lamps in that *Ein Sof*. All these lights and lamps depend upon it for their existence, yet are incapable of grasping. The one who knows and does not know is none but supernal Will, concealed of all concealed, *Ayin*. (*Zohar* 2:239a)

Many zoharic texts focus specifically on the emergence of the second *sefirah Ḥokhmah* from *Keter*. As we have already seen, *Ḥokhmah*'s chief symbolic designations include point, thought, and beginning. To these we should also add *yesh*/being; whence the phrase *yesh me-ayin*, creation from nothing, came to signify the emergence of *Ḥokhmah* from *Keter*. It is perhaps not inaccurate to suggest that a central goal of zoharic meditation or praxis is precisely the attainment in one's own thought of this original and continuous divine breakthrough—from *ayin* to *yesh*, from nothingness to being, *Keter* to *Ḥokhmah*. The following passage is among the most famous for describing this breakthrough:

> תישארב (*Be-Reshit*), *In the beginning* (Genesis 1:1). At the head of potency of the King, He engraved engravings in luster on high. A spark of impenetrable darkness flashed within the concealed of the concealed, from the head of Infinity—a cluster of vapor forming in formlessness, thrust in a ring, not white, not black, not red, not green, no color at all. As a cord surveyed, it yielded radiant colors. Deep within the spark gushed a flow, splaying colors below, concealed within the concealed of the mystery of *Ein Sof*. It split and did not split its aura, was not known at all, until under the impact of splitting, a single, concealed, supernal point shone. Beyond that point, nothing is known, so it is called תישאר (*Reshit*), Beginning... (*Zohar* 1:15a)
>
> The Light Not Existing in Light engraved, and the Spark of All Sparks flashed, striking within the Will of Wills, hidden within, unknown.
>
> When this Will desired to extend, this Spark—concealed within Will, befitting and not befitting to exist as color—flashed forth. When this Will extended, this Spark—

> splaying color and no color—struck, entering into
> that extension, splaying forth in its colors, ascending,
> becoming actualized through its ascent within Will and
> the extension.... (*Zohar Ḥadash* 57a, *Qav ha-Middah*)

Nothingness does not appear by name in these passages, though the first *sefirah Keter* is most certainly present, in the first instance as the luster on high and then as Will. Both passages culminate with the emergence of *Ḥokhmah*, described as "point" and "beginning," and as "extension" variously. Of chief significance for our purposes is the mysterious action within nothingness—the spark of impenetrable darkness operative within *Keter*. I cannot go into detail here about the *botsina de-qardinuta* and its role in mapping the emanation of divinity. My intent is merely to highlight that the first *sefirah Keter*, the divine nothing, which in the *Zohar's* imagination is coeternal with and surrounds infinity, is not an absolute nothing in the Parmenidean sense, but rather a domain beyond (divine) being containing within itself the potential and desire for all being. Indeed, the flashing forth of the spark has strong erotic tones (Wolfson, 1995, pp. 60-69). Infinity, nothingness, being, and desire—these are the core terms of zoharic theogony and of Der Nister's modernist myth.

3. Der Nister's Primordium: Being and Nothingness in a Modernist Yiddish Key

Der Nister's myth surely counts among the strangest and most obscure creations of Yiddish modernism. Dismissed by the great master Y.L. Perets, who didn't understand it,[4] Der Nister's "Der kadmen," published in 1910 in his little booklet *Hekher fun der erd* (Higher than the Earth) is a kabbalistically suffused, modernist, hyperanthropomorphic myth about

---

[4] A postcard to Shmuel Niger dated December 2, 1909, recounts the following: "I broke with Perets. I sent him several chapters of Kadmen. He answered me with an angry letter, saying that he is not an expert, that he doesn't understand. If I saw him, I would tell him the words of the great Rabbi Aharon Karliner: 'You can, but you don't want to.' Yes, he doesn't want to. His angry letter testifies to it. It contains a sentence such as this: 'perhaps I am too grey for you, and perhaps you for me—too green.' God be with him! I am not downhearted, because the one who believes in himself doesn't need to believe in God, and certainly not...in Perets." (Translation from Bechtel, 1990, p. 33; see Novershtern, 1993, pp. 163, 181; Der Nister, 1957, p. 283.)

creation. Telling the story of God's becoming, and the transformation of what is not into what is, Der Nister's myth is less cosmogony than theogony—a story about the birth of the god, indeed, the Jewish God, though it is unlike any other Jewish myth. Over the course of 10 dense and dazzling chapters, brimming with startling imagery and cryptic, liturgical rhythms, Der Nister's tale takes the reader deep into the mind of God preceding creation—though nowhere does he mention God explicitly. Der Nister's myth, rather, focuses on a being referred to as *der Kadmen*, the Primordium, and narrates his precarious and tortured quest for self-consciousness and expression. Theogonic yet monotheistic, the plot of the myth is fundamentally internal and psychological. Tracing the Primordium's maturation across cosmic eons in the face of his own doubts and fear, and in the face of cosmic silence and nothingness, Der Nister's "Der Kadmen" is a daring and sophisticated exploration of the relationship between being and nothingness.[5]

Born Pinkhas (Pinye) Kahanovitch in the illustrious town of Barditshev (Berdychiv) in 1884, Der Nister—the Hidden One, a pen name brimming with kabbalistic meaning and associations—occupied a place at the very center of the Yiddish literary pantheon.[6] Be it for his symbolist short stories which marked his first great creative phase, or for his socialist-realist novel, the saga *The Family Mashber*, Der Nister remains one of the most enigmatic and enticing of modern Yiddish masters.[7] His short stories in particular, written between 1913 and 1929

---

[5] As far as I am aware, the only scholarly examination of the story in any language is by Delphine Bechtel (1990, pp. 50-68; 1992, pp. 38-54.). Bechtel's analysis is very insightful though as a non-Kabbalah scholar, she misses some key concepts and allusions. For a Hebrew translation, see Sadan (1963, pp. 67-84).

[6] The Hidden One, or the one who fathoms the hidden, the esoteric. The Jewish mystical tradition, the Kabbalah, is known as *torat ha-nistar*, the hidden/concealed Torah. In the popular imagination of traditional and especially Hasidic Jews, a *nistar* is a hidden saint, a concealed messiah in potential. The origins of the pen name may derive from his living under an assumed name for 12 years to avoid conscription into the Tsar's army, or his absence (hiddenness) from birth lists for the same reason. Be that as it may, the pen name reflected both his personality and his obscure writings. It was Shmuel Niger (1922, pp. 22-31) who placed him at the center of Yiddish modernism.

[7] On Der Nister's life and his symbolist period in particular, see Bechtel (1990); Mantovan (1993). Both of these works contain extensive bibliographies of Der Nister's works and key Yiddish essays about him. Khone Shmeruk's Hebrew introduction remains seminal (1963, pp. 9-52). The most accessible and insightful English overview is David Roskies (1996, pp. 191-229). For recent treatments, see Estraikh, Hoge and Krutikov, eds. (2014). Der Nister died in a Soviet gulag in 1950, two years before the night of the murdered poets.

in Zhytomyr, Kyiv, Moscow, Kovno, Berlin, Hamburg, and Kharkiv, and published collectively in *Gedakht* 1922-23 and *Fun mayne giter* 1929, earned him the reputation as the mystic of modern Yiddish literature. Shmuel Niger, for example, the leading literary critic of his day, noted that Der Nister "bewitched and cast spells with the secrets and allusions of the Kabbalah" and that his tales were packed "with the symbolism and age-old language of the *Zohar* and similar holy books" (Niger, 1958, p. 368; cited in Bechtel 1990, p. 24). Avraham Golomb, the celebrated Yiddish pedagogue and writer, described his stories as "akin to secrets of Torah, difficult to understand, indeed, an esoteric Torah" (Golomb, 1952, p. 249; cited in Bechtel, 1990, p. 24).

Although Der Nister's myth presents itself as the lost Yiddish pages of *Sefer Yetsirah*, the theogony draws on, and indeed is structured by, a special myth from the *Zohar*—the myth of the failed primordial worlds, *almin qadma'ei* and primordial kings, *malkhin qadma'in*. This foundational zoharic myth is found in the most esoteric strata of the *Zohar*—*Sifra di-Tsni'uta*, the *Idra Rabba* and the *Idra Zuta*. The zoharic myth is complex and subtle, though at its core focuses on the idea of failed, aborted, or destroyed emanations and stirrings of being prior to the stable configuration of reality.

> Before the world was created, they did not gaze face-to-face; and therefore primordial worlds were destroyed, and primordial worlds were fashioned in disarray. That which is disarrayed is called "flashing sparks"—like a blacksmith pounding an iron tool, scattering sparks in every direction; and those flying forth flash and scintillate and are immediately extinguished. These are called Primordial Worlds. Thus they were destroyed and did not endure, until the Holy Ancient One was arrayed and the Artisan proceeded to His artistry. (*Zohar* 3:292b (*IZ*)[8]

---

[8] The origins of the motif are in *Bereshit Rabbah* 3:7: "Rabbi Yehudah son of Rabbi Simon said, 'It is not written *Let there be evening*, but rather *There was evening* [*and there was morning*] (Genesis 1:5). From here we know that a time-order existed before this [i.e., understanding the clause to mean *there already had been evening*].' Rabbi Abbahu said, 'From here we know that the blessed Holy One kept creating worlds and destroying them until He created these [i.e., heaven and earth]. Then He declared, "These please Me, those do not."'" Cf. *Bereshit Rabbah* 12:15.

The primordial worlds are the beginning before the beginning that never became a beginning—rough drafts of creation, inchoate stirrings that never attained existence, preconscious fluctuations, miscarriages of divine consciousness that arose in the divine only to sink and dissolve into infinity from whence they came (Hellner-Eshed, 2021, pp. 174-184; Har-Shefi, 2014). It is precisely Der Nister's use of this zoharic myth as a refrain throughout the story that bestows hypnotic and mythical grandeur on his composition:

> And generations and eons, without vision or hearing, and unseen and unheard, while being became nothing, became from nothing, came to nothing, and not beginning, ended. And eunuch-generations and barren-eons, life without content and power without substance, without end and without measure, without shape and without form, while being came to nothing and stagnant passed away.
> And generations without history and worlds without tradition, without confession, without testament, without an heir and without a trace lived, liked so came to life, flickered, withered and were lost. (Der Nister, 1910, pp. 4, 10, 25)

As noted, Der Nister's narrative focuses on a being called the Primordium (*der Kadmen*) and his coming to self-consciousness and expression across cosmic aeons. Nowhere are we told explicitly who this being signifies, though the term clearly points to *Adam Qadmon* (Primordial Adam/Man), which Der Nister seems to be using in its zoharic sense, as a name for the totality of the male sefirotic edifice, from *Ḥokhmah*

See *Zohar* 3:128a (*IR*): "It has been taught: Before the Ancient of Ancients, Concealed of the Concealed, had prepared adornments of the King and crowns of crowns, there was neither beginning nor end. He engraved and gauged within Himself, and spread before Him one curtain, in which He engraved and gauged kings, but His adornments did not endure. As is written: *These are the kings who reigned in the land of Edom before a king reigned*—Primordial King—*over the Children of Israel*, the Primordial One (Genesis 36:31). All those who had been engraved were called by name, but they did not endure, so He eventually put them aside and concealed them. Afterward, He ascended in that curtain and was arrayed perfectly."

In addition to the *Zohar*, the theme of previous worlds and failed emanations appears in the writings of Moses Cordovero, and inspired Isaac Luria's theory of "the breaking of the vessels."

through to *Yesod—Adam Qadma'ah* in the *Zohar*'s Aramaic.[9] The other main character in the myth is the female Silence (*di shtilkeyt*), the cosmic silence, the silence of nothingness. Again, Der Nister does not tell us whom she signifies, though a number of hints make it clear that he is imagining her as a more primordial aspect of divine being above and beyond the Primordium. "Boundlessly empty and infinitely quiet," and with the appearance of "before everything" and "after everything," Der Nister's Silence is none other than the kabbalistic *Ayin* / nothingness (with some important original characteristics), and his myth as whole an account of the relationship between male Being-in-its-becoming (let us say, *Yesh*) in relation to *Ayin* / Nothingness, personified as female Silence pregnant with the seeds of potential being.

As befits a myth describing the passage from that which is not into that which is, the narrative begins with a string of negations, and though Maimonides and Wallace Stevens remind us that "the cancellings, the negations are never final,"[10] Der Nister manages to evoke the primordial nothing and take the reader to the beginning before the beginning:

> *Bereshit*—In the very beginning—no beginning, no first, no many and no one, no whole and no part, no thought, no utterance.[11]
>
> *Bereshit*—In the very beginning—no truth, no legend, no imagination, no dream, not even sleep.

---

[9] For overviews on Adam Qadmon, see Horodetsky (1928); Idel (1980); Scholem (1946, p. 265); Tishby (1989, pp. 295-298).

On *adam qadma'ah* in the *Zohar*, see for example: 1:91b; 2:167b (*SdTs*); 3:88b, 162b, 174b, 193b.

On *adam qadmon* in *Tiqqunei ha-Zohar*, see *TZ* 42a, 120a; *ZH* 114c-d. Ḥayyim Vital's *Ets Ḥayyim* begins with a discussion of *adam qadmon*.

[10] The negations are conveyed through the Yiddish article קיין *keyn*, no, none. As will become clear at the end of the account, Der Nister has the Hebrew negation אין *ein*, in mind too. The Wallace Stevens phrase is from "The Auroras of Autumn."

The negations recall the famous zoharic homily on the opening word of the Torah. See *Zohar* 1:15a: "not white, not black, not red, not green, no color at all."

[11] "Utterance" renders the Hebrew *ma'amar*, pointing to the ten utterances of creation in Genesis 1. According to M *Avot* 5:1, "The world was created through ten utterances." See BT *Rosh ha-Shanah* 32a and *Megillah* 21b: "The ten utterances by which the world was created. What are these? The expressions *And [God] said* in the first chapter of Genesis. But there are only nine! The words *In the beginning* are also an utterance, since it is written: *By the word of YHVH the heavens were made* (Psalms 33:6)."

"Thought" renders *rayen/ ra'ayon*. The very beginning which is not yet a beginning is prior to any idea or conception. Being does not yet exist even in potential within the divine mind.

Bereshit—In the very beginning—no number, no weight or size, no time or place, no color, no voice, not even silence.

Bereshit—In the very beginning—no thing, no anything, no life, no aspiring, no wanting, no aims, not even Nirvana.

And *Bereshit*? In the very beginning the End grew tiresome for the Beginning.... And with as yet unbegun, but supernatural young-man-strength, the Beginning spat the End from out of its mouth; but even before the Beginning motioned to shut its mouth, the End—lightning-fast, as with violently-elongated and frighteningly-tensiled circle-steel—suddenly did a terrifying jerk-and-fly right back into the mouth of the Beginning and shackled its throat with fetters.... And from the mighty and speedy fly-through of the Wheel-of-End-and-Beginning the eternal legend was created.[12]

And...when the legend opened its eyes it already found the Primordium lying on the great ancient-primeval foundation stone....[13]

---

[12] Alluding to the ancient mythological image of the of a serpent biting its tail, known as "uroboros," from the Greek *ouroboros* ("devouring its tail"). The uroboros appears in the opening chapter of *Sefer Yetsirah*: "Ten *sefirot belimah* (numerals of nothingness, entities of emptiness). Their measure is ten, yet infinite. Their end is embedded in their beginning, their beginning in their end, like a flame joined to a burning coal." In alchemy the uroboros is sometimes drawn around the Greek motto *Hen to pan* (All is One). Der Nister's startling image appears to point to a momentary fracturing in the closed circle of infinity, *Ein Sof*—the precondition necessary for any action whatsoever. Indeed, following this momentary fracture the "eternal legend" is created. Whom this eternal legend refers to is never stated, and this mysterious figure does not appear again in the myth. Perhaps the eternal legend is the mythos itself, or the possibility of a vantage point outside of infinity capable of witnessing the theogony. The wheel of end and beginning might also be understood in psychological terms (Jung and Neumann) as describing the uroboric stage in consciousness—undifferentiated, infinite, preego and preindividuation.
    Der Nister's imagery here also recalls the Hebrew phrase: סוֹף מַעֲשֶׂה בְּמַחֲשָׁבָה תְּחִלָּה (*sof ma'aseh be-maḥshavah teḥilah*), "last in deed, first in thought," best known in Solomon Alkabets' kabbalistic hymn *Lekha Dodi*. See also Yehudah ha-Levi, *Sefer ha-Kuzari* 3:73 citing Arabic philosophers: "The first thought includes the final deed."
[13] According to midrashic tradition, the world was created from the Foundation Stone, וְבֶן היתשה (*even ha-shtiyah*), the omphalos of the world, located in the Holy of Holies in the Temple in Jerusalem. See M *Yoma* 5:2; *Tosefta Yoma* 2:14; JT *Yoma* 5:2, 42c; BT *Yoma* 54b; *Targum Yerushalmi, Exodus* 28:30; *Targum, Song of Songs* 4:12; *Vayiqra Rabbah* 20:4; *Pesiqta de-Rav Kahana* 26:4; *Pirqei de-Rabbi Eli'ezer* 35; *Tanḥuma, Qedoshim* 10.

And generations without count, and power without
measure, without themselves and without a shadow,
knowing not themselves, knowing nothing—were in
themselves and in their own unknowing sunken.
And the Primordium was already lying on the great
ancient foundation stone, only un-thinking, only un-
pondering, still without anything, still without a single
thing, still without self even, not having yet self, not
possessing self—he-the-foundation-stone-not-he, not-
he-he-the-foundation stone. For he and all else outside-
he was still only he. (Der Nister, 1910, pp. 3-4)[14]

The narrative arc of the myth is difficult to convey in shorthand (the tale
is nearly 10,000 words); though at its core, we follow the titular character
in his quest for consciousness, self-understanding, and clarity of purpose:

There was no day, no night came, no suns rose, no suns
set—and yet something stirred and overflowed: as from a
long and distant-distant sleep, slowly-slowly, awakening
and calmly-calmly coming to itself; as from a far-far
sleep-height, from the highest height, effortlessly and
slowly descending through its own breath, leaving it
behind,— so did the Primordium feel himself descending
from his previous, distant and unknowing height as into
his intimate, his own and knowing now....
And the Primordium's heart sensed in itself some sort of
unease, as though originating from itself, to itself foreign
and not understood...some kind of restlessness and non-
satisfaction, which is owed something but doesn't know
what, which wants, it seems, nothing, and yet demands
its due, which feels itself both guilty and vindicated to
itself....
And the Primordium's heart set off to itself, wanted to
discover and know itself, to grasp itself and understand.
And the Primordium's heart began turning around itself,

---

[14] There is as yet nothing outside of or beyond the Primordium. Presumably, Der Nister
has in mind the Lurianic idea of Infinity filling all primordial space before the *tsimtsum*,
the divine contraction into itself, to enable the space for Being outside of Infinity.

as though spinning around after its own tail, running after it, chasing it and wanted to catch it. Spun around, ran— fast and angry. Faster, angrier—ran to one side, tried the other—and…nothing: didn't reach any beginning and didn't arrive at any end. The Primordium's heart remained at itself, at itself and at its own impotence. (Der Nister, 1910, pp. 4-6)

Eons pass until:

One time—not day, not night or twilight—without any point and without any reason, but suddenly, of its own accord, the Primordium together with his brain shivered and quivered with divine-delight: Aha!... I know!...

…It was one of the great by-chance-moments which by chance is discovered, by chance is identified, when suddenly by chance is sensed the awesome terror of chance…. It was one of the moments when the creator then feels himself as his own creation; one of the moments when the creator then delights in himself alone, in himself as his own creation, and in his great and holy idea of creation, sanctifies himself, prides himself and loves himself…. The Primordium experienced then the divinely-immense and eternally-creative delight- moment. It was the first great creation-thought.

And…in that moment the eternal chaos-and-void was supposed to take on colour and form; in that moment the innumerable and infinite zeros were supposed to add a one to themselves; in that moment the first and greatest world-poem was supposed to receive its truest rhythm, its clearest expression, only… together with the first creation-thought—doubt was born…and as soon as the great delight-moment had passed, so the doubt came before the Primordium's brain, stationed itself cold and calm directly opposite, and with a cold and cynical smirk asked him a question: You know? Go on then, try saying what?...

> The first solid and sharp creation-thought as though
> slipped from its own hands, as soon as ascended up to the
> brain, was there undone, became something immaterial
> and insubstantial, and disappeared. (Der Nister, 1910,
> pp. 8-9)

The remainder of the myth outlines the process by which the creation-thought is reclaimed and traces the Primordium's moments of existential insight (that "by himself and within himself he has nothing for himself, that not within himself will he find himself"; ibid., p. 13), though overwhelmingly focuses on his moments of doubt, confusion, fear, and despair. Indeed, the central drama of the myth turns on whether the Primordium will manage to overcome his own self-enclosed apathy and solipsistic madness to realize his purpose. Der Nister's story proceeds with Kafkaesque rhythms of failed starts and impossible quests.

Although more primordial than the Primordium, the Silence makes her first appearance relatively late in the myth, and only following the Primordium's first stirrings of stable (but fleeting) consciousness. She appears initially as a sensation, then as cosmic entity and divine hypostasis:

> At that moment there rested in the Primordium such a
> silence, that the quietest and deepest nights, the loneliest
> and far-furthest deserts, and the purest and holiest
> morning-skies have no conception of such a silence,
> have not even a tradition of such a silence....
> Never had there yet been a silence so silent and deep;
> never had there yet been a silence so immensely endless
> and limitless—indeed, never had silence yet surrounded
> and fathomed itself as at that moment; indeed, never had
> silence yet so penetrated and understood to the roots
> of its own hair its own immensity as at that moment...
> Deep and sharp until brain-ache, foundationally and
> profoundly until abyss and absurdity did the Silence
> understand itself at that moment.
> The Silence understood infinity infinitely—but no
> more; the Silence comprehended itself boundlessly-
> limitlessly—but no more: there was no more, She was

no more, there could be no more!... This bothered the
Silence and she strained her brain yet more strenuously.
(Der Nister, 1910, pp.14-15)

Note that, unlike the Primordium, the Silence understands herself fully. She
also grasps infinity—as does *Ayin* in the *Zohar* (see above). Significantly,
like the Primordium, she seems bothered by nonexistence. In the face
of the Primordium's becoming, she realizes that the moment of decision
has arrived—will she allow being to become? As readers we of course
know that being has become and is, though the role of nothingness in
this becoming is mysterious. Was nothingness opposed to being? Is being
the result of a theomachy of sorts between them. Has being vanquished
nothingness?

> The Silence sensed that the great, prodigious moment
> of decision was approaching, and—either she herself
> must stand to the side, and allow to happen that which
> must happen, and remain eternally silent in her eternally
> silent opinion about it, —or—not let out anything
> outside herself, and rather remain great and united in
> her own greatness and unity, and with only herself, with
> her immense unity stand and stand like so eternally,
> eternally.... (Der Nister, 1910, p. 15)

Nothingness, it seems, has much to lose in the face of becoming and
being.

Master storyteller Der Nister maintains the tension between
the Silence and the Primordium until the very last sentence. At times it
seems she seeks to thwart the Primordium. Witnessing the Primordium's
imbecility and apathy in the face of debilitated chaos-and-void—which for
Der Nister stands for unrealized being-in-potential—she grows disgusted
by the Primordium and thinks up "a menacing and malicious thought"
(Der Nister, 1910, p. 20). On another occasion she appeals directly to
him: "Clumsy oaf! Why don't you ask yourself where you are, who you
are and what you are? Why don't you ask yourself how and in what way
you came here? And where and what your purpose is?" (ibid., p. 21).
What does she want? For being to be or not to be?

In the final chapter, with the Primordium on the verge
of an eternal coma, in which case "would then transpire
eternally-eternally what already transpired eternally
eternally before the Primordium's waking up" (ibid.,
p. 28), namely—nothingness for all time, the Silence
appears before the Primordium:

At that moment the Silence stood boundlessly empty and
infinitely quiet.... And at that moment the Silence looked
as though still before everything, and as though already
after everything;[15] within her was the strained, heavy
catching-breath of before creation and the emptiness
of after.... And here with his ear to the Silence the
Primordium lingered, paid attention and listened within.
And the Primordium imagined that as though for his
sake, as though with him specifically in mind, the Silence
seemingly grew yet more and more silent. The Silence
muted throughout the entire extent of her immense
domain.... And with her eternal-silent far upon her eternal-
silent wide and long, with her immense silent-keeping-
silent upon her immense profundity[16]—the Silence then
presented with herself—herself alone: the one and only
real truth, the one and only true reality, whose greatest
proof is her own being, whose greatest demonstration is
her herself.... The Silence then presented with herself—
the eternal, first and greatest heresy, the eternal heresy
against the First and Greatest; the deepest and most silent
heresy, whose greatest proof is that *it* does indeed exist,
and she, nevertheless, thinking—can deny—and does
think, can smile heretically—and does smile: "As if it
never was".... The most silent and deepest heresy whose

---

[15] "Before everything" and "after everything" recalls *Adon Olam*, the poem (attributed
to Solomon ibn Gabirol) which closes the Sabbath liturgy: *Adon olam asher malakh
be-terem kol yetsir nivr'a* (Master of the universe who reigned before any creation was
created) / *Ve-aharei kikhlot ha-kol levado yimlokh nor'a* (And after all is ended, He, the
Awesome One, alone will reign.)

[16] The references to the dimensions of Silence's domain: wide and long and high and deep
recall *Sefer Yetsirah* 1: "Ten *sefirot belimah*. Their measure is ten, yet infinite, Depth of
beginning, depth of end, depth of good, depth of evil, depth of below, depth of east, depth
of west, depth of north, depth of south."

greatest demonstration is *it* itself, that it already is, that
it already must be, that it already cannot not be... (Der
Nister, 1910, pp. 30-31)

Der Nister's logic here is complex. Unlike the Primordium and Being
and Creation, Silence and Nothingness *cannot not be*. Whereas one can
conceive of creation not taking place or Being not being, one cannot
conceive of the Nothingness not being. Indeed, the mere thought of
Nothingness, the idea there didn't need to be something, but that there
had to be nothing, bestows priority on the Nothingness (not merely
temporally but ontologically) and challenges the regime and dominion
of being. Nothingness is prior to and superior than Being, says the teller
of the tale, and so, the Silent Nothingness is the eternal heresy against
God—"the first and greatest."

Der Nister's view on the ultimacy of nothingness is thus the polar
opposite of Parmenides, who, at the very dawn of Western philosophy,
denied the possibility of thinking or speaking of nonbeing:

Come now, I will tell thee—and do thou hearken to my
saying and carry it away...namely, that It is [Being is],
and that it is impossible for anything not to be [non-
Being to be].... For you cannot know what is not—that
is impossible—nor utter it (Fragment 2; see also Plato's
The Sophist 237a-e)

In fact, Der Nister's view accords quite precisely with Daoist
understandings on the impossibility of the nonbeing of Nothingness:

Brilliance queried nothingness, saying: 'Are you, sir,
being or are you nothing?' Brilliance, unable to get a
response, carefully regarded the other's appearance—a
far-reaching vacuity. He gazed the entire day and saw
nothing, listened but heard no sound, reached out but was
unable to grasp anything. Brilliance said: 'How perfect!
Who can be as perfect as this! I can grant the fact of
nothingness but not the non-being of nothingness. As
for nothingness, how can one realize such perfection!'
(*Zhuangzi* 22; emphasis added; see Chai, 2019, pp.1-30)

The Silent-Nothing is Being's heresy. She will deny the Primordium and thwart his becoming:

> That which you hear, that which you see, I, I Silence, am now, for all eternity was, and for all eternity will be. Outside of me was not...is not...and will not be—not you, not someone, not anyone.... Not! You were not.... You are not.... You will not be.... I, I Silence am your heresy!... I, I Silence deny you.... I, I was for all eternity, am now, and for all eternity will be. Who can deny me?... Who can be my heresy?... Who?! (Der Nister, 1910, pp. 31-32)

Note that Silence/Nothingness employs language usually associated with God to describe herself: I am, was, will be. How will being emerge?

> The denouement of the myth is astounding:
> Serene and sure, looking at the Primordium, the Silence repeated her question again: Who can deny me? Who can be my heresy? Who?! And as if provokingly and incitingly, silent, cold and mockingly asked the Primordium another question: Maybe... you? The Primordium could no longer bear it. In a single moment he jumped up on the foundation stone...pierced all worlds and generations with a single glance of the eye and, like the first and mighty thunder of a young and fresh May-Breast, the first sound and word erupted from the Primordium's heart: Me!!! Triumphantly-silent-smilingly the Silence retreated: Me!—The Primordium expressed himself, because... at that moment the first atom collided with the second! (Der Nister, 1910, p. 32)

Provoked into action and full self-consciousness by the Silence, the Primordium announces *ikh* (I, me), whereupon creation ensues. Although Der Nister uses the Yiddish word איך (*ikh*), he is undoubtedly also thinking of the Hebrew word אני (*ani*), "I," which has the same letters as אין (*ayin*), nothingness and *ein*, the particle for negation, with which the myth began. Der Nister's theogony thus concludes with the transformation of nothingness and not into being, *ayin* into *ani*, which in classical kabbalistic sources signifies the final *sefirah*, the culmination of the divine edifice—*Malkhut*.[17] According to Bible and the Rabbis, the world was created through speech, whether with many words, one word or even by a single letter. According to Der Nister and following kabbalistic myth, Being is the result of the speaking of the divine "I"—an affirmation of being in the face of the heresy of nothingness. Although I cannot elaborate here, it is interesting to note that in claiming his consciousness and I-hood, Der Nister's Primordium also recalls Friedrich Schelling's philosophical theogony in his *Die Weltalter, Ages of the World* where the Absolute posits itself and emerges into being and time only after a crisis where its own nonbeing is experienced as unbearable and as a loss (Žižek and Schelling, 1997, p. 17).[18]

Has being then vanquished nothingness? No! One small phrase holds the key to the entire myth. Following the divine self-expression and the emergence of stable being, we read that the Silence retreats "triumphantly-silent-smilingly." Only now do we learn that this is what she had wanted all along! Here we must ask: Why does Silence-Nothingness desire being's becoming? After all, had the Primordium drifted into his coma of indifference and imbecility, and had she not prodded him to consciousness and expression, she would have remained all that is, "with only herself, with her immense unity stand and stand like so eternally, eternally." Why then does she desire being?

Because she is a pregnant mother—pregnant with pulsating and precarious potential, and if being does not become, if the Primordium does not affirm his I-hood, then the "burning tangle of creation-stuff"—the chaos and void, the *tohu va-vohu*, of Genesis 1—cannot become manifest:

---

[17] See *Zohar* 1:204a: "Who is *I*? The blessed Holy One, holy Kingdom of Heaven"; 1:65b: "Come and see: Everywhere *ani* becomes a body for the soul, receiving what is above... *ani, I,* standing revealed, verging on being known; *ani, I,* throne to what is above... *Va-Ani, And I,* encompassing male and female as one." The earliest attestation of *ayin/ani* as *Keter* and *Malkhut* seems to be in Gikatilla's *Sha'arei Orah*; see Scholem (1946, pp. 216-18).

[18] The parallels between Der Nister's myth and Schelling's philosophy are not as surprising as one might imagine. As has been demonstrated by numerous scholars, Schelling was profoundly influenced (albeit indirectly) by Kabbalah.

And on both shores of the eternal abyss there stood then young-men-worlds on one side and maiden-times on the other—stood, looked, yearned for one another, longed for one another, but were unable to come to one another. And they stretched their hands, bodies and necks out taut towards one another, and with wild eyes, suffocated breath and mouths agape, body yearned for body, heart pined for heart, and with all their might they convulsively gravitated to one another....

And at that time the chaos-and-void...looked out and implored unceasingly: ...Eh...eh...just one cold drop... one cold spurt...eh...eh...---......---And at that moment the burning tangle of creation-stuff implored before the Primordium, before the eternal creator: Almighty! Take us apart! Almighty! Conceive us! Almighty! Create us, suffer with us, rejoice with us and give us a name and give us your name. (Der Nister, 1910, p. 26)

Der Nister does not say explicitly that the Silence is pregnant with the formless chaos. However, when we consider that both the Silence and the chaos are referred to as "endless" and that the chaos is described as "silent darkness," and above all that the Silence says of herself, "all contents in me and me no one's content," a compelling case emerges for understanding his mythical geography in this way. Der Nister's nothingness is thus not a true nothing (absolute nonbeing in a Parmenidean vein) devoid of any content, but a domain of no-thing-ness, a plenitude of undifferentiated being-in-potential brimming with erotic yearning to become and attain actuality. And to attain actuality, to be manifest in being, the Silence must force the Primordium's hand. Alone, the Primordium / *Yesh* / Being-in-its-becoming is caught in an antagonistic vortex of drives—one expansive, desiring to encounter that which is not he, and the other constrictive, desiring to remain within himself.[19] Only Mother-Silence-Nothingness

---

[19] The expansive drive: "He understood deeply, and with the depth of his heart felt, that he alone is insufficient for himself, that he alone exceeds himself, that he alone cannot be his own measure... that he and all outside of he is outside of him." (Der Nister, 1910, p.13)

The constrictive drive: "Remember, you should eternally-eternally remain only at yourself—at your self only and only at your eternal and almighty possibility.... Remember, you should not set out from your own hands.... Remember, that you alone are all and in you alone is all, but outside of you is all, all, only not you!" (Ibid., p. 27).

can catapult the Primordium to become. This is her "first and greatest mission to the first and most innocent birth" (Der Nister, 1910, p. 16)— the birth of being.

Although as readers we only come to understand Silence's desire at the very end of the myth, in fact, her decision to enable being had been made at her very first encounter with the Primordium:

> And—notwithstanding how much seriousness Silence has on her own, at her own disposal, and how much eternal seriousness there is in being and not being—the eternal seriousness and the immense and eternal responsibility for all dangers for all times and generations, worlds and creatures at the moment of birth and death—at that moment, the Silence perceived and understood and nevertheless, with the clearest and deepest knowing took all of it upon herself. (Der Nister, 1910, p. 17)

Why is there something rather than nothing? Because Mother Nothing made sure it was so. She is the hero of the myth. She is ultimate mother of being. From a classical kabbalistic perspective, Der Nister's personification of the Silent-Nothingness as mother is surprising. Recall that in the *Zohar*, *Ayin*, the first *sefirah Keter* is either understood as male (think of *Attiqa Qaddisha*), or beyond gender. As a Yiddish modernist, Der Nister was not bound by tradition, and so his Silence-Nothingness artfully combines aspects of *Keter* with characteristics of *Binah*—the third *sefirah*, the supernal mother and womb of being. Be that as it may, what is crucial in Der Nister's myth is the view of nothingness as ultimate, as mother, and as working with and through being to establish a stable configuration of reality. Two atoms, Nothingness and Being, Mother and Father.

4. By Way of Conclusion

In the same year that Der Nister published his myth in Warsaw, another Warsaw resident, the famed scholar-author-journalist-mystic Hillel Zeitlin published his essay on the "Foundations of Hasidism." "Because the Nothing is the essence of Creation and its innermost soul" he wrote, "it—the Nothing—is in fact the real Being, true existence, essential reality" (see Green, ed., 2012, p. 76). For Zeitlin, what we call Being— "the sensory, visible to the eyes of flesh and grasped by the rational mind" is "blindness of the senses, illusory existence" (ibid.). I am not sure that Der Nister would have agreed with this second sentiment, though Zeitlin's view of the Nothing as ultimate Being resonates strongly with Der Nister's myth. I imagine that he would have smiled triumphantly-silently, though, when reading Hillel's son, the kabbalistic Yiddish poet, Aaron Zeitlin's poems—*Visn dem Gornisht*/ Knowing the Nothing, and *Der Nisht* / The Nothing:

> One thing I call dust, another—gold.
> But which is dust? Which is gold? This I know not.
> Not even a jot.
> O, would that I knew, in place of knowing nothing,
> Knew the Nothing,
> From which You create dust and gold,
> And me too, the something, who wishes to know that Nothing-Not,
> But doesn't know anything, not even a jot!

(Zeitlin, 1970, p. 481)

> The number is prior to the word.
> I went after the number—
> And perceived a path, that is
> Infinitely wide, infinitely slender.

> And did perceive, that mount is vale.
> And did perceive, that vale is mount.
> Like a child I went in search
> Of her, of her, for mother number-count.

> And mother number led me on
> To small which is from small-being—vast,
> And brought me to herself in land,
> And on her knees set me holding fast.

And she brought me to zero-nil
And she led me unto the limit, until.
And I know: The nothing, the hollow nothing,
Can every moment become full, infill.

And I glimpsed into the source,
And it wave-fizz refreshed me, gushing.
The nothing becomes every moment—all,
The all becomes every moment—nothing.

Ibid., pp. 290-91

References

Azriel of Gerona (1942) *The way of faith and the way of heresy* [*Derekh ha-emunah ve-derekh ha-kefirah*, Scholem, G. (ed.) in 'Seridim hadashim mi-kitvei R. Azriel mi-Gerona. In Assaf, S. and Scholem, G. (eds.) *Sefer zikkaron le-Asher Gulak ve-liShmu'el Klein*. Jerusalem, Hebrew University, p. 207.

Bechtel, D. (1992) Der Nister's "Der Kadmen": A metaphysical narration on cosmogony and creation. *Yiddish,* 7(2), pp. 38–54.

Bechtel, D. (1990) *Der Nister's Work 1907-1929: A study of a Yiddish symbolist*. Berne, Switzerland: Peter Lang.

Chai, D. (2019) *Zhuangzi and the Becoming of Nothingness*. Albany: SUNY Press.

de León, M. (1911) *Sheqel ha-Qodesh*. Edited by Greenup, A.W. London.

Der Nister (1957) *Dertseylungen un eseyen*. New York: Ikuf.

Der Nister (1963) *Ha-nazir ve-ha-gdiyah: sippurim, shirim, ma'amarim*. Translated by Dov Sadan. Jerusalem: Mossad Bialik.

Der Nister (1910) *Hekher fun der erd*. Warsaw: Farlag Progres.

Estraikh, G., Hoge, K. and Krutikov, M. (eds.) (2014) *Uncovering the Hidden: The Works and Life of Der Nister*. London: Legenda.

Gikatilla, J. (1883) *Sha'arei Orah*. Warsaw: Orgelbrand.

Golomb, A. (1952) Fun zeyer onheyb, zikhroynes. In Opatoshu, J. and Leivick, H. (eds.) *Zamlbikher,* 8, pp. 249-256.

Green A. (ed.) (2012) *Hasidic Spirituality for a New Era: The religious writings of Hillel Zeitlin*. New York: Paulist Press.

Har-Shefi, A. (2014) *Malkin qadma'in: Ha-beri'ah ve-ha-hitgalut be sifrut ha-'Idrot shel ha-Zohar*. Los Angeles: Cherub Press.

Hellner-Eshed, M (2021) *Seekers of the Face: Secrets of the Idra Rabba (The Great Assembly) of the Zohar*. Translated by R. Dascalu. Stanford, CA: Stanford University Press.

Horodetsky, S.A. (1928) Adam qadmon. *Ha-goren,* 10, pp. 94-121.

Idel, M. (1980) Demut ha-adam she-me-al ha-sefirot. *Da'at,* 4, pp. 41-55.

365

Kaplan, L. (2013) Faith, rebellion and heresy in the writings of Rabbi Azriel of Gerona. In Schwartz, D. and Sagi, A. (eds.) *Faith: Jewish Perspectives*. Boston: Academic Studies Press, pp. 278-301.

Kister, M. (2007) Tohu wa-bohu, primordial elements and creatio ex nihilo. *Jewish Studies Quarterly,* 14, pp. 229-256.

Langermann, Y.T. (2002) On the beginnings of Hebrew scientific literature. *Aleph,* 2, pp. 169-189.

Mantovan, D. (1993) Der Nister and his symbolist short stories (1913-1929): Patterns of imagination. Ph.D. diss., Columbia University.

Matt, D.C. (2000) Ayin: The concept of nothingness in Jewish mysticism. In Fine, L. (ed.) *Essential papers on Kabbalah.* New York: NYU Press, pp. 67-108.

Matt, D.C. (1997) Varieties of mystical nothingness: Jewish, Christian and Buddhist. *Studia Philonica,* 9, pp. 316-31.

Niehoff, M.R. (2006) Creatio ex nihilo theology in Genesis Rabbah in light of Christian exegesis. *Harvard Theological Review,* 99, pp. 37-64.

Niger, S. (1922) Moderner mitos. *Dos naye leben,* 2, pp. 22-31.

Niger, S. (1958) *Yidishe shrayber in sovet-rusland.* New York: Sh. Niger bukh-komitet baym altveltlekhn yidishn kultur-kongres.

Novershtern, A. (1993) Igrotav shel Der Nister el Shemuel Niger. *Huliot,* 1, pp. 159-244.

Pachter, M. (2004) The root of faith is the root of heresy. In Pachter, *Roots of Faith and Devequt: Studies in the History of Kabbalistic Ideas.* Los Angeles: Cherub, pp. 13-51.

Roskies, D. (1996) Der Nister: The storyteller as high priest. In Roskies, *A Bridge of Longing: The Lost Art of Yiddish Storytelling.* Cambridge, MA: Harvard University Press, pp. 191-229.

Scholem, G. (1946) *Major Trends in Jewish Mysticism.* New York: Schocken Books.

Scholem, G. (1987) *Origins of the Kabbalah.* Translated by A. Arkush. New York: Princeton University Press.

Shmeruk, K. (1963) Der Nister: Ḥayyav ve-yetsirato. In Der Nister, *Ha-nazir ve-ha-gdiyah: sippurim, shirim, ma'amarim.* Translated by Dov Sadan. Jerusalem: Mossad Bialik, pp. 9-52.

Tishby, I. (1989) *The Wisdom of the Zohar,* vol. 1. Translated by D. Goldstein. London: Littman Library of Jewish Civilization.

Wasserstrom, S.M. (2002) Further thoughts on the origins of *Sefer Yeṣirah. Aleph,* 2, pp. 201-221.

Wasserstrom, S.M. (1993) *Sefer Yeṣira* and early Islam: A reappraisal. *Jewish Thought and Philosophy,* 3, pp. 1-30.

Weiss, T. (2018) *Sefer Yeṣirah and Its Contexts.* Philadelphia: University of Pennsylvania Press.

Wolfson, E.R. (1995) *Circle in the Square: Studies in the Use of Gender in Kabbalistic Symbolism.* Albany: SUNY Press.

Wolfson, E. R. (2019) Heidegger's seyn/nichts and Kabbalistic Ein Sof. In Wolfson, *Heidegger and Kabbalah: Hidden Gnosis and the Path of Poiesis.* Bloomington, IN: Indiana University Press, pp. 97-123.

Zeitlin A. (1970) *Lider fun khurbn un lider fun gloybn,* vol. 2. New York: Bergen Belsen Memorial Press.

Žižek, S. and Schelling, F.W. (1997) *The Abyss of Freedom/Ages of the World.* Translated by J. Norman. Ann Arbor, MI: University of Michigan Press.

Made in the USA
Columbia, SC
14 October 2024

b4041f0a-0944-4b2e-b52e-e163cc99d6e2R01